WineTrails
OF WASHINGTON

A guide for uncorking your memorable wine tour

Anne & Alf
Enjoy !
Vic & Bonnie

Washington Wine Highway
Chateau Ste Michelle
May 25th 2008

by Steve Roberts

South Slope
Productions

MORE WINE ▶

WineTrails of Washington
A guide for uncorking your memorable wine tour

Published by
South Slope Productions
9311 SE 36th Street; Suite 108; Mercer Island, WA 98040
(206) 660-5200
www.winetrailsnw.com

Readers should also be aware that maps and directions as well as other tasting room attributes (e.g., hours of operation, tasting fees, etc.) may have changed since this book was printed. Readers are advised to contact the winery in advance to verify the information. Remember to drink responsibly; drive responsibly.

Library of Congress Cataloging-in-Publication Data available.

⚜️WINE TRAILS NW   WineTrails Northwest logo by Beth Hayes, King Salmon Creative Designs

Edited by Sunny Parsons and Seattle Publishing, Inc.

Cover and interior design by Lisa J. Pettit, Lisa Pettit Designs

Photos by Steve Roberts, South Slope Productions

Layout and Production by Seattle Publishing, Inc.

First Edition
ISBN 13 - 978-0-9792698-0-6
ISBN 10 - 0-9792698-0-6

Printed in China by C&C Offset Printing Co., Ltd.

Acknowledgements & Dedication

My research for *Wine Trails of Washington* introduced me to hundreds of wine-makers and other winery personnel too numerous to list here. To them I am greatly indebted for their willingness to share their craft and their unbridled joy in producing wine. Along the way, I also relied heavily on the experience and thoughtful insights of a variety of industry leaders. In particular, I wish to thank Amy Mumma, program coordinator and instructor for Central Washington University's World Wine Program; Ronald Irvine, Vashon Winery's owner and winemaker and co-author of *The Wine Project, Washington State's Winemaking History*; Stanley Clarke, coordinator of Walla Walla Community College's Institute for Enology and Viticulture program; and Mike Lempriere, creator of *Mike L's Guide to Washington State Wineries*.

Early on, Beth Hayes of King Salmon Creative Designs was instrumental in creating the WineTrails Northwest logo and color scheme. I owe Beth a huge dose of gratitude for her branding talents. I am especially indebted to my editor extraordinaire, Sunny Parsons. She transformed my rather ungainly draft manu-script into readable text and somehow managed to preserve my voice. To the amazingly talented Lisa J. Pettit, who created the cover and designed the inte-rior, I am most thankful. Her design talents resulted in the book's striking look and easy navigation. To the team at Seattle Publishing Inc. that was responsible for the production of this book, I am greatly indebted. I want to give particular thanks to my friend and mentor Rob French, who invested many hours (and bottles of wine) providing sage advice.

I thank my family and especially my children, Alex and Meg, for their patience and love throughout this process. To their mom, Pat Leach, I thank her for be-ing an important part of my life. To my siblings—Carole Nicholas, Noyes Rob-erts, Libby Kennedy and Gayle Vaughn—and their spouses, as well as a host of cousins, nieces, nephews, and friends who have supported me throughout the process, I am immeasurably grateful. I wish my parents were alive; they would have been most proud. I really owe everything to them.

I thank Kathleen von Reumont for her loving support throughout this amaz-ing venture. Her belief in me kept me going. Her timely advice and opinions regarding the myriad details in this book are blessedly evident throughout.

Lastly, I dedicate the book to Doug Carver—my best friend. Doug never failed to ask how the book was coming along or note to other friends and acquain-tances that I was producing a guidebook. His premature death reminds me to live each day to its fullest. Doug, your seat next to me at Husky Stadium will forever be empty.

Washington Wine Country Regions

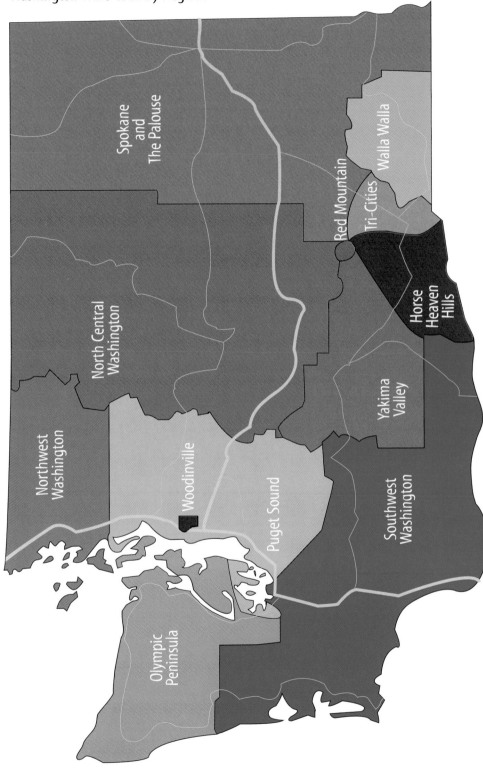

Contents at a Glance

Contents at a Glance

Cave B Inn and Winery in Winter

Detailed Table of Contents

North Central Washington Wine Country

Spokane Wine Country

Appendices

Listening to My Tongue

"Hold your question, I'll be right back," winemaker Don Corson said as he went to another room to turn up the music. The local radio station was celebrating Beethoven that weekend, and it was clear that Don, owner/winemaker of Camaraderie Cellars, didn't make wine in isolation. He needed classical music. Lots of it. He handed me a wineglass with a generous pour of cabernet sauvignon and exclaimed, "Wine goes with the good things in life." I swirled, stuck my nose in the glass, and smelled the aroma. I took in a mouthful and knew immediately that I was dealing with a big Washington red: powerful, dark berry flavor up front, followed by a velvet feel to the tongue and remarkable spice notes at the finish. Don was right, Beethoven did sound better. What's more, I wanted to share this wine with friends, family, and a hearty meal, be it steak au poivre or a cheeseburger—the good things in life.

Don led me to the barrel room and, using his "thief," extracted some still-aging merlot from a French oak barrel. While he filled my glass, he talked about the Eastern Washington vineyards where he acquires his fruit, the steps he takes from crush to fermentation, his use of oak, the cleaning or "racking" the barrels, and aging the wine. Balancing wine glass and notepad, I madly scribbled, "Winemaking is more craft than art; more science then guessing." I could see that to be a good winemaker, you needed to pay attention to detail, be well

Camaraderie Cellars, Port Angeles

organized, keep a journal, and maintain a clean workspace. But as Don clearly stated, it all starts with the fruit: Good grapes give the promise of good wine.

My visit to Camaraderie Cellars revealed that to be a great winemaker, it takes more than textbook know-how—it takes soul. Call it zeal or call it a personal mantra, Don Corson was making wine for a reason and that reason resonated with me: to enjoy wine with the good things in life. I discovered this same passion wherever I went on the WineTrails, from the threadbare winemaking operations to the well-heeled winery giants. I never knew what I would experience when I walked into each of the myriad tasting rooms I visited, but one commonality stood out. Whether the winemakers were making Bordeaux-style blends or fruit wine from cranberries, they took an obvious and often unbridled joy in their creations.

1

Camaraderie Cellars was one of the first wineries I visited in mid-January 2006. Two months earlier, I had mentioned to a friend that what the world needed was a good guidebook to the wine tasting rooms of Washington. Although I found some wonderful books about Washington's wines, these tomes either focused on one particular wine region of the state or they described wine varieties and their tastes. I couldn't find a comprehensive book that covered the entire state, addressed the tasting rooms themselves, and was written for would-be wine tourists. I also turned to the Web and found a similar problem: outdated information, a narrow focus, and limited assistance in planning my own wine tour getaway.

Mona the camel, near San Juan Vineyards

I figured that the beauty of tackling a subject of which I knew little was the chance to exercise gray matter, meet new people, and, in this case, sip my way through Walla Walla. One rainy evening, while dining out on phad Thai and contemplating the Washington wine conundrum, I was struck by the realization that soon I would be on a trail of discovery about wine, in particular, Washington wine. At the time, I had no idea where my journey would lead or what fun I would have. I didn't know that I would walk through rows of lush green vineyards in the Horse Heaven Hills, have dinner with the owner of Tsillan Cellars at Lake Chelan, be stranded at the Cave B resort during a snowstorm, or make the acquaintance of Mona the camel while visiting San Juan Vineyards.

China Bend Winery

Sometimes we take on more than we can chew (or in my case, drink). But *naïveté* can be a good thing. Do you really think that the Corps of Discovery would have left St. Louis if Lewis and Clark had known about the Bitterroot Mountains? What, I reasoned, would be the difficulty in visiting wine tasting rooms and sampling a little merlot here and some cabernet sauvignon there? Little did I know that my quest would lead me to more than 200 wineries in the course of a year, sampling wine in basements, barns and doublewides; racking up 30,000 miles on my car; spending sleepless nights in noisy motel rooms; and deflating my already shrinking wallet. I had heard of the "wine bug" before; I just didn't know that I had caught it. But that's what passion does: It drives you. For example, I was more than willing to make the long drive to China Bend Winery, located in the state's northeast corner and within a stone's throw of Canada. Upon my arrival, I mentioned to the tasting room server that the journey getting to the winery was amazing and that I hadn't seen the beauty of Lake Roosevelt before. She stopped what she was doing and said, "The journey's great, but the destination is better." I thought then that the chardonnay she was pouring would be splendid. It was: refreshingly crisp, with apple and tropical flavors, full to the mouth and only slightly sweet.

Why I wrote this book

People do things for crazy reasons, like those guys going over Niagara Falls in a barrel. What were they thinking? Or consider the army of workers that built the Panama Canal despite the fact that they were dropping like flies from yellow fever and dengue fever. Was the pay *that* good? And then there is me, a self-confessed "wineaux," visiting more than 200 wineries in a year because he wanted an inside look at the Washington wine scene. Crazier still were the countless hours devoted to writing the profiles for each winery visited, inputting data, organizing photos, and editing maps. Meanwhile, my dog stared longingly at her leash begging for a walk, my business that pays the bills went neglected, and I forgot my sisters' birthdays. But I was driven to tell the story of the Washington winemaking industry, spurred by some pretty interesting statistics:

- Washington is the second-largest producer of premium wines in the U.S.
- There are 500 bonded wineries in the state, and the number is growing.
- The wine industry contributes more than $3 billion towards the state's economy.
- The industry generates 14,000 jobs.
- There are more than 30,000 acres of *vinifera* vineyards in the state.
- Washington state has nine American Viticultural Areas (AVAs), designated by the U.S. Tobacco Tax and Trade Bureau as uniquely suited for growing wine grapes.

These numbers are all factual, but they don't capture the tender care taken by the vineyard manager as he prunes in early spring, the intense green of Horse Heaven Hills under July skies, the crush of handpicked cabernet sauvignon grapes in the fall or the eager anticipation of wine-loving fans at a vintage release party. It's this attention to detail, this drive to make better wines year after year, that has critics from around the world heaping praise on Washington's

Benson Vineyards at Lake Chelan

wines. None other than Robert Parker's *The Wine Advocate* gave Snohomish's Quilceda Creek a perfect score of 100 two years in a row. In April 2006 the

3

same publication noted, "Washington State's Columbia Valley, long described as having great potential, has fulfilled many expectations, and its future is as bright today as any viticultural region's on Earth." These are powerful words. So is the Washington Wine Commission's quotation about Washington having "the perfect climate for wine." I love that line.

Yes, I wanted to describe the Washington wine industry—its size and scope as well as the great quality of its product. But more than that, I wanted the rest of the world to savor what I have experienced. I'm an average bloke, and if I found a visit to a winery's tasting room to be an excellent weekend getaway or just a fun Saturday-afternoon jaunt, then I wanted to tell that story. I met some engaging people who work their wineries in their spare time and keep their day jobs to pay the bills. I saw amazing landscapes, including the San Juan archipelago, the basalt cliffs of the Columbia River Gorge, and Glacier Peak in the North Cascades. I tasted great wine and learned that there are dozens of other Washington wine varieties besides merlot and cabernet sauvignon. And in the process, I also learned to let go of my inhibitions and listen to what the wine enthusiasts had to say. I swirled and sipped like the best of them and found myself having a great time. I was the "accidental wine taster" and I was compelled to share my experiences. I needed to let people know that my special memories could also be theirs.

In large part, I wrote this book so you won't make the same mistakes I did. I succeeded in making a barrel room full of mistakes. For example, I was forever getting lost and, reluctant to ask for directions, I wasted a lot of time and many neurons. About half the wineries charge a small tasting fee (usually $2 to $5), and I often forgot to bring cash. In my search to find ATMs in such places as Quincy, Lyle, and Kettle Falls, I accrued enough information to write a guidebook on the ATMs of Washington. Sometimes I arrived at my destination winery only to

Alexandria Nicole Cellars, Horse Heaven Hills

discover it had run out of wine—a good lesson to call ahead. I bought wine when it was 100 degrees outside and didn't have a cooler in the hot car in which to store it. Sometimes I would go to an area and wander from one winery to another, only to discover later that there was a logical circuit to follow. On many a wine expedition, I wasn't sure where I would spend the night, let alone where I would eat dinner. Trust me, you don't want to be in Mattawa when it's 9 at night and you're not sure if you should go north or south.

From these mistakes grew the idea of creating "WineTrails," essentially grouping wine tasting rooms into geographic clusters, allowing you to experience each group in a day or more. Much like a book focusing on hiking in the Cascade Mountains or a walking tour of San Francisco, *WineTrails* provides details about which wineries to see, when to visit, how to get there, and tips on dining and lodging—all the information you need to plan your next weekend-getaway wine tour.

How to Use This Guidebook

I've organized this book by 12 "Wine Country Regions," and within these regions I have identified 32 WineTrails with more than 200 winery destinations. The wineries included in this book are open to the public and have regular tasting room hours. That accounts for about half of the wineries in the state. The other wineries require an appointment or are not open at all (unless your last name is Gates or you publish a magazine titled *Wine Spectator*). See the sidebar discussion on this topic.

Use this guidebook and its companion website, www.winetrailsnw.com, to plan your wine tour. Decide where you want to go and when. Winetrailsnw.com includes event information and up-to-date information about each winery, including tasting room hours, tasting fees, locations, and more.

Washington's WineTrails

As noted, each WineTrail is a cluster of wineries that form a natural geographic group. I gave each WineTrail a name that describes the general area of the winery. I admit that the name "Walla Walla WineTrail South" isn't very sexy, but it is functional. Some WineTrails are loop trails, allowing you to easily plan the sequence of wineries for a day trip.

Choosing the Wineries to Include in the Book

I chose more than 200 winery tasting rooms to include in *WineTrails of Washington*. This represents only half the wineries in the state! So the first question that might pop into your head is why did you leave out half of the state's wineries? The answer is simple: ***WineTrails of Washington* focuses only on those wineries that have tasting rooms open to the public with regular tasting room hours.** The remaining wineries are open "by appointment only" or not open at all. I encourage you to visit the appointment-only wineries as well (see Appendix A for contact information). Often a visit to the "by appointment only" wineries will give you the opportunity to talk one-on-one with the winemaker. Many of the state's renowned wineries are not open to the public and require calling in advance to set up an appointment. These wineries include Quilceda Creek Vintners, DeLille Cellars, Soos Creek Wine Cellars, Cayuse Vineyards and many others. However, not to worry, my fellow WineTrail enthusiasts. Many of the publicly accessible wineries are the best of the best, according to wine critics.

Many of the wineries are within easy walking distance of each other. Others are scattered across miles of terrain (or water), which requires more travel time. For many of your treks, you will need a car or a hired limo to get from one winery to another.

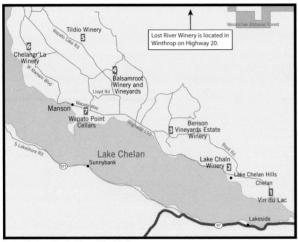

Lake Chelan North Shore WineTrail

This guidebook is a "glove box" book for taking with you on your tour. Included are detailed driving directions from the nearest highway for each winery, photos of the winery, and a brief description that highlights something unique about the winery—the winemaker's philosophy for making wine, the architecture of the building, the use of estate grapes, or other unique descriptors. Armed with this information, you can better shape your wine tour and know what to look for (and taste).

I've chosen purposefully to avoid any ratings of wine. This book is about wine touring and the experience associated with getting out there and swirling. More often than not, I discovered that a visit to a tasting room housed in a double-wide trailer is just as fun and memorable as a visit to a tasting room located in a chateau. Thus, the focus is on the overall experience of visiting the winery without passing judgment on the wine itself. Often, "good wine" is in the eye of the beholder. Why else would a wine not receive accolades in one competition and get high marks in another from a different set of judges. At times I do gush about a tasting room's ambiance—a panoramic view, a well-stocked gift shop or a splendid place to picnic. For example, you can't visit Maryhill Winery on the Columbia River Gorge and not come away knowing that this is one of the top views in Washington. That gets my "Favorite" vote.

David Cowan of Cowan Vineyards

To answer questions about my favorite wineries to eat, sleep, picnic, shop, view scenery, and get hitched, I have included my list of favorites in the next section. This list is bound to cause some contention, but the great thing about being the author of this book is that I get to choose. I am judge and jury. However, because of the dynamic nature of Washington's wine industry, with new wineries continually emerging and big bucks being invested in "wine villages" and resort destinations, the lists are subject to periodic review. Your voice is important. I am interested in knowing your opinion about what you consider "the best," via the WineTrails Northwest website.

My hope is that you will experience the joys of Washington's tasting rooms that I found. From Woodinville to Walla Walla (and everywhere in between) I personally visited each winery and met with as many winemakers as possible. What I discovered is a very passionate group of individuals strongly committed to producing the best wine possible. Most winemakers keep their day job and work the "hobby that got out of control" at night and on the weekends. They are not rich—many are just getting by. They're not snooty either. In fact, most folks I encountered were down to earth and driven by a passion to make great wine.

Zin and the Art of Wine Tasting

The key to tasting wine is to slow down and concentrate.

Beyond that, you just need to swirl, smell and taste. A visual check of the wine simply informs your brain what you are about to taste. Shades of red wine range from purple, ruby red, deep red, red brown, mahogany, to brown. White wine hues range from yellow green, straw, gold, yellow-brown, amber brown, to brown. It's a good idea to hold your glass up to

The Label

Now is a good time to study the wine's label and learn where the grapes came from, the wine's vintage, the grape varietals, the amount of alcohol by volume, and if the wine is bottled at the winery (estate bottled). With respect to the source of the grapes, you may discover that you enjoy cabernet sauvignon from Red Mountain or cabernet franc from a particular Yakima Valley vineyard.

The vintage year of a wine is important to note, because the quality of a wine in large part depends on the variant weather of the Pacific Northwest. For example, it is no accident that 2004 Walla Walla wines used grapes from outside Walla Walla. During 2004, the Walla Walla Valley suffered a deep freeze that essentially ruined the grape crop for winemaking. Vineyards at higher elevations or near temperate rivers made out just fine. Another useful piece of information is the varietal designation of the wine. The correct term is variety of wine or the grape's species. If the label states that the wine is "cabernet sauvignon," you know that at least 75 percent of the grapes used in the production of the wine were of the cabernet sauvignon variety. The remaining 25 percent may be syrah, merlot, cabernet franc or some other variety that the winemaker used for blending.

Increasingly we witness the emergence of "hot" wines. These wines have an alcohol content of 14.5 percent or higher and often cause a burning sensation in the back of the mouth if the alcohol is not masked by the wine's flavor.

a white background (a wall or a napkin) to judge the color of the wine. Where the wine is on the color palette informs your brain and gives your taste buds a heads up for what they are about to experience. If, upon uncorking, you find a wine to be bad, the chance of it being caused by oxidation is like winning the lottery: remote. More likely the problem is "cork taint," which occurs when wine is exposed to a diseased cork containing 2,4,6-trichloroanisole (TCA). Increasingly, wineries are moving to screw caps, plastic bags (boxed wines) and synthetic corks to avoid this problem. For my money though, I still need the sound of the cork popping out of the bottle.

Once the wine is poured, some folks like to tilt the wine glass and observe how the wine flows down the inside of the glass. However, there is no correlation between the "legs" or "tears" on the inside of the glass and the taste itself.

WineTrail Note: The crystals you often find at the bottom of your wine glass are harmless tartrate crystals and should not reflect negatively on the wine. These "wine diamonds" are more of an aesthetic issue. Filtering these crystals may take away some desirable flavor characteristics.

Swirling

A wine just poured needs to stretch its legs and aerate. Swirling lets the wine open up and release aromas. Up to this point, oxygen has been a bad thing; now, oxygen is the wine's best friend. It allows the wine to open up and create a bouquet. Most tasting rooms provide wine glasses roomy enough to swirl the wine without spillage. You need that space between the wine and your nose to smell the aroma. If you chance upon a winery that uses little plastic cups or tiny "orange juice glasses," you might consider shortening your visit and moving on to the next winery.

Smelling

The aroma given off by a wine is referred to as its "nose." Right after a vigorous swirl, quickly smell the wine by sticking your nose into the glass. Get your nose as far down as possible. Concentrate and let your imagination run wild as you attempt to describe what you smell. In time, descriptions such as sweaty saddle, cat pee (no kidding), tar, kerosene, burnt match, and asparagus may enter your smelling lexicon. Researchers say that flavor is made up

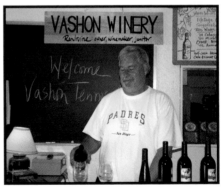

Ron Irvine, Vashon Winery

of 75 percent smell and 25 percent taste. No wonder food tastes bland when you have a cold. You can't smell it. Washington varietals, such as merlot and cabernet sauvignon, have a distinctive smell. I often pick up dark berry smells and hints of chocolate, mineral, and smoked cedar when I take in the aroma of a Washington cabernet sauvignon. To me, California cabernet sauvignons don't have the intense nose that Washington's cabernet sauvignons do.

Tasting

Most of us grew up with the understanding that the tongue has certain regions that taste salt, bitter, sweet, and sour. Have you ever seen those drawings of the tongue that depict which part of the tongue tastes what? But according to current research, all taste buds can taste salt, bitter, sweet, and sour to varying degrees. Taste buds are on the front of the tongue and the back. That's why you see sommeliers and wine connoisseurs vigorously swishing the wine around their mouths; they are getting the maximum exposure throughout their mouth, to taste the wine. While swishing, your brain is also registering other sensations, such as heaviness, roundness, finish, and astringency from the tannins found in the wine. Concentrate for a few seconds while the wine is in your mouth. Swirl it around your mouth and attempt to suck a little air in—without committing a gagging *faux pas*—to pick up the wine's full flavors.

Red Sky Winery tasting room, Woodinville

Remember, slow down and concentrate.

Tasting Room Etiquette—Do's and Don'ts

There are definite rules of the road when it comes to visiting tasting rooms, and most involve common sense. Moderation is a good thing. At the Hedges Winery tasting room in Red Mountain, I struck up a conversation with a fellow wine trekker and learned that he had visited 17 other wineries *that same day*. His wife sheepishly admitted that she couldn't remember any of the wineries after no. 8. Not surprising. Those little ounces add up. So have a strategy ahead of time and try to stick to it. With apologies to Heloise, here are my "Hints from Steve" with respect to tasting room etiquette, a list of do's and don'ts the WineTrails have taught me:

Do:
- **Drink responsibly**—designate a driver or hire a limo.
- **Spit or dump as much as you want**—that's what those spittoons are for. You've already experienced the taste of the wine and if you have five more wineries to visit, or you're counting calories, or you simply don't care for the wine, it's OK not to swallow.

- **Have patience with the wine pourer**—don't poodle your way forward with outstretched hand begging for another fill; they'll get to you.
- **Have a tasting strategy**—choose which wines you would like to sample. If you are only interested in the reds, let your pourer know.
- **Ask questions**—tasting room staff are passionate about their wines and anxious to tell you why.
- **Purchase wine if you want to**—assuming it is in your budget and you like it, spring for it. This is especially true in small wineries where the winery itself may be the only place to purchase the wine.

Dunham Cellars' Three-Legged Red was named after owner Eric Dunham's dog, Port

- **Be open to wines that you believe you will not like**—reds, whites, port wines. You might be surprised to learn how delicious grapes grown in the Puget Sound region can be or how a fruit wine might be a perfect accompaniment to the pound cake you plan to serve (e.g., Harbinger's blackberry wine).
- **Let them know if you like their wine**—there's a reason that the pourer is staring at you with an expectant look in their eyes. If you like it, tell them. Winemakers live for such moments.

Don't:
- **Ask for a second helping**—unless you are contemplating purchasing a bottle or you need a second helping to clarify what you just tasted, it's considered most piggish to ask for another sample.
- **Feel that you have to purchase a bottle of wine**—the winery's primary goal is to provide you a positive experience so you tell your friends and family about it.
- **Wear perfumes or colognes**—your nose needs to smell the wine.
- **Attempt to engage the tasting room staff in esoteric debates**—save the Hungarian versus American oak debate for a conversation with the winemaker, not the poor pourer.
- **Take anything**—the wine glasses are theirs, not yours, as are those medallions draped around wine bottles and the family wine dog. **WineTrail Note:** The exception to this rule is Glacier Peak Winery in Rockport, where your $5 tasting fee entitles you to keep the engraved wine glass.
- **Drink excessively**—again, an ounce here and an ounce there add up. Keep your wits.

Ready, Set, Enjoy!

"We could have used your book today," exclaimed a leather-clad biker at Dusted Valley Vintners in Walla Walla. She had overheard my conversation with the tasting room pourer and wanted to know more about the book. There's something conspicuous about lugging around a Nikon D200 camera and scribbling notes in a wire bound notebook not made for left-handers. I didn't get their names, but the two motorcycle couples had ridden down to Walla Walla from the Tri-Cities that morning and we struck up a conversation when curiosity got the better of them.

Biking tourists at Dusted Valley Vintners

I must confess that there were many times that I felt obvious with my writing accoutrements; people would look at me with that "Who's the cork dork with the notepad?" look. I asked the motorcyclists if they had visited the wineries along Highway 14 in the Columbia River Gorge. They replied that they hadn't yet, but when they do they could really use my book. To that group of bikers at the Dusted Valley Vintners, please contact me and I will see that you get a copy. Hey, I'll even autograph it in the Dusted Valley Vintners' description.

To other WineTrail enthusiasts, use *WineTrails of Washington* to plan your wine tour getaway, but don't forget to take this guidebook with you, along with cash, a bottle of water, a cell phone, a camera, and a cooler (in the summer). If you plan to purchase wine and you're packing a terrific picnic, please don't hesitate to invite me! Just kidding…sort of. Before venturing out, it is also a good idea to call ahead to verify tasting room hours, go over directions, and ask about special events or the likelihood that the winemaker will be there when you visit.

After any of your WineTrail excursions, let me know how it went and how I can improve *WineTrails of Washington* for future editions. The wine-industry landscape is constantly changing, and I attempt to stay current and provide accurate information. Please take a moment to visit winetrailsnw.com and shoot me a message at sroberts@winetrailsnw.com.

Happy WineTrails to you!

Steve Roberts

Reininger's barrel room

Favorites

When I tell friends and acquaintances about *WineTrails of Washington*, I pause for a few seconds before the inevitable questions come my way, asking about the best place to picnic, shop, eat or stay. For example: "Hey Steve, we're heading to Walla Walla for our anniversary. Is there a winery where we can stay?" Or: "My husband's really into wine. Is there a winery in Woodinville where I can get him a gift?" At first, I ducked these questions, mainly because "the best place to picnic" or the "best winery view" is truly subjective. Besides,

Patio view of Lake Chelan from Nefarious Winery

I still need to remain on friendly terms with *all* wineries. Then I realized that there aren't many people crazy enough to visit more than 200 wineries in one year, fill up five notebooks, snap a gazillion pictures, and live to tell about it. I figured that I owed it to folks to tell them which wineries offer the best in shopping, eating, sleeping, picnicking, and tying the knot. I decided to take the plunge and render an opinion on such matters. Without further ado, here are *my* favorites.

Favorite Destination Wineries

When I refer to a "destination winery," I'm talking about a winery that offers a place to stay and dining options—from ordering off the menu to breaking out the spaghetti pot in your guest suite. You can drive to a destination winery, unpack and not leave for a weekend (or two). In Washington, such one-stop destination wineries are rare. More common are the growing number of

Basel Cellars Estate Winery

travel-related businesses that cater to wine tourists; Walla Walla's Marcus Whitman Hotel, Woodinville's Willows Lodge, Leavenworth's Visconti's Restaurant, and Yakima's Birchfield Manor Gourmet Restaurant & Inn are examples that come to mind. Right now, I can't give you my top 10 destination wine resorts because there aren't 10. However, that picture is rapidly changing. In the next 10 years, we will

13

witness the emergence of a number of wine resorts. In the meantime, you do have a small number of great choices:

1. **Abeja** (Walla Walla)—The Inn at Abeja is a stunning turn-of-the-century farmstead restored with loving care. With wonderful breakfasts and attentive staff, the Abeja experience is romantic, relaxing, and memorable.
2. **Cave B Estate Winery** (Quincy)—Go to the spa in the afternoon and enjoy a concert under the stars at night. Both *Luxury Travel Magazine* and *Condé Nast* gush about Cave B.
3. **Basel Cellars Estate Winery** (Walla Walla)—Basel Cellars was voted best destination winery by *Seattle Magazine* in 2005 and 2006.
4. **Desert Wind Winery** (Prosser)—Ample guestrooms with flat-screen televisions and a bridal suite Jacuzzi make for a relaxing getaway. Conveniently located off I-82.
5. **Eagle Creek Winery & Cottage** (Leavenworth)—Guests choose a bottle of wine from the well-stocked cellar to enjoy while overlooking the vineyard.
6. **China Bend** (Kettle Falls area)—Pack your croquet mallet to take to this relaxing wine resort. Enjoy breathtaking views and organic cuisine fresh from the garden.
7. **Tefft Cellars** (Outlook)—In the heart of Rattlesnake Hills wine country, Outlook Inn Guest Villa includes a full kitchen and three bedrooms. There is a minimum two-night stay.

Favorite Wineries for Dining

From menus that feature a full-course dinner to chalkboards listing appetizer specials, select wineries provide the perfect atmosphere to enjoy wine paired with Northwest cuisine. Some wineries serve *al fresco*, weather permitting, so don't drop by in February and expect to eat. But whether the dining space is inside or outside, if you're hitting the WineTrails and your tummy begins to rumble, check out these choice wineries:

Tagaris Winery & Taverna Tagaris

1. **Cave B Estate Winery** (Quincy)—Tendrils Restaurant, situated in Cave B's architecturally splendid inn, serves up five-star regional fare under the direction of celebrated executive chef Fernando Divina.
2. **Vin du Lac Winery** (Lake Chelan)—This old orchard farmhouse, remodeled in a country French style, serves delicious fare. Ideal for lunch or a late-afternoon snack, this outdoor Lake Chelan bistro emanates charm.
3. **Wapato Point Cellars** (Lake Chelan)—Winemaker's Grill pairs Nebraskan steaks and wonderful wine. The grill also features live music most weekends.

4. **Tsillan Cellars** (Lake Chelan)—Open when the weather's warm, Tsillan's outdoor wine bistro serves up delectable food paired with exceptional views and wonderful wines.

5. **Lake Chelan Winery** (Lake Chelan)—Barbecue never tasted so good as it does in the wine garden at this North Shore location. Don't worry; there are plenty of napkins to accompany the baby back ribs.

6. **Desert Wind Vineyard** (Prosser)—A full-service kitchen, attentive wait staff, and warm hues of reds and browns are combined with marvelous wine and food choices at this location.

7. **Alexandria Nicole Cellars** (Prosser)—In this setting, bacon-wrapped scallops pair wonderfully with crisp sauvignon blanc.

8. **Tagaris Winery & Taverna Tagaris** (Richland)—The taverna, a Mediterranean-style restaurant, serves local fare. Patio Kouzina offers a great place for a glass of wine or lighter fare in warm weather.

9. **Bookwalter Winery** (Richland)—This winery serves artisan regional cheeses and *charcuterie* both indoors and outside under umbrellas. Inside, warm earth tones go perfectly with light fare and wine.

10. **Caterina Winery** (Spokane)—The winery features appetizer specials on weekend nights along with music and wine.

Favorite Winery Views

Because of Washington's diverse landscapes, selecting wineries for the "best views" category is difficult. It's far easier to come up with my top 50 winery views than limiting it to 10. I enjoy desert vistas, mountain ranges, lush valleys, ocean shores, and rolling wheat fields *equally*. However, if forced to narrow it down to my top 10, I'd pack a camera when visiting the following wineries:

1. **Cave B Estate Winery** (Quincy)—Astonishing sweeping views of sky, water, canyon, and vineyard. *Gorgeous.*

2. Tying for second place: **Tsillan Cellars, Nefarious Cellars, and Chelan Estate Vineyards & Winery** (Lake Chelan, south shore)—Although they pose a danger and can wreak havoc, local summer forest fires also create red skies at night and wonderful sunsets.

View of Columbia River Gorge from Maryhill Winery

3. **Benson Vineyards Estate Winery** (Lake Chelan, north shore)—Pinch yourself and repeat after me, "I'm not in Italy, I'm not in Italy, I'm not in Italy."

4. **Maryhill Winery** (Goldendale)—Located next to the Columbia River Gorge, this winery offers dramatic views of vineyards leading down to the river. Oregon's Cascade Mountain range fills the canvas beyond.

5. **Wind River Cellars** (Husum)—Situated in the Columbia River Gorge, this winery's deck has stunning views of both Mount Adams and Mount Hood.
6. **Saint Laurent Winery** (Malaga)—Saint Laurent offers marvelous views of the Columbia River and distant mountains.
7. **Martin-Scott Winery** (East Wenatchee)—Located on a bluff above the Columbia River, this winery has some breathtaking views.
8. **Glacier Peak Winery** (Rockport)—Aptly named, the winery's location on the scenic North Cascades Highway offers dazzling larger-than-life views of Glacier Peak.
9. **Arbor Crest Wine Cellars** (Spokane)—Views of Spokane Valley never looked so good.
10. Tying for 10th place: **Terra Blanca Winery & Estate Vineyard, Hedges Family Estate, Tapteil Vineyard Winery, Hightower Cellars, Kiona Vineyards Winery** (Red Mountain)—All of these Red Mountain wineries face the golden beauty of Horse Heaven Hills.

The following wineries fall into the "honorable mention" bucket, but if you gave me a glass of Barnard Griffin Reserve Cabernet Sauvignon, they could easily move into the top 10:

- **Basel Cellars Estate Winery** (Walla Walla)—This hilltop location presents magnificent views of the Blue Mountains.
- **China Bend Winery** (Kettle Falls area)—The scenery at this winery, found on the west side of Lake Roosevelt 20 miles north of Kettle Falls, is drop-dead gorgeous.
- **Preston Premium Wines** (Pasco)—Preston Premium Wines' elevated tasting room and outdoor deck provide a ringside seat to its 160-acre vineyard.
- **Cascade Cliffs Winery & Vineyard** (Highway 14, milepost 88.5)—Basalt cliffs jetting skyward and rows of manicured vineyards complement each other beautifully.
- **Steppe Cellars** (Zillah)—At night, the lights of the lower Yakima Valley farmland sparkle like diamonds.
- **Silver Lake Winery at Roza Hills** (Zillah)—Panoramic views of the Rattlesnake Hills AVA vineyards are beautiful, no matter what the season.

Favorite Winery Gift Shops

Is there someone on your holiday list who seems impossible to buy for? If that person appreciates the grape, a wine-related gift might be just the answer. A number of wineries offer merchandise to satisfy any wine lover's taste, from the whimsical (e.g., aprons that read, "I love to cook with wine; sometimes I even include it in the recipe") to elegant Riedel stemware. Take along your Visa to these wineries:

Olympic Cellars gift shop

1. **Columbia Winery** (Woodinville)—Purchase wine and complete your holiday shopping in one visit (as I did).
2. **Chateau Ste. Michelle** (Woodinville)—A cornucopia of well chosen merchandise is available.
3. **Maryhill Winery** (Goldendale)—The buyer for this gift shop has an excellent eye.
4. **Latah Creek Winery** (Spokane Valley)—Eastern Washington's top gift shop.
5. **Lake Chelan Winery** (Lake Chelan)—The variety of wine-related merchandise dazzles.
6. **Three Rivers Winery** (Walla Walla)—This gift shop is the best in Walla Walla wine country, hands down.
7. **San Juan Island Vineyards** (Friday Harbor)—An old schoolhouse provides the perfect ambiance for shopping (although the chalkboard is not for sale).
8. **Olympic Cellars** (Port Angeles)—This is a winery that caters to women, and the goodies in the gift shop reflect this focus.
9. **Sagelands Vineyard** (Wapato)—This gift shop emphasizes quality over quantity.
10. **Preston Premium Wines** (Pasco)—Preston Premium Wines is the place to go in the Tri-Cities area for wine merchandise.

Favorite Places to Picnic

Most wineries offer a place to spread a blanket or a nearby picnic table. With good wine and a hoagie sandwich in hand, what more could you want? Nevertheless, there are some nuances to the picnicking experience, which I've flushed out in my top 10 "pack a picnic" wineries:

Three Rivers Winery

1. **Chateau Ste. Michelle** (Woodinville)—The biggest challenge here is where to throw the picnic blanket.

2. **Tsillan Cellars** (Lake Chelan)—Nosh and take in amazing views amidst landscaped waterfalls.
3. **Cave B Estate Winery** (Quincy)—Picnic on a basalt cliff overlooking the Columbia River. A bottle of SageCliffe Semillon completes the perfect picture.
4. **Columbia Crest** (Paterson)—In Horse Heaven Hills, fields of vineyards present a bucolic setting for a picnic.
5. **Terra Blanca** (Red Mountain)—Views of Horse Heaven Hills in this shaded, cool space make a perfect setting for uncorking a bottle.
6. **Three Rivers Winery** (Walla Walla)—The winery overlooks a mini three-hole golf course and the Blue Mountains.
7. **Snoqualmie Vineyards** (Prosser)—Deck furniture surrounded by Pacific Northwest–inspired landscaping makes this winery a great place to break out the cheese and baguette.
8. **San Juan Vineyards** (Friday Harbor)—Bring plenty of food; you'll want to spend all day out on the deck.
9. **Wind River Cellars** (Husum)—Wind, river, mountains, whitewater rafting: Picnicking here is a celebration of life Columbia River Gorge style.
10. **Camaraderie Cellars** (Port Angeles)—The Corsons have created a marvelous setting to enjoy wine and food.

Favorite Places to Wed

The vast majority of wineries do not allow weddings; either they don't have the facilities or they choose not to deal with the angst that usually accompanies the wedding day. But some wineries do accommodate weddings, either in a dedicated space within the winery or outdoors next to the vineyard. Those establishments that do permit weddings can suggest florists, caterers, limousine services and more, and they often have dedicated dressing rooms for the bride and groom. For weddings, call well ahead of time,

Columbia Winery

because most wineries are booked a year in advance. Ask about availability, amenities, size limits, suggested caterers, and more. If you or someone you know has a wedding in the future, check out these wineries:

1. **Columbia Winery** (Woodinville)—Weddings can take place inside or outdoors, with nearby accommodations for guests; a lovely place to toss a bouquet.

2. **Basel Cellars Estate Winery** (Walla Walla)— Basel Cellars offers overnight accommodations, great views, and, outdoor pool for everyone to jump into.

3. **Desert Wind Winery** (Prosser)—This winery offers dedicated his-and-her changing rooms with full-length mirrors, a nice touch.

Beresan Vineyard in Walla Walla

4. **Icicle Ridge Winery** (Leavenworth)—Weddings are performed outside, next to the vineyard and fruit orchards, amongst lovely views of surrounding mountains.

5. **Martin-Scott Winery** (East Wenatchee)—Get married with amazing views of the Columbia River in the background.

6. **Saint Laurent Winery** (Malaga)—Opposite Martin-Scott Winery, Saint Laurent offers terrific views of the Columbia River.

7. **Bethany Vineyards** (Ridgefield)—A beautiful little lake is the backdrop for the nuptials.

8. **Tsillan Cellars** (Lake Chelan)—Located on the south shore of Lake Chelan, Tsillan offers first-class amenities.

9. **Pleasant Hill Estate** (Carnation)—A charming old farmhouse and beautiful grounds present the perfect setting to host rehearsal dinners and the wedding itself.

10. Tied for 10th place: **San Juan Vineyards** (Friday Harbor)—Guests will enjoy getting there via ferry and spending time on San Juan Island. **China Bend** (Kettle Falls area), **Hyatt Winery** (Zillah), **Novelty Hill** and **Jamuik Winery** (Woodinville), and **Wind River Winery** (Husum)—Small, intimate settings for weddings, hosted in selected instances.

You might be wondering what my top 10 tasting rooms are. That's a fair question. However, I'm exercising the Fifth Amendment, which gives authors the right not to incriminate themselves. When it comes to tasting rooms, I like them all. I should have a bumper sticker that reads, "I brake for ALL wine tasting rooms." Admittedly, if pressed, I could come up with a list of my top 10 wine tasting rooms, but why would I do that? In doing so, I would alienate hundreds of other tasting rooms—not a good idea. I'd like to be welcomed back. On this one, I'm as neutral as Switzerland.

Northwest Washington
WINE COUNTRY

Challenger Ridge

On the Northwest Washington WineTrail, diversity rules and our palates celebrate. Nine establishments offer fruit wines, hard ciders, wine from local crops, and Bordeaux-style products made from Eastern Washington grapes. Often the best time to visit these wineries is in the spring during the annual Tulip Festival in Skagit County. Miles of red, orange, purple, and yellow tulips greet you in the valley, as do the tasting room hosts as visitors flock to enjoy their fresh spring releases.

From Bellingham to La Conner, there are plenty of places to stay and dine while on the mainland. We suggest that you budget at three days for the Northwest Washington WineTrail. Cheers.

Northwest Washington WineTrail

1 Pasek Cellars Winery
2 Carpenter Creek Winery
3 Tulip Valley Vineyard & Orchard
4 Glacial Lake Missoula Wine Co.
5 Samson Estates Winery
6 Mount Baker Winery
7 Eagle Haven Winery
8 Challenger Ridge Vineyard & Cellars
9 Glacier Peak Winery

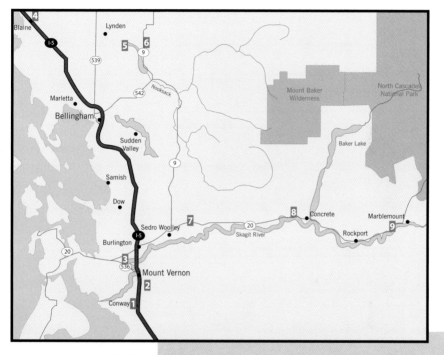

Region:	**Northwest Washington Wine Country**
# of tasting rooms on tour:	**9**
Estimated # of days for tour:	**3**
Getting around:	**Car**
Key events:	❏ **Skagit Valley Tulip Festival in April—see www.tulipfestival.org for details.**
Tips:	❏ **During April, many wineries participate in Tulip Festival and it is a great time to visit.**
	❏ **Take in the North Cascade Highway (US-20), the east/west highway from Burlington to Winthrop. Explore Eagle Haven Winery, Challenger Ridge Vineyards & Winery and Glacier Peak Winery. US-20 to Winthrop is closed during winter.**
	❏ **Pasek Winery is colocated with a deli and also has a second tasting room in Leavenworth.**
Best:	❏ **Best View: Glacier Peak Winery**

23

Pasek Cellars Winery

Cork dorks might make the mistake of passing by Pasek's Mount Vernon tasting room, located right off I-5's exit 221, because the winery's focus is on making

fruit wine. But that would be their loss. While Pasek Cellars makes several traditional wines, including syrah and merlot, it is known for making exceptional fruit wines. Its list of fruit wines reads more like a fruit smoothie menu board: blackberry, cranberry, raspberry, loganberry, guava, pineapple, and passion fruit. Incidentally, the raspberry, loganberry, and blackberry also come as dessert-style port wines to be enjoyed separately, or

drizzled on vanilla ice cream or (my favorite) pound cake. According to Gene Pasek, they had a "tiger by the tail" from the start, and demand for their fruit wines often exceeds supply.

Which wine do you think is Pasek's most popular? If you guessed cranberry, you are correct. And when asked which food pairs the best with cranberry wine, you may be surprised by Gene's answer: everything!

WineTrail Note: A visit to Pasek Winery puts you smack dab in the middle of Skagit Valley's famous tulip area. Come April, the fields are painted with reds, yellows, and other tulipy colors for miles, with an occasional red barn popping up in the distance. Each year an original painting is selected to represent the Tulip Festival and the chosen image adorns the label on Pasek's "Tulip Red" merlot-cabernet. Folks come from all over to purchase the "Tulip Red" blend and many feel as though they're getting two for one, a great wine and a terrific label.

For the sake of convenience, Pasek's tasting room shares a building with an eatery that features deli-style sandwiches, snacks and teriyaki. Hey, maybe the cranberry wine goes with chicken teriyaki. However, if you find yourself a hundred miles east in the übertown of Leavenworth, you will find a second Pasek tasting room, located on 939 Front St., where Pasek has partnered with Willow Crest Winery to offer an inviting space for sampling wine.

And remember: Once you get those bottles of fruit wine home, be sure to serve it chilled.

PASEK CELLARS WINERY
opened: 1995
winemaker(s): Gene Pasek
location: 18729 Fir Island Road
Mount Vernon, WA 98273
phone: 888-350-9463
web: www.pasekcellars.com
e-mail: pasekwinery@hotmail.com
picnic area: Yes
gift shop: Yes
fee: Complimentary wine tasting
hours: Daily 11–5

Pasek Cellar's Cranberry Wine

DIRECTIONS: From I-5 take exit 221 and head west toward Conway. Just west of the freeway, look for the Conway's Skagit Red Barn where the tasting room is located adjacent to Conway Deli.

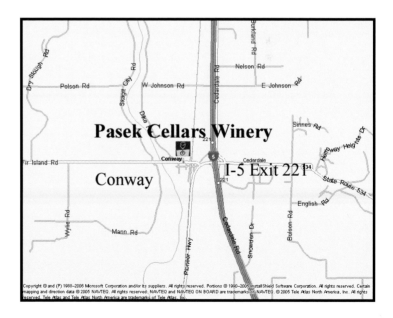

Carpenter Creek Winery

When you think of Skagit County, perhaps your mind doesn't conjure up images of wine tasting but instead visualizes tulips blooming in April across the valley. Au contraire, trekker! Mount Vernon is also home to Carpenter Creek Winery, where winemaker/owner Jeffrey Hammer specializes in handcrafted premium wines. The approach to Carpenter Creek Winery is a nice surprise in

itself. The winery is nestled amongst tall firs and cedar trees, just far enough off the beaten path that you can hear Carpenter Creek gurgling in the background.

Carpenter Creek Winery produces about 3,000 cases of wine each year and focuses on Eastern Washington varietals, including riesling, sauvignon blanc, chardonnay, semillon, syrah, and cabernet sauvignon. The awards draping many of the wine bottles are a testament that you have arrived at the right place for tasting. Be sure to try Jeff's estate-grown siegerrebe. These German grapes don't do well in the hot, dry climates east of the Cascades, but thrive in the cool, damp climates found in the Puget Sound region. You might also find other unique wines, including perhaps a semillon ice wine, which, by the way, would be a perfect partner with fresh peaches and pound cake.

WineTrail enthusiasts will zero in on the distinctive long-stem wine glasses that Carpenter Creek Winery uses in the tasting room. They're gorgeous and remind one of a tulip in shape. Coincidence? I think not.

Speaking of tulips, April is a special time of the year to visit the winery and enjoy its Spring Wine and Tulips Festival. Carpenter Creek Winery provides hors d' oeuvres, barrel tasting, new releases, and daily specials in the gift shop. There might even be some "brats" to go with the cabernet. You definitely want to pick up a bunch of tulips and a case of wine while you are at this WineTrail favorite. Enjoy!

CARPENTER CREEK WINERY
opened: 2001
winemaker(s): Jeffrey W. Hammer
location: 20376 East Hickox Road
Mount Vernon, WA 98274-7730
phone: 360-848-6673
web: www.carpentercreek.com
e-mail: wwcinfo@carpentercreek.com
picnic area: Yes
gift shop: Yes
fee: Complimentary wine tasting
hours: 10–6 Friday and Saturday; 11–6 Thursday
through Monday during April

DIRECTIONS: From I-5 take exit 225—Anderson Road exit. Take the first right onto Cedardale Rd. Proceed on Cedardale for approximately 1 mile. Turn left on Hickox Rd. Follow Hickox Rd for 1 mile. Carpenter Creek Winery is the last driveway on the right.

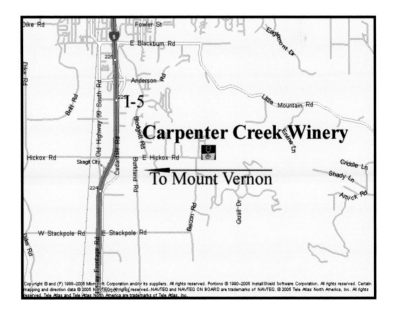

Tulip Valley Vineyard & Orchard

The old 1920s barn is being renovated, but when it's ready in the spring of 2007 the Tulip Valley tasting room will be a "must stop" along the Northwest Washington WineTrail. Currently Tulip Valley's three partners—Ector Deleon, Drew Zimmerman, and Carl Inglebreath—are slogging their way through a major remodel of the supersized barn. In the meantime, they have set up

a temporary tasting room in a cozy corner of the barn, complete with a portable toilet outside. It's everything that a diehard WineTrail enthusiast would love!

The truly wonderful thing about the Northwest Washington WineTrail is the variety of wines you encounter. At Tulip Valley Vineyard & Orchard you will find traditional wines such as chardonnay and pinot noir, in addition to some award-winning apple-cider wines made from local fruit. The champion of the cider wines is Drew Zimmerman, and if you are lucky enough to visit the winery when Drew is there, you are in for an eloquent spiel about the noble apple and how its sugary liquid converts into hard cider. Of course inhabitants of the Normandy region of France and the Welsh countryside already know about the virtues of cider wine. But it is somewhat surprising that in the "apple capital of the world" we don't have a lot of experience with fermented apple juice. Drew is out to correct that, and you might find yourself toting away a bottle of his Jonagold semi-dry or his award-winning "Red Barn Fire Barrel" cider.

By the way, in terms of cider-wine food pairings, consider ham-and-cheese crepes. Hard cider (which is actually only 7 percent to 8 percent alcohol) also goes nicely with a number of cheeses such as Brie, Cougar Gold cheddar, and fontina. Chicken and seafood are also strong candidates. But for me a glass of "Fire Barrel" cider and a couple of cinnamon doughnuts from Seattle's Mighty-O Donut Shop are a hit.

WineTrail Trivia: Across the street from Tulip Valley is Washington State University's Mount Vernon Research and Extension Center. For many years, this WSU agricultural service has worked collaboratively with the grape growers of the Puget Sound region to develop and promote cool-weather grapes such as Madeleine Angevine and siegerrebe, which is actually a cross between Madeleine Angevine and gewürztraminer. From Vashon Island to San Juan Island, grape growers have lauded the efforts of WSU's extension program.

Drew Zimmerman

TULIP VALLEY VINEYARD & ORCHARD
opened: 2006
winemaker(s): Carl Inglebreath; Drew Zimmerman and Ector Deleon
location: 16163 State Route 536
Mount Vernon, WA 98042
phone: 360-428-6894
web: www.redbarncider.com
e-mail: drewzimmer@comcast.net
picnic area: No
gift shop: No
fee: Complimentary wine tasting
hours: Please call ahead

DIRECTIONS: From I-5 take exit 226 [WA-536] west toward Kincaid St. Go .2 miles. Turn left on Kincaid St. and go .2 miles. Turn right on S. 3rd St. and go .3 miles. S. 3rd St. becomes W. Division St.—go .8 miles. W. Division St. becomes WA-536—go 1.3 miles. Arrive at 16163 State Route 536 on the right. Look for large red barn on right and sign for wine/cider tasting.

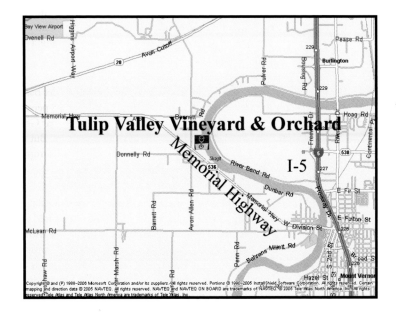

29

Glacial Lake Missoula Wine Co.

Tucked away in the northwest corner of Washington is a winery that's just minding its own business. Glacial Lake Missoula Wine Co. isn't trying to pick a fight with other wineries, but it might succeed nevertheless. At the very least, Blaine-based Glacial Lake Missoula would be shunned in Walla Walla, where an organic viticultural practice called biodynamics is all the rage.

Tom Davis

Briefly, the owners and winemaker Tom Davis at Glacial Lake Missoula "subscribe to the thesis of Australian wine scientist Chris Somers that red wine quality can be objectively measured and can be achieved by maximally extracting grape phenols in an ideal wine matrix." Thus, good winemaking practice relies on sound scientific knowledge rather than the current trends.

Ironically, despite the employment of a huge dose of science in the creation of these wines, Glacial Lake's black-and-white labels, depicting a rushing wall of water, are exceptionally pleasing for their aesthetic quality. Moreover, the poetically named "Deluge" was the perfect choice for a wine that celebrates the Ice Age floods of eastern Washington. These floods, combined with thousands of years of strong winds, resulted in rich soils perfect for growing premium wine grapes.

I'm not sure what an ideal wine matrix is, but the folks at Glacial Lake Missoula Wine Co. are quite willing to explain their winemaking practice in detail. In fact, bring your notebook and no. 2 pencil, and be prepared to take copious notes. The "Science of Winemaking" class is now in session.

GLACIAL LAKE MISSOULA WINE CO.
opened: 2002
winemaker(s): Tom Davis
location: 1625 Boblett Street
Blaine, WA 98230-9260
phone: 360-332-2097
web: www.lakemissoulawine.com
e-mail: sales@lakemissoulawine.com
picnic area: No
gift shop: No
fee: Complimentary wine tasting
hours: 12–6 Saturdays or by appointment

DIRECTIONS: From I-5 heading toward Vancouver BC take exit 275 onto SR-543 and proceed .7 miles. Turn right (east) onto H St. and continue .3 miles. Turn right (south) onto Ludwick Ave. and proceed .2 miles. Turn right (west) on Boblett St. and continue .1 miles to arrive at the winery.

31

Samson Estates Winery

Samson Estates Winery brings a fresh face and a willingness to think outside the traditional barrel. In fact, owner and winemaker Rob Dhaliwal does not use oak in the production of either reds or whites. He is part of a small but

growing minority of winemakers who want to preserve the taste of the grape and not confuse it with wood.

He's also a big-time producer of fruit wines, with Samson Estates' raspberry wine outselling its other award-winning wines, including chardonnay, other fruit wines, dessert wines, riesling, merlot, a red-blend Meritage, and even a wine called "Oro," which is made from fermented hazelnuts. With a family history of farming, Rob grew up surrounded by 200 acres of raspberries. In fact, the family farm is the source of the berries for Samson Estates' raspberry wine. For the number-crunchers among us, let the record show that an astounding 3 pounds of raspberries go into producing one bottle of raspberry wine. No wonder it tastes like biting into a big handful of fresh raspberries picked at their zenith. This is not your grandma's fruit wine. By the way, Rob's father, Sam, still tends to the 200-plus acres of fruit, and Rob honors his dad in the winery's name: Sam-son.

People want alternatives and they want good value, too. How's this for value? Most of the Samson Estates wines sell for around $10 a bottle. Its most expensive wine is its delicious red Meritage, which sells for $19 a bottle. That's still way below the amount you would shell out for a similar quality of wine found in Woodinville or Walla Walla.

Bring a friend and split a carafe of wine near the cozy fireplace or, weather permitting, sit outside on the comfortable deck chairs and enjoy stunning views of the Twin Sisters Mountain in the distance. To paraphrase the Beatles, "Raspberry fields forever."

SAMSON ESTATES WINERY
opened: 2002
winemaker(s): Rob Dhaliwal
location: 1861 Van Dyk Road
Everson, WA 98199
phone: 360-966-7787
web: www.samsonestates.com
e-mail: info@samsonestates.com
picnic area: Yes
gift shop: No
fee: Complimentary wine tasting
hours: Daily 11–6 from June 1 through September 30;
11–5 Friday through Sunday from October through
May; 11–3 Wednesday and Thursday, 11-5 Friday
through Sunday, December 1 through December 23,
or by appointment. CLOSED December 24 through
December 26 and December 31

DIRECTIONS: From I-5 take exit 255 and head east onto SR-542 [Mt. Baker Hwy] 4.7 miles. Turn left onto Everson-Goshen Rd and proceed 6 miles. Turn right onto SR-544 [Everson-Goshen Rd] and continue 1 mile. Turn left onto Van Dyk Rd for about 1 mile and arrive at Samson Estates Winery at 1861 Van Dyk Rd.

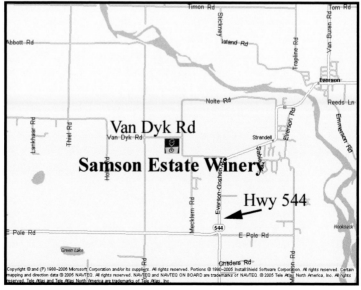

Mount Baker Winery

This is the story of one man's passion for growing and making wine. Randy Finley, owner of Mount Baker Vineyards, purchased the winery/vineyard in 1989. Prior to that, he gained fame as the creator of Seattle's Seven Gables Theatre in the U District. However, a year's sojourn in France gave him the wine bug, and upon his return, he purchased Mount Baker Vineyards. Now,

years later, he is able to look back and reminisce. In a *Whatcom County Business Pulse* article in June 2002, he quipped, "They say if you start with a really large winery and handle it just right, it'll be small in no time." Mother Nature has a way of humbling us all.

Having a sense of humor is a prerequisite for a grape grower in northwest Washington near Mount Baker. Most years, the Nooksack Valley provides a long, mild growing season for the production of varietals favored by Mount Baker Vineyards. Randy's 6 acres produce cool-weather grapes including chasselas, Madeleine Angevine, Müller-Thurgau, pinot noir, pinot gris, and siegerrebe. However, if the summer weather remains too cool, you do not get enough sugar. And, as we all know, without sufficient sugar, it is hard to make that all-important ingredient of good wine: alcohol. Likewise, a harsh winter can wreak havoc on the roots. Then too, the surrounding maple trees produce a powdery mildew that can ruin the grapes and negatively affect crop production.

A great way to mitigate the risk is to import Eastern Washington grapes to produce award-winning wines, such as cabernet sauvignon, merlot, lemberger, and syrah. That is precisely what Mount Baker Vineyards does. Including his estate wines, Randy is able to produce 8,000 cases per year, which requires a small army of helpers for crushing, fermenting, and bottling. Mount Baker Vineyards sells most of its wine at the winery, but you can find it in local grocery stores, wine shops, and restaurants. What's more, Randy is quite willing to offer private-label wines and co-produce the wine, as he recently did with Kaspar Donier for Seattle-based Kaspar's Special Events and Catering.

The other key partner to this endeavor is Randy's spouse, Patricia Clark Finley. Her distinctive artwork adorns the walls of the tasting room and graces the wine labels of many of their releases. This convergence of land, wine, art, friends, and family defines Mount Baker Vineyards.

Northwest Washington WineTrail

MOUNT BAKER WINERY
opened: 1989
winemaker(s): Randy Finley
location: 4298 Mount Baker Highway
Everson, WA 98247
phone: 360-592-2300
picnic area: Yes
gift shop: Yes
fee: $2 tasting fee
hours: Daily 11–5

DIRECTIONS: From I-5 take exit 255 and travel east on SR-542 [Mt. Baker Hwy] about 15 miles outside Bellingham. Look for Mount Baker Winery on your left.

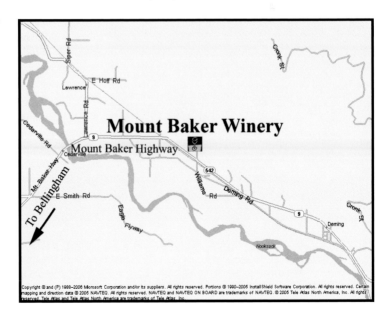

Eagle Haven Winery

A celebration of Northwest fruit, Eagle Haven Winery is the collaboration of owners Tom and Jim Perkins (father and son), Fred Vochatzer, and winemaker Chuck Jackson. Their creation is a tribute to the surrounding apple orchards, grape fields, nearby rivers, and animal habitats. These guys are hard-working, salt-of-the-earth types who haven't forgotten how to have a good time after a good day's work. The motif of the winery is intentionally "Old West," and its large tasting room boasts an expansive tasting bar that surely took much of the Northern Hemisphere's forests of knotty pine to construct. The result is a welcoming environment most suitable for tasting wine and striking up a conversation with other WineTrail enthusiasts.

The winery is located 4 miles east of Sedro-Woolley in the foothills of the North Cascade Mountains. Here in this Eddie Bauer setting is the Eagle Haven Winery, surrounded by 40 acres of orchards containing 50 apple varieties. Next to the winery is a charming garden area with outdoor furniture, the perfect place to uncork a bottle of Eagle Haven's Madeleine Angevine and siegerrebe blend to enjoy with Gouda cheese and nutty crackers.

Since 2004, winemaker Chuck Jackson has been producing unique fruit wines (winter pear, red apple, blackberry, and black currant), a crisp white wine using a blend of Madeleine Angevine and siegerrebe grapes, and a syrah using grapes from the Columbia Valley. Chuck has 30 years of experience fashioning premium wines.

By the way, Fred Vochatzer and Jim Perkins typically do the honor of pouring wine for visitors, and their running commentary will convince you—as it did me—that the black currant wine has a distinctive evergreen forest smell. Passion has a way of doing that.

Tom Perkins, Fred Vochatzer and Jim Perkins
(l to r)

EAGLE HAVEN WINERY
opened: 2004
winemaker(s): Chuck Jackson
location: 8243 Sims Road
Sedro-Woolley, WA 98284-7990
phone: 360-856-6248
web: www.eaglehavenwinery.com
e-mail: info@eaglehavenwinery.com
picnic area: Yes
gift shop: Yes
fee: Complimentary wine tasting
hours: 11–6 Friday through Monday, or by appointment

DIRECTIONS: From I-5 take exit 230 and travel east toward Burlington on SR-20 [Avon Cutoff]. Continue on SR-20 approximately 10 miles and turn right onto Sims Rd. Follow signs to Eagle Haven Winery (.3 miles) on your left just past the orchards.

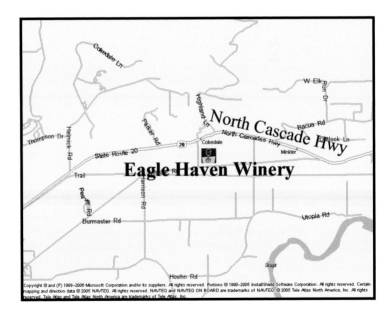

Challenger Ridge Vineyard & Cellars

Challenger Ridge Vineyard & Cellars is the story of eight partners investing in a dream. Initially started in 2002 by French transplants Louis and Dominique Dially, the winery was sold to the partners in 2006. Now equipped with nearly 10 acres of prime pinot noir and a great deal of unbridled energy, the partners are poised to take Challenger Ridge to the next level.

Using a combination of estate grapes as well as fruit from Yakima Valley, Red Mountain, and Horse Heaven Hills, partner and head winemaker Randy Bonaventura is prepared to coax the *terroir* from these grapes, just as he did as Mount Baker Winery's winemaker. For now, the current inventory is largely the responsibility of Louis Dially, but in the near future, that inventory will be expanded to include estate-grown chardonnay. In time, Randy hopes to grow the current annual production from 3,000 to 10,000 cases, but no more.

Randy is a very hands-on winemaker; he still wants to be involved in every step of the process, from pruning the vineyard to punching down the must. When production reaches more than 10,000 cases, he believes the winemaker's role changes from being intimately involved to managing others. That's not his cup of tea, as he learned first-hand from a previous stint at a New Zealand–based winery that produced more than 1,000,000 cases annually. There, he learned the antithesis of "artisan." As he describes it, they used dump trucks instead of standard bins and 6-inch pipes instead of 1-inch pipes.

The new owners have exciting plans in store for Challenger Ridge visitors, including the hosting of weddings, jazz concerts, and other events. In addition, as a member of the fledgling Skagit Winery Association, Challenger Ridge will, in coordination with other local wineries, work to entice WineTrail enthusiasts to make the drive east on Highway 20 to its winery near Concrete. Seeing a name like "Concrete," you would not expect to discover a truly beautiful setting for a winery. Nestled on a Cascade foothill right off Highway 20, Challenger Ridge Vineyard & Cellars is close to the beautiful Skagit River. We suspect that many visitors will be taken by its charm and drop in often.

CHALLENGER RIDGE VINEYARD & CELLARS
opened: 2000
winemaker(s): Randy Bonaventura
location: 43095 Challenger Road
Concrete, WA 98237-9416
phone: 360-853-7360
web: www.challengerridge.com
e-mail: randybon@earthlink.net
picnic area: Yes
gift shop: Yes
fee: Complimentary wine tasting
hours: Daily 11–5 from Memorial Day weekend
through November; 11–5 Saturday and Sunday from
November through May

Randy Bonaventura

DIRECTIONS: From I-5 take exit 232 (north of Burlington). Go east to US-20. Approximately 25 miles to Milepost 85. Before Concrete turn onto Challenger Rd. Proceed to Challenger Ridge Winery at 43095 Challenger Rd.

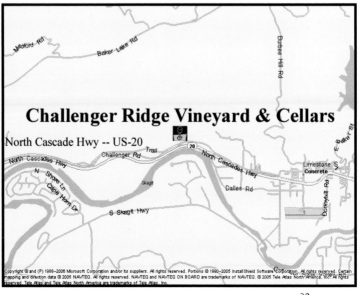

Glacier Peak Winery

Take one part magnificent beauty, one part truly nice people and add a dash of Hungarian grapes and you have the makings of Glacier Peak Winery. Steve and Susan Olson opened their tasting room in 2005 along the Cascade Loop Highway in Rockport, Washington, surrounded by mountain peaks. One of those peaks is Glacier Peak—one of five active volcanoes in Washington. Fortunately for WineTrail trekkers, Glacier Peak has not stirred for nearly 200 years.

Winemaker/viticulturist Steve Olsen produces a combination of wines using fruit from the Yakima Valley as well as several estate wines. His estate wines feature pinot noir, siegerrebe, and a unique Hungarian varietal called Agria. By itself, Agria offers a robust flavor that pairs nicely with Northwest seafood. However, Steve takes it a step further by blending Agria with siegerrebe to create a delicious wine he calls "Glacier Sunrise." Steve's Eastern Washington grapes go into the production of rich, full-bodied cabernet sauvignon, syrah, and merlot. Together he makes about 1,000 handcrafted cases per year and he wants to keep it that way—"quality over quantity," he notes. Given the accolades wine connoisseurs have given Steve recently, he must be doing something right.

When Steve and Susan first opened their tasting room, they encountered bureaucratic paperwork and had not received the appropriate water permit necessary for cleaning wine glasses. Not to be derailed, the Olsens purchased 1,300 wine glasses with the idea that they would charge a tasting fee to recover the cost of the wine glasses. Tasters not only got to sample great wine but also kept the wine glass. For most folks, the $5 tasting fee became a good deal. Consequently, the tasting fee and you-keep-the-glass idea stuck, and today the Olsens still have the tasting-fee policy, even though they have long since obtained the water permit. Necessity is the mother of invention.

The beauty of the upper Skagit River Valley, great wine, and wonderful people all conspire to make this a mandatory stop along the Cascade Loop Highway.

Steve Olsen

GLACIER PEAK WINERY
opened: 2005
winemaker(s): Stephen Olsen
location: 58575 SR-20
Rockport, WA 98283
phone: 360-770-9811
web: www.glacierpeakwinery.com
e-mail: gpwinery@msn.com
picnic area: Yes
gift shop: No
fee: Complimentary wine tasting
hours: 11–5 Saturdays, Sundays and holidays, May
through October, or by appointment

⭐ **BEST Views**

DIRECTIONS: From I-5 take exit 232 (north of Burlington). Go east to US-20. Approximately 45 miles to Milepost 104. Vineyard and tasting room is on the left side of Hwy 20.

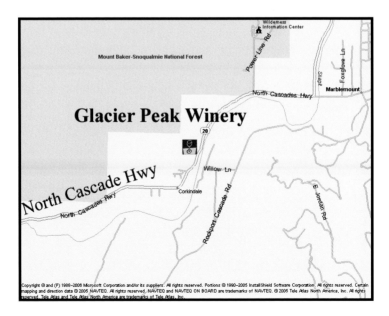

San Juan and Lopez Island
WineTrail

San Juan Vineyards

The San Juan and Lopez Island WineTrail includes only two wineries, but you will need to budget time for getting to and from the Islands via the Washington State Ferry service. Actually, for most of us mainlanders—that's a good thing. The ride is spectacular and it's a short hop from Friday Harbor to Lopez Island. Along the way, you will discover the charm of Friday Harbor and the quaintness of Roche Harbor. **WineTrail Note:** the Lime Kiln Café at Roche Harbor is famous for their cake doughnuts baked daily. You might want to have a crisp riesling on hand—we discovered that it paired superbly with a still warm sugar doughnut.

Both San Juan and Lopez Island offer a number of places to satisfy your getaway needs. The San Juan and Lopez Island WineTrail is a day trip that you will likely extend to a long weekend.

1 Lopez Island Vineyard &
  Winery   **2** San Juan Vineyards

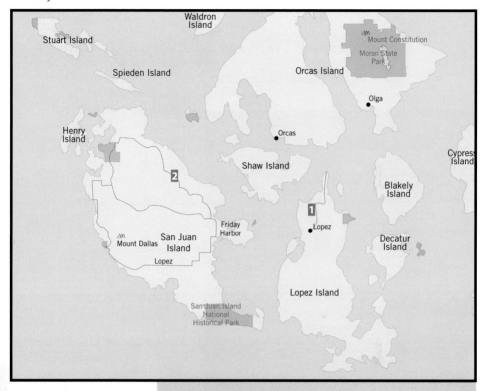

Region:	**Northwest Washington Wine Country**
# of tasting rooms on tour:	**2**
Estimated # of days for tour:	**1 or 2**
Getting around:	**Car, ferry and bike**
Tips:	❑ **Friday Harbor offers a variety of places to eat.** ❑ **A side trip to Roche Harbor is recommended; close by is Westcott Bay Orchards for hard cider wine— appointment only.** ❑ **American Camp is great for picnicking, beach combing, and views of the Straits of Juan de Fuca.** ❑ **Lopez Island's town village offers shopping and a variety of restaurants.**
Best:	❑ **Best Gift Shop: San Juan Vineyards** ❑ **Best Picnicking: San Juan Vineyards**

Lopez Island Vineyard & Winery

A short 10-minute drive from the ferry dock takes you to the small stone-and-timber winery that is Lopez Island Vineyards. The grapes in the vineyards are cool-weather grapes suitable for the Puget Sound viticultural area and include Madeleine Angevine and siegerrebe. These grapes go into Lopez Island's estate white wines. For better-known wines such as merlot and cabernet sauvignon, winemaker Brent Charnley uses grapes from the renowned Crawford Family

Vineyards in the lower Yakima Valley. In addition, Lopez Island Vineyards makes fruit wine using berries and stone fruit from nearby organic farms. The winery rotates its fruit wines; one year it might be raspberry wine, the next year, wild Himalayan blackberry wine.

This winery is first and foremost about using organic farming techniques and natural winemaking practices to produce food (i.e., wine) that is "clean and healthy." This has been its focus since the beginning back in 1986. The goal, in part, is sustainability, which it defines on its website to be "capable of being maintained indefinitely; capable of meeting the environmental, economic and social needs of current generations without compromising the ability of future generations to meet their needs."

When on Lopez Island, do as the Lopez Islanders do: Slow down and enjoy these wines. It is no surprise that just outside the winery are a number of Adirondack chairs begging you to sit down and relax. Wound-up city dwellers need to take in the moment and breath slowly; really taste the wine, notice the vineyard's canopy growing skyward, hear the birds, and notice how the sunlight plays on the glass window. Heck, the ferry won't depart for another four hours. Just chill and enjoy.

LOPEZ ISLAND VINEYARD & WINERY
opened: 1987
winemaker(s): Brent Charnley
location: 724 Fisherman Bay Road
Lopez Island, WA 98261-8499
phone: 360-468-3644
web: www.lopezislandvineyards.com
e-mail: winery@lopezislandvineyards.com
picnic area: Yes
gift shop: Yes
fee: $3 tasting fee
hours: 12–5 Saturdays in April and from October
through December 18; 12–5 Friday and Saturday
May, June and September; 12–5 Wednesday through
Saturday July through August

DIRECTIONS: From Lopez Island ferry terminal take Ferry Rd 2.5 miles. The road name changes to Fisherman Bay Rd. Look for Lopez Island Vineyard and Winery sign on the right at 724 Fisherman Bay Rd. See www.wsdot.wa.gov/ferries/ for ferry schedule.

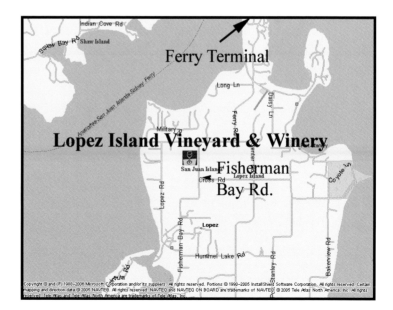

45

San Juan Vineyards

If you should find yourself on the Washington State ferry to Friday Harbor, don't pass up the chance to visit San Juan Vineyards. A mere 10 minutes from the ferry landing, San Juan Vineyards is located 3 miles north of Friday Harbor on Roche Harbor Road.

San Juan Vineyards was the creation of Steve and Yvonne Swanberg, who, together with their insurance-agency partner, Tim Judkins and his daughter

Madison, founded the winery in 1996. Sadly, Steve was later diagnosed with cancer, and he lost his battle with the disease in mid-2006. Today, Yvonne manages the winery.

You'll find the San Juan Vineyards compound has some rather unusual features. A turn-of-the-century one-room schoolhouse houses the tasting room and a well-stocked gift shop. The 1896 schoolhouse features original hardwood floors, a blackboard, and plenty of chalk to write: "I will not throw wine corks at Jimmy anymore." Outside the tasting room is an ample deck with outdoor furniture, perfect for picnicking and enjoying a glass of wine. From the deck, you can see across the road to a grassy field where a horse and a camel lazily graze. Did we say "camel"? Yep. Her name is Mona, and you don't need to worry about being spit upon— she's friendly. Evidently, the banana-belt climate of San Juan Island agrees with camels. Also on the grounds is a replica of a church found on the Hawaiian island of Molokai.

Recently Chris Primus joined San Juan Vineyards to take on the duties of winemaker. Chris will be responsible for producing 4,000 cases of wine annually, including a full line of white and red wines. Oh, and one rosé wine called "Afterglow Blush." Hmmm. San Juan Vineyards' estate wines feature siegerrebe and Madeline Angevine grapes, both grown in the winery's 7-acre vineyard. The grapes used to produce the winery's Bordeaux- and Rhone-style wines hail from the Columbia Valley and the Columbia River Gorge.

WineTrail students, class is in session!

SAN JUAN VINEYARDS
opened: 1996
winemaker(s): Chris Primus
location: 3136 Roche Harbor Road
Friday Harbor, WA 98250
phone: 360-378-9463
web: www.sanjuanvineyards.com
e-mail: sjvineyards@rockisland.com
picnic area: Yes
gift shop: Yes
fee: Small tasting fee
hours: Daily 11–5 in summer; 11–5 Wednesday
through Sunday in fall and spring; January and
February by appointment

⭐ BEST Gift shop and picnicking

DIRECTIONS: **From Friday Harbor,** travel toward Roche Harbor on Roche Harbor Rd. About 3 miles outside of Friday Harbor look for San Juan Vineyards on the right side of the road. Watch for the schoolhouse and chapel on the right.
From Roche Harbor Resort, take Roche Harbor Rd toward Friday Harbor; San Juan Vineyards is on left about 6 miles down the road.

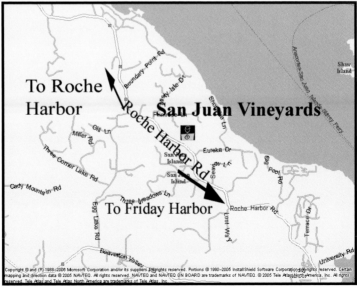

Olympic Peninsula
WINE COUNTRY

Whidbey Island–Port Townsend
WineTrail

Greenbank Cellars

On the Whidbey Island–Port Townsend WineTrail, you will become familiar with the Washington State Ferry schedule and enjoy great wine to boot. Don't be surprised if you find yourself volunteering to pick grapes at Whidbey Island Vineyard and Winery, or eager to bottle wine at FairWinds Wineries. Factor in lunch and/or dinner in Langley or Port Townsend with the knowledge that restaurants feature local wines. You might also want to bring along a bicycle—there are plenty of gentle hills and spectacular views to experience by bike.

1 Whidbey Island Vineyards
  & Winery

2 Greenbank Cellars
3 FairWinds Winery

4 Sorensen Cellars

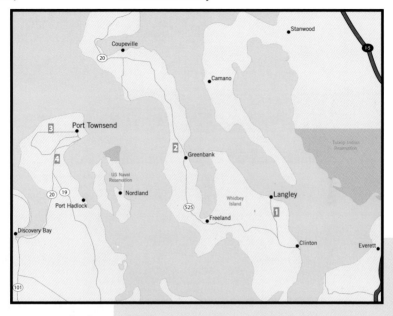

Region:	**Olympic Peninsula Wine Country**
# of tasting rooms on tour:	**4**
# of satellite tasting rooms:	**1—Greenbank Farm on Whidbey Island offers wines from Whidbey Island Vineyards & Winery, Olympic Cellars, Mount Baker Vineyards, Bainbridge Island Vineyards & Winery, Lopez Island Vineyards & Winery, Lost Mountain Winery, FairWinds Winery, Cameraderie Cellars, Sorensen Cellars, Black Diamond Winery and Pasek Cellars**
Estimated # of days for tour:	**1 to 2**
Getting around:	**Car, ferry and bike**
Key events:	❑ **Wineries are part of the North Sound Wineries Association—3 key annual events: Spring Barrel Tasting (Memorial Day Weekend); Passport Wine Tour (Veterans Day Weekend); and Red Wine & Chocolate (February).**
	❑ **See www.northsoundwineries.org/ for event times and tickets.**
Tips:	❑ **Get to know Washington State Ferry schedule—see www.wsdot.wa.gov/ferries.**
	❑ **Budget time to explore Langley and Port Townsend—both offer a variety of restaurants and overnight accommodations.**
	❑ **For walking on the beach and picnicking explore Fort Casey Park near the ferry terminal to Port Townsend, and Fort Worden State Park just outside of the town.**

Whidbey Island Vineyards & Winery

I'll let you in on a secret: It doesn't rain all the time on Whidbey Island. Contrary to popular belief, the growing season is quite dry, and the northern latitude means long summer days with cool nights. Add to the equation the proximity of Puget Sound and you get mild winters, creating unique conditions

for grape growing. Owner and winemaker Greg Osenbach planted Whidbey Island Vineyards' first grapes in 1986, and today the winery produces unique white wines that are a perfect complement to Northwest seafood. As Osenbach states on his website, "We plant varieties from the cooler parts of Europe—France's Loire Valley and Alsace, Germany, and Eastern Europe. The resultant wines are delicate, crisp, and fragrant."

Today the 7 acres of grapes include some lesser-known varietals, such as Madeleine Angevine and siegerrebe. These grapes make delicious white wines that you won't find in Yakima Valley. Make sure you try the winery's "Island White" wine. This "durable blend" of Madeleine Sylvaner and Madeleine Angevine remains Whidbey Island Winery's most popular white. The "Island White" would pair wonderfully with pecan-crusted halibut, but it's also delightful by itself, sipped on the back porch in the summertime—or, in the case of Whidbey Island, on the beach with a picnic.

WHIDBEY ISLAND VINEYARDS & WINERY
opened: 1992
winemaker(s): Greg and Elizabeth Osenbach
location: 5237 South Langley Road
Langley, WA 98260
phone: 360-221-2040
web: www.whidbeyislandwinery.com
e-mail: winery@whidbeyislandwinery.com
picnic area: Yes
gift shop: Yes
fee: Small tasting fee may apply
hours: 12–5 Wednesday through Monday from July
through December; 12–5 Wednesday through Sunday
from October through June

Greg Osenbach

DIRECTIONS: From Clinton Ferry Terminal proceed on SR-525 for 2 miles and go right onto Langley Rd. Continue on Langley Rd 1.9 miles and look for Whidbey Island Vineyards and Winery sign on the right.
From Langley, take Langley Rd toward Clinton 1 mile and arrive at 5237 Langley Rd—look for winery sign on your left.
See www.wsdot.wa.gov/ferries for Washington State ferry schedule to and from mainland.

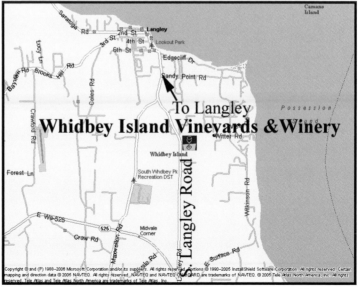

Greenbank Cellars

Greenbank Cellars is a celebration of the finer things in life, and if WineTrails adventurers want to join the celebration, they would be wise to pack a picnic for this experience. Yes, Greenbank Cellars produces outstanding wines, but Frank and Betty Rayles have built Greenbank Farms to offer fine wines, showcase lovingly restoredantique cars and display Betty's fine art.

Greenbank's tasting room is housed in a 100-year-old barn. If you should pay a visit, make sure you note the outstanding wine bar, which was brought from Nebraska in 1905. Many of the wines that winemaker Frank Rayle creates come from Greenbank's own vineyards, including Müller-Thurgau, Madeleine Angevine, siegerrebe, Madeleine Sylvaner, and pinot noir. Make a point of swirling, sniffing, and tasting some of these estate wines, because the vast majority of wineries in Washington don't make wine from cool-climate grapes. Greenbank Cellars makes Alsatian-style whites without oak; as a result, these wines have dry, fresh, crisp, citric flavors. Try the riesling and feel the tingling on your tongue—not too sweet, with an excellent finish.

Frank Rayle also produces some fine European oak-aged reds, including a pleasant, full-flavored cabernet sauvignon and a cabernet franc that features the predominant taste of dark cherries. Equally refreshing is the loganberry wine made from Willamette Valley grapes. Imagine having this with an assortment of cheeses and crusty French bread. Relish the experience, but don't forget to take a look at some antique cars and fine Northwest artwork before unpacking the picnic basket.

The winery gets a steady stream of visitors and is especially popular during the three main events of the North Sound Winery Loop: Red Wine and Chocolate in February; Spring Barrel Tasting during Memorial Day Weekend; and Passport to Wine in November (ticket price is $20 each). Consult www.northsoundwineries.org for details.

GREENBANK CELLARS
opened: 1998
winemaker(s): Frank Rayle
location: 3112 Day Road
Greenbank, WA 98253-9728
phone: 360-678-3964
web: www.whidbey.com/wine
e-mail: wine@whidbey.com
picnic area: Yes
gift shop: No
fee: Complimentary wine tasting
hours: 11–5 Thursday through Monday, or
by appointment

DIRECTIONS: 20 minutes from Clinton ferry; 10 minutes from Keystone ferry on US-525. **From US-525**, go .5 mile west on Bakken Rd in Greenbank. Located on the corner of South Day and Bakken Rds. See www.wsdot.wa.gov/ferries for Washington State ferry schedule to and from mainland.

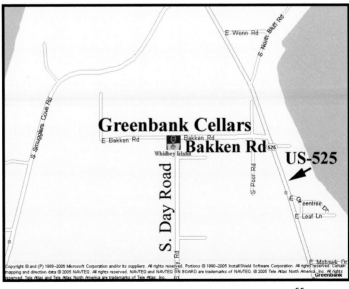

FairWinds Winery

Sure, we all love those mainstream merlots and chardonnays, but for a delightful change of pace check out a little gem of a winery located on the outskirts of Port Townsend: FairWinds Winery. Its owners, Michael and Judy Cavett,

are committed to producing unusual varietals along with more well-known wines, and pricing them within most folks' reach. To this end, FairWinds is the only Washington winery to produce aligote (a white Burgundy). And while aligote's color will remind you of chardonnay, it has its own unique taste and aroma. Even its legs seem to drip down a little quicker than a chardonnay. **WineTrail Note:** Aligote makes a great accompaniment to chicken marsala or a summer salad.

FairWinds Winery also features mead, a sweet white wine that can be drunk by itself or paired with dessert. Mead is associated with the word "honeymoon" because the beverage was drunk during a bride and groom's honeymoon in ancient Scandinavian times. Note: The word "honeymoon" originated in an ancient Northern European custom in which newlyweds, for the first month of their married life, drank a daily cup of honeyed wine, i.e., mead.

One of the treats of visiting FairWinds is the winery tour routinely given by Michael. As you take in the sights, you can easily imagine all his volunteers assisting during crush or squeezing corks into skinny necks bottle by bottle. The winery gets a steady stream of visitors and is especially popular during the three main events of the North Sound Winery Loop: Red Wine and Chocolate in February; Spring Barrel Tasting during Memorial Day Weekend; and Passport to Wine in November (tickets are $20 each).

FairWinds Winery was established in 1993 by two retired Coast Guard couples, and the tasting room was opened in 1996. Eventually Michael and Judy took sole possession of the winery. The FairWinds name and label are nods to Michael's Coast Guard past. Smooth sailing!

Michael Cavett

FAIRWINDS WINERY
opened: 1993
winemaker(s): Michael Cavett
location: 1984 Hastings Avenue West
Port Townsend, WA 98368-9638
phone: 360-385-6899
web: www.fairwindswinery.com
e-mail: info@fairwindswinery.com
picnic area: Yes
gift shop: Yes
fee: Complimentary wine tasting
hours: Daily 12–5 from Memorial Day to Labor
Day; 12–5 Monday through Friday from September
through May

DIRECTIONS: From SR-20 just outside the Port Townsend city limits, turn west on Jacob Miller Rd
and go 2 miles to Hastings Ave. W. Turn right on Hastings. Winery driveway is your first left.

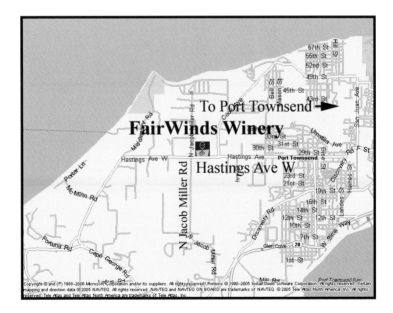

57

Sorensen Cellars

Along the Whidbey Island–Port Townsend WineTrail, just outside of beautiful Port Townsend, is Sorensen Cellars, another wine oasis for WineTrail trekkers. Established in 1998, Sorensen Cellars is a small, family-owned and -operated winery dedicated to the production of premium wines. The knowledgeable pouring staff makes you feel more at ease with each tasty sample. With the philosophy that all winemaking begins in the vineyard, winemaker and owner Richard Sorensen seeks out premium grape growers, such as Candy Mountain Vineyards near the Tri-Cities for its sangiovese, the Ciel du Cheval Vineyard for its merlot, and Windy Ridge Vineyard in the Horse Heaven Hills appellation.

Sorensen Cellars produces two labels: its premium label, Sorensen, and its more light hearted, value-oriented Townsend Bay label. Be sure to try the pinot gris, merlot, sangiovese, and cabernet sauvignon under the Sorensen label. Richard uses only French oak for these premium wines. The skins touch his cabernet franc rosé for only 24 hours, and the result is a dry (only 1 percent residual sugar), peach-colored treat. Think of this paired with summer salad and lemon-pepper chicken. Are you salivating yet?

Check out the Sorensen website for events and newsletter tidbits at www.sorensencellars.com. Like its distinct wines, the winery's website is different from the norm, using a picnic basket theme with links to navigate through the website—a nice approach.

SORENSEN CELLARS
opened: 1998
winemaker(s): Richard Sorensen
location: 274 Otto Street, Building S
Port Townsend, WA 98368
phone: 360-379-6416
web: www.sorensencellars.com
e-mail: info@sorensencellars.com
picnic area: No
gift shop: Yes
fee: Small tasting fee
hours: 12–5 Friday through Sunday from March
through May, or by appointment; daily 12–5 from
June through August; 12–5 Friday through Sunday
from September through mid-November; December
through mid-February, closed

DIRECTIONS: Located off US-20 approximately 1 mile south of the Port Townsend city limits, in Glen Cove Industrial Park. Sorensen Winery can be found on Otto St., which parallels US-20, between Fredericks St. and Seton Rd. Turn right (east) off US-20 onto Seton Rd. if approaching from the south.
Coming from Port Townsend, turn right (east) onto Fredericks St., go to Otto St. and follow the signs. See www.wsdot.wa.gov/ferries for Washington State ferry schedule to and from mainland.

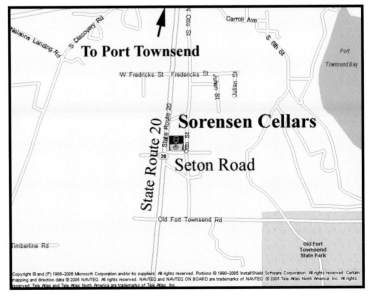

Olympic Peninsula
WineTrail

From Bordeaux-style blends to wines that rely on rhubarb and plums, get ready for variety when it comes to the Olympic Peninsula WineTrail. Here you will discover that Port Angeles offers the perfect climate to ferment hot weather Eastern Washington grapes. Along the way, we suspect that you will find a wonderful beach to uncork a cabernet franc, or a fine restaurant that features local wines. From Sequim to Port Angeles there are plenty of places to stay and eat (especially seafood), not to mention quick access to the Olympic National Park via Hurricane Ridge.

1 Lost Mountain Winery   **3** Black Diamond Winery   **5** Harbinger Winery
2 Olympic Cellars   **4** Camaraderie Cellars

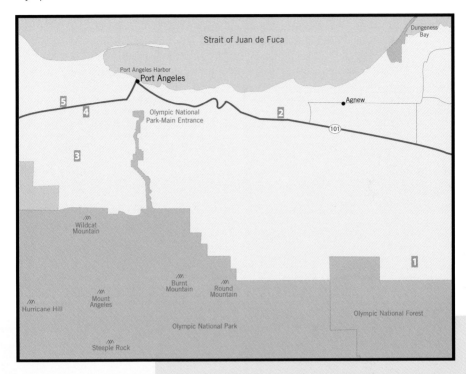

Region:	**Olympic Peninsula Wine Country**
# of tasting rooms on tour:	**5**
Estimated # of days for tour:	**1 to 2**
Getting around:	**Car**
Key events:	❑ **Wineries are part of the North Sound Wineries Association—3 key annual events: Spring Barrel Tasting (Memorial Day Weekend); Passport Wine Tour (Veterans Day Weekend); and Red Wine & Chocolate (February). See www.northsoundwineries.org/ for event times and tickets.**
Tips:	❑ **Budget time to walk along the beach and visit Olympic National Park.**
	❑ **Ferry service twice a day to Victoria, BC. See www.cohoferry.com/schedules.htm.**
	❑ **Many restaurants feature local wines.**
	❑ **Harbinger Winery also features kayaking excursions and gear.**
Best:	❑ **Best Gift Shop: Olympic Cellars**
	❑ **Best Picnic: Camaraderie Cellars**

61

Lost Mountain Winery

Tucked in the foothills above Sequim, on the Olympic Peninsula, is the Lost Mountain Winery, and for WineTrail enthusiasts, a visit is an absolute must. The small, intimate tasting room provides a comfortable setting to enjoy some "big reds," typically poured by co-owner Sue Conca. And while the focus

here is on the artisan "non-sulfite" wines produced by Steve Conca, the two also mix in some levity with wines named "Cellar Rat Red" and "Distinguished Dago Red." Also included in the tasting bonanza are a hearty zinfandel (made from California grapes), merlot, syrah, cabernet franc, and a wonderfully named "RainForest Red" blend. The grapes for most of their wines come from the Tri-Cities area and Red Mountain.

As pointed out on the Lost Mountain website, "Our grapes are hand-picked at the peak of ripeness and rushed to the winery where they are gently crushed and slowly fermented in small lots. The new wine is aged in oak barrels for 12–24 months, then carefully bottled and labeled by hand. The natural, unfiltered and unrefined style allows these dry red wines to retain their rich and distinct varietal flavors. We specialize in the classic red varieties of cabernet sauvignon, merlot, syrah, and cabernet franc that regularly receive gold and silver medals in wine competitions."

Lost Mountain line-up including Cellar Rat Red

No kidding: Gold, silver, and bronze medals are found on many of the bottles that grace the tasting room.

Steve and Sue Conca inherited the winery from Steve's father, Romeo Conca, following his death in 1997. Prior to his father's passing, Steve had actively participated for many years as an assistant wine maker at Lost Mountain. Steve and Sue have continued Lost Mountain's tradition of producing hand crafted red wines, a tradition that began in the Conca family's native Italy.

Family, tradition, fun, great setting, warm ambiance, award-winning wines: These are the reasons that the Lost Mountain Winery is a definite stop along the WineTrails path.

Entrance to Lost Mountain Winery

LOST MOUNTAIN WINERY
opened: 1981
winemaker(s): Steve Conca
location: 3174 Lost Mountain Road
Sequim, WA 98382-7918
phone: 360-683-5229
web: www.lostmountain.com
e-mail: wine@lostmountain.com
picnic area: Yes
gift shop: Yes
fee: Complimentary wine tasting
hours: Daily 11–5 from mid-June through
mid-September; 11–5 Saturday and Sunday from
mid-September through November; 11-5 Friday
through Sunday on Thanksgiving weekend; closed
November 28 through December 9; December 10
and 11, Holiday Open House, weather permitting;
from December 13 through April 1, call for seasonal
hours; 11–5 Saturday and Sunday from April 1
through mid-June

DIRECTIONS: On US-101 about 2.5 miles past Sequim heading west, turn left onto Taylor Cutoff Rd. Proceed 2.7 miles and turn right onto Olson Rd, then immediately turn left onto Lost Mountain Rd. Follow signs to winery at 3174 Lost Mountain Rd. Lost Mountain Winery is approximately 6 miles off Hwy 101.

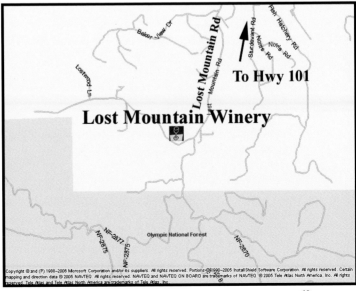

Olympic Cellars

Located in a huge old barn on Highway 101, 9 miles west of Sequim, Olympic Cellars is dedicated to "Wines for Women Who Want It All." The owners of Olympic Cellars—Kathy Charlton, Molly Rivard, and Libby Sweetser—comprise the "Olympic Women in Wine." Kathy states, "I knew that to survive as a very small player in the wine industry, we needed to focus on a niche market. We couldn't compete on price, there was no way economies of scale would kick in, and like any industry, major acquisitions were taking place, making it even harder to compete. So we played to our strengths, we are women, we know what we like, so we created the Working Girl wines and self-proclaimed them the Official Wine of Working Women."

Olympic Cellars gift shop

Although it's not a wise strategy to buy wine based on the label alone, it is hard to resist a "Rosé the Riveter" bottle of wine from Olympic Cellars. Beyond the label, however, is the fact that "Rosé the Riveter" is a refreshing, well-balanced wine that goes well with sliced turkey and havarti.

Olympic's award-winning Working Girl series ("Working Girl" white, "Go Girl" red, and "Rosé the Riveter") is designed to be distinct, yet affordable for sharing with co-workers after a long day in pantyhose and pumps. Depending upon availability, check out its premium La Dolce Vida line of wine, which includes five varietals that are produced in small quantities (150 to 200 cases each). La Dolce Vida wines, as the name implies, are intended to be shared during those special occasions when we take time to reflect on the fruits of our labors and share the good life. A third line of Olympic wines is the Dungeness series, which includes the heritage and artist series of labels, which were first made in 1980. The Dungeness white is a semi-sweet riesling, and the Dungeness red is a Beaujolais-style lemberger.

The generous gift shop features a world of wine-related items guaranteed to satisfy that hard-to-buy-for aunt.

Olympic Cellars is a key member of North Sound Wineries Association and participates in its events, including Spring Barrel Tasting (Memorial Day Weekend); Passport Wine Tour (Veterans Day Weekend); and Red Wine & Chocolate (February). In addition, Olympic Cellars produces its own special events throughout the year; and be sure to check out its outstanding website in advance for upcoming events and other tidbits. You go, girl!

Olympic Cellars' distinctive red barn tasting room

OLYMPIC CELLARS
opened: 1979
winemaker(s): Benoit Murat
location: 255410 Highway 101
Port Angeles, WA 98362
phone: 360-452-0160
web: www.olympiccellars.com
e-mail: wines@olympiccellars.com
picnic area: Yes
gift shop: Yes
fee: Small tasting fee
hours: Daily 11–6 from May through October; 11–5
Monday through Saturday, 12–5 Sunday, from
November through April

 **BEST Gift shop**

DIRECTIONS: **From Port Angeles**, head east on US-101. Go about 7 miles. Winery is on right at 255410 Hwy 101 in the huge old barn.
From Sequim, head west on US-101. Go about 9.4 miles. Winery is on left at 255410 Hwy 101. Look for large barn.

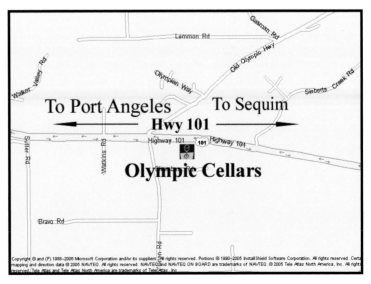

Black Diamond Winery

Located in the foothills of the Olympic Mountains southwest of Port Angeles, Black Diamond Winery specializes in making fruit wines, the kind you might describe as "back-porch" wines. Despite the proliferation of Bordeaux-style wineries around the state, Black Diamond owners Lance and Sharon Adams haven't deviated from their specialty wines, which they began perfecting 20 years ago.

Black Diamond vineyard—early spring

Leaving the road, you make the short 200-yard drive up to the winery and catch sight of their orchard and small 2-acre vineyard. In the summer, you can see the plums, raspberries, and rhubarb ripening for harvest. Either Lance or Sharon will greet you in the small tasting room situated at the end of the building that houses the winery, just above Tumwater Creek. By paying a nominal tasting fee, you have the opportunity to try their Ridge white wine; a Müller Thurgau wine (the grapes are from Whidbey Island Vineyard); Shiro plum, rhubarb, loganberry, cranberry, and raspberry wines; and "Sharon's Blush," a blend created from red and white grapes grown in the Adams' vineyard.

Lance and Sharon's passion for making their fruit wines can be tasted in every sip you take. Each berry picked, each pressing made, each vintage bottled represents an enormous amount of labor. Black Diamond Winery produces an impressive 800 cases of wine a year. For visual impact, check out the photos on the tasting-room wall showing the ripe Shiro plums ready to be picked and the huge stalks of rhubarb being pulled during the harvest. One can almost feel the aching arm muscles that would come at the end of a day picking those babies.

Now, one final mental exercise: Imagine raspberry wine poured over French vanilla ice cream. Ahhh.

BLACK DIAMOND WINERY

Black Diamond barn

opened: 1999
winemaker(s): Lance and Sharon Adams
location: 2976 Black Diamond Road
Port Angeles, WA 98363-9443
phone: 360-457-0748
web: www.pages.prodigy.net/sharonlance
e-mail: bdwinery@prodigy.net
picnic area: Yes
gift shop: No
fee: Small tasting fee
hours: 10–5 Thursday through Saturday, 11–4
Sunday and Monday, from February through
December, or by appointment

DIRECTIONS: **Depart Port Angeles on US-101** [N. Lincoln St.]. Turn left (south) onto Black Diamond Rd. Arrive 2976 Black Diamond Rd.

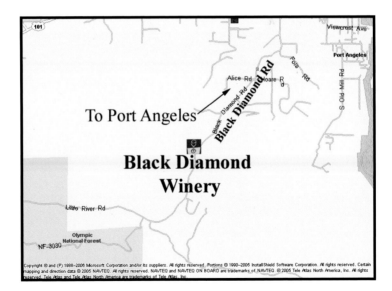

Camaraderie Cellars

In 1992, Don Corson and his wife, Vicki, formed Camaraderie Cellars with a "combination of hope, a small new building, great vineyard connections, and a family philosophy that the best things in life are meant to be shared." OK,

they had me at "hope," but what distinguishes Camaraderie is this sense of community and the belief in sharing the good things in life. You see this reflected in the beautiful gardens that greet you when you arrive, the handcrafted outdoor furniture, and the new tasting room topped with a beautiful weathervane. This, my fellow WineTrails lover, is one winery with many a photo op.

Camaraderie Cellars wines are made to complement many types of cuisine. You find yourself wondering how steak *au poivre* would taste with Camaraderie's hearty merlot blend or how Beethoven might sound as one of Don's Bordeaux-style red blends is swishing around your palate. It's no wonder select restaurants and wine bars include Camaraderie Cellar Wines on their wine lists.

Don is routinely asked why he chose to locate his winery in Port Angeles. He responds that the area's cool marine air and mild summers offer the perfect conditions for grapes to ferment in the winery's French barrels. But he adds that great wine begins with the best fruit, and to that end, Camaraderie is fortunate to get its grapes from the Artz Vineyards on Red Mountain and Champoux Vineyards in the Horse Heaven Hills AVA. The contrasting elements of Eastern Washington's dry, hot climate and Western Washington's mild, wet climate work magic on the grapes. Yin and yang. Hearty stew and cabernet sauvignon. Beethoven and a red Bordeaux blend. It doesn't get any better than that.

CAMARADERIE CELLARS
opened: 1992
winemaker(s): Don Corson
location: 334 Benson Road
Port Angeles, WA 98363-8492
phone: 360-417-3564
web: www.camaraderiecellars.com
e-mail: info@camaraderiecellars.com or
corson4@tenforward.com
picnic area: Yes
gift shop: No
fee: Complimentary wine tasting
hours: 11–5 Saturday and Sunday from May through
October, or by appointment; also available at The
Tasting Room in Seattle

BEST Picnic

DIRECTIONS: **From Port Angeles**, head west on US 101 [N. Lincoln St.]. Go 2.6 miles on Hwy 101 and turn left (south) onto Benson Rd. Arrive 334 Benson Rd.

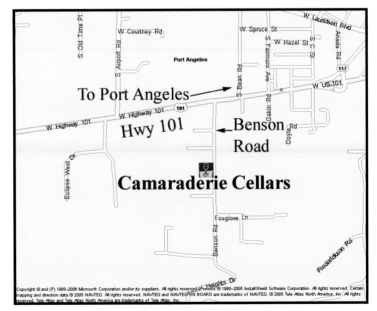

Harbinger Winery

Harbinger *n.* – one that indicates or foreshadows what is to come; a forerunner.

In 2004, Sara Gagnon and Tammi Hinkle experienced a traumatic event that proved to be life altering: They survived a plane crash. Tragically, the pilot of the small plane died, but Sara and Tammi managed to get out of the crash with their lives. The accident proved to be the impetus for living each day as if it were their last. Indeed, emblazoned across the Harbinger sign inside the winery is their mantra, "Step forth and be the harbinger of your dreams."

And after that close call, harbingers of their dreams they became! Sara had been the chief winemaker at nearby Olympic Cellars, which gave her considerable exposure to the commercial side of the business. Her dream was to have her own winery. Tammi had been a kayaking guide and harbored notions of owning her own kayaking business. After the plane crash, both women decided to act on their dreams and together they launched Harbinger Winery. As winemaker, Sara spends most days tending to myriad winery duties. Tammi, on the other hand, invests most of her time in her "baby": Adventures Through Kayaking guide service.

Harbinger's winery and tasting room are located just west of Port Angeles on the south side of Highway 101 in a large blue metal building that looks "suspiciously like an old logging-truck shop." Inside the winery, the atmosphere is "Northwest comfort," with Buddha statues serving as decoration, a huge gold couch, and kayaks hanging on the wall. The concrete floors provide cool comfort even on the hottest days of the summer. However, we're here for the tasting and with a $2 tasting fee, visitors enjoy a smorgasbord of reds and whites. Depending upon availability, get ready for "Dynamo White" (a blend of riesling, chardonnay, and semillon), "Dynamo Red" (a blend of syrah, cabernet sauvignon, and merlot), syrah, cabernet franc rosé, a surprising "Cranberry Bliss" (a blend of cranberry and chardonnay), and "Blackberry Bliss," which borrows from Sara's family recipe for blackberry wine. "Dynamo Red" has turned out to be the winery's best-seller, and your taste buds will undoubtedly agree with the consensus.

WineTrail lovers are indebted to Sara and Tammi for living their dream. As that famous American philosopher Dr. Seuss once wrote, "Be who you are and say what you feel because those who mind don't matter and those who matter don't mind."

HARBINGER WINERY
opened: 2006
winemaker(s): Sara Gagnon
location: 2358 W. Highway 101
Port Angeles, WA 98363-9420
phone: 360-452 4262
web: www.harbingerwinery.com
e-mail: info@harbingerwinery.com
picnic area: No
gift shop: Yes
fee: $2 tasting fee
hours: 11–6 Memorial Day through Labor Day;
contact winery for other hours

DIRECTIONS: Follow Hwy 101 west out of Port Angeles about 3 miles. The winery is on the south (left) side of the road in a large blue metal building.

Bainbridge Island–Hoodsport-Shelton
WineTrail

Bainbridge Island Vineyards & Winery

The Bainbridge Island–Hoodsport-Shelton WineTrail will expose you to top-notch syrah and wines that rely on "cool climate grapes" with interesting names like Madeleine Angevine or siegerrebe. Just when you thought Washington wines were dependent upon Eastern Washington grapes, the folks at Bainbridge Island Vineyards and Winery will set the record straight. This WineTrail will take you along glorious Hood Canal and then on a ferry ride between Bainbridge and Seattle. With plenty of restaurants and overnight accommodations to choose from, your challenges will be to remember to pack a corkscrew and bring plenty of film for the camera (at least those digitally challenged).

1 Bainbridge Island
Vineyards & Winery

2 Hoodsport Winery

3 Walter Dacon Wines

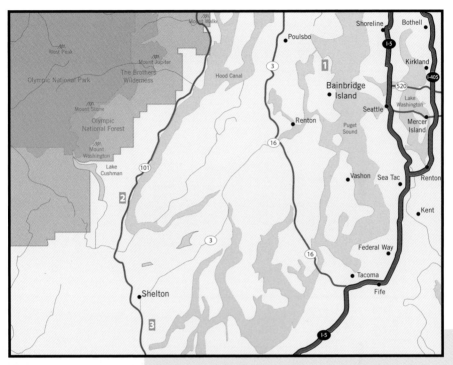

Region:	**Olympic Peninsula Wine Country**
# of tasting rooms on tour:	**3**
Estimated # of days for tour:	**1 or 2**
Getting around:	**Car and ferry**
Key events:	❏ **Bainbridge Island Vineyards and Winery is part of the North Sound Wineries Association—3 key annual events: Spring Barrel Tasting (Memorial Day Weekend); Passport Wine Tour (Veterans Day Weekend); and Red Wine & Chocolate (February). See www.northsoundwineries.org for event times and tickets.**
Tips:	❏ **Gerard Bentryn leads tours of the vineyard and winemaking process on Sundays beginning at 2 pm.** ❏ **There are plenty of great restaurants in Winslow.** ❏ **Time visit to Walter Dacon to coincide with OysterFest held during the first full weekend in October.**

Bainbridge Island Vineyards & Winery

Do you realize that you are just a short ferry-boat ride away from experiencing Puget Sound–area estate wines? It may be true that 98 percent of the grapes in Washington come from the east side of the Cascades, but Gerard and Jo Ann

Bainbridge Island Vineyards in early spring

Bentryn have proven that you can grow grapes and produce some wonderful wines west of the Cascades as well. Don't be surprised to hear Jo Ann note that "we make 101 percent estate-grown wine" at Bainbridge Island Vineyards & Winery. Essentially their wines are a convergence of viticulture philosophy with the cool-climate grapes that thrive in Western Washington. The winery's "Ferryboat White" is a perfect example of this pairing.

The Bentryns' 8 acres of grapes produce some unusual Washington wines, including Müller-Thurgau, Madeleine Angevine, and siegerrebe (which I love hearing—when pronounced correctly). You're not here to sample conventional Bordeaux wines but rather some high-country Alp-like wines made in the traditional Alsace style. Müller-Thurgau will remind you of a spicy riesling and would be a perfect dance partner with a four-star Thai dish. However, if you are looking for a back-porch wine to quaff on a perfect summer day, try the Ferryboat White, which presents a nice balance of citrus flavors and acidity while remaining dry. Also of note is Bainbridge Island Winery's Madeleine Angevine, which has its roots in the Loire Valley of France. With its citrus flavors and bright finish, this white wine will remind you of a sauvignon blanc.

WineTrail Tip: On Sunday afternoons at 2 p.m., Gerard leads anyone who happens to be visiting on a tour of the vineyard. He walks visitors through the entire wine-making process, from growing the grapes to uncorking Mother Earth at the dinner table.

BAINBRIDGE ISLAND VINEYARDS & WINERY
opened: 1977
winemaker(s): Gerard Bentryn
location: 8989 East Day Road
Bainbridge Island, WA 98110-1398
phone: 206-842-9463
web: www.bainbridgevineyards.com
e-mail: info@bainbridgevineyards.com
picnic area: Yes
gift shop: Yes
fee: Small tasting fee
hours: 11–5 Friday through Sunday, or
by appointment

DIRECTIONS: **From Seattle** take Bainbridge Island Ferry from Coleman Dock Station. Then drive 4 miles on US-305. At the traffic light, turn right onto Day Rd E. and go .5 miles. Vineyards are on the right. Take next driveway on the right. Winery is at the end of the driveway.
See www.wsdot.wa.gov/ferries for Washington State ferry schedule to and from mainland.

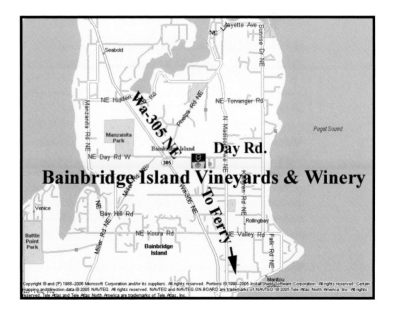

Hoodsport Winery

Hoodsport Winery's label recently underwent a significant change as part of its distinctive "Orca" series of wines. It's a dramatic change for a winery that has been a steady producer of fine wines for more than 30 years. Fortunately for consumers, only the label has changed—the quaint tasting room, friendly staff, and great views of Hood Canal all remain the same.

Dick Patterson continues as Hoodsport's winemaker even though the winery has recently inked a strategic marketing arrangement with Washington Wine & Beverage Company (parent company of Silver Lake Winery and Glen Fiona). Perhaps this new strategic relationship has updated its image but the bread-and-butter basics remain the same.

Hoodsport produces a unique red wine called "Island Belle" (part *Labrusca* and part *vinifera).* The vines for this varietal are found on Stretch Island near Olympia and are about 100 years old, as noted in the *Wine Project Book* by Ron Irvine and Walter J. Clore. It's worth asking if Hoodsport has this wine available for tasting, because you will not find it anywhere else.

After you sample some of the vinifera varietals (e.g., syrah, cabernet franc, cabernet sauvignon, chardonnay, gewürztraminer, chenin blanc, riesling, sauvignon blanc, semillon, and merlot), you might want to end your tasting experience on a "sweet" note with a taste of Hoodsport's fruit wine. Hoodsport specializes in raspberry, rhubarb, and loganberry wines. The raspberry wine has made off with some top honors and can be enjoyed by itself or soaked up in pound cake accompanied by fresh raspberries.

With majestic views of the Olympic Mountains and Hood Canal, the Hoodsport Winery is a mandatory stop along Route 101.

Hoodsport tasting room

HOODSPORT WINERY
opened: 1978
winemaker(s): Dick Patterson
location: North 23501 Highway 101
Hoodsport, WA 98548-0000
phone: 360-877-9894
web: www.hoodsport.com
e-mail: wine@hoodsport.com
picnic area: No
gift shop: Yes
fee: Complimentary wine tasting
hours: Daily 10–6

DIRECTIONS: Located just 1 mile south of the town of Hoodsport on US-101 on Hood Canal. Hoodsport wines can also be enjoyed at the Silver Lake tasting room in Woodinville.

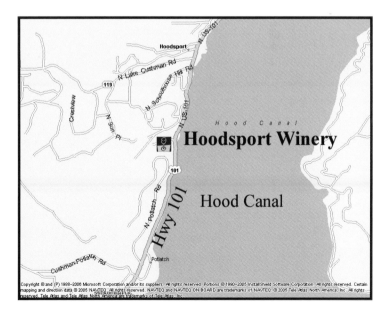

Walter Dacon Wines

WineTrail enthusiasts who enjoy syrah will want to plan a visit to Walter Dacon Winery. But we're not talking about a trip to Walla Walla or even Woodinville. We're talking Shelton. "Shelton?" you ask. Yep, Shelton, Washington. Set in

the heart of Mason County, Walter Dacon Winery produces about 1,000 cases of syrah per year, as well as small lots of sangiovese. Conveniently located, Walter Dacon Winery is a short drive from Highway 101, taking the SE Lynch Road exit.

Upon starting his winery in 2003, owner/winemaker Lloyd Anderson named it after his grandfather Walter Dacon. Lloyd's background is in forestry, having had a career at Weyerhaeuser and owning his own logging-related enterprises. But after the logging industry took a downturn, Lloyd turned to his passion—making wine. Together with his wife, Ann, the Andersons have managed to distinguish their young winery from the slew of other wineries and received awards and feel-good accolades.

Before launching Walter Dacon Winery, Lloyd learned his winemaking skills from the best with a stint at McCrea Cellars. But ever the tinkerer and hands-on do-it-yourselfer, Lloyd has taken his skills much further, employing European winemaking techniques not practiced elsewhere in the state. For example, following de-stemming, Lloyd uses frozen carbon dioxide to cold-stabilize the syrah grapes. And, remaining true to Rhone-style wines, he makes liberal use of blending. However, Lloyd defers to Ann's sensitive palate for the taste test.

When it comes to Walter Dacon syrah, check out its "C'est Syrah Belle" (aged in French oak), "C'est Syrah Beau" (a more robust flavor from aging in American oak), and "C'est Syrah Magnifique" (barrel select). All Walter Dacon wines exhibit tamed tannins and are much smoother than many of the syrahs Washington is known for. These wines pair wonderfully with lamb, duck, or salmon, yet are delicious sans food. It's no wonder the winery's Le Grand Crew Wine Club has grown significantly since its birth in mid-2006. *C'est fantastique!*

WALTER DACON WINES
opened: 2003
winemaker(s): Lloyd Anderson
location: 50 SE Skookum Inlet Road
Shelton, WA 98584
phone: 360-426-5913
web: www.walterdaconwines.com
e-mail: winemaker@walterdaconwines.com
picnic area: Yes
gift shop: Yes
fee: Complimentary wine tasting
hours: 12–6 Wednesday through Sunday, or
by appointment

Lloyd Anderson

DIRECTIONS: **From SR-3** south of Shelton take SE Lynch Rd (east) approximately 1.5 miles. Turn right onto SE Skookum Inlet Rd and arrive at Walter Dacon Wines.

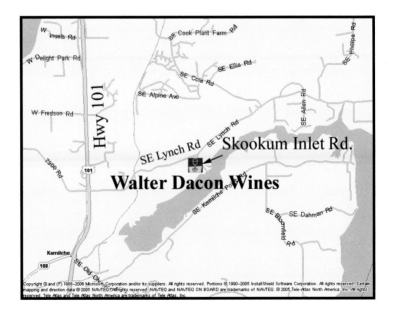

Puget Sound
WINE COUNTRY

Seattle
WineTrail

During the second Saturday of each month, four wineries in South Seattle open their doors for tasting—Fall Line Winery, O•S Winery, :Nota Bene Cellars, and Cadence Winery. If you happen to be in Seattle on one of those lucky Saturdays, make sure you are in or near the Pike Place Market. There, you can experience a number of wineries under one roof at The Tasting Room–Wines of Washington. Also, drop in on tiny Market Cellars Winery. It is amazing to realize that there are an untold number of non-bonded "wineries" throughout Seattle in garages and basements. Members of the Boeing Wine Club purchase over 50 tons of grapes each year for their winemaking hobby. The wineries of Seattle WineTrail represent the select few that have gone beyond being "garagistes" to fulfill their dreams on a commercial scale.

1 The Tasting Room–Wines of Washington

2 Market Cellar Winery

3 Fall Line Winery

4 O•S Winery

5 Cadence Winery

6 :Nota Bene Cellars

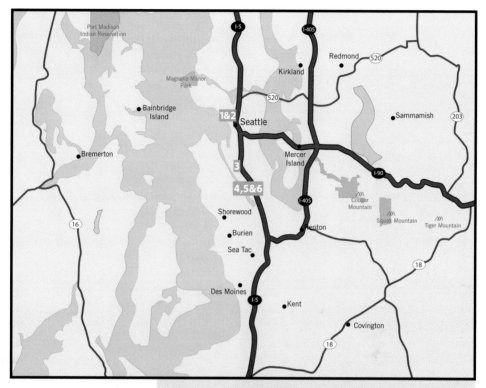

Region:	**Puget Sound Wine Country**
# of tasting rooms on tour:	**6**
Estimated # of days for tour:	**3 or 4**
Getting around:	**Car and ferry**
Tips:	❑ **Consider hiring a limousine—especially if your plans include Woodinville.**
	❑ **Both Market Cellar Winery and The Tasting Room–Wines of Washington are located at the Pike Place Market. There are plenty of places to stay and eat nearby.**
	❑ **The Tasting Room–Wines of Washington offers bistro fare.**

The Tasting Room—Wines of Washington

Take seven outstanding Washington wineries of which winemaker and owner for each are one and the same, put them in an historic building in the heart of Seattle's Pike Place Market, and you have The Tasting Room—Wines of Washington. The brainchild of one of the seven owners/winemakers, Paul

Beveridge of Wilridge Winery, The Tasting Room is a perfect spot for those who want to sample great wine without driving to Port Angeles or Walla Walla.

Within its cozy setting, The Tasting Room features Apex Cellars, Camaraderie Cellars, Harlequin Wine Cellars, JM Cellars, Latitude 46 N, Wilridge Winery, and Wineglass Cellars. You can sample wines for a small fee or buy a glass to enjoy with the selection of gourmet meats and cheeses it offers. **WineTrail Note:** Speaking of cheese, The Tasting Room has collaborated with Pike Place Market neighbor Beecher's Handmade Cheese to offer "Mac-n-Cheese Mondays." Who knew that this classic staple would dance so well with a reserve red?

The Tasting Room goes out of its way to educate and inform wine enthusiasts about making wine. It also hosts events that place their wines center stage. For example, you can join winemaker and owner Don Corson of Camaraderie Cellars and blend your own signature wine in his "Palate and Palette Blending" series. The Tasting Room also does an excellent job of making you feel like a member of its community through emails that alert you to winemaker dinners, special events, and good buys on wine. Private parties and corporate events are welcome at The Tasting Room, where its space can accommodate 50 sit-down guests.

From de-stemming to crushing, fermenting to racking, these winemakers have been intimately involved in their wines every step of the way. They are proud parents of their own "offspring," but are quick to acknowledge each other's accomplishments and special gifts. Any time of the year, The Tasting Room is a place for friends and business associates to gather, kick back, and enjoy the low-hanging fruits of Washington.

THE TASTING ROOM—WINES OF WASHINGTON
winemaker(s): Various winemakers
location: 1924 Post Alley, Pike Place Market
Seattle, WA 98101
phone: 206-770-9463
web: www.winesofwashington.com
e-mail: info@winesofwashington.com
picnic area: Yes
gift shop: Yes
fee: Small tasting fee—$2 to $3
hours: Daily 12–8

DIRECTIONS: The Tasting Room is located in the heart of Seattle's famous Pike Place Market at 1924 Post Alley (between Stewart and Virginia Streets, next to Kell's Irish Pub and across from the Pink Door Restaurant). Pedestrian-only traffic—find nearby street or garage parking.

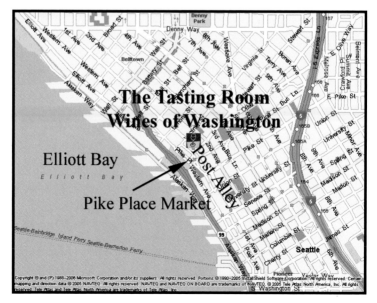

85

Market Cellar Winery

Located in Seattle's historic Pike Place Market on Western Avenue, the Market Cellar Winery is a labor of love from a man who decided that he didn't want to retire after laying brick for 50 years. Now in his 80s, John Farias engages you with his bright eyes and that this is his third business since "retiring." Slowed by arthritis, John produces less than 500 cases annually from the winery of cabernet sauvignon, gewürztraminer, chardonnay, and merlot. (He also sells homemaking beer kits and gets a steady stream of beer aficionados sprinkled with wine purchasers.) John is such a likeable man that WineTrail enthusiasts are warned to resist the urge to hug him.

As part of the Seattle WineTrail, Market Cellar Winery is located just a few blocks from The Tasting Room–Wines of Washington. As you go between the two locations, you will experience flying fish, the laughing sounds of daycare children, and tourists clicking pictures left and right. This is the real Seattle, and at $9.20 a bottle for cabernet sauvignon, you have discovered a great value crafted by a true artisan. His grapes are from Sunnyside's Upland Vineyard, which was planted in 1971, making it one of the oldest vinifera vineyards in Washington.

John B. Farias

MARKET CELLAR WINERY
opened: 1996
winemaker(s): John Farias
location: 1432 Western Avenue
Seattle, WA 98101
phone: 206-622-1880
web: www.marketcellarwinery.com
e-mail: marketcellar@qwest.net
picnic area: No
gift shop: No
fee: Complimentary wine tasting
hours: 11–6 Monday through Saturday

DIRECTIONS: Located near the Pike Place Market on Western Ave. **From downtown Seattle**, go west on Madison St. and turn right onto Western Ave. toward the Pike Place Market. Market Cellar Winery is located at 1432 Western Ave.—look for their sign. Street and garage paid parking is available.

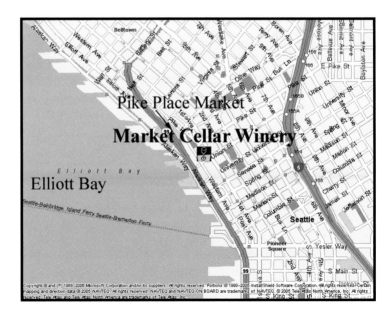

87

Fall Line Winery

I missed the KING-TV film crew by a few days. They were doing a story on winemakers who live duo lives, pursuing their passion of making wine in their spare time while maintaining interesting careers. Tim Sorenson, winemaker and co-owner of Fall Line Winery, is the perfect candidate for such a story. Tim

is a professor of economics at Seattle University by day and a winemaker by night (and on the weekends). To my knowledge, he is the only winemaker in Washington to have a PhD from Harvard University. A nosey interviewer (me) discovered this little factoid during our visit, but Tim is the kind of person who carries no airs and is remarkably friendly. His passion is winemaking, and he cares what you think.

Tim bounces back and forth from the Seattle University campus to his 4,000-square-foot winery in South Seattle (Georgetown). The place is spotless; I'm not sure you would want to eat off the floor, but you could. He assures me, however, that when he and his wife and co-owner, Nancy Rivenburgh, took possession of the office park space, it was essentially a shell with hanging wires, clutter, and dust. A healthy dose of elbow grease, new walls and paint, and many shekels for the equipment transformed the space. Early on, they decided to call their winery "Fall Line" in recognition of their other great passion—skiing. As they note on their website, "'fall line' evokes the alluring image of a perfectly balanced skier, gracefully descending a slope of deep, fluffy powder—leaving behind a beautifully carved swoosh."

Tim is grateful to his friend and mentor, Ben Smith of nearby Cadence Winery, for teaching him the craft of making wine, introducing him to elite grape growers in the Columbia Valley, and giving his ongoing support and friendship. Ever the economist, Tim has an Excel spreadsheet full of cash flow analyses, income projections, and balance sheets. However, he hasn't looked at the spreadsheet for some time. Instead, he's guided by a belief in his product and the confidence that his small winery will be self-sustaining in time. When you taste Fall Line wines, you'll agree.

FALL LINE WINERY
opened: 2003
winemaker(s): Tim Sorenson
location: 6122 Sixth Avenue South
Seattle, WA 98108-3308
phone: 206-768-9463
web: www.falllinewinery.com
e-mail: mail@falllinewinery.com
picnic area: No
gift shop: No
fee: $5 tasting fee refundable with purchase
hours: 1–5 second Saturdays of the month from
February through August; open selected other
Saturdays in November and December: consult
www.ssaw.info for details

Tim Sorenson

DIRECTIONS: From I-5 take exit 162 [Corson Ave./Michigan St.] and bear right (west) onto S. Michigan St. and proceed .2 miles. Turn right (north) onto 6th Ave. S. and go .1 miles and arrive at 6122 6th Ave. S.

O•S Winery

When Republican ex-banker Rob Sullivan joined forces with liberal Democrat winemaker Bill Owen in 1997 to create Owen Sullivan Winery, you would have put money on a short-lived partnership. But you would have been wrong.

Now, nearly 10 years later, the recently renamed O•S Winery is clearly a success story, as measured by the frequent appearance of the words "SOLD OUT" next to the winery website's list of wines. Or by the following comment from *Wine Spectator*'s Harvey Steiman: "From their jury-rigged winery in a nondescript business park near Seattle-Tacoma Airport, Bill Owen and Rob Sullivan are making some of Washington's plushest and headiest reds. … They make small lots that just keep getting better with each vintage." Powerful words.

World traveler, restaurateur, and winemaker-in-training, Bill Owen had toyed with the notion of launching his own winery. He asked an acquaintance, a banker, if he knew of a financial type who could assist him with his business plan. It turns out the person he asked was Rob Sullivan, who, after a full career of banking and with a longstanding love of wine, was eager to try something new. A review of the pro forma statement, followed (we suspect) by a glass of wine or two, and Rob Sullivan and Bill Owen were business partners.

When it comes to wine naming, O•S Winery takes the cake. With names like BSH, R3, and M, the monikers are unabashedly simple—although some of the names require a secret decoder ring. The name "M" comes from the fact that merlot is the primary ingredient in this wine. The "R3" moniker comes from the use of three reds (merlot, cabernet sauvignon, and cabernet franc). But the *crème de la crème* is "BSH," which Bill Owen, a lover of big, full-flavored wines, accidentally coined when he exclaimed that a still-in-the-barrel red wine was built like a **B**rick **S**h-t **H**ouse.

Yin and yang. You say "potāto," I say "potăto." But as one Sydney J. Harris noted, "Opposites attract because they are not really opposites, but complementaries."

O•S WINERY
opened: 1997
winemaker(s): Bill Owen
location: 1501 South 92nd Place, Suite B
Seattle, WA 98108
phone: 206-243-3427
web: www.oswinery.com
e-mail: mail@oswinery.com
picnic area: No
gift shop: No
fee: $5 tasting fee refundable with purchase
hours: 1–5 second Saturdays of the month from
February through August; open selected other
Saturdays in November and December: consult
www.ssaw.info for details

Rob Sullivan, co-owner

DIRECTIONS: From Seattle going southbound on I-5, take exit 162 onto Corson Ave. S. [Corson Ave./Michigan St.] and go about 1.3 miles. Bear left (southeast) onto E. Marginal Way S. and proceed for .7 miles. Turn right (south) onto 16th Ave. S. and proceed .5 miles and then bear right onto 14th Ave. S. Turn left (east) onto S. Director St., then immediately turn right (south) onto 15th Pl. S.

If heading northbound toward Seattle on I-5 take exit 156 to Hwy 599. Go north on Hwy 599 (which becomes 99) to the 14th S exit. Turn right (east) onto S. Director St. then immediately turn right (south) onto 15th Pl. S.

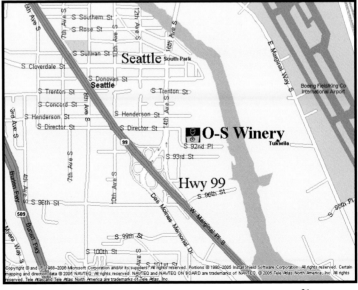

Cadence Winery

Little Cara Smith's feet don't touch the foot pedals of the forklift—at least not yet. But we suspect that in about 10 years, Cara will be the chief cellar rat for Cadence Winery in South Seattle. She may be destined for that role, given the fact that Ben Smith and his wife, Gaye McNutt, owners of Cadence Winery,

Gaye McNutt and Ben Smith

named their 10-acre Red Mountain vineyard in their daughter's honor: Cara Mia Vineyard. Like Cara, the vineyard is young and full of promise, with maturing cabernet sauvignon, merlot and cabernet franc grapes managed by Ryan Johnson of Ciel du Cheval fame.

The name "Cadence" reflects the qualities of balance, harmony, and precision. And these qualities are precisely what Ben Smith and Gaye McNutt aspire to achieve: a harmony of blended red varieties. A graduate of Ohio State University, Ben made his way west and worked for Boeing in Seattle. While there, he immersed himself in Boeing's winemaking club and volunteered at Chris Camarda's Andrew Will Winery on Vashon Island. Encouraged by winemaking friends at Boeing, Ben decided to make wine commercially and in 1997, Cadence Winery was born. Today, Cadence Winery is one of 13 bonded wineries in Washington started by Boeing employees, which demonstrates just how much engineers love to tinker. Gaye recently left her legal position with Microsoft to be a key part of the winemaking operations.

In early 2007, Ben and Gaye moved their winemaking operations to a South Seattle industrial park within a stone's throw of OS Winery and :Nota Bene Cellars. The winery's high ceiling and 4,000-plus square feet of space provide an ideal environment for blending reds and creating luscious flavors exhibiting lots of fruit and spice. Cadence Winery is certain to continue receiving high marks from *Wine Spectator* and other publications. But when asked if he would eventually move family and operation to Red Mountain, Ben replies, "It's not in the cards. I'm sure my wife would object to that." It appears this transplanted couple likes the Puget Sound region's harmonic blend of salt air and lush evergreens.

CADENCE WINERY
opened: 1987
winemaker(s): Benjamin Smith and Gaye McNutt
location: 9320 15th Avenue South; Unit CF
Seattle, WA 98108
phone: 206-381-9507
web: www.cadencewinery.com
e-mail: info@cadencewinery.com
picnic area: No
gift shop: No
fee: $5 tasting fee refundable with purchase
hours: 1–5 second Saturdays of the month from
February through August; open selected other
Saturdays in November and December: consult
www.ssaw.info for details

Ben Smith

DIRECTIONS: From I-5 take exit 158 (Boeing Access Rd/E. Marginal Way). Merge onto Pacific Hwy
S. [Tukwila: International Blvd] and proceed .5 miles. Take ramp onto SR-99 [W. Marginal Way]
and go 1.5 miles. Turn left onto ramp toward 14th Ave. S. Turn right (south) onto W. Marginal Pl.
S., then immediately turn left (east) onto S. 95th St. Road name changes to 15th Ave. S. Arrive
at 9320 15th Ave. S.

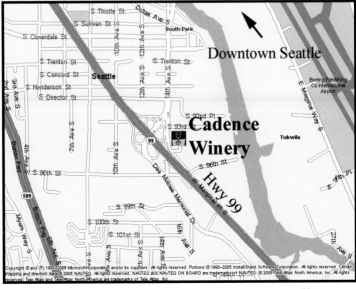

:Nota Bene Cellars

Being meticulous doesn't guarantee great results, but let's face it, gold medal winners and sloppy winemaking don't mix. The best winemakers are painstakingly fussy: They monitor fermentation like a hawk and religiously keep detailed records. The production facility itself is clean and well organized, comparable to what you would find in a top-notch Lexus or Cadillac service center. To such perfectionists, winemaking is much more of a craft than an art. It's much more science than guesswork. These winemakers are "left brain" types. And, assuming the grapes are from premium vineyards, the results are predictable: great wine. Such is the case with :Nota Bene and its chief winemaker, Tim Narby.

:Nota Bene is Latin for "note well" and happens to be associated with the first letter of :Nota Bene owners' respective surnames: "N" for Narby and "B" for Tim's wife, Carol Bryant. Tim, a Boeing systems analyst for more than 30 years, joined the Boeing Employees' Wine and Beermaking Club years ago to learn first-hand the ingredients necessary for creating premium wines. Along with all those 767s, Boeing has been cranking out winemakers, who have gone on to establish wineries such as Soos Creek Wine Cellars, Eagle Haven Winery, Cadence Winery, Austin Robaire Vintners, Crutcher Family Cellars, Willis Hall Winery, and Pleasant Hill Winery. Unlike many of his Boeing brethren, however, Tim isn't an engineer by background. Rather, Tim joined Boeing fresh out of the University of Washington with a degree in zoology. That zoology training serves him well when it comes to understanding the microbiology of what *Saccharomyces cerevisiae* (yeast) does to sugar.

:Nota Bene is a red-wine zone, represented by Bordeaux blends and syrah. With the help of assistant winemaker Mark Rashap, Tim relies on grapes harvested from a who's who of vineyards: Ciel du Cheval, Portteus Vineyard, Alder Creek, Champoux Vineyards, Artz Vineyard, Conner Lee Vineyard, and Stillwater Creek. The fact is, Tim prefers the option of selecting his grapes from various Washington vineyards and, like a gourmet chef, deciding which ingredients to include in a featured entrée. Tim is most intrigued by this blending or "linking" of disparate vineyard grapes. The name "Abbinare," which is one of :Nota Bene's Bordeaux blends, is the Italian word for "to link." His "Ciel du Cheval Vineyard" combines grapes from the vineyard of the same name but features four different varietals. "Miscela," Italian for "blend," contains a heavy dose of merlot, but also includes several other red varietals.

If you are looking for a lively discussion about topics such as volatile acidity distillation, titratable acidity, pH, malolactic paper chromatography, residual-sugar-by-pill test, and percentage of alcohol by ebulliometer, Tim is the person to see. We suggest, however, that you skip the technical process and go right to the wine—in the name of scientific research, of course.

:NOTA BENE CELLARS
opened: 2001
winemaker(s): Tim Narby
location: 9320 15th Avenue South, Unit CC
Seattle, WA 98108
phone: 206-459-2785
web: www.notabenecellars.com
e-mail: info@notabenecellars.com
picnic area: No
gift shop: No
fee: $5 tasting fee refundable with purchase
hours: 1–5 second Saturdays of the month from
February through August; open selected other
Saturdays in November and December: consult
www.ssaw.info for details

Tim Narby (r) and assistant winemaker

DIRECTIONS: From I-5 take exit 158 (Boeing Access Rd/E. Marginal Way). Merge onto Pacific Hwy
S. [Tukwila: International Blvd] and proceed .5 miles. Take ramp onto SR-99 [W. Marginal Way]
and go 1.5 miles. Turn left onto ramp toward 14th Ave. S. Turn right (south) onto W. Marginal Pl.
S., then immediately turn left (east) onto S. 95th St. Road name changes to 15th Ave. S. Arrive
at 9320 15th Ave. S.

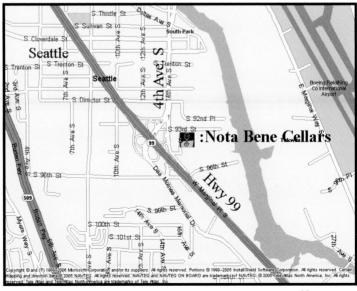

Around the Sound Wine Trail

Sky River Meadery

The Puget Sound region has more than 60 wineries, excluding Woodinville. But just a handful offer tasting rooms with regular hours. The wineries included in the Around the Sound WineTrail stretch from Tacoma to Sultan with a foray by ferry to Vashon Island. Along the way, you will discover the deep roots of Washington wine history, the passion of Puget Sound grape growers, and a variety of styles and types of wine that will surprise you. And, with plenty of places to stay and eat, your biggest challenge will be keeping track of the time.

1 E.B. Foote Winery

2 Vashon Winery

3 Vino Aquino Winery

4 Blackthorn Mountain Winery

5 Sky River Meadery

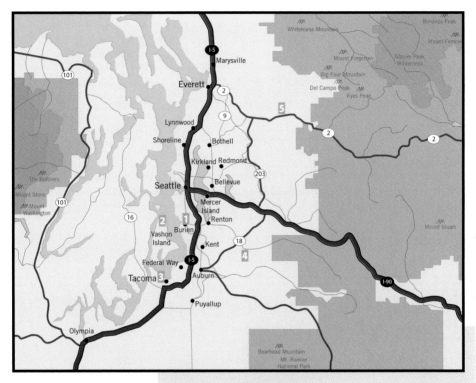

Region:	**Puget Sound Wine Country**
# of tasting rooms on tour:	**5**
Estimated # of days for tour:	**3 or 4**
Getting around:	**Car and ferry**
Tips:	❑ **E.B. Foote Winery in Burien hosts plays such as "Gone with the Wine"—see www.ebfootewinery.com for event times.** ❑ **A variety of restaurants to choose from in Vashon Island village.** ❑ **Consider hiring a limousine—especially if your plans include Woodinville.**

E.B. Foote Winery

Burien's E.B. Foote Winery is all about fun and enjoying life. Owners and winemakers Rich Higginbotham and Sherrill Miller wouldn't have it any other way. To this end, you'll discover quirky quotes throughout the winery and plenty of convivial conversation at the tasting room bar. You can also join Rich and

Sherrill for the Breeders Theater, which takes place twice yearly, in January and three weekends in July. Of course, the winery will provide the wine (as well as hors-d'oeuvres) to accompany the plays, which are described as "wacky, silly, and just plain fun." With titles such as "Gone with the Wine," you can count on an evening of laughter. And be quick with your ticket purchases; these plays often sell out.

When it comes to wine, however, E.B. Foote gets serious with a full offering of reds and whites made from Eastern Washington grapes. Rich and Sherrill's focus is on reds, and despite having zero winemaking experience (she was a schoolteacher and he worked for King County) when they bought the winery in 1991, they have managed to amass a number of accolades along the way. Their "Perfect à Trois" red blend of cabernet sauvignon, merlot, and cabernet franc is a delicious example of their school-of-hard-knocks winemaking skills. Perhaps the Louis Pasteur quotation on one of the winery's walls applies to this taut, fresh red blend: "The flavor of wine is like delicate poetry."

Located in Burien, west of Sea-Tac Airport, this small working winery is in the "cellar" of a retail building. Here, assisted by a small army of volunteers lovingly referred to as "Volunteer Vintners," Rich and Sherrill haul, crush, press, ferment, bottle, label, and sell their wines. They produce about 2,500 cases per year, with 90 percent of their wine sold directly from the winery.

In addition to the annual plays, E.B. Foote Winery hosts Red Wine and Chocolate; Red, White and Blue Days; Spring Barrel Tasting; Father's Day Weekend Special; Summer Celebration; and Christmas Open House. Consult E.B. Foote's website for a calendar of events.

Sherrill Miller and Richard Higginbotham

E.B. FOOTE WINERY
opened: 1978
winemaker(s): Rich Higginbotham and Sherrill Miller
location: 127-B SW 153rd Street
Burien, WA 98166-2311
phone: 206-242-3852
web: www.ebfootewinery.com
e-mail: winemaker@ebfootewinery.com
picnic area: Yes
gift shop: Yes
fee: Complimentary wine tasting
hours: 7–9 Tuesday and Thursday, 10–4 Friday through Saturday, or by appointment

DIRECTIONS: From I-5 take exit 154 and head west toward Sea-Tac Airport and Burien on SR-518. Proceed about 3 miles. Go past SR-509 and at the light turn left onto 1st Ave. S. getting into the right lane. Go 3 blocks and turn right onto 153rd St. The E.B. Foote Winery is located to your left in the cellar of the retail strip mall. Access the winery via the fenced stairway.

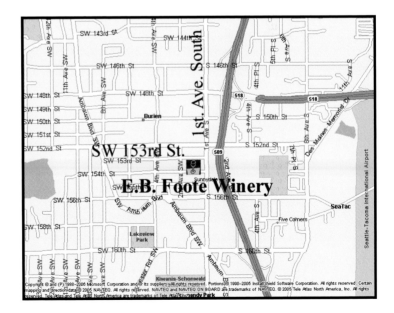

99

Vashon Winery

WineTrail trekkers, you don't need an excuse to take the short ferry ride to picturesque Vashon Island, but if you're looking for one, try Vashon Winery. Ron Irvine is the proprietor and winemaker for this gem of a winery, which

he himself describes as "boutique" and he's happy to keep it that way.

The road to Ron's purchase of Vashon Winery in 2001 includes a number of wine-related ventures. Any student of the Washington wine industry will likely recognize Ron Irvine as the co-author of *The Wine Project*, which traces the history of the state's wine industry, from pioneer grape growers to modern-day movers and shakers. The other author of *The Wine Project* was none other than Walter J. Clore, who is generally credited as the father of Washington's modern-day wine industry. (Incidentally, you can purchase *The Wine Project* at Vashon Winery, and we suspect that Ron would be happy to autograph it.)

Included on Ron's résumé is the little fact that he was a wine retailer for many years as the owner of Pike and Western Wine Shop at the Pike Place Market. Working in the trade no doubt reinforced his winemaking style, which uses neutral oak to create smooth (i.e., soft) wines.

At the Vashon Winery, visitors have an opportunity to sample Ron's full portfolio of reds and whites as well as his European-style hard ciders. For his reds, Ron relies on the grapes from Yakima Valley–based Portteus Vineyards, which include cabernet sauvignon, cabernet franc, and merlot. The white wines, such as Ron's smooth and crisp semillon and sauvignon blanc, are made from grapes grown by Eastern Washington growers. For a real treat, check out his wonderfully named "Isletage" (rhymes with Meritage), which is a blend of Puget Sound–area grapes: Madeline Angevine, siegerrebe, and Müller-Thurgau. He also makes wine from a relatively obscure island-grown varietal called chasselas, best known in Switzerland.

In addition to teaching for South Seattle Community College's wine program, Ron is actively involved with the Puget Sound Grape Growers Association. Despite his wealth of credentials, Ron is an amazingly approachable and fun individual. Even inexperienced wine tasters feel at ease with Ron. In Vashon Winery's barn-like tasting room, a chandelier hangs from the rafters, a basketball hoop graces the wall, and the sign above the tasting bar reads, "Ron Irvine, owner, winemaker, janitor." A whimsical guy, but one serious winemaker.

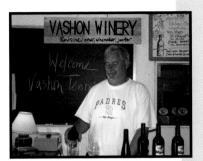

Ronald Irvine of Vashon Winery

VASHON WINERY
opened: 1995
winemaker(s): Ron Irvine
location: 10317 SW 156th Street
Vashon, WA 98070
phone: 206-567-0055
web: www.vashonwinery.com
e-mail: vashonwinery@yahoo.com
picnic area: Yes
gift shop: No
fee: Complimentary wine tasting
hours: 2–5 Saturdays April 1 to October 1, or by
appointment; Friday night BBQ and music during
summer: call to confirm

DIRECTIONS: From Seattle, take the Fauntleroy-Vashon Island Ferry westbound—see www.wsdot.
wa.gov/ferries/ for ferry schedule. Arrive Vashon Island and take Vashon Hwy SW (south) about
3.5 miles. Turn right onto SE 156th St. and proceed about .25 miles. Vashon Winery will be on
your left in a big red barn.

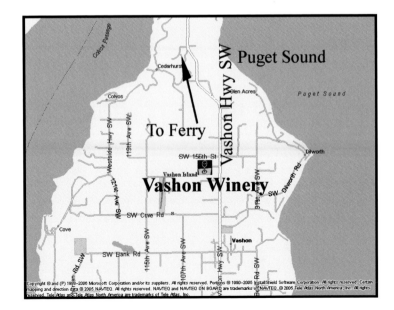

Vino Aquino Winery

Rich Aquino and his business partner, Stan Jordan, are out to prove that anyone can become a winemaker. For about $75, you can purchase one of their equipment kits, add juice from a box, and let the fermentation begin. They sell their own wine, too. In fact, sales of their wine outnumber the sales of winemaking kits and starter juice boxes combined. They must be doing something right. WineTrail enthusiasts who aren't convinced are encouraged to

try their "Port of Tacoma" chocolate-flavored port, a dessert wine and their number-one seller. Take a few sips and you'll understand its popularity.

You will not find French oak barrels or any special yeast cakes at Vino Aquino. The grape juice comes right out of the box, and in six to eight weeks, you have cabernet sauvignon, pinot noir, or one of 40 other types of wine. Ever wonder what peach apricot chardonnay

Stan Jordan and Rich Aquino (l to r)

tastes like? This is the place to come to satisfy your curiosity. As Rich Aquino points out, "We love wine snobs. They usually come here with a particular mindset and after a few samples, their attitude melts away."

Since launching Vino Aquino in 2001, both Rich and Stan have survived major health scares. Now they both find that each day working at the wine shop is a joy. Their mission is to end the mystique that surrounds the art of winemaking and celebrate life along the way. And they succeed.

In addition to making wine and selling winemaking kits, Vino Aquino offers creative wine labels customized for corporate events, nonprofit auctions, wedding parties, and the like. The wine shop also hosts a steady stream of private parties and functions.

Vino Aquino is a unique stop on the Greater Seattle WineTrail, one that has something to teach while giving a big boost to your spirits. And that attitude adjustment may come in handy when you have to explain to your spouse why there's an 8-gallon pail and 6-gallon carboy in the back of your car.

Rich Aquino and Stan Jordan (l to r)

VINO AQUINO WINERY
opened: 2001
winemaker(s): Rich Aquino
location: 2607 6th Avenue
Tacoma, WA 98406
phone: 253-272-5511
web: www.vinoaquino.com
e-mail: vinoaquino@mcleodusa.com
picnic area: No
gift shop: Yes
fee: Complimentary wine tasting
hours: 10–6 Monday through Saturday

DIRECTIONS: From I-5 take exit 132 onto Hwy 16 toward Gig Harbor/Bremerton/Sprague Ave. Take S. Sprague Ave. exit and continue 1.3 miles. Turn left onto 6th Ave. and travel about .3 miles. Vino Aquino Winery is on the right at 2607 6th Ave.

Blackthorn Mountain Winery

There are myriad home winemakers, but few break through to the commercial realm. The regulatory paperwork is daunting. The equipment needed is costly. Despite this, Alistair and Sally Sloley of Black Diamond followed their guts (and discerning palates) and launched Blackthorn Mountain Winery in 2005. Producing approximately 500 cases annually, their winery is tiny when compared to other commercial wineries. The Sloleys take pride in Blackthorn Mountain's reputation as an "artisan winery."

Their winemaking style relies on old-world techniques, including sustained maceration and extended lees aging, also known as sur lie aging. Rather than racking the wine or transferring it to a clean barrel for aging, the fermented wine remains in its original barrel and matures on the gooey muck (or "lees") on the bottom of the barrel. Reds and whites are aged in neutral oak. The effect is an amazingly different wine-tasting profile that few Washington wineries emulate. Perhaps closest in taste would be the wines of White Heron Cellars, Saintpaulia Vintners, and Black Canyon Vintners, which rely on similar winemaking styles.

I first met Alistair (Alex) at the 2007 Taste Washington event in Seattle. At the time, I had a hummus-covered cracker to munch on while I swirled and sipped his merlot. I had sampled many other wines that evening prior to sampling Blackthorn Mountain wine, but the distinctive flavor cut through. I could taste the chocolate and blackberry notes, and it actually paired nicely with the hummus. It was then that Alex gave me the explanation for the sur lie aging process, and I thought to myself that it must have taken a great deal of courage to adopt a winemaking philosophy very different from the pack. If you are looking for a unique tasting experience, a richness of flavor different from others, check out Blackthorn Mountain Winery in Black Diamond.

Alex Sloley

BLACKTHORN MOUNTAIN WINERY
opened: 2005
winemaker(s): Alistair (Alex) Sloley
location: 25318 Kanaskat Drive
Black Diamond, WA 98010
phone: 360-886-2308
web: www.blackthornmountainwinery.com
e-mail: wine@blackthornmountainwinery.com
picnic area: No
gift shop: No
fee: Complimentary wine tasting
hours: 12–4 first Saturday of each month

DIRECTIONS: **From SR-169** [SE Maple Valley Hwy] take Black Diamond Ravensdale Rd exit and continue .7 miles. Turn left (north) onto Kanaskat Dr. and proceed .3 miles and look for winery signs.

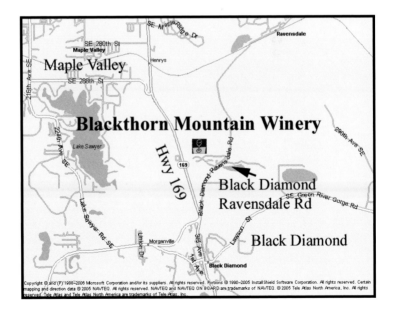

Sky River Meadery

Denice Ingalls, owner of and winemaker for Sky River Meadery, has a sweet thing going. Using select honeys, she employs advanced techniques refined at Cornell University to create honey wine (a.k.a. mead). This is a non-tannin

zone: You won't find any grapes around its Sultan production facility. Instead, what you will find are three different premium honey wines: Sky River Sweet Mead (6 percent residual sugar); Sky River Semi-Sweet Mead (3 percent residual sugar) and Sky River Dry Mead (less than 1 percent residual sugar). Choosing among the three wines depends upon your taste preferences and what's for dinner. The Sky River Sweet Mead is excellent as an aperitif, whereas the Sky River Dry Mead pairs nicely with pan-Asian cuisine and Northwest seafood. Each mead sells for around $12 a bottle.

Working with a variety of honey suppliers from around the world, Denice chooses honeys for color, flavor, aromatics and sugars, not unlike traditional winemakers working closely with grape growers. However, her "farmers" are bees, rather than growers from the Columbia Valley. At wine tasting events, she is surrounded by traditional grape wine vintners who go to great lengths to explain why their merlot is different from their neighbor's. Denice, however, has no explaining to do. Honey wine is unique, and her product alone sets her apart.

It also helps that mead wine is rich in lore from ancient Europe. For example, Greeks called mead "ambrosia" or nectar of the gods, believing that gods drank mead. Consequently, the Greeks thought that mead had magical and sacred properties. The term "honeymoon" comes from the ancient tradition of giving bridal couples a moon's worth of honey wine. For a quick and interesting read, there are a number of other honey-wine-related tales and anecdotes noted on the Sky River Meadery website (see www.skyriverbrewing.com).

SKY RIVER MEADERY
opened: 1999
winemaker(s): Denice Ingalls
location: 32533 Cascade View Drive
Sultan, WA 98294
phone: 360-793-6761
web: www.skyriverbrewing.com
e-mail: denice@skyriverbrewing.com
picnic area: No
gift shop: Yes
fee: Complimentary wine tasting
hours: 10–4 Monday through Friday

DIRECTIONS: From US-2 in Sultan, take Cascade View Drive (south) .2 miles and arrive at Sky River Meadery on the left. If traveling east, Cascade View Drive will be a right turn off of US-2 just past the Sultan town center.

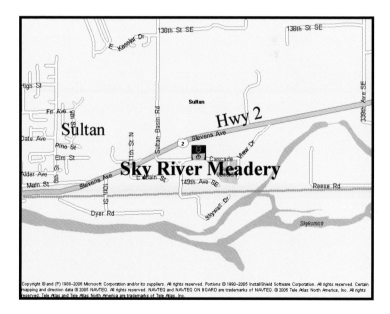

Woodinville
WINE COUNTRY

Woodinville
WineTrail North

Along Woodinville WineTrail North, you will discover that business parks are not what they used to be. This is the suburban equivalent to city garage winemakers or garagistes. These boutique wineries transform grapes from Eastern Washington into award-winning wines that continually receive accolades from connoisseurs. Two major business parks account for most wineries in this WineTrail. Simply park your car and follow the signs. A few wineries require a drive but won't disappoint.

Woodinville WineTrail North

1 Edmonds Winery
2 Cuillin Hills Winery
3 Des Voigne Cellars
4 Mark Ryan Winery
5 Page Cellars Winery

6 Red Sky Winery
7 Arlington Road Cellars
8 Saintpaulia Vintners
9 Chatter Creek Winery
10 Covington Cellars

11 Stevens Winery
12 Woodinville Wine Cellars
13 DiStefano Winery

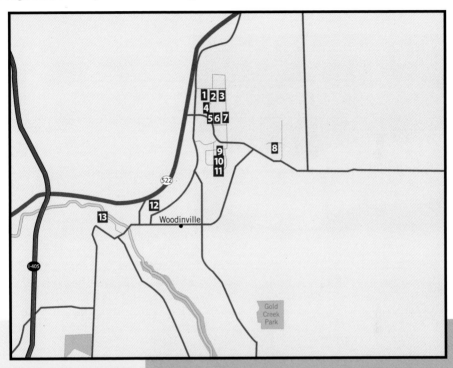

Region:	**Woodinville Wine Country**
# of tasting rooms on tour:	**13**
Estimated # of days for tour:	**3**
Getting around:	**Car and foot**
Key events:	❑ **St. Nicholas Day Open House (first weekend in December) and Passport to Woodinville (typically the first weekend in April)—both sponsored by Woodinville Wine Country. See www.woodinvillewinecountry.com for details and ticket information.**
Tips:	❑ **Woodinville offers a variety of restaurants: Some popular places include The Golden Goat, the Barking Frog, Pasta Nova, Garden Café, The Herbfarm at Willows Lodge, Italianissimo R-storante, and Purple Café & Wine Bar.** ❑ **Consider hiring a limousine service, such as Bon Vivant 206-437-1298, Bayview Limo Service 206-223-6200 Washington Wine Tours 206-794-0565, or Gray Line of Seattle 206-624-5077.**

Edmonds Winery

Located in the same business park where a number of other Woodinville WineTrail North wineries are found, Edmonds Winery is a relatively new "micro" winery founded by owner/winemaker Doug Peterson. Working

closely with his wife, Lael, their goal "is to make our wines in a lighter fashion, for the most part just letting the wine make itself, with minimal intervention. We handcraft our wines in small, open-top fermentation tanks and age in small oak barrels."

You're in for a treat if you venture to Edmonds Winery, because Doug is usually doing the pouring honors. You'll get to sample some truly excellent wine while engaging in a conversation with Doug. And talk with Doug can go in many directions, thanks to his diverse work background. His current day job is as a computer specialist with Group Health Cooperative, but he has also dabbled in a variety of other careers. **WineTrail Note:** Tasting-room enthusiasts run into a lot of winemakers who keep their day jobs while following their passion for making great wine. Doug embodies this renaissance characteristic to the nth degree.

You will swirl, smell, and have a hard time spitting out Doug's Bordeaux-style blends. Of note is a cabernet sauvignon he has dubbed "Mystery," because it has a smell and taste that you won't find in any other wine. However, call it serendipity or just dumb luck, but one WineTrail enthusiast who was there when we were visiting exclaimed that the smell was reminiscent of geraniums. To which the eight tasters in attendance agreed that she had nailed it. Mystery solved, perhaps?

Edmonds Winery is an active member of the Woodinville Wine Country Association and, in collaboration with other Woodinville wineries, participates in the Passport to Woodinville (the first weekend of April) and the St. Nicholas Open House (first weekend of December) events. Visit www. woodinvillewinecountry.com for details. The winery also enjoys hosting new-wine-release parties, an annual crush party, a winery anniversary party, spring barrel tasting, and a number of other excuses to party. You get the picture. Fellow WineTrail enthusiasts, a stop at Edmonds Winery, along the Woodinville North WineTrail, is a must.

EDMONDS WINERY
opened: 2002
winemaker(s): Doug Petersen
location: 19501 144th Avenue NE Suite D-500
Woodinville, WA 98072
phone: 425-774-8959
web: www.edmondswinery.com
e-mail: info@edmondswinery.com
picnic area: No
gift shop: No
fee: Complimentary wine tasting
hours: 12–4 Saturdays; occasional Sundays (call ahead)

Doug Petersen

DIRECTIONS: From SR-522 take NE 195th St. exit. The road name changes to NE North Woodinville Way. Turn left (north) onto 144th Ave. NE and arrive at 19501 144th Ave. NE—Edmonds Winery is located inside the Woodinville Park North business complex in Suite D-500.
From Woodinville Center, depart on NE 175th St. [NE Woodinville Duvall Rd] heading east. Turn left (west) onto NE North Woodinville Way and go about .2 miles. Turn right (north) onto 144th Ave. NE and arrive at 19501 144th Ave. NE, Suite D-500.

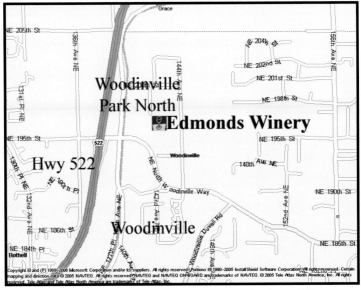

Cuillin Hills Winery

According to the Cuillin Hills Winery (pronounced Coo-lin) website, the winery was conceived "when a Scottish girl and a wine-loving bagpiper found themselves in the Highlands of Scotland; a place where dreams and possibilities are realized," and where a hobby suddenly changes its path and a winery is born.

Woodinville Passport at Cuillin Hills

The bagpiper is Derek Des Voigne, who honed his winemaking skills as the assistant winemaker at Vin du Lac Winery in Lake Chelan.

For the wine enthusiasts making the rounds of the Woodinville WineTrail North tasting rooms, a visit to Cuillin Hills Winery is a special treat, because you get a nice two-for-one surprise. Derek and his brother Darren Des Voigne, founder of Des Voigne Winery, chose to colocate their wineries in the same suite of the same business park.

Being a new winery, Cuillin Hills focuses on small lot production of ultrapremium, hand-crafted wines. And what great wines they are! No wonder Cuillin Hills Winery was featured in the April 2006 issue of *Seattle Magazine* as a "hot-off-the-press winery making a splash at Taste Washington." By limiting his production to 600 cases of wine, Derek is able to focus on syrah, sangiovese, and claret red. His primary focus is on complex, full-finish syrahs, and we suspect that the folks from *Seattle Magazine* were sampling this beauty.

The tasting room is fairly plain, the wines are complimentary, and wearing a kilt is optional. But we suspect that you will take home a bottle of Cuillin Hills syrah, pop in your copy of *Braveheart*, and uncork this wine. Your clan will truly enjoy this with a large pepperoni-and-sausage pizza.

Derek Des Voigne

CUILLIN HILLS WINERY
opened: 2005
winemaker(s): Derek Des Voigne
location: 19501 144th Avenue NE Suite C-200
Woodinville, WA 98072-4409
phone: 425-415-VINO
web: www.cuillinhills.com
e-mail: info@cuillinhills.com
picnic area: No
gift shop: No
fee: $5 fee credited toward wine purchase
hours: 12–4 Saturdays, Sundays by appointment

DIRECTIONS: From SR-522 take NE 195th St. exit. The road name changes to NE North Woodinville Way. Turn left (north) onto 144th Ave. NE and arrive at 19501 144th Ave. NE—Cuillin Hills Winery is located inside the business complex in Suite C-200.

From Woodinville Center, depart on NE 175th St. [NE Woodinville Duvall Rd] heading east. Turn left (west) onto NE North Woodinville Way and go about .2 miles. Turn right (north) onto 144th Ave. NE and arrive at 19501 144th Ave. NE, Suite C-200.

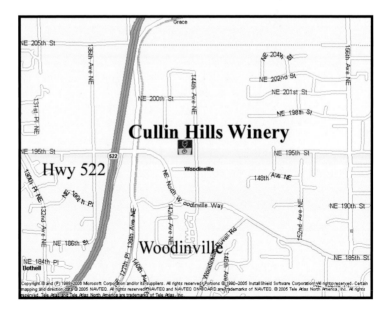

Des Voigne Cellars

Get ready for another one of those Woodinville WineTrail North business park wineries—but with a twist. Or perhaps we should say "twists," because here you get a two-for-one tasting room. Darren Des Voigne, founder of Des Voigne Winery, and his brother Derek Des Voigne, owner of Cuillin Hills Winery, have

opted to share winemaking facilities and tasting room. Fortunately, they are not twin brothers; otherwise WineTrail enthusiasts might be really confused.

Des Voigne Cellars is one of Woodinville's newest boutique wineries,

Getting sample at Des Voigne tasting room

founded by Darren and Melissa Des Voigne. The Des Voignes' goal is to produce small quantities of "Tuscany-inspired" premium wines from select Washington vineyards. Just out of the gates, Darren's first-year crop of wines netted 400 cases of sangiovese, syrah, cabernet franc, merlot as well as a newly released red blend they have dubbed "Solea." "Solea" is an Andalusian word for the flamenco. (Darren named the blend after a song by Miles Davis, not because he is studying to be a flamenco dancer.) The "Solea" is a blend of cabernet sauvignon, merlot, cabernet franc, and malbec, all from Washington's prized Red Mountain area. This would be great wine with a summertime barbeque or a wet winter Seattle night with red beans and rice and smoked sausage and a splash of jazz in the background. All Des Voigne vintages are noteworthy, but for those who lean toward the spicy syrah, we encourage you to check out the Des Voigne version. It would make a perfect complement to a peppercorn steak and grilled corn on the cob.

Because Des Voigne Cellars is similar to the other business-park wineries, don't bother to pack a picnic or plan to shop in the gift shop. Just bring your palate for great wine tasting in a relaxed but somewhat Spartan environment. Des Voigne Cellars is truly a destination spot along the WineTrail journey.

Darren Des Voigne

DES VOIGNE CELLARS
opened: 2005
winemaker(s): Darren Des Voigne
location: 19501 144th Avenue NE Suite C-200
Woodinville, WA 98072-4409
phone: 425-415-VINO
web: www.desvoignecellars.com
e-mail: info@desvoignecellars.com
picnic area: No
gift shop: No
fee: $5 fee credited toward wine purchase
hours: 12–5 Saturdays, Sundays by appointment

DIRECTIONS: From SR-522 take NE 195th St. exit. The road name changes to NE North Woodinville Way. Turn left (north) onto 144th and arrive at 19501 144th Ave. NE—Des Voigne Cellars is located inside the business complex in Suite C-200.
From Woodinville Center, depart on NE 175th St [NE Woodinville Duvall Rd] heading east. Turn left (west) onto NE North Woodinville Way and go about .2 miles. Turn right (north) onto 144th Ave. NE and arrive at 19501 144th Avenue NE, Suite C-200. Des Voigne Cellars is colocated with Cuillin Hills Winery.

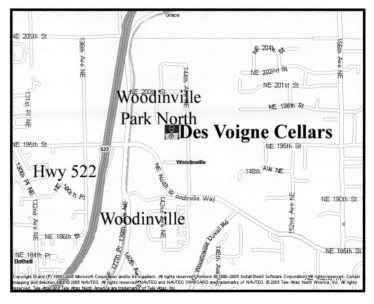

117

Mark Ryan Winery

What's in a name? By any other name, a wine would taste just as good, to paraphrase a guy in England a few centuries back. Nevertheless, to WineTrail enthusiasts a name is very important, because it represents a certain attention

to detail. Carefully chosen names can be a good barometer for gauging how carefully the winemaker has considered every step of the winemaking process, from selecting the growers to choosing the perfect yeast. Thus, when you hear the names of Mark Ryan wines, we suspect that you will want to sample the whole lot. And what names they are! With names such as "Wild Eyed Syrah," "Long Haul," "Dead Horse," and (our favorite) "The Dissident," you know that winemaker/owner Mark Ryan McNeilly has given great thought and care to what's in the bottle.

He's obviously got a sense of humor, with the "Dead Horse" wine being a prime example. "Dead Horse" is a play on words associated with the grapes being from the famed Ciel du Cheval vineyard; in English, "Ciel du Cheval"

Lovers at Mark Ryan—was it the wine?

loosely translates to "Horse Heaven." But as Mark points out, "No horses were hurt during the production of this wine, and it was tested on humans." Phew.

Mark and his winery staff like to party and do so with the release of each of their wines. Tasting-room trekkers are invited to come celebrate the release of selected vintages during the year. Check the Mark Ryan website for open-house dates. So ride in on your horse and find a hitching post close to the winery's business park bay. You'll want to avoid a long haul for all the wine you'll be bringing back to the wild-eyed wine drinkers in your life.

Mark Ryan McNeilly

MARK RYAN WINERY
opened: 1999
winemaker(s): Mark Ryan McNeilly
location: 19501 144th Avenue NE Suite F-900
Woodinville, WA 98072
phone: 206-295-6796
web: www.markryanwinery.com
e-mail: mark@markryanwinery.com
picnic area: No
gift shop: No
fee: Complimentary wine tasting
hours: 12–4 Saturdays

DIRECTIONS: From SR-522 take NE 195th St. exit. The road name changes to NE North Woodin-ville Way. Turn left (north) onto 144th and arrive at 19501 144th Ave. NE—Mark Ryan Winery is located inside the business complex in Suite F-900.
From Woodinville Center, depart on NE 175th St. [NE Woodinville Duvall Rd] heading east. Turn left (west) onto NE North Woodinville Way and go about .2 miles. Turn right (north) onto 144th Ave. NE and arrive at 19501 144th Ave. NE, Suite F-900.

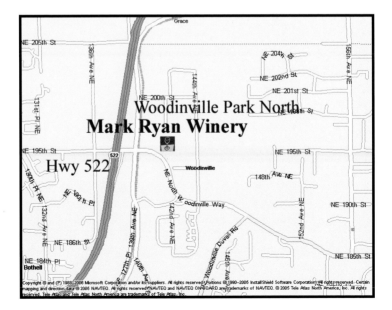

Page Cellars Winery

We all have a special person in our life who makes us feel at home when we visit. They're attentive to our needs and genuinely interested in making sure we're comfortable. They talk to us as if there was no one else in the room. Such is the gift of Rothelle Page as she welcomes visitors to Page Cellars' tasting room, and her warm reception makes this visit especially memorable. (This gift must be infectious, because her able staff, including longtime family friend John, also engage you with attentive eyes.)

Page Cellars's Woodinville location

Rothelle is a self-described winery diva, responsible for managing the tasting room, wine distribution, marketing, public relations, paying bills and making sure the glasses are clean at the end of the day. She's pressed (no pun intended) into service because her husband, Jim Page, is a corporate pilot when he isn't a winemaker in training. While Jim's racking up virtual frequent flyer miles, Rothelle is tending the fire back home. And what a nice fire it is!

Experiencing Page Cellars is like going to a Mariners game and watching a rookie called up to the majors and hitting three homers in his first game. Despite the fact that Jim is still learning the ropes, Page Cellars has brought home hardware from several prestigious wine-tasting events, including the Indiana State Fair as well as competitions in Florida and Texas. As you sample Page Cellars' delicious "Preface" cabernet sauvignon or its "Luscious" syrah, you quickly realize why the winery is winning such accolades. Ever one to be humble, Rothelle is quick to point out that the medals are a result of using the best grapes harvested from Red Mountain and Yakima Valley and the best winemaking talent, in particular Matt Loso of Matthews Cellars fame. Currently, Matt is the lead winemaker at Page Cellars, and Jim is the apprentice. Guidance from other winemakers, such as Eric Dunham and Greg Lill, has also been of great help.

WineTrail trekkers are advised that they will be treated with great care when they visit Page Cellars. But unlike home, you won't need to take your shoes off at the front door.

Jim Page

PAGE CELLARS WINERY
opened: 2000
winemaker(s): Jim Page and Matthew Loso
(Consultant Winemaker)
location: 19495 144th Avenue NE; Suite B-235
Woodinville, WA 98072
phone: 253-232-9463
web: www.pagecellars.com
e-mail: info@pagecellars.com
picnic area: No
gift shop: No
fee: $5 tasting fee
hours: 12–4 Saturdays

DIRECTIONS: From SR-522 take NE 195th St. exit. The road name changes to NE North Woodinville Way. Turn left (north) onto 144th Ave. NE and arrive at 19501 144th Ave. NE—Page Cellars is located inside the business complex in Suite B-235.
From Woodinville Center, depart on NE 175th St. [NE Woodinville Duvall Rd] heading east. Turn left (west) onto NE North Woodinville Way and go about .2 miles. Turn right (north) onto 144th Ave. NE and arrive at 19501 144th Ave. NE, Suite B-235.

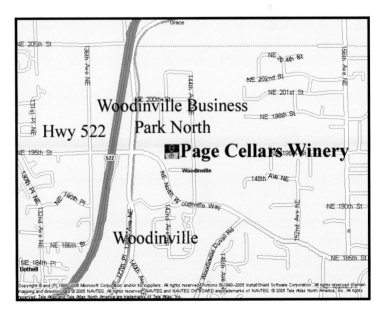

121

Red Sky Winery

Enjoying a glass of wine under a red-sky sunset in Eastern Washington, Jim and Carol Parsons made the decision to start a winery. They clinked their glasses in a toast to their dreams on that evening in 1999, and Red Sky Winery was born.

The Parsons' love affair with wine began back in 1982 when they opened a retail wine and cheese shop in Seattle. Eventually they collaborated with friends to produce 50 cases of Red Sky wine in their Bellevue basement in 1999. It must have tasted pretty good, because they haven't looked back.

Red Sky Winery tasting room, Woodinville

They began with the idea that it all begins with the fruit. WineTrail lovers will appreciate the fact that the grapes come from such vineyards as Boushey, Conner Lee, Dineen, Klipsun, Pleasant, Pepper Bridge, Rosebud, and Sheridan vineyards. To coax the best flavors from these grapes, the Parsons needed a great winemaker, which they found in John Ogburn (Boeing's master chef for its ship. Yes, Virginia, Boeing has a seagoing vessel, and of course it needs a great chef to get its passengers through those rough seas in the Strait of Juan de Fuca). John recently handed the reins to Carol, but during his stint, he helped the couple expand production to 1,000 cases of rich and elegant Red Sky wines.

You won't find picnic benches or great views at this Woodinville business park, but you will discover great wine. Resident artist Gretchen is a wonderful guide for sampling Red Sky wines during your visit. Check out her artwork on display at the winery and get a peek at the artwork that will soon grace Red Sky's labels.

RED SKY WINERY
opened: 1999
winemaker(s): John Ogburn
location: 19495 144th Avenue NE, Suite B-220
Woodinville, WA 98072
phone: 425-481-9864
web: www.redskywinery.com
e-mail: redskywinery@comcast.net
picnic area: No
gift shop: No
fee: Complimentary wine tasting
hours: 12–4 Saturdays

DIRECTIONS: From SR-522 take NE 195th St. exit. The road name changes to NE North Woodin-
ville Way. Turn left (north) onto 144th Ave. NE and arrive at 19501 144th Ave. NE—Red Sky
Winery is located inside the business complex in Suite B-220.
From Woodinville Center, depart on NE 175th St. [NE Woodinville Duvall Rd] heading east. Turn
left (west) onto NE North Woodinville Way and go about .2 miles. Turn right (north) onto 144th
Ave. NE and arrive at 19501 144th Ave. NE, Suite B-220.

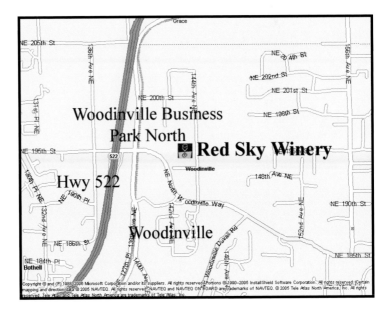

Arlington Road Cellars

While a huge number of adults have a dream of starting their own business, few act on it. Whether it's the risk of financial ruin or simply because there are not enough hours in the day, most would-be entrepreneurs let go of the dream and stick to their daily routine.

Ken and Robin Nydam visiting with winemaker consultant Matthew Loso on far left

Ken and Robin Nydam are different. They followed their dream.

While keeping their day jobs—Ken works for a telecommunications company and Robin works for a software company—the Nydams took the plunge to create their own winery. In 2002, Arlington Road Cellars was born and in due course the couple leased space in a north Woodinville business park for the future winery. A subsequent trip to France gave them a first hand look at the layout and design of a number of successful wineries. From this experience, they were able to create the design of Arlington Cellars, even down to the sparkles you see embedded in the concrete walls of the barrel room. These are reminiscent of the caverns they saw in France.

Not having a lick of winemaking knowledge, they realized early on that they could either go to the library and get a bunch of books on winemaking or hire a consultant winemaker. They chose the latter, hiring Matthew Loso, of nearby Matthew Cellars fame, as a consultant. When asked why they chose Matthew, Ken quickly responds, "We simply liked his wines the best. We wanted our wines to reflect his winemaking style." There is little doubt that Arlington Cellars will focus on Bordeaux-style blends like those Matthew Cellars produces. In fact, its 2007 portfolio is primarily reds, including Arlington Road Cellars' flagship "Monolith" vintage, a Bordeaux blend with huge berry flavors, full-bodied feel, and lasting finish.

Eventually, Ken and Robin will devote all of their attention to Arlington Road Cellars. In the meantime, Ken will continue to get calls from Matthew urging him to leave his unexciting systems engineering meeting to assist with that day's bottling. Although Ken's heart lies with the winery, the bills still need to be paid.

Perhaps one day, someone will approach Ken and Robin and exclaim that they have a dream of making wine and ask if they would be available for consultation. I would love to see their expressions when it happens.

Ken and Robin Nydam

ARLINGTON ROAD CELLARS
opened: 2002
winemaker(s): Ken Nydam and Matthew Loso
(Consulting Winemaker)
location: 19495 144th Avenue NE, Suite A-115
Woodinville, WA 98072-4427
phone: 425-482-1801
web: www.arlingtonroadcellars.com
e-mail: wine@arlingtonroadcellars.com
picnic area: No
gift shop: No
fee: Tasting fee may apply
hours: 12–5 Saturdays

DIRECTIONS: From SR-522 take NE 195th St. exit. The road name changes to NE North Wood-
inville Way. Turn left (north) onto 144th and arrive at 19495 144th Ave. NE—Arlington Road
Cellars is located inside the business park in Suite A-115.
From Woodinville Center, depart on NE 175th St. [NE Woodinville Duvall Rd] heading east. Turn
left (west) onto NE North Woodinville Way and go about .2 miles. Turn right (north) onto 144th
Ave. NE and arrive at 19495 144th Ave. NE, Suite A-115.

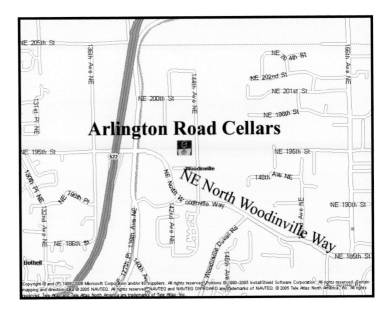

Saintpaulia Vintners

With his lofty goal "to produce wine that is complex and worthy of cellar space," Paul Shinoda, winemaker and proprietor of Saintpaulia Winery, sets the bar high for his wines and focuses on creating red wines that are distinctly different. One visit to this Woodinville WineTrail North business park location

will convince you that Paul's wines do stand out from most other wines. And to the point about being "worthy of cellar space," you will note that he is pouring wine from bottles that bear the vintage 1995, 1999, and so on. This isn't wine bathed in oak for 18 months and made ready for the masses. With the motto "I will pour no wine before its time," Paul hits you with a knowing smile as you swirl, smell, and sample.

"Saintpaulia" is the botanical name for the African violet and it pays homage to Paul's flower-growing past. A 1959 graduate from the University of California–Berkeley, Paul received his bachelor of science degree in plant pathology and worked for many years with his father at San Lorenzo Nursery in Santa Barbara, California.

Paul's botanical background becomes evident as you work your way through his vertical flight of cabernet sauvignons; he will spend most of the time talking about the growing of the grapes and the fact that stressed grapes are the true flavor enhancers. For growing his grapes, he works closely with Black Canyon Vineyard in the Red Mountain area, near Benton City. As he points out, "It doesn't matter what the leaves look like; they could all be brown and crinkly. What matters are the grapes, because that is where the plant is focusing its remaining energy."

In the tasting room, take a moment to look around and be sure to note the photographs on the wall. These pictures reveal the heart and soul of Saintpaulia Winery, the family and friends who are dedicated to it. Even the distinctive purple labels were created by a friend of his daughters! As Paul puts it, "We are a stealth winery because we fly below the wine world radar. We're a family-owned winery that takes great pride in producing fine quality, special wines."

Paul Yahiro Shinoda, Jr.

SAINTPAULIA VINTNERS
opened: 1993
winemaker(s): Paul Shinoda Jr.
location: 14522 NE North Woodinville Way
Woodinville, WA 98072
phone: 360-688-8585
web: www.saintpauliavintners.com
e-mail: paulshinoda@msn.com
picnic area: No
gift shop: No
fee: Complimentary wine tasting
hours: 12–5 Saturdays

DIRECTIONS: **From SR-522** take NE 195th St. exit. The road name changes to NE North Woodinville Way. Go up the hill to 14522 NE North Woodinville Way up the hill across from Shurgard Storage.
From Woodinville Center, depart on NE 175th St. [NE Woodinville Duvall Rd] heading east. Turn left (west) onto NE North Woodinville Way and go up the hill to 14522 NE North Woodinville Way.

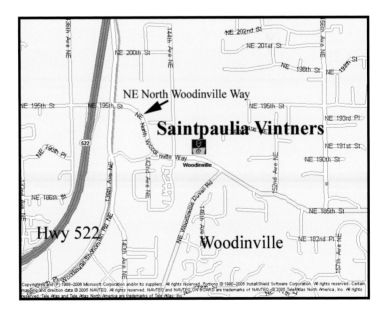

Chatter Creek Winery

A self-described "terroirist" and curmudgeon, Gordon "Gordy" Rawson isn't your typical winemaker. His personality is reflected in his distinctive single-vineyard wines, his eye-catching labels, and his anything-goes manner of speaking. As a Seattle boy, Gordy would seem ill suited to toil amongst the chardonnay-and-Brie crowd in suburban Woodinville. But he has managed to make the SR 520 commute for many years, which included a stint as the cellar master at Columbia Winery working with David Lake and company. He

Chatter Creek "Wine Diva" visitors

now makes the daily commute to the new Chatter Creek location along the Woodinville WineTrail North.

Gordy's portfolio of wines includes pinot gris, viognier, grenache, syrah, cabernet franc, and cabernet sauvignon, from vineyards such as Lonesome Spring Ranch, Clifton Hill, and Alder Ridge. These wines exhibit the true *terroir* of the different viticulture areas of Washington. Chatter Creek produces about 2,000 cases of wine per year.

Whereas Gordy's reds have been described using adjectives such as "youthful," "creamy and rich," and "full-bodied and well-balanced," his production of grenache represents a departure and an acknowledgement that tastes have shifted to softer fruit-forward wines. Gordy calls his grenache an excellent "red-white" wine, because it is easy to drink and won't grab your tongue like some of the merlots and syrahs. Here's how one reviewer described the Chatter Creek grenache: "A very pretty wine in the glass, light ruby in color, very clear and bright. The nose is full of the aromas of cranberry, fresh bread, and strawberry. Racy acid in the forward palate combines with the flavors of cranberry, raspberry, peach, and a bit of hazelnut, resulting in a well-balanced, classic grenache." I'm not sure this WineTrail trekker picked up on the aroma of "fresh bread," but I did pick up a bottle of the grenache to pair with a meal of minestrone soup and "gnarly" artisan bread.

Buon gusto!

CHATTER CREEK WINERY
opened: 2000
winemaker(s): Gordon Rawson
location: 18658 142nd Avenue NE, Building "E"
Woodinville, WA 98072-8521
phone: 206-985-2816
web: www.chattercreek.com
e-mail: gordy@chattercreek.com
picnic area: No
gift shop: No
fee: Complimentary wine tasting
hours: 11–5 Saturdays

Gordon Rawson

DIRECTIONS: From SR-522 take NE 195th St. exit. The road name changes to NE North Woodin-ville Way. Turn right onto 142nd Ave. NE and arrive at 18658 142nd Ave. NE—Chatter Creek Winery is located inside the business complex.

From Woodinville Center, depart on NE 175th St. [NE Woodinville Duvall Rd] heading east. Turn left (west) onto NE North Woodinville Way and go about .5 miles. Turn left (southwest) onto 142nd Ave. NE, go .3 miles, and arrive at 18658 142nd Ave. NE. Look for Building "E" in the Woodinville Commerce Center. The winery is in the lower portion of Building "E" at the far end.

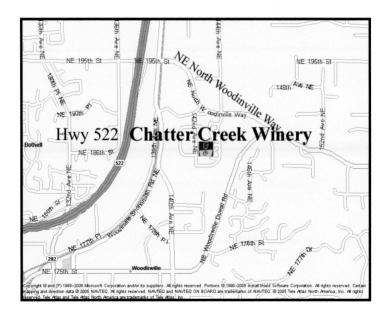

Covington Cellars

Covington Cellars is a family affair and a true labor of love. Founded in 2002 by David and Cindy Lawson, Covington Cellars is the story of a beer guy who meets a wine woman and falls in love with both her and the wine. Ever the tinkerer, David began experimenting with winemaking at the Lawsons' house in Covington. One success led to another, and with a few University of

California–Davis courses under David's belt, Covington Cellars was born.

Cindy is usually working the Tuscan-inspired tasting room while David and David Jr. are handling the ongoing winemaking chores in the back. The warm colors of the tasting room are a pleasant contrast to the asphalt parking lot at the 142nd Avenue business park where the tasting room is located. And while David's day job as an elevator mechanic is up and down, his winemaking duties often have him going back and forth as he travels to Walla Walla and Yakima Valley to collaborate with Covington's growers. Among them are Seven Hills, Les Collines, Kestrel, Destiny Ridge, and Klipsun.

David explains that Covington Cellars is a "hobby gone mad" and is quick to point out that it is Cindy who is the business brains behind the operation. David is also involved with the Naval Reserve, and he views his winemaking efforts as an opportunity to give back. To this end, David produces a "Rough House Red" as a tribute to the U.S. Armed Forces. This wine is dedicated to the men and women who serve in the Armed Forces and their families. **WineTrail Note:** If you are active-duty military or a veteran, you will receive a 10 percent discount on "Rough House Red" wines. Nice touch.

David's loyalties to family and to country have in turn spawned a loyal following of Covington Cellars buyers. At Passport to Woodinville, the line to sample his reds snaked out the tasting room to the outside parking lot. The Lawsons must be doing something right. Check it out. That's an order!

David Lawson and son

COVINGTON CELLARS
opened: 2002
winemaker(s): David Lawson
location: 18580 142nd Avenue NE
Woodinville, WA 98072-8520
phone: 425-806-8636
web: www.covingtoncellars.com
e-mail: cindy@covingtoncellars.com
picnic area: No
gift shop: No
fee: $5 tasting fee refundable with purchase
hours: 1–5 Saturdays

DIRECTIONS: From SR-522 take NE 195th St. exit. The road name changes to NE North Woodinville Way. Turn right onto 142nd Ave. NE and arrive at 18580 142nd Ave. NE—Covington Cellars is located inside the business complex.

From Woodinville Center, depart on NE 175th St. [NE Woodinville Duvall Rd] heading east. Turn left (west) onto NE North Woodinville Way and go about .5 miles. Turn left (southwest) onto 142nd Ave. NE, go .3 miles, and arrive at 18580 142nd Ave. NE.

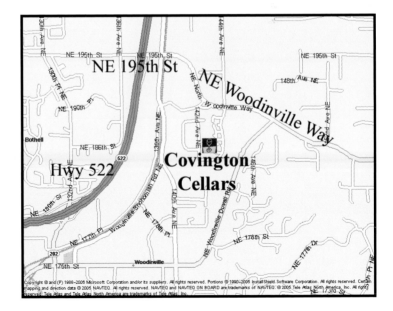

Stevens Winery

WineTrail trekkers know two things are common among most wineries: First, the vast majority of winemakers/owners are friendly people with a healthy dose of passion. Second, winemakers have divergent backgrounds and often

arrive at winemaking from different paths. Such is the case with Stevens Winery, where owners Tim and Paige Stevens welcome each visitor to their Woodinville tasting room with a friendly "glad to see you" smile. Prior to launching Stevens Winery, Tim had been a commercial artist, dabbled in the restaurant business, concentrated on an English degree, and got his fingers dirty at Sheridan Vineyards in Zillah. It was at Sheridan Vineyards, under the tutelage of Scott Greer, that Tim caught the wine bug. From there, he went on to become an assistant winemaker under Matt Loso at Matthews Cellars as well as the recipient of some friendly mentoring from Chris Camarda of the famed Andrew Will Winery on Vashon Island.

Like most of the wineries along the Woodinville WineTrails North, Stevens Winery is not about winery side ventures, such as gift shops or picnic grounds. Rather, it is focused on the wine—especially big reds. Using grapes from the Yakima Valley, Tim crafts premium syrahs, cabernet sauvignons, merlots, and cabernet francs. In addition, Stevens Winery has gained a reputation for its "STEVENS424" red blend (named for the fact that Stevens Winery is the 424th bonded winery in Washington). But with plenty of Northwest seafood demanding a special white wine, Stevens Winery also produces a limited quantity of delicious sauvignon blanc, meaning if you like it, buy it, because it sells out fairly quickly.

Incidentally, remember the previous reference to Tim Stevens' graphic arts background? Well, for each wine produced, Tim creates original artwork for each label. It's just one more role for Tim the winemaker/artist/grower/English major/father/husband/waiter. Cheers!

STEVENS WINERY
opened: 2002
winemaker(s): Tim Stevens
location: 18510 142nd Avenue NE
Woodinville, WA 98072
phone: 425-424-9463
web: www.stevenswinery.com
e-mail: info@stevenswinery.com
picnic area: No
gift shop: No
fee: Complimentary wine tasting
hours: 12–4:30 Saturdays

Tim and Paige Stevens

DIRECTIONS: From SR-522 take NE 195th St. exit. The road name changes to NE North Woodin-ville Way. Turn right onto 142nd Ave. NE and arrive at 18510 142nd Ave. NE—Stevens Winery is located inside the business complex on the left.
From Woodinville Center, depart on NE 175th St. [NE Woodinville Duvall Rd] heading east. Turn left (west) onto NE North Woodinville Way and go about .5 miles. Turn left (southwest) onto 142nd Ave. NE, go .3 miles and arrive at 18510 142nd Ave. NE.

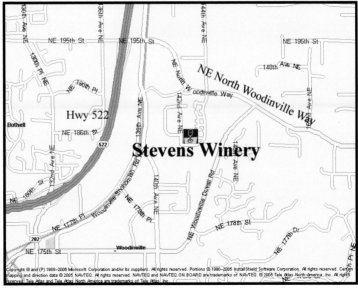

Woodinville Wine Cellars

According to Merriam-Webster's Dictionary, an artisan is one who produces something (such as cheese or wine) in limited quantities, often using traditional methods. Bingo. That describes Woodinville Wine Cellars' *raison d'être*. With its custom-made Lacanche kitchen ranges (which you will covet) and its handcrafted wines, Woodinville Wine Cellars invites you to experience the best in artisan wares, most especially, the wares of artisan winemaker Sean Boyd.

Visitor at Woodinville Wine Cellars

Situated by Little Bear Creek near downtown Woodinville, the winery and tasting room are a little off the beaten path. To WineTrail lovers, that translates into an oasis without the crowds. Woodinville Wine Cellars possesses none of the business-park feel or the chateau-like experience. Rather, it has an elegant, showroom-like quality that just happens to feature a great place to enjoy a picnic. The warm colors of the tasting room highlight a perfect environment to sample the winery's reds: syrah, cabernet sauvignon (if not sold out), merlot, and a terrific red blend called "Ausonius," named after a fourth-century Roman poet who also happened to manage his own vineyard. The winery also produces a sauvignon blanc that may be just what the sommelier ordered for your picnic. As Woodinville Wine Cellars points out on its website, "Each wine is fermented in small lots and barrel aged in French and American oak. Each lot and individual wine barrel is meticulously monitored from the moment the fruit is hand harvested, to the day the wine is gently bottled by hand. This artisan approach allows us to preserve the delicate balance of aromas and unique characteristics of each wine."

Each summer, Woodinville Wine Cellars hosts a Summer Celebration and Gourmet BBQ. Everyone is invited, but space and tickets are limited. (Woodinville Wine Cellars Club members get a break on the ticket prices.) The wine flows, the band rocks, and good wine complements the edibles. It's the perfect opportunity for fellow artisan enthusiasts to unite!

WOODINVILLE WINE CELLARS
opened: 1999
winemaker(s): Sean Boyd
location: 17721 132nd NE Avenue
Woodinville, WA 98072
phone: 425-481-8860
web: www.woodinvillewinecellars.com
e-mail: winesales@woodinvillewinecellars.com
picnic area: Yes
gift shop: No
fee: $5 tasting fee refundable with any wine
purchase
hours: 12–4 Saturdays from April through
September, or by appointment

DIRECTIONS: From SR-522 take the first Woodinville exit (Hwy 202 east to Woodinville/Redmond).
At the top of the ramp go right and immediately get in the left turn lane. Turn left onto NE 177th
Pl. [Little Bear Creek Pkwy]. Take the first left onto 132nd Ave. NE. The winery is located at
17721 132nd Ave. NE.
From Woodinville Center, depart on NE 175th St. [NE Woodinville Duvall Rd] heading west and
go about .5 miles. Turn right (north) onto SR-202 [131st Ave. NE], then immediately turn right
(east) onto NE 177th Pl. [Little Bear Creek Pkwy]. Take the first left onto 132nd Ave. NE.
Woodinville Wine Cellars is located at 17721 132nd Ave. NE.

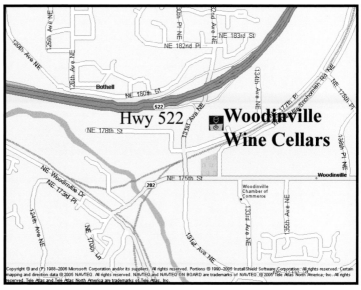

DiStefano Winery

As Mark Newton, owner and winemaker of DiStefano Winery states, "The DiStefano wines are a gift to my wife, Donna, and offered in tribute to her family—a family combining great personal and business integrity with a strong sense of tradition."

Donna Newton

And what a tribute it is. This surprising find is located within a small industrial park in Woodinville. It's not the wines that are surprising; DiStefano Winery already enjoys an outstanding reputation for producing fine wines. It's the inviting ambiance of the tasting room, with its warm colors and view of the barrel room, that's an unexpected treat. Equally warm is the tasting-room staff, which includes Mark's wife, Donna.

The non-reserved wine samples are complimentary, but we would suggest springing for the reserve wines. At a cost of $5, sampling the reserves is a very good value and gives you access to the full menu of wines, including merlot, syrah, "Syrah R," "Ottimo," rosé of cabernet, "Saint John" (sauterne style), sauvignon blanc, semillon, "Sogno" (cabernet franc), "Sweet Catherine" (sauterne style), and both a red and white Meritage. Mark's focus has been on Bordeaux-style wines but with the addition of syrah and other wines, he has expanded his repertoire. Be sure you try the "Sogno," a cabernet franc blend that displays all the flavors of this varietal while keeping its smooth, supple finish. Also, as you taste the sauterne-style "Sweet Catherine," ask yourself how good this would be with caramel-drizzled pound cake. Hmmm.

Like a number of top winemakers in Washington, Mark started his career as an engineer before plunging into winemaking. You often find that mathematicians make very good musicians. Well, the same holds true for engineers and winemaking, and Mark Newton is proof positive.

DISTEFANO WINERY
winemaker(s): Mark Newton
location: 12280 Woodinville Dr. SE
Woodinville, WA 98072
phone: 425-487-1648
web: www.distefanowinery.com
e-mail: info@distefanowinery.com
picnic area: No
gift shop: No
fee: Complimentary wine tasting except $5 for
reserve wines
hours: 12–5 Saturday and Sunday, or by
appointment; During the summer, the tasting room
is open on Fridays 12–4

DIRECTIONS: From SR-522 take first Woodinville exit onto SR-202 [131st Ave. NE]. Turn right
(west) onto SR-2-2 [NE 175th St.] and go about .3 miles. At the four-way stop, go right onto
Woodinville-Redmond Rd NE and go .3 miles and take a right into the industrial park—look
for the DiStefano sign on the road. Follow the road to the right .1 miles and arrive at DiStefano
Winery in the industrial complex.

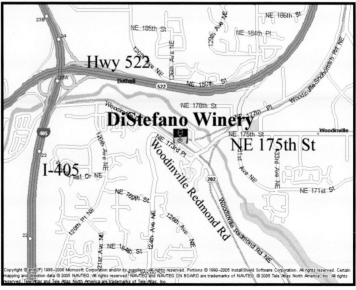

Woodinville
WineTrail South

Woodinville wine country is home to the magnificent Chateau Ste. Michelle Winery as well as the Columbia Winery, but many people are surprised to learn that a number of other wineries are tucked away in unexpected locations. With a half dozen wineries composing this WineTrail, don't be surprised if two or more excursions to Woodinville are needed. With the magnificent grounds of Chateau Ste. Michelle, bringing a blanket and a picnic to go with your wine is a prerequisite.

WineTrail tip: Consult Chateau Ste. Michelle's website for event information including their summer concert series.

Woodinville WineTrail South

1 Chateau Ste. Michelle	**4** Novelty Hill	**7** Matthews Cellars
2 Columbia Winery	**5** Woodhouse Family Cellars	**8** Brian Carter Cellars
3 JM Cellars	**6** Facelli Winery	

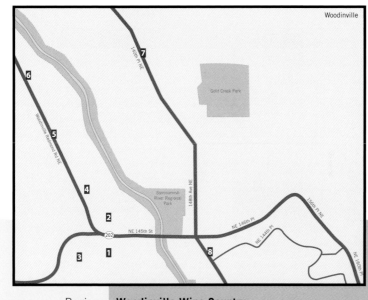

Region:	**Woodinville Wine Country**
# of tasting rooms on tour:	**8**
# of satellite tasting rooms:	**1—Silver Lake tasting room, which also features Glenn Fiona and Hoodsport Winery.**
Estimated # of days for tour:	**2**
Getting around:	**Car**
Key events:	❑ **St. Nicholas Day Open House (first weekend in December) and Passport to Woodinville (typically the first weekend in April)—both sponsored by Woodinville Wine Country. See www.woodinvillewinecountry.com for details and ticket information.**
Tips:	❑ **Woodinville offers a variety of restaurants: Some popular places include The Golden Goat, the Barking Frog, Pasta Nova, Garden Café, The Herbfarm at Willows Lodge, Italianissimo Ristorante, and Purple Café & Wine Bar.** ❑ **Consider hiring a limousine service, such as Bon Vivant 206-437-1298, Bayview Limo Service 206-223-6200, Washington Wine Tours 206-794-0565, or Gray Line of Seattle 206-624-5077.**
Best:	❑ **Best Picnicking: Chateau Ste. Michelle** ❑ **Best Gift Shop: Chateau Ste. Michelle and Columbia Winery** ❑ **Best for Weddings: Columbia Winery**

139

Chateau Ste. Michelle

Many a would-be WineTrail enthusiast heads for Woodinville with the express purpose of visiting four or five wineries and ends up going to just one—Chateau Ste. Michelle.

Chateau Ste. Michelle

A visit to Chateau Ste. Michelle usually entails a walk around its well-manicured grounds, a visit to the fishponds, and a stroll by the old Stimson family residence. During the summer, pack a picnic and a blanket and sprawl on the spacious lawn (with wine of course). You can also time your visit to coincide with the winery's summer concert series, which attracts such artists as Elvis Costello, Lyle Lovett, Pink Martini, and Bonnie Raitt.

However, the main reason you're here is for the wine and to discover (or reinforce) why *Wine Enthusiast Magazine* named Chateau Ste. Michelle "American Winery of the Year" in 2004. But before you head to the tasting room, we suggest that you take a complimentary guided tour through the facility (throughout the day from 10:30 a.m. to 4:30 p.m.). On the tour, you learn about its estate vineyards, discover that the reds are made in Eastern Washington and the whites are made in Woodinville, and get the details about their partnership with Eroica (riesling) and Col Solare. Private tours are also available for a charge and might be the perfect answer to entertaining out-of-town guests or a visiting corporate officer you are trying to impress.

The tour conveniently ends at the tasting room, where, by now, you are salivating at the thought of a cabernet sauvignon or a sauvignon blanc. If you are overcome by an urge to shop, the spacious tasting room includes elegant wine merchandise (don't count on finding cocktail napkins with cute sayings such as "No Whining Zone") to pair with any wine purchases. But gravitate toward the ample wine bar, where well-trained staff is ready to give you a Nordstrom-like experience. This is good, because you might be here for a while, given the winery's extensive portfolio of reds and whites. As servers pour, they will inform you of where the grapes were grown (typically one of four estate vineyards in Eastern Washington: Canoe Ridge, Horse Heaven, Cold Creek, and Indian Wells vineyards). Eventually you will glance at your watch and realize that you'll have to bag going to the other Woodinville wineries. They'll be there for another visit.

CHATEAU STE. MICHELLE
opened: 1934
winemaker(s): Bob Bertheau
location: 14111 NE 145th Street
Woodinville, WA 98072
phone: 425-488-1133
web: www.ste-michelle.com
e-mail: info@ste-michelle.com
picnic area: Yes
gift shop: Yes
fee: Complimentary wine tasting; premium and
reserve tastings available for a fee
hours: Daily 10–5, except New Year's Day, Easter,
Thanksgiving, and Christmas Day

BEST Picnicking and gift shop

DIRECTIONS: From SR-522 take first Woodinville exit onto SR-202 [131st Ave. NE]. Turn right (west) onto SR-202 [NE 175th St.] and go about .3 miles. Turn left (southeast) onto SR-202 [Woodinville-Redmond Rd NE] and go 1.7 miles. Chateau Ste. Michelle is located on the right as you round the corner. Follow signs to parking.

From Woodinville center, head west on NE 175th St [NE Woodinville-Duvall Rd] for .3 miles. Turn left (southeast) onto SR-202 [Woodinville-Redmond Rd NE] and go 1.7 miles. Chateau Ste. Michelle is located on the right as you round the corner.

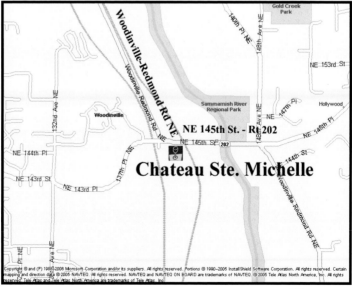

Columbia Winery

Founded in 1962, Columbia Winery is one of the oldest and most prestigious wineries in the state. From great wines to banquet rooms to cooking classes to a well-stocked gift shop, Columbia Winery offers the whole package. You would be proud to host a wedding reception here: You wouldn't have to worry about parking (there's plenty), or be concerned about the size of the tasting room (it

 boasts the largest tasting room bar in the state), or panic over whether the garden will be in ship-shape condition (it will be—it appears the winery employs a small army of gardeners).

From humble beginnings in a garage in Seattle's Laurelhurst neighborhood, Columbia Winery was the creation of Dr. Lloyd Woodburne and nine other wine enthusiasts. They were Washington's original "garagistes,"
making their first wines with grapes from what would become Washington's Columbia Valley viticulture region. It was this pioneering spirit that showed the world that Washington's location, soil, and climate could create world-class grapes similar to those of the Bordeaux region of France, which just happens to run along the same northern parallel.

David Lake, Columbia Winery's master of wine, joined the winery in 1979. His close working relationship with the premium grapes growers of Washington has spearheaded the production of many award-winning wines and introduced a number of varietals and blends new to consumers' palates. For example, he is credited for being the first winemaker to produce several varietals in Washington, including syrah, cabernet franc, and pinot gris. Columbia Winery's fruit is harvested from a who's who of Washington vineyards, including Otis, Sagemoor, Wyckoff, and Red Willow vineyards. As part of its tasting room experience, Columbia Winery offers an all-star lineup of award-winning wines, including David Lake's Signature Series of fine wines.

With Columbia's annual production of more than 160,000 cases of wine, you might wonder about the quality of its wine. However, as your tastebuds will discover, quality can be found in every bottle, thanks to the strict production control of David Lake and his team of vintners.

WineTrail Tip: During the weekdays, tours are conducted at 2 and 6 p.m., so plan accordingly. Also, on the weekends, tours commence every 45 minutes.

COLUMBIA WINERY
opened: 1962
winemaker(s): David Lake
location: 14030 NE 145th Street
Woodinville, WA 98072-6994
phone: 425-488-2776
web: www.columbiawinery.com
e-mail: contact@columbiawinery.com
picnic area: Yes
gift shop: Yes
fee: Complimentary wine tasting; reserve tasting available for a small fee
hours: Daily 10–6

 **BEST Gift shop and weddings**

DIRECTIONS: From SR-522 take first Woodinville exit onto SR-202 [131st Ave. NE]. Turn right (west) onto SR-2-2 [NE 175th St.] and go about .3 miles. Turn left (southeast) onto SR-202 [Woodinville-Redmond Rd NE] and go 1.7 miles. Columbia Winery is located on the left as you round the corner.
From Woodinville center, head west on NE 175th St [NE Woodinville-Duvall Rd] for .3 miles. Turn left (southeast) onto SR-202 [Woodinville-Redmond Rd NE] and go 1.7 miles. Columbia Winery is located on the left immediately after you round the corner.

JM Cellars

JM Cellars is open to the public only on the first Saturday of the month. However, a reward awaits those WineTrail followers who time their Woodinville excursion accordingly. Leave the crowds behind at the big wineries and drive up the hill. Talk about relaxed: After leaving your vehicle with a valet parking attendant, you follow the shrub-lined path to the tasting room. Yes, the tasting

fee is a bit steep ($10), but you get it back with a purchase of wine. And odds are you won't be able to resist these treasures.

John and Peggy Bigelow began JM Cellars in 1998 in the basement of their Laurelhurst home. In 2001, the Bigelows moved their operation and home to Woodinville. Like so many other "artisan" winery owners, John Bigelow has kept his day job and finds time at night and on the weekends to produce some lovely blends of red wines. His distinctive, full-bodied wines reflect their source: grapes from the Red Mountain viticulture area near the Tri-Cities. They also reflect the recipes of one of America's top winemakers and his mentor, Mike Januik of Januik Winery and Novelty Hill Winery fame. As noted on the JM Cellars website, "By combining old-world artisan techniques with new-world style, John crafts his wines one barrel at a time, striving for wines that show both power and finesse, and exemplify the well-balanced fruit, tannic structure and acidity that has made Washington wine a recognized player on the world stage of fine wines." Nice.

While enjoying your visit with John and Peggy, check out these beauties: Klipsun Vineyard sauvignon blanc, cuvée viognier, "Bramble Bump" Red (named after the location of their home/winery), Columbia Valley merlot, "Tre Fanciulli" blend, cabernet sauvignon, and syrah. If you like big, full-bodied wines, you are in for a treat. Soon the crowds in lower Woodinville will be a distant memory.

John and Peggy Bigelow

JM CELLARS
opened: 1998
winemaker(s): John Bigelow
location: 14404 137th Place NE
Woodinville, WA 98072
phone: 206-321-0052
web: www.jmcellars.com
e-mail: john@jmcellars.com
picnic area: No
gift shop: No
fee: $10 tasting fee, waived on purchase of wine
hours: 12–4 the first Saturday of each month

DIRECTIONS: From SR-522 take first Woodinville exit onto SR-202 [131st Ave. NE]. Turn right (west) onto SR-202 [NE 175th St.] and go .3 miles. At the four-way stop, go left onto Woodinville-Redmond Rd NE and go 1.6 miles and bear right onto NE 145th. Road name changes to 137th Pl. NE. Continue up the hill (west) and look for JM Cellars sign on the left. Please note that due to limited parking, JM Cellars provides valet parking.

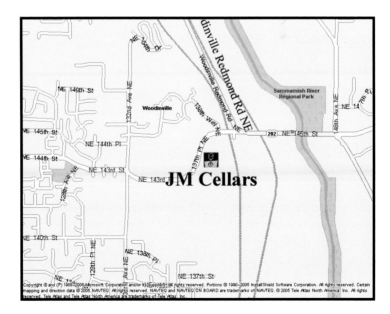

Novelty Hill and Januik Winery

I would like to ask everyone to clear out of the new Novelty Hill and Januik Winery. The reason? I'd like to live there. I relish the thought of living in a contemporary fusion of glass, wood, and stylish concrete. This would be the perfect space to kick back, relax, and wonder how the other half lives. Oh, and

one other thing. I'd need the key to the wine cellar. A glass of Novelty Hill merlot every day for a year would suit me just fine.

Opened in the spring of 2007, the new winery occupies more than 33,000 square feet on 3.1 acres in Woodinville. The fact that the parking lot can accommodate 100 vehicles speaks volumes for anticipated sippers eager to sample Novelty

Novelty Hill and Januik Winery

Hill and Januik wines. However, you might think that visitors would overlook the winery, given that their neighbors to the south are Columbia Winery and Chateau Ste. Michelle. But I think not. The public already is familiar with the elegance of these wines. And the fact that the facility is earth-friendly by design simply adds to the allure of Novelty Hill and Januik Winery.

Within this modern structure, WineTrail enthusiasts experience two different wineries: Novelty Hill and Januik Winery. Although they are two different wineries, they share one big common denominator: Mike Januik, winemaker extraordinaire. Novelty Hill owners Tom Alberg and Judi Beck turned to Mike Januik for his award-winning expertise. With 25 years of winemaking experience, including 10 years as the chief winemaker for Chateau Ste. Michelle, Mike knows what to do with the grapes. In addition, he enjoys a solid relationship with many of the state's finest premium grape growers.

When not making wine for Novelty Hill, Mike focuses on creating his own wine under the Januik Winery label. Bearing names such as Lewis Vineyard syrah, Champoux Vineyard cabernet sauvignon, and Cold Creek chardonnay, Januik wines are created from the finest ingredients.

Premium grapes, high-quality ingredients, and a sleek, modern facility harmonize to create excellent winemaking *feng shui* for Novelty Hill and Januik Winery.

NOVELTY HILL AND JANUIK WINERY
opened: 2000
winemaker(s): Mike Januik
location: 14710 Woodinville-Redmond Road
Woodinville, WA 98072
phone: 425-481-5502
web: www.noveltyhillwines.com
e-mail: info@noveltyhillwines.com
picnic area: Yes
gift shop: No
fee: Columbia Valley Tasting $5; King Cab Tasting
$10; Single Vineyard Tasting $15—fees waived for
Cellar Circle members; Ask winery for details
hours: Daily 11–5

DIRECTIONS: From I-405 heading north, take exit 20B and bear right (east) onto NE 124th St.
Continue on NE 124th St. for 2.3 miles. Turn left (north) onto SR-202 [Woodinville-Redmond Rd
NE] and proceed 1.6 miles. Turn left (west) onto SR-202 [NE 145th St.] and continue .6 miles.
Arrive at Novelty Hill and Januik Winery on your right.

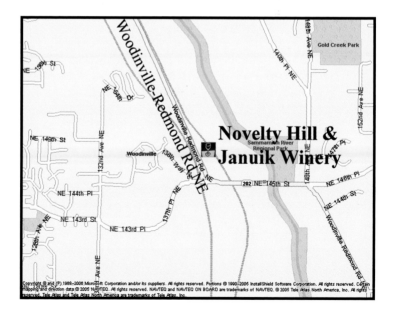

Woodhouse Family Cellars

Question: What do Darighe, Dussek, Kennedy Shah, Maghie, and Hudson have in common (besides being blessed with great names)? Answer: They all are wines produced by Woodhouse Family Cellars under the winemaking direction of 30-year veteran Tom Campbell. At Woodhouse Family Cellars, wine-tasting trekkers have an opportunity to sample a variety of wines in a spacious room

lit by chandeliers. Woodhouse Family Cellars is a partnership between Bijal and Sinead Shah and winemaker Tom Campbell, Sinead's uncle. The winery debuted with 100 cases of its 1998 vintage of "Darighe," a Bordeaux-style blend that sold out three months after its release in 2001. This secured a small but loyal following for the winery that has grown in time. Woodhouse Family Cellars also produces small allocations of two other premium wines, "Dussek Family Cellars" cabernet and "Maghie Cellars" merlot.

More recently the owners have added "Kennedy Shah" to their line-up of wines. Kennedy Shah is the name of Bijal and Sinead Shah's daughter. Part of the proceeds from the sale of "Kennedy Shah" goes toward supporting local women's and children's organizations.

Unlike many tasting rooms where you need to keep your wineglass close to your chest when the throngs arrive, at Woodhouse Family Cellars there is plenty of space to mill around and explore. You can check out the barrel room, enjoy wine in the intimate banquet area, and note the many chandeliers as you gaze upward.

Just when you were beginning to think that all Woodinville-based business-park winery settings were the same, Woodhouse Family Cellars shatters that image. It offers a top-notch tasting room designed to encourage its visitors to relax and enjoy its wines. That makes it a mandatory stop along the Woodinville WineTrail South route. Enjoy!

Visitors at Woodhouse

WOODHOUSE FAMILY CELLARS
opened: 2001
winemaker(s): Tom Campbell
location: 15500 Woodinville-Redmond Road, #C600
Woodinville, WA 98072
phone: 425-527-0608
web: www.woodhousefamilycellars.com
e-mail: Victoria@woodhouse-usa.com
picnic area: No
gift shop: No
fee: $5 tasting fee applied to purchase
hours: 12–4 Fridays; 12–5 Saturday and Sunday, or
by appointment

DIRECTIONS: From SR-522 take first Woodinville exit onto SR-202 [131st Ave. NE]. Turn right (west) onto SR-202 [NE 175th St.] and go about .3 miles. Turn left (southeast) onto SR-202 [Woodinville-Redmond Rd NE] and go 1.2 miles. Woodhouse Family Cellars is on the left in an industrial complex at 15500 Woodinville-Redmond Road. Look for the Woodhouse Family Cellars tasting room sign. Turn right into our driveway and take an immediate left, then a quick right— look for the trellis and wine barrels.

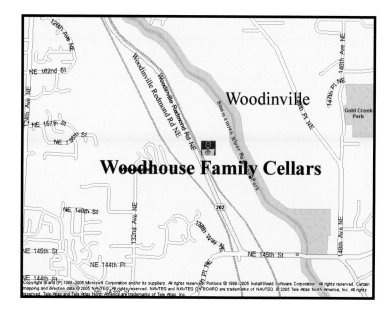

Facelli Winery

Located in one of Woodinville's many business parks is a gem of a winery: Facelli Winery. This family-owned and -operated winery prides itself on producing outstanding reds and offering an especially friendly welcome to the many visitors who frequent the winery. Its varietals include cabernet sauvignon, merlot, syrah, sangiovese, cabernet franc, lemberger, chardonnay, and fumé blanc. Some wines are only available at the winery. All grapes are grown by renowned Columbia Valley growers and are hand-picked, hand-sorted, and processed with gravity flow. Winemaker Louis Facelli celebrates

more than 20 years of experience with Washington grapes and, more often than not, Lou himself is there to autograph your purchased bottle of wine. With an annual production of 4,500 cases, Louis Facelli has gone through a lot of Sharpies®.

Especially unusual is Facelli's late-harvest syrah. This after-dinner treat contains 4 percent residual sugar, yet it doesn't seem overly sweet, which is a tribute to the syrah's rich flavors and overall tasting experience. Also, a warning to the hungry wine sampler: The sangiovese is created from grapes from the famous Red Willow Vineyard, and this Italian-style wine conjures up images of fresh mozzarella and basil drizzled with extra-virgin olive oil, as well as other Italian fare with which this wine pairs so nicely.

FACELLI WINERY
opened: 1988
winemaker(s): Lou Facelli
location: 16120 Woodinville-Redmond Road NE,
Suite 1
Woodinville, WA 98072-9090
phone: 425-488-1020
web: www.facelliwinery.com
e-mail: facelliwinery@msn.com
picnic area: No
gift shop: No
fee: Complimentary wine tasting
hours: 12–4 Saturday and Sunday; groups by
appointment only

DIRECTIONS: From SR-522 take first Woodinville exit onto SR-202 [131st Ave. NE]. Turn right (west) onto SR-2-2 [NE 175th St.] and go about .3 miles. Turn left (southeast) onto SR-202 [Woodinville-Redmond Rd NE] and go about .75 miles. At the "Riverfront" business park, turn left. (Facelli Winery sign out on weekends). The Facelli Winery is around the back of the second building on the right.

Matthews Cellars

Every once in a while along the WineTrail path, you run into a really serious winemaker whose wines grab you. When this happens, you usually find a supporting cast of evangelical self-proclaimed cellar rats and eager volunteers.

Such is the case you will likely witness at Matthews Cellars in Woodinville.

Winemaker and owner Matthew Loso concentrates his efforts on producing Bordeaux-style blends using grapes grown in the finest Columbia Valley vineyards. Matt's winemaking skills were honed from practical experience rather than the textbooks of University of California–Davis and the like. He must be doing something right, as the number of awards and accolades garnered by his wines continue to grow. And just as Matt has learned from other winemakers at nearby Chateau Ste. Michelle and Columbia, he, in turn, passes along his knowledge to other boutique-style winemakers. In fact, you are likely to hear his name and note a tip of the hat from other fledging winemakers in the Woodinville area.

Matthews Cellars is located on an 8-acre estate in the heart of Woodinville. The tasting room opens to a spacious production facility. To the WineTrail trekker, the size of the facility itself communicates that Matt's venture is not that of a weekend warrior. Matt's day job is Matthews Cellars, so everything is riding on what goes into each bottle. At $10, the tasting fee is a bit steep, but you get it back with any purchase. And, if you are like this WineTrail enthusiast, you won't leave there empty handed.

Get ready for some spectacular red blends as well as delicious sauvignon blanc, late harvest viognier, and cabernet franc rosé. Value hunters (who isn't?) are strongly encouraged to sample Matthews Cellars claret. Selling for half the price of its ultra-premium red wines, the claret is made from leftover picks blended together and aged in once or twice used French oak barrels for 12 to 14 months, rather than the standard 22 to 24 months. Call me a cheap date, but you can use this wine to make some delicious "cabernet burgers" and then polish off the bottle while munching on those freshly grilled burgers and tossed salad. Cheers!

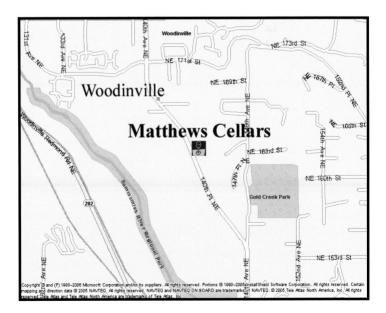

MATTHEWS CELLARS
opened: 1993
winemaker(s): Matthew Loso
location: 16116 140th Place NE
Woodinville, WA 98072
phone: 425-487-9810
web: www.matthewscellars.com
e-mail: wine@matthewscellars.com
picnic area: No
gift shop: No
fee: $10 tasting fee refundable with purchase
hours: 12–4 Saturdays

Matthew Loso

DIRECTIONS: From SR-522 take ramp (right) onto SR-202 [131st Ave. NE]. Turn left (east) onto NE 175th St. and go about .5 miles. Turn right (south) onto 140th Ave. NE. The road name changes to 140th Pl. NE. Proceed to 16116 140th Pl. NE. Matthews Cellars Winery is on the left.

Brian Carter Cellars

"A passion for the art of blending": With that tagline, Brian Carter Cellars stakes its claim on European-style (primarily red) blends. With more than 25 years of winemaking experience, noted vintner Brian Carter finally has his own label under which to showcase his talents. During those 25 years, Brian Carter managed to pick up "Winemaker of the Year" twice by Washington Magazine. His résumé includes stops at Paul Thomas, Hedges Cellars, Silver Lake Winery, McCrea Cellars, Kestrel Vineyards, and most recently Apex and Bridgman wineries. Along the way, he has captured a number of awards and won critical acclaim.

The winery's tasting room is located in an amiable little red house next to the soon-to-be-developed Woodinville Village, where the new Brian Carter Cellars will reside. When it comes to "a passion for the art of blending," think beyond wine. Rather, expand the "blending" idea to encompass landscape photography by Woodinville native John Shephard, which gracefully hangs in the tasting room. Also note the wine labels themselves. Artist Stephen Black's dramatic paintings strike a chord with the liquid art inside the bottle. I know we shouldn't buy wine based on the label alone, but there are exceptions and this is one of them.

Brian Carter Cellars offers five blended wines: "Oriana," a white blend of three varieties; "Tuttorosso," a sangiovese-based Tuscan-style blend; "Byzance," a Southern Rhône–style blend of grenache and syrah; "L'Etalon," a robust blend of five classic Bordeaux varieties; and "Solesce," the winery's signature Bordeaux-style blend. "Abracadabra" is its second-tier wine and reflects the goal of producing a "magical" red blend. The name "Abracadabra" itself conjures magical beliefs and has its origin in ancient Greece. People who were ill would wear an amulet around their neck that contained a piece of parchment. Inscribed on the parchment was a triangular formula derived from the word: A B R A C A D A B R A

Interestingly, the term "hocus pocus" is derived from Latin and is thought to mean "Stop at Brian Carter Cellars next time you are in Woodinville."

BRIAN CARTER CELLARS
opened: 2006
winemaker(s): Brian Carter
location: 14419 Woodinville-Redmond Road
Woodinville, WA 98072
phone: 425-806-WINE
web: www.briancartercellars.com
e-mail: info@briancartercellars.com
picnic area: Yes
gift shop: Yes
fee: $5 tasting fee applied toward purchase
hours: 12–5 Thursdays; 12–6 Friday through Sunday

Visitors at Brian Carter's tasting room

DIRECTIONS: From I-405, take exit 20B, and go east on NE 124th St. Continue on NE 124th St. 2.3 miles and turn left onto SR-202 [Woodinville-Redmond Rd NE]. Proceed 1.5 miles and arrive at Brian Carter Cellars on your left.

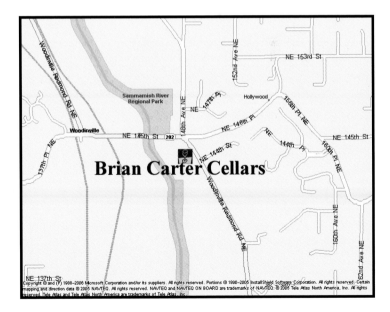

Southwest Washington
WINE COUNTRY

Southwest Washington
Wine Trail

The Southwest Washington Wine Trail includes a number of wineries from Vancouver to Chehalis. Many have a rich history of winemaking and offer a combination of wines using grapes that are prevalent in Oregon, such as pinot noir, and Bordeaux or Rhone-style blends using grapes from Eastern Washington. Here diversity rules and that's what makes the Southwest Washington Wine Trail so unforgettable. From a visitor's standpoint, there is no shortage of terrific places to stay and eat in the Portland metropolitan area. Because of the distance between these wineries, budget a couple of days to enjoy this Wine Trail.

Southwest Washington WineTrail

1 Heymann Whinery
2 Widgeon Hill Winery

3 Salishan Vineyards
4 Bethany Vineyard & Winery

5 English Estate

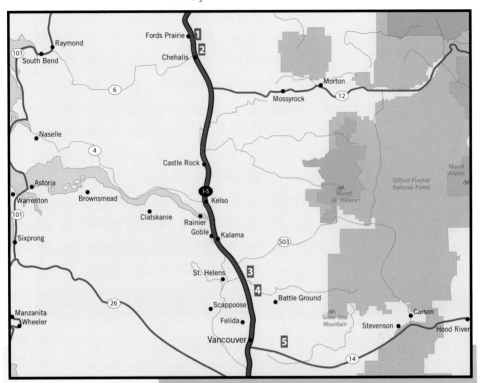

Region:	**Southwest Washington Wine Country**
# of tasting rooms on tour:	**5**
Estimated # of days for tour:	**2**
Getting around:	**Car**
Key events:	❏ **Consult individual winery websites for events.**
Tips:	❏ **Portland metro area offers an abundance of places to stay and eat.** ❏ **Bethany Vineyards hosts weddings.**
Best:	❏ **Best Picnicking: Bethany Vineyards & Winery and English Estates** ❏ **Best Gift Shop: Heymann Whinery**

Heymann Whinery

With the slogan "We can help you Whine!" Bob and Flossie Heymann clearly convey their vision for Heymann Whinery: Don't take things—including wine—too seriously. Heymann Whinery's new tasting room location is in Centralia, on South Tower. As you will discover, it is much more than a tasting room. Yes, you can sample winemaker Bob's many berry wines and Bordeaux-style wines, but you also can purchase a wide variety of wine- and beer-related merchandise. This is also where you can purchase beer- and wine-making equipment and supplies. Heymann has everything you need to be the neighborhood winemaker.

From refrigerator magnets (the type with quotations like "I love to cook with wine. Sometimes I even put it in the food.") to Betty Boop wine stoppers, Scorned Woman's Fudge, wine jelly, and sweet 'n' hot mustard, it's easy to shop for your favorite wine- (and beer-) loving uncle. But many visitors come to Heymann Whinery for Bob's fruit wines, which include cranberry, raspberry, cherry, apricot, and blackberry wines, all made from Washington state fruit. However, for those WineTrail trekkers who want to stick with grape wines, Bob relies on grapes from the Yakima Valley to make his chardonnay, cabernet sauvignon, merlot, sauvignon blanc, and riesling.

Warning: Cork dorks will need to check their attitude at the door; you're entering a No Whining Zone.

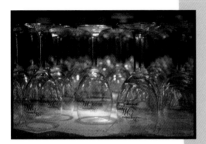

HEYMANN WHINERY
opened: 2004
winemaker(s): Bob Heymann
location: 105 South Tower Ave.
Centralia, WA 98531
phone: 360-623-1106
web: www.heymannwhinery.com
e-mail: h-whinery@comcast.net
picnic area: No
gift shop: Yes
fee: Complimentary wine tasting
hours: 11–6 Tuesday through Friday, 9–5
Saturday, 1–5 Sunday

BEST Gift shop

DIRECTIONS: From I-5 take exit 82 and travel toward Centralia on Harrison Ave. Proceed about .75 miles and bear left onto W. Main St. and continue for .5 miles. Turn left onto Tower Ave. and arrive at 105 S. Tower Ave. Look for the Heymann Whinery storefront on the left.

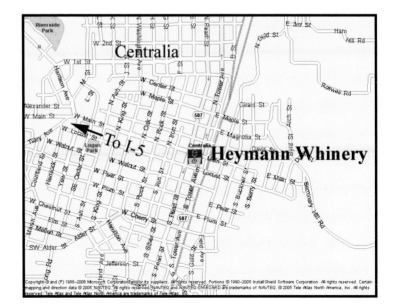

Widgeon Hill Winery

wid-geon *n.* – a freshwater duck (*Anas americana* of North America) having a grayish or brownish back and a white belly and wing coverts.

Established in 1991 by father and son Rhett and Joel Mills, Widgeon Hill Winery is located about 4 miles east of I-5 via exit 81 between Chehalis and Centralia. It's a little off the beaten path, but a short 10-minute drive brings you to a cozy tasting room/winery where Joel will make you feel at home with

a full range of reds and whites. Joel has been the sole winemaker/owner of Widgeon Hill since 2005, following the unexpected death of his father. Suddenly saddled with managing a winery and keeping his day job as a real estate appraiser, Joel's winemaking passion has kept the winery going.

With annual production at nearly 1,000 barrels of wine, Joel gets his grapes primarily from the Prosser/Grandview area of Yakima Valley. For a small winery, Widgeon Hill offers an impressive array of wines, including merlot, syrah, chenin blanc, chardonnay, sauvignon blanc, and late-harvest viognier. However, of particular note is the elegant labeling used to hallmark the reserve merlot, syrah, and cabernet sauvignon. The fruit comes from Bouchey Vineyards and HRP Ranch (which Rhett Mills nicknamed "Area 51" because you don't see the 60-acre vineyard until you arrive at a knoll on the country road and it suddenly appears before you).

Legend has it that the old-timers feasted on the widgeon duck that populated the Salzer Valley watershed, where Widgeon Hill is located. Now, the new timers can feast on "Area 51" syrah and other varietals at Widgeon Hill Winery. When you think about it, a bottle of Widgeon Hill merlot would pair nicely with roasted duck!

Joel Mills

WIDGEON HILL WINERY
opened: 1991
winemaker(s): Joel Mills
location: 121 Widgeon Hill Road
Chehalis, WA 98532
phone: 360-748-0432
web: www.widgeonhill.com
e-mail: widgeonhill@localaccess.com
picnic area: No
gift shop: No
fee: Complimentary wine tasting
hours: Daily 11–5

DIRECTIONS: From I-5 take exit 81 and travel toward Centralia center on SR-507 [Mellen St.] for .5 miles. Turn right onto Woodland Ave. and proceed about .5 miles. Bear left onto (W) Summa St. and continue .75 miles. The road name changes to Salzer Valley Rd. Proceed 1 mile. Turn right onto Centralia Alpha Rd and continue almost 2 miles and turn right onto Widgeon Hill Rd. The winery is on the left.

Salishan Vineyards

Joan Wolverton is an amazing woman. A handful of people are responsible for the emergence of the Washington wine industry. Joan, the creator and loving caretaker of Salishan Winery, is counted among them.

Salishan was the first *vinifera* vineyard and winery established in southwest Washington state. Armed with 50 years of weather data from Burgundy, Joan

and her economist husband, Lincoln, set about finding a location in Washington having a similar climate. They settled on a plot of land outside the small town of La Center, and Salishan Vineyard was born in 1971. They bonded the winery and released their first estate pinot noir in the early '80s. Thirty years and many awards later, the 10-acre vineyard is producing high-quality fruit. This should come as no surprise; the climate is similar to the north Willamette Valley of Oregon, where there is an army of winemakers fervently devoted to world-class pinot noir.

However, despite her impact on the Washington wine industry, this self-effacing person finds it easier to dish out credit than to receive it. The now-faded Salishan logo on the side of the winery greets visitors. Inside the combined tasting/barrel room, local newspaper articles and other memorabilia cover the walls and provide a synopsis of Salishan Winery. Joan herself is a former newspaper reporter from Seattle, and a visit with her reveals that she must have been a terrific writer. Her inquisitive mind made it possible to investigate stories for the *The Seattle Times* and *Seattle Post-Intelligencer*, and she's applied that same approach to learning about the viticulture and winemaking world. The fact is, prior to planting her 10 acres, she knew next to nothing about farming.

The Salishan languages are a group of Native American languages of western Canada and the Pacific Northwest that are characterized by an astonishing variety of consonant clusters. Sample these wines and your consonants and vowels will spell out enthusiastic words of praise.

WineTrail Note: Salishan's prices are low. A bottle of its 2002 pinot noir sells for $12 and reflects Joan's philosophy of giving her customers good value.

SALISHAN VINEYARDS
opened: 1982
winemaker(s): Joan Wolverton
location: 35011 NE North Fork Avenue
La Center, WA 98629
phone: 360-263-2713
picnic area: No
gift shop: No
fee: Complimentary wine tasting
hours: 1–5 Saturdays from May through December,
or by appointment

Joan Wolverton

DIRECTIONS: From I-5 north or south, take exit 16 and travel toward La Center on NW La Center Rd about 1.5 miles. Turn right onto Aspen Ave. and bear right for about .75 mile. The road name changes to NE Fork Ave.—continue up the hill and arrive at 35011 NE North Fork Ave. Salishan Winery is on the right.

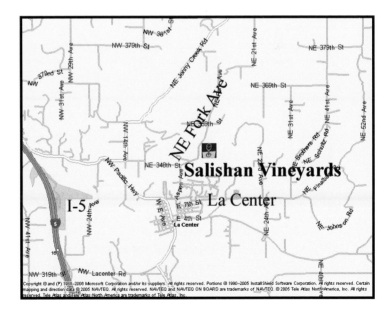

Bethany Vineyard & Winery

Walt Houser named his vineyard and winery after the love of his life: his wife, Bethany. Another great love of his is wine, making it not with the aim of winning awards, mind you, but for the sheer joy of it. In his younger years, Walt focused on berry wines, but quickly moved to making premium grape wines. Nevertheless, he still makes berry wines and manages to sell a lot of blackberry, blueberry, and raspberry wines.

But it is Walt's vinifera wines that cause WineTrail lovers to take Exit 14 off I-5 and head east to the Bethany Vineyard and Winery. The vineyard grows 15 different varieties of wine grape that are suitable for southwestern Washington's cool climate. Walt is proud of the fact that all Bethany Vineyard wines include some grapes from his vineyard, which surrounds his winery and tasting room. The other grapes come from Eastern Washington and go into making cabernet sauvignon, merlot, and syrah. Preferring to emphasize the taste of the grape, Walt will transfer his wine, after just seven months in new oak, to older neutral oak barrels. He then allows the wine to remain in the barrels for an additional two years or longer, depending upon the varietal. The result is handcrafted, ultrapremium wines, and his no. 1 seller is his pinot noir.

Walt and Bethany present a meticulously kept winery and tasting room worthy of a navy admiral's inspection. Inside the small tasting room, visitors can view barrels in the backroom resting comfortably between racking. During the summer, visitors flock to the winery to enjoy four music concerts featuring local artists. The concerts take place next to the winery's private lake (which is also the setting for outdoor weddings held with weekend regularity). But the big bash is held every August when Walt and Bethany sponsor an organ-donor fundraiser dinner in support of Oregon's donor program. Two hundred and fifty guests pay $60 each toward this life-giving cause. Bethany Vineyards and friends provide the food, wine, and entertainment for the event, donating nearly 100 percent of the proceeds to this worthwhile cause. Walt and Bethany know from personal experience the importance of organ transplantation. In 2002, Bethany was stricken with a life-threatening liver disorder. Fortunately, and in the nick of time, she became the recipient of a donor liver while at the Oregon Health & Science University Hospital.

Walter Houser Jr.

BETHANY VINEYARD & WINERY
opened: 2002
winemaker(s): Walter Jay Houser
location: 4115 NE 259th Street
Ridgefield, WA 98642-9749
phone: 360-887-3525
web: www.bethanyvineyards.com
e-mail: beth@bethanyvineyards.com
picnic area: Yes
gift shop: Yes
fee: Complimentary wine tasting
hours: 11–6 Saturdays, or by appointment

 **BEST Picnicking**

DIRECTIONS: From I-5 take exit 14 and head east on SR-501 [Pioneer St.]. Road name changes to S. 65th Ave. Continue on S. 5th St. for 1 mile and turn right onto NE 10th Ave. and proceed about .25 miles. Turn left onto NE 259th St. and proceed 1.5 miles. Look for Bethany Vineyard & Winery on the right.

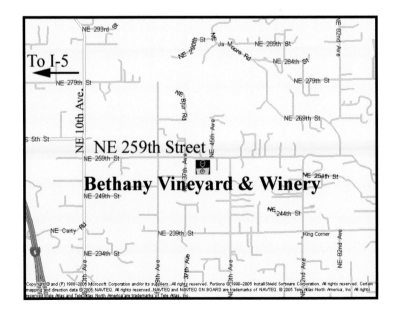

English Estate

English Estate's owner/winemaker Carl English rolled the dice and decided to offer premium wines in a box. That's right, that same box that got a bad rap 20 or 30 years ago. Cheap wine in a box translates into bad taste in the mouth. However, imagine if you could have premium cabernet sauvignon or pinot noir one glass at a time over a period of months and the taste would never change. How? Because, thanks to a bag within the box, those nasty little oxygen molecules don't touch the wine. For those wine drinkers who enjoy a glass of wine a day, the bag in a box just might be the right solution.

But English Estate Winery takes the bag concept one step further by offering a bag in a *beautiful* box, or BIBB. And indeed the outer wooden box shell with the attractive engraving presents a look elegant enough to adorn Emeril's kitchen. Each box holds 3,000 ml of wine, or the equivalent of four bottles of wine. No worry of corkage here—there ain't no cork. Nevertheless, for those among us who love the bottle-opening ritual and its obligatory popping cork, English Estate Winery offers all its fine wines in a bottle.

Housed in a 1913 dairy barn, Vancouver, Washington–based English Estate Winery is the closest vineyard and winery to Portland. Many of the wines offered are estate wines made from grapes (especially pinot noir) harvested from their own vineyard, Gravel Mine Vineyards. Other grapes come from nearby vineyards that enjoy the confluence of the Columbia and Willamette rivers and the special *terroir* of the Columbia River Gorge.

With a red barn providing a bucolic background, the winery grounds offer an out-of-the-ordinary respite from the urban world. Speaking of respite, English Estate has a growing community of fans known as the English Estate Purple Thistle Wine Club whose mission is a simple one: to have fun and celebrate life. To give an example, the "Dogs of English Estate" offers a photo op for wine-loving club members and their dogs. Woof!

ENGLISH ESTATE
opened: 2001
winemaker(s): Carl English
location: 17806 SE 1st Street
Vancouver, WA 98684
phone: 360-772-5141
web: www.englishestatewinery.com
e-mail: sales@englishestatewinery.com
picnic area: Yes
gift shop: No
fee: Complimentary wine tasting for 3 wines; $5 to sample all
hours: 12–6 Friday through Sunday from April through December; January through March, by appointment only

BEST Picnicking

DIRECTIONS: From SR-14 [Lewis and Clark Hwy] take exit 8 and head north onto SE 164th Ave. Travel 2.1 miles and turn right onto SE 1st St. and proceed about .75 miles. English Estate Winery is on the left.

169

Columbia River Gorge
WineTrail

Cascade Cliffs Vineyard

Going east from Vancouver, the Columbia River Gorge WineTrail takes you through the territory made famous by Lewis and Clark. However, the Columbia River is far tamer now than what they experienced in the fall of 1805. Today, we have plenty of windsurfers, destination resorts, vineyards and wineries to check out during our expedition. Your discovery will introduce you to wineries with names like Wind River, Marshal's, Syncline, Maryhill, and Waving Tree. In between wine tasting, there are spots for sleeping such as the Skamania Lodge and the Lyle Hotel and Restaurant. For sightseeing, check out the Stonehenge Memorial or the Maryhill Museum, or go white-water rafting along the White Salmon River. Pack your camera too—there are photo ops galore.

Columbia River Gorge WineTrail

1 Wind River Cellars
2 Bad Seed Cider House
3 Syncline Wine Cellars
4 Cor Cellars

5 Illusion Winery
6 Marshal's Winery
7 Cascade Cliffs Winery and Vineyard

8 Maryhill Winery
9 Waving Tree Winery

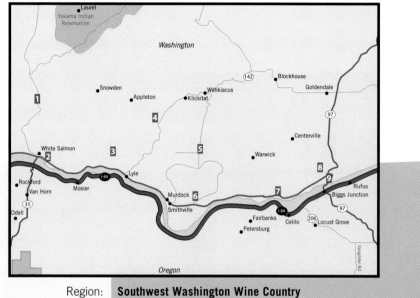

Region:	**Southwest Washington Wine Country**
# of tasting rooms on tour:	**10**
# of satellite tasting rooms:	**1—Wind River Wines are also found at Bad Seed Cider House**
Estimated # of days for tour:	**2**
Getting around:	**Car**
Key events:	❑ **Columbia Gorge Wine Celebration (early September). See www.columbiagorgewine.com for details.**
Tips:	❑ **Visit Maryhill Museum and Stonehenge Memorial near Maryhill Winery.** ❑ **Maryhill Winery sponsors a summer concert series at their outdoor amphitheater—see www.maryhillwinery.com for schedule and tickets.** ❑ **Cross over to Oregon if time permits to visit wineries that are part of the Columbia Gorge winery association.** ❑ **Limited time? Check out the wine bar in downtown Bingen across from Bad Seed Cider House.**
Best:	❑ **Best View: Wind River Cellars, Cascade Cliffs Winery and Vineyard and Maryhill Winery** ❑ **Best Gift Shop: Maryhill Winery** ❑ **Best Picnicking: Maryhill Winery and Wind River Cellars**

171

Wind River Cellars

The views are stunning. The wine is magnificent. The hospitality is first-rate. Wind River Cellars has it all.

With magnificent views of Mount Hood to the south and Mount Adams to the east, visitors to Wind River Cellars have license to use the word "stunned."

This is the perfect setting to get married (which they do) or to enjoy a catered lunch on the deck after a day of white water rafting (which they also do). Wind River Cellars owners Joel and Kris Goodwillie love being in the Columbia River Gorge and being residents of the tiny town of Husum. A visit there might have you packing your bags as well and taking up windsurfing.

Joel Goodwillie handcrafts about 3,500 cases annually using grapes from his vineyard, other local growers (including Celilo Vineyard), and Horse Heaven Hills. Joel produces the wine but Kris is the marketing/number-crunching brains behind the operation. They make a good team. He states that the Columbia Gorge grapes have more acid than grapes from other wine growing areas of Washington and therefore you get that clean, crisp, lively finish on the tongue. However, the word "velvety" came to mind when we sampled our way through a fairly ambitious list of Wind River wines: riesling, gewürztraminer, pinot gris, cabernet sauvignon, merlot, pinot noir, syrah, lemberger, tempranillo and a "save room for dessert" Port of Celilo. By the time this WineTrail adventurer got to tempranillo, Joel had a very strong resemblance to Hollywood star Kiefer Sutherland. However, Joel assured me that they weren't separated at birth.

If you are fortunate to be the only one visiting the tasting room (rare in the summer time), Joel can provide you a tour of the barrel room. Cross your fingers that he brings along his thief for barrel tasting. If he's too busy pouring, rumor has it that their two boys Connor and Adam will provide the guided tour. Cellar rats unite!

WIND RIVER CELLARS
opened: 1995
winemaker(s): Joel Goodwillie
location: 196 Spring Creek Road
Husum, WA 98623
phone: 509-493-2324
web: www.windrivercellars.com
e-mail: info@windrivercellars.com
picnic area: Yes
gift shop: Yes
fee: $5 waived upon wine purchase
hours: Daily 10–6; closed December 15 to January 1

Joel Goodwillie

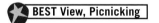 **BEST View, Picnicking**

DIRECTIONS: From SR-14 go north onto SR-141 (toward Husum). Proceed about 6.5 miles remaining on SR-141 and turn left (west) onto Spring Creek Rd a little past Husum town center. Continue on Spring Creek Rd for 1.5 miles and arrive at Wind River Cellars. (Note: Wind River Cellars wines can also be sampled at the Bad Seed Cider House tasting room in nearby Bingen.)

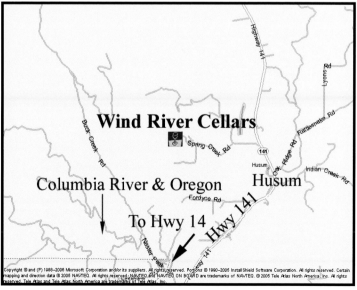

Bad Seed Cider House

How's this for a slogan: "For the Bad Seed in all of us." We love it. Indeed, an angry red-faced apple emblazons Bad Seed Cider's beer-size bottles. Along with the mad apple, Bad Seed Cider also ferments the mighty pear. Both varieties

weighing in at 5.8 percent alcohol, Bad Seed Cider comes in a convenient six-pack and is a perfect antidote for a hot summer day kayaking, whitewater rafting, golfing, or hiking in the Gorge.

As you might suspect, Bad Seed Cider is all about fun, and its Bingen tasting room reflects a carefree attitude. No swirling needed here—it's more about quaffing than sipping. Every second Saturday night (May through September) is free movie night at Bad Cider. And, as you might expect, frequent bands are guests of the cider house.

Despite the relaxed environment, the staff is serious about their hard ciders and proud of the fact that they use locally grown fruit. The quip found on the Bad Seed label, "How do you like them apples?" says it all. It's easy to close your eyes and imagine a ham-and-cheese crepe to go with Bad Seed Cider.

Incidentally, the Bad Seed Cider tasting room also features wines from Wind River Cellars. For a $3 tasting fee, you can enjoy Joel Goodwillie's award-winning wines. However, if you're wanting wine and time permits, make the short car drive to the Wind River Cellars in Husum and enjoy stunning views and the full lineup of Wind River Cellars wines.

BAD SEED CIDER HOUSE
opened: 1997
winemaker(s): Craig Sawyer
location: 415 West Steuben Street
Bingen, WA 98605
phone: 509-493-3881
web: www.badseedcider.com
e-mail: info@badseedcider.com
picnic area: No
gift shop: Yes
fee: Complimentary wine tasting
hours: Daily 11–6

Bad Seed Cider's Craig Sawyer

DIRECTIONS: Travel on SR-14 to Bingen and arrive at 415 W. Steuben St.where the Bad Seed Cider House tasting room is located.

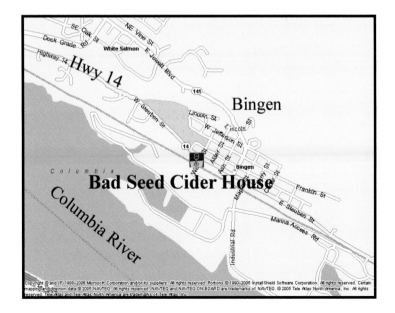

Syncline Wine Cellars

syn•cline *n.* a trough of stratified rock in which the beds dip toward each other from either side.

If your car trek takes you through the Columbia River Gorge, you'll likely spot a dramatic 300-foot rock wall jutting out beside the Columbia River. Known

as the "Coyote Wall Syncline," this is the namesake of Syncline Wine Cellars.

It's no accident that Syncline Wine Cellars makes great wine. Yes, winemaker James Mantone starts out with great fruit, but his background as a microbiologist and organic chemist has ingrained him with a strong attention to detail, which truly pays off when it comes to fine-tuning the fermentation process.

James and Poppie Mantone are transplants from other parts of the country. They met and fell in love at LaVelle Vineyards in the Willamette Valley. Settling on the Washington side of the Columbia River Gorge, they started Syncline in 1999. Most recently, they relocated from beautiful downtown Bingen and opened a new facility in the metropolis of Lyle.

Syncline Wine Cellars' focus is on Rhone-style wines and that aforementioned attention to detail may help explain why a growing number of wine lovers call Syncline their favorite wine. This is high praise considering the winery's short history and its initial shoestring budget. With current production running fewer than 3,000 cases annually, the winery primarily produces syrah, grenache, roussanne, and viognier. The Mantones acquire their grapes from a who's who of growers, including Alder Ridge Vineyards, Celilo Vineyard, Clifton Vineyard, Coyote Canyon, Destiny Ridge, McKinley Spring, Northridge, Pheasant Vineyard, Sundance Vineyard, and Steep Creek Ranch (their own vineyard). Not surprisingly, James is also the winemaker for McKinley Spring in the Horse Heaven Hills, which is where he gets his syrah grapes.

Hard work, passion and a scientific background all conspire to create distinctive Rhone-style Syncline wines.

SYNCLINE WINE CELLARS
opened: 1999
winemaker(s): James and Poppie Mantone
location: 111 Balch Road
Lyle, WA 98635
phone: 509-493-4705
web: www.synclinewine.com
e-mail: info@synclinewine.com
picnic area: Yes
gift shop: No
fee: $5 fee waived upon wine purchase
hours: 11–5 Friday through Sunday from Memorial Day through September; closed rest of year

Columbia River Gorge

DIRECTIONS: From SR-14 heading east as you approach Lyle turn onto County Road 1230 [Lyle White Salmon Rd] and proceed about 3 miles. Turn left onto Balch Rd and proceed .3 miles and arrive at 111 Balch Rd.
If heading west on SR-14 turn right onto Lyle Snowden Rd and proceed 1.2 miles. Keep straight onto Lyle White Salmon Rd and proceed 1.1 miles. Turn right onto Balch Rd and proceed .3 miles to Syncline Wine Cellars tasting room.

Cor Cellars

If a stranger turns to you and says, *"Bonum vinum laetificat cor hominis,"* don't throw a punch at him. He's simply exercising his Latin by saying, "Good wine gladdens the human heart." Such are the words that Luke Bradford embraced when he started Cor Cellars in 2005. Luke is one of a growing number of young winemakers who have splashed onto the Washington wine scene.

Despite his youth, this graduate of Evergreen State College doesn't lack winemaking experience. He worked at a relative's winery in Italy (which helps to explain the Latin connection) as well as stints with Wind River Cellars and Syncline Winery. He gives particular credit to James Mantone at Syncline for mentoring him in the chemical and microbiological aspects of making wine. In addition, Luke is grateful to the many growers with whom he collaborates, including McKinley Springs Vineyard in Horse Heaven Hills, Underwood Mountain Vineyards, Lonesome Spring Ranch, and Evergreen Vineyard.

Samples of Luke's wines include cabernet sauvignon, chardonnay, sauvignon blanc, riesling, and pinot blanc. However, his aptly named red table wine called "Momentum" reflects Luke's "movement, impulse, and effort" to make great wine. Everything about Cor Cellars reflects the promise of youth: a startup winery, a recently planted vineyard adjacent to the winery, and a youthful vintner. For those who celebrate life's pleasures (especially wine), it will be fun to watch the maturation of Cor Cellars.

COR CELLARS
opened: 2005
winemaker(s): Luke Bradford
location: 151 Old Highway 8
Lyle, WA 98635-9308
phone: 509-365-2744
web: www.corcellars.com
e-mail: corcellars@yahoo.com
picnic area: Yes
gift shop: No
fee: $3 tasting fee refundable upon purchase
hours: 11–6 Wednesday through Sunday, from
Memorial Day through Labor Day

Luke Bradford

DIRECTIONS: Driving east on US-14 go 4 miles out of Bingen. Take a left onto Old Hwy 8, go 5 miles and look for Cor Cellars sign and winery on the left.
Driving west on US-14 through Lyle, cross the Klickitat River, take first right onto Old Hwy 8 and go 1.5 miles. Cor Cellars is on the right.

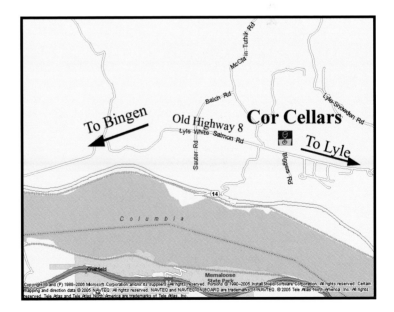

Illusion Winery

In the summer of 2007, Illusion Winery moved its operations from Black Diamond to a location in southwest Washington near Lyle. As with humor, timing is everything, and unfortunately, this new location was not open at the time of this writing. Nevertheless, from taking a sneak peak at the pictures on the Illusion Winery website, the views from the new facility of a nearby vineyard, canyons, and a sliver of the Columbia River offer WineTrail trekkers another reason to head to the Columbia River Gorge.

I first met David and Dina Guest at the 2007 Taste Washington! event in Seattle. A constant stream of loyal followers eager to sample the Guests' new vintage prevented me from asking them insightful questions such as "Why the heck do you do this?" or even better, "Where do you hope to take it?" So I didn't. Instead, I really want to make the trek to their new winery and experience the new digs. I want to ask those questions in the quiet of the tasting room without the crowds. I want to concentrate on the fruits of their labor (especially their red blend wine with the enchanting name of "Apparition") and give it quality time. Thus, I'm excited to visit their new Lyle location this coming summer and report my findings in the second edition of the guidebook. (I know this is a shameless way to plug the next edition but, hey, that's my job.)

David Guest

ILLUSION WINERY
opened: 2002
winemaker(s): David Guest
location: 31 Schilling Road
Lyle, WA 98635
phone: 206-261-1682
web: www.illusionwine.com
e-mail: illusion@sprintmail.com
picnic area: No
gift shop: No
fee: Complimentary wine tasting
hours: 11–5 during select summer weekends; call ahead or check website for details

DIRECTIONS: From SR-14 heading east, turn left onto 3rd St. in Bingen and head north. The road name changes to Columbia Ave. Turn right (east) onto Keasey Ave., then immediately turn left (north) onto Centerville Hwy. Proceed on Centerville Hwy for 10 miles. Turn left (north) onto Schilling Rd and proceed .3 miles to winery.

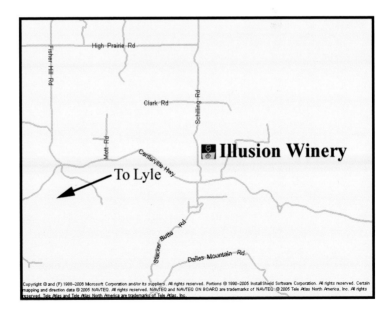

Marshal's Winery

Just past The Dalles Bridge on Highway 14, watch for the signs that lead you to Marshal's Winery. As you wind your way up to Marshal's, check out the rock formations jutting out; with a little imagination, you might see a stone face on one.

Ron Johnson, known as "RonJohn," named the winery after his son Marshal upon its launch in 2001. RonJohn is what you call a "vigneron," meaning that he produces wines from bud to bottle, and he has the good fortune of owning a south-facing vineyard to help him in that task. A visit to this "mom and pop" winery (as RonJohn calls it) becomes a truly memorable experience if you are lucky enough to visit with Ron. With his engaging smile and dulcet voice, RonJohn, accompanied by his dog, leads you on a tour of the production area. Please note the wine-stained walls near the fermentation tanks. RonJohn was

there when the tank exploded and still has the grape-shrapnel-stained shirt to prove it. If you are there during crush, be prepared to hit the ground.

RonJohn's diminutive wife, Lilie, originally from the Philippines, manages the tasting room. She has brought with her rich cultural traditions, including the hosting of big parties where a farm animal of some type ends up on the barbecue. Such is the case when they host and roast at the annual "Swine and Wine" event in the summer. With live music playing in the background, a glass of Marshal's wine in hand, and barbecued pork on your plate, you have the makings of a memorable day. On Thanksgiving, 13 turkeys are barbecued, giving visitors an opportunity to discover which wine pairs best with this delectable bird.

RonJohn makes some of the more traditional wines, such as riesling, cabernet sauvignon, and cabernet franc. He also makes a red table wine blend called "Stone Face Red," named for those unusual rock formations you saw driving in. However, RonJohn is also known for other, more remarkable creations, including a "hot tub wine" called "Black Homberg," made from 100-year-old vines and very appealing to those with a sweet tooth; "Sweet Anna Marie," a port-like wine made without brandy, resulting in a restrained alcohol level of 13.5 percent; and an Italian barbera. As you sample Marshal's wines, check out the lantern-adorned labels on its bottles. Created by RonJohn, the lantern drawing includes the words "Put a little light in your life." RonJohn and family live by those words every day.

MARSHAL'S WINERY
opened: 2001
winemaker(s): Ron Johnson
location: 150 Oak Creek Road
Dallesport, WA 98617
phone: 509-767-4633
web: www.marshalswinery.com
e-mail: marshalswinery@gorge.net
picnic area: Yes
gift shop: No—some logo wear
fee: Small fee waived upon purchase
hours: Daily 9–6

Ron Johnson

DIRECTIONS: .25 miles east of The Dalles Bridge—**from SR-14** take Dalles Mountain Rd north away from the Columbia River. Then immediately go left onto Oak Creek Rd and proceed 1 mile. Arrive at Marshal's Winery on the right.

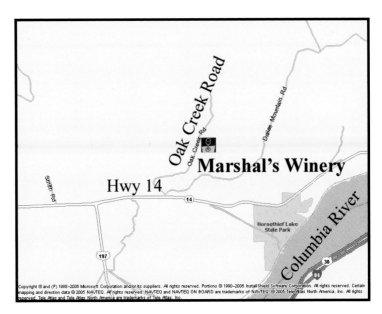

Cascade Cliffs Winery and Vineyard

At mile marker 88.5 on Highway 14, look for a red, white, and green wine barrel. It marks the entrance to Cascade Cliffs Vineyard and Winery. We know it looks like a fruit-packing shed, but that's part of Cascade Cliffs' charm. Named

for the basalt cliffs rising 400 feet on the north side of the vineyard, Cascade Cliffs is the creation of owner/winemaker Bob Lorkowski. The geography, which includes the Columbia River and surrounding cliffs, creates a microclimate well suited to the 23-acre vineyard. Lots of heating units combined with a long growing season translate into the perfect climate for grapes of Mediterranean origin.

So how is your Italian? You may be speaking it with a Piedmont accent by the time you depart Cascade Cliffs. This is the home to outstanding barbera, nebbiolo, and dolcetto. Bob also produces a red blend called "Goat Head Red" composed in part of barbera and nebbiolo. In the process, Bob manages to use American, French, and Hungarian oak to create a kaleidoscope of flavors that he blends to create his award-winning wines. However, not to neglect the French, Bob also produces small quantities of petite syrah, zinfandel, syrah, and cabernet sauvignon. But don't be surprised to find that many of these wines are not available for tasting; they often sell out. That's OK, WineTrail lovers are here for Bob's renowned light and fruity Italian wines.

WineTrail Tip: Pick up a large Four Cheese Decadence pizza from Sahara Pizza nearby in The Dalles, Oregon (918 West Sixth Street; 541-296-0099). Claim a table outside the Cascade Cliffs tasting room and uncork one of its Italian wines for a delicious experience. *Buon gusto!*

CASCADE CLIFFS WINERY AND VINEYARD
opened: 1985
winemaker(s): Robert Lorkowski
location: 8866 Highway 14
Wishram, WA 98673
phone: 509-767-1100
web: www.cascadecliffs.com
e-mail: cascadecliffs@gorge.net
picnic area: Yes
gift shop: No
fee: Complimentary wine tasting
hours: Daily 10–6

 BEST View

DIRECTIONS: Cascade Cliffs Winery & Vineyard is located at Milepost 88.5 on US-14.

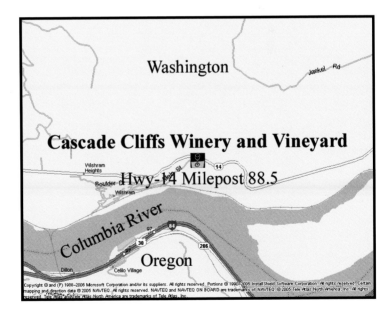

Maryhill Winery

There are many reasons to make a journey to Maryhill Winery. Many visitors stop for the view, and why not? With stupendous views of Mount Hood to the west and the Columbia River Gorge below, visitors are so entranced they might forget to sample Maryhill Wine. Then too, many trekkers come here for the summer concert series at Maryhill's outdoor amphitheater. Past performers include none other than Bob Dylan; B.B. King; Crosby, Stills & Nash; Amy

Grant; and ZZ Top. With the stars above you and ZZ Top rocking on stage, a glass of Maryhill's zinfandel would complete the picture.

Maryhill may be the wine-event capital of the world. Throughout the year, Maryhill Winery hosts such events, from crush to bottling and everything in between. It even takes time in August to celebrate "verasion," when the white grape varieties turn from opaque to translucent, and when the red grape varieties turn from green to deep red. However, many tourists are here simply because they love the wine. They note the view, browse the well-stocked gift shop, but make a quick beeline for the tasting bar.

The tasting bar is the centerpiece of the spacious tasting room. Built in the early 1900s, the massive Brunswick bar is 20 feet long and 12 feet high, with inset mirrors and wood carvings. The same crew responsible for the Egyptian pyramids must have moved this wine bar into position. Behind the bar, the well-trained staff pours and educates. The $5 fee for sampling reserve wines is well worth it, especially if you are thinking of purchasing a bottle or two; the fee applies to purchases of $20 or more. Maryhill Winery features a whole slew of dry to sweet white wines and a variety of classic reds. Cross your fingers that its popular "Fort Rock Red" is not sold out.

Owners Craig and Vicki Leuthold and family members Donald Leuthold and Cherie Brooks launched the winery in 2000. With an annual production of 35,000 cases, Maryhill Winery is one of the largest family-owned wineries in the state. Their slogan is "Passion, Patience, and Balance." However, they could easily switch it for the motto, "Fun, Celebrate, Drink," and WineTrail enthusiasts would understand. Come for the music, the view, or an event, but realize that without the wine, the setting would be just another windy photo op along Highway 14.

View of Columbia River Gorge from Maryhill
Winery

MARYHILL WINERY
opened: 1999
winemaker(s): John Haw
location: 9774 Highway 14
Goldendale, WA 98620
phone: 509-773-3733
web: www.maryhillwinery.com
e-mail: maureenl@maryhillwinery.com
picnic area: Yes
gift shop: Yes
fee: $5 tasting fee for reserved wines waived for
purchase of $20 or more on wine
hours: Daily 10–6

★ BEST View, gift shop, picknicking

DIRECTIONS: Travel east on SR-14 to Milepost 97 just past Maryhill Museum to Goldendale. Maryhill Winery is on the right.

Waving Tree Winery

If you are looking for a different wine tasting experience, check out the Waving Tree Winery tasting room. The room is in a log cabin located across from Maryhill State Park. From the outside, it looks like a visitor information center and, indeed, once inside you'll find rows of colorful tourist brochures touting Columbia River Gorge attractions, of which there are many. But your mission is

not to get directions to Stonehenge Memorial. Rather, you're here to sample Terrance Atkins' estate wines.

For Waving Tree wines, Terrance chose a unique blue-and-green label with the phrase "The wind was once created by the trees waving back and forth to one another" printed in

Author outside Waving Tree tasting room

big block letters on the bottle. There's plenty of wind in the Gorge, after all, and someone had to explain it.

Terrance is usually at the tasting room pouring mainly reds, which are made from the grapes in his 60-acre vineyard. Because Waving Tree produces only about 1,000 cases of wine per year, there's a good chance that one of his vintages will be sold out. However, with a little luck, WineTrail trekkers can sample cabernet sauvignon, cabernet franc, sangiovese, barbera, grenache, syrah, and viognier. As Terrance puts it, "Ninety percent of good wine is due to the vineyard." Terrance is a veteran viticulturist and winemaker in the Columbia River Gorge appellation. As you swirl and sip, don't pass up the opportunity to learn about the region's wine history and many of the characters who shaped this appellation.

Armed with this information and perhaps a bottle or two of Waving Tree wines, you can now take on the Stonehenge Memorial. It's just 4 miles east of the Maryhill Art Museum, as the brochure states.

Terrance Atkins

WAVING TREE WINERY
opened: 2002
winemaker(s): Terrance Atkins
location: 2 Maryhill Highway
Goldendale, WA 98620
phone: 509-773-6552
web: www.wavingtreewinery.com
e-mail: atkins@gorge.net
picnic area: Yes
gift shop: No
fee: Complimentary wine tasting
hours: Daily 9–5 from Memorial Day through Labor
Day; 9–5 Friday through Sunday from April through
May and September through November

DIRECTIONS: From US-14 take US-97 south toward Columbia River and Oregon. The Waving Tree
tasting room is located in the log cabin across from Maryhill State Park off US 97, just north of
the Biggs Bridge.

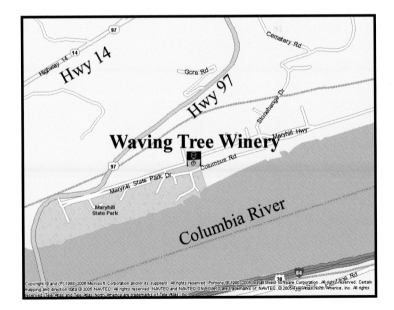

North Central Washington

WINE COUNTRY

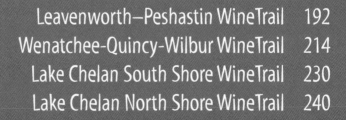

Leavenworth–Peshastin
WineTrail

The Leavenworth–Peshastin WineTrail will take you through the heart of Washington's Bavarian-inspired village that is fun to visit in any season. This is arguably the most majestic location in Washington. Here, you'll discover friendly pouring staff and tasting rooms within walking distance of each other. With names like Berghof Cellars, Eagle Creek, Napeequa Vintners, Icicle Ridge and Wedge Mountain, the Leavenworth–Peshastin WineTrail takes the cake for great names and good times. In addition, a number of wineries (e.g., Kestrel, Glenn Fiona, Silver Lake, Pasek, and Willow Crest) have satellite tasting rooms in downtown Leavenworth.

Leavenworth–Peshastin WineTrail

1 Boudreaux Cellars
2 Okanogan Estate and Vineyards
3 Windfall Winery
4 Ryan Patrick Vineyards
5 Berghof Keller Winery
6 Napeequa Vintners
7 Eagle Creek Winery & Cottage
8 Cascadia Winery
9 Icicle Ridge Winery
10 Wedge Mountain Winery

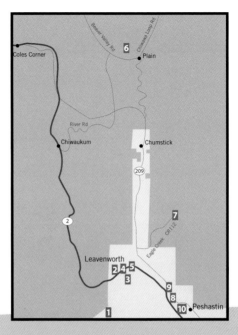

Region:	**North Central Washington Wine Country**
# of tasting rooms on tour:	**10**
# of satellite tasting rooms:	**5—Kestrel, Silver Lake, Glenn Fiona, Pasek, and Willow Crest. Note: Okanogan Winery is located north near the Canadian border in Oroville. Okanogan also has a separate tasting room in Oroville.**
Estimated # of days for tour:	**2**
Getting around:	**Car and foot**
Key events:	❑ **Red Wine and Chocolate (mid-February) sponsored by the Columbia Cascade Winery Association.** **See www.columbiacascadewines.com for details.** ❑ **Christmas Lighting Festival during December weekends in Leavenworth.**
Tips:	❑ **Eagle Creek Winery and Cottage offers overnight accommodations.** ❑ **Leavenworth offers a variety of places to eat and sleep.** ❑ **Consider hiring a limousine service such as Leavenworth Winery Tours 509-670-3607.** ❑ **Plan visit to the area by clicking on www.leavenworth.org or call 509-548-5807.**
Best:	❑ **Best Destination: Eagle Creek Winery & Cottage** ❑ **Best View: Wedge Mountain Winery** ❑ **Best Picnicking: Icicle Ridge** ❑ **Best for Weddings: Icicle Ridge Winery**

193

Boudreaux Cellars

I could listen to Rob Newsom all day. He has that Louisiana Cajun thing going on with his voice. But, despite his Southern heritage, he's been here long enough to embrace certain Northwest trappings; note the Seahawks flag, pictures of Rob ice climbing, and of course, Washington wines. Still, you half expect Rob to offer you a cup of chicory coffee rather than a taste of his cabernet sauvignon.

Boudreaux Cellars is located 7.7 miles from Leavenworth on Eightmile Creek, just a few miles past the Sleeping Lady Conference Center. As you go over the bridge to Boudreaux Cellars, look for Rob's chocolate lab, Roux, to greet you.

Downtown Leavenworth

It's all homespun magic, but then again, so are his wines.

Although Rob welcomes visitors, he doesn't post winery hours for the public. He wants to keep his family-run operation small. Also note that the road to Boudreaux Cellars can be tricky to navigate in the winter. Thus, visitors to his winery need to call in advance. However, Rob is usually there tending to myriad vintner duties, in between playing fetch with Roux, of course. Inside the tasting room is a large, honey-colored pine bar where Rob pours from distinctively heavy French bottles. Depending upon availability, he will dispense samples of his chardonnay, merlot, cabernet sauvignon, and syrah. He's likely to inform you of sources of his grapes (which includes many of Washington's top vineyards), his winemaking training in Walla Walla, his style, and other interesting details. But being the modest man that he is, Rob will probably leave out the fact that in 2007, *Seattle Magazine* named Boudreaux Cellars the "Best New Winery of the Year" and Rob Newsom as the "Best New Winemaker of the Year."

If time permits, climb down the ladder to the barrel room. There's something comforting about the musky smell emanating from 150 barrels of wine, the soft light given off by the wall sconces, and the dulcet sound of Rob's voice as he presents his future vintages.

BOUDREAUX CELLARS
opened: 2001
winemaker(s): Rob Newsom
location: 4551 Icicle Creek Road
Leavenworth, WA 98826-9300
phone: 509-548-5858
web: www.boudreauxcellars.com
e-mail: rob@boudreauxcellars.com
picnic area: Yes
gift shop: No
fee: Complimentary wine tasting
hours: Call ahead to schedule—visitors welcome

DIRECTIONS: From US-2 on the west end of Leavenworth, turn south onto Icicle Rd. Continue 7.7 miles and arrive at Boudreaux Cellars on your left. The winery is located on Eightmile Creek in the heart of beautiful Icicle Canyon.

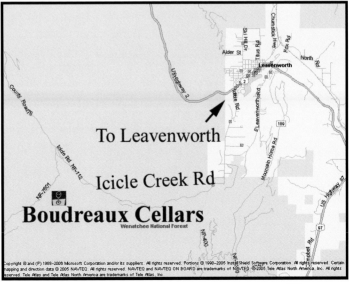

Okanogan Estate and Vineyards

Okanogan Winery offers two different tasting locations to sample its estate wines: One is in Leavenworth and the other is in Oroville, near British Columbia.

Most visitors experience Okanogan Winery at the Wine & Gift Shoppe in Leavenworth on Highway 2. By your third sip of Okanogan wine, you might

be surprised to learn that the fruit used for its wines comes from the winery's estate vineyards in the Okanogan Valley. Its orchards (along with the winery and tasting room) are located north on Highway 97, before you enter Canada's premier wine-growing region in British Columbia's Okanagan. (By the way, that's not a typo. On the American side, it's spelled "Okanogan," but on the Canadian side, it's spelled "Okanagan.") As stated in the winery's brochure, "The vineyards are located on the valley's sandy, desert sage benches and on the sunny slopes amongst the orchards of this fruitful valley that sits at the edges of beautiful Lake Osoyoos." Wow, a desert-like climate in northern Washington? Yep.

But if Leavenworth is the end of the WineTrail North for you, the Wine & Gift Shoppe offers a full slate of Okanogan's dry and sweet white wines (e.g., pinot grigio, riesling, gewürztraminer, and late-harvest sauvignon blanc) as well as classic reds (e.g., merlot, pinot noir, and "Bench Rock" blend). Formerly using the moniker "Gold Diggers Cellars," named after its fruit orchards, the renamed Okanogan Winery is proud of the fact that its wines don't rely on grapes trucked in from Yakima Valley or other points south. The friendly tasting room staff also can advise you on where to eat, sleep, and shop in Leavenworth.

If, however, your wine-related travels take you north on Highway 97, Okanogan Winery's downtown Oroville location is a fun pit stop. Oroville is an old mining town, and you'll want to budget time to experience Oroville's charm. Just dig around a bit to discover its nuggets.

OKANOGAN ESTATE AND VINEYARDS
opened: 2000
winemaker(s): Michael P. Buckmiller
location: 285 Highway 2
Leavenworth, WA 98826
phone: 509-476-2736
web: www.okanoganwine.com
e-mail: winery@golddiggerscellars.com
picnic area: Yes
gift shop: Yes
fee: Complimentary wine tasting
hours: 11–5 Sunday, Monday, Thursday, 11–7 Friday
and Saturday, from January through April; 11–6
Sunday through Thursday, 11–7 Friday and Saturday,
from May through December

DIRECTIONS: If traveling from west of the Cascades (Stevens Pass), take US-2 to Leavenworth. The tasting room is located on the right just as you enter Leavenworth on US-2.
If traveling from the east, arrive in Leavenworth and continue to 285 US-2 located on the left. The tasting room is located across from Kristall's Restaurant and right next door to Leavenworth Properties. Note: Okanogan Estate and Vineyards' other tasting room is located in Oroville.

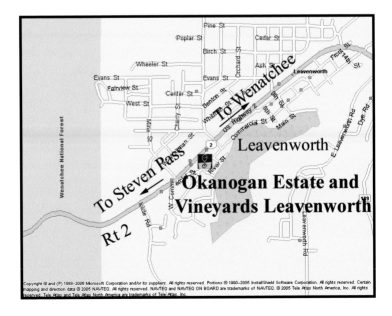

Windfall Winery

While in Leavenworth, don't miss the opportunity to visit the Kestrel Vintners satellite tasting room on Front Street. Here you get a two-for-one opportunity to sample Kestrel Vintners wines including their "Lady in Red" wines as well as Windfall Winery's AP wine. The Kestrel tasting room is the only location for sampling Windfall's AP (i.e., Asian Pear) wine. Served cold, AP is a surprisingly dry wine to enjoy by itself or paired with food.

Staff at Kestrel Tasting room in Leavenworth pouring Windfall's AP

Windfall Winery is the brainchild of San Juan Island–based Larry Soll who put his science background and love of making fruit wines into the creation of AP. During the 1980s, Larry sold his biotech company and moved to San Juan Island, where "retirement" was not to be. Among other endeavors, Larry was active making a variety of fruit wines. His friends and neighbors convinced him that the Asian Pear wine was the best and he should go commercial. However, lacking the production facility, Larry was fortunate to have Ray Sandidge of Kestrel Vintners fame offer his production facility in Prosser for the converting pear juice to pear wine. During the process, the pear wine (which checks in at 11 to 12% alcohol by volume) is aged in oak for two months. This gives AP a more wine-like taste and feel on the tongue, ready to take on grilled chicken or pecan crusted halibut.

With your purchase of AP, you also get a two-for-one benefit. You get the golden bottle of AP wine with its distinctive label plus you get a good feeling knowing that 100% of the profits are invested in low-income housing. Larry Soll is an ardent supporter of the "community land trust model" that provides affordable housing for low-income families who otherwise won't enjoy home ownership. Many non-profit housing organizations benefit from AP sales including SHARE Community Land Trust in Leavenworth and San Juan Island Community Land Trust which Larry helped found. Your purchase of AP is a windfall for yourself and for those in need.

WINDFALL WINERY
opened: 2004
winemaker(s): Larry Soll
location: 843 Front Street
Leavenworth, WA 98828
phone: 800-481 3712
web: www.windfallwine.com
e-mail: larry@windfallwine.com
picnic area: No
gift shop: No
fee: Complimentary wine tasting
hours: Daily 11–5

DIRECTIONS: **If traveling from west** of the Cascades (Stevens Pass), take US-2 to Leavenworth. Take a right onto Front St. as you enter Leavenworth. The Windfall Tasting Room is colocated with the Kestrel Tasting Room at 843 Front St.
If traveling east on US-2 take a left onto 9th St. followed by a right onto Front St. The Windfall Tasting Room is colocated with the Kestrel Tasting Room at 843 Front St.

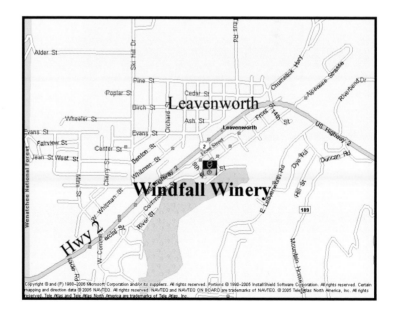

Ryan Patrick Vineyards

Although its winemaking facilities are in nearby Rock Island, Ryan Patrick Vineyards' tasting room is in the heart of Bavarian-inspired Leavenworth. From time to time, you can find owner Terry Flanagan pitching in at the new tasting room, but you are more likely to find his wife, Vivian, pouring. When not at the

tasting room, Terry is often making wine at their Rock Island facility or tending to his vineyards. The winery is the namesake of the couple's two sons, Ryan and Patrick.

Most of the wines produced here are estate wines, using fruit grown from three separate family-owned vineyards: The Bishop's Vineyard, The Homestead Vineyard, and Vivian's Vineyard. Together the three vineyards make up 58 acres of outstanding varietals, including chardonnay, cabernet sauvignon, merlot, cabernet franc, malbec, nebbiolo, and barbera. Low yields in the vineyard, combined with prime locations for heat and sunlight, produce concentrated fruit for Terry.

For fans of white wine, be sure to sample the *vin d'été* (summer wine), a white Bordeaux blend of sauvignon blanc and semillon. And for the fans of red wine, Ryan Patrick Vineyards offers two traditional Bordeaux-style blends of cabernet sauvignon, merlot, and cabernet franc. If your loyalties are divided, go for both reds and whites.

The tasting room offers plenty of space for the tourists who flock to Leavenworth. Featuring exposed brick and comfy chairs, the tasting room is a nice oasis in which to kick back and enjoy wines that are only found in select restaurants and wine shops. On one wall are a series of photographs demonstrating the winemaking process. From grape harvest, crush, and punch down, the pictures depict the labor that goes into each 750-milliliter bottle.

Vivian and Terry Flanagan

RYAN PATRICK VINEYARDS
opened: 1996
winemaker(s): Craig Mitrakul
location: 900 Front Street
Leavenworth, WA 98826
phone: 509-888-2236
web: www.ryanpatrickvineyards.com
e-mail: Terry@ryanpatrickvineyards.com
picnic area: No
gift shop: No
fee: Complimentary wine tasting
hours: Daily 11–5:30

DIRECTIONS: **If traveling from west of the Cascades** (Stevens Pass), take US-2 to Leavenworth. Take a right onto Front St. The tasting room is located at 900 Front St.
If traveling east on US-2 take a left onto 9th St. followed by a left onto Front St. The winery is on the left at 900 Front St.

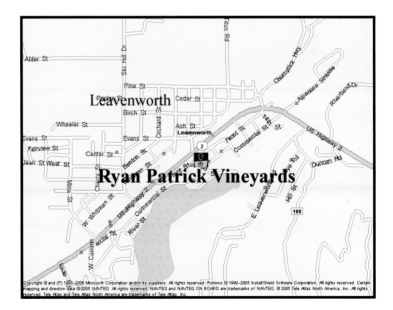

Berghof Keller Winery

Achtung, WineTrail trekker! Surely you would know that any Bavarian-style village worth its salt (or grapes, in this case) would have German wines. If there wasn't a winery making German-style wines, we'd be tempted to start one. But Bob Duncan beat us to the punch.

Bob's construction and orchardist backgrounds gave him the experience he needed to get started. First, with the downturn of the fruit industry, Bob made the tough decision to pull his fruit trees and replace them with riesling, gewürztraminer, and lemberger—all varietals suitable for this cooler region, which shares the same latitude as Germany's wine region. Then Bob transformed his two-story construction facility into a winery and tasting room, with a cobblestone façade and Bavarian-style motif reflecting the Leavenworth look.

Now all he needed was a suitable name, and a friend suggested "Berghof," which is German for a mountainous state. Berghof Cellars was born.

Berghof Cellars is located just off Highway 2 east of downtown, in the shadow of a mountain aptly named Mountain Home. A stenciled sign on the outside of the winery reads "*Herzlich Willkommen*" (German for "Hearty Welcome"). Bob greets visitors to the winery and provides generous pours. Standing more than 6 feet tall, his commanding presence belies the fact that Bob has a special way of making visitors feel welcome; in a word, he's charming. The first floor houses the tasting room and production area. Plans call for transforming the second floor into a 2,000-square-foot event center for hosting winemaker dinners, wedding receptions, and other events.

Bob relies on estate fruit for his riesling, gewürztraminer, and lemberger. However, for his siegerrebe and Spätburgunder (pinot noir), he acquires his fruit from other Washington grape growers. Working with winemaker Martin Sieloff, their goal "is to make small quantities of excellent German wine with a minimum of equipment." Their bestseller is the gewürztraminer ("gewurz" means "spice" in German), which we suspect was fermented to pair with sausage and sauerkraut. A close second must be the "Red Baron" blend (love the label) with its full flavor and easy drinking. Enjoy German-style wines without the hassle of flying to Rhine country—and don't forget to pack your lederhosen!

Bob Duncan

BERGHOF KELLER WINERY
opened: 2004
winemaker(s): Martin Sieloff
location: 11695 Duncan Road
Leavenworth, WA 98826-9329
phone: 509-548-5605
web: www.berghofkeller.com
e-mail: berghofkeller@msn.com
picnic area: No
gift shop: No
fee: Complimentary wine tasting
hours: 1–5 Tuesdays through Saturdays

DIRECTIONS: If traveling from west of the Cascades (Stevens Pass), take US-2 to Leavenworth. Just past Leavenworth bear right (south) onto Duncan Rd. Turn right to stay on Duncan Rd. Arrive at 11695 Duncan Rd.
If traveling from the east take a left on Duncan Rd just as you enter Leavenworth. Turn right to stay on Duncan Rd. Arrive at 11695 Duncan Rd.

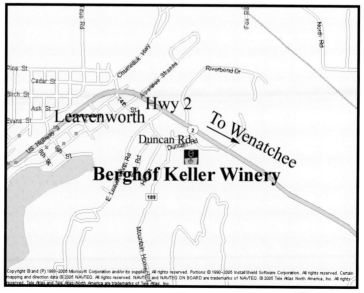

Napeequa Vintners

Plain, Washington? Who thinks of starting a winery in a small village 15 curvy miles north of Leavenworth? It isn't exactly a major crossroads—you have to have a reason to go to Plain. But as this wine tourist discovered, winemaker/owner David Morris and partners Ann Hathaway and Michael Mann had

Napeequa—Your Friends, Your Food, Our Wine

a good reason. It's called community. While waiting for David to return from nearby Plain Hardware, where he had gone to fetch a latte, a dozen visitors trickled into the tasting room as if they were coming home. They seemed to know one another. Friendly. Relaxed. It struck me that the owners of Napeequa Vintners could have chosen Woodinville for the location of their winery; instead they chose Plain. Here, they could be a key part of the community—a village watering hole—where friends and acquaintances could mingle and enjoy good wine. Their slogan, "Your Friends, Your Food, Our Wine," is more than mere words.

Winemaker David Morris relies on small lot vineyards in the Columbia and Yakima valleys to create wines that are "different and intriguing." Balancing winemaking with his Lake Stevens chiropractic practice, David talks about his goal of perfecting the best wine for food and friends. He pays homage to his volunteer experience at Quilceda Creek in 2002, which added to his winemaking résumé. He also thanks his mentor, Ray Sandidge (of C.R. Sandidge Wines fame), whom he affectionately refers to as Master Po with himself as Grasshopper, a bow to the hit TV show *Kung Fu*. David's science background lends itself to experimenting. For example, he is currently working with a California cooperage firm to test hybrid barrels composed of American and French oak. Interesting concept, but when your goal is to create wines that are different and intriguing, you step outside the norm.

David wants his wine to be fruit-forward. "It should be the first thing you experience when tasting Napeequa wines," he states. By keeping production small (fewer than 2,000 cases), David can focus on stylish red and white wines. His current '06/'07 offerings include "Randonee" (chardonnay), "Trailhead" (a red blend), sangiovese, malbec, merlot, gewürztraminer ice wine (wonderfully sweet with a long finish), and a dessert wine called "Glissade," which is a gewürztraminer made in the Trockenbeerenauslese (say that 10 times) style to pair with chocolates and cheesecakes.

A short drive north of the touristy village of Leavenworth drops you into Plain, where country stores, a small schoolhouse, and friendly neighbors create the perfect setting for making great wine.

David Morris and team member

NAPEEQUA VINTNERS
opened: 2005
winemaker(s): David Morris
location: 18820 Beaver Valley Road
Plain, WA 98826
phone: 206-930-7501
web: www.napeequa.com
e-mail: sales@napeequa.com
picnic area: No
gift shop: No
fee: Complimentary wine tasting
hours: 11–5 Saturdays, 12–4 Sundays, May through
November; call to confirm

DIRECTIONS: From US-2 on the eastside of Leavenworth turn north onto Chumstik Hwy. Continue about 14 miles and arrive in Plain. Turn right (north) onto Beaver Valley Rd and arrive at Napeequa Vintners on the left.

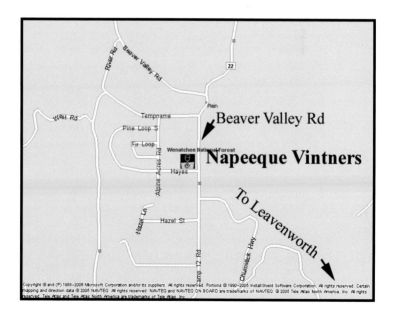

Eagle Creek Winery & Cottage

Note the name. It's not simply Eagle Creek Winery. Rather, it's Eagle Creek Winery & *Cottage*. Owners Ed and Pat Rutledge must have a penchant for the finer things in life. The cottage provides a homey atmosphere in which to relax and read by the fire or play a board game or gaze outside at the vineyard adjacent

to the property. There's also a fully equipped kitchen for those who want to cook their own meals. The cottage can also serve as a home base for outdoor activities or shopping in nearby Leavenworth. No need to worry about going to town for a bottle of wine, however.

As a perk of your stay, you can choose a bottle of wine from the downstairs cellar. It's one of many nice touches that cottage guests enjoy.

Winemaker Ed Rutledge produces about 4,000 cases annually of both red and white wines. Ed's chardonnay is produced from grapes grown in Eagle Creek's own vineyard, but his other wines use grapes from the Columbia Valley. His red wines include cabernet sauvignon, merlot, cabernet franc, and Bordeaux-style blends. Ed employs a combination of American and Hungarian oak.

To sample Eagle Creek wines, visitors enter the downstairs tasting room at the rear of the building. The tight quarters lend a "cozy" feeling to the room, yet it's the type of place where visiting with others comes easily. You soon find yourself joining other visitors on a field trip to the barrel room and cellar adjacent to the tasting room. You realize that this is where guests of the cottage come to select their bottle of wine, and if you're like this WineTrail adventurer, you find yourself turning a little green with envy.

EAGLE CREEK WINERY & COTTAGE
opened: 2002
winemaker(s): Ed Rutledge
location: 10037 Eagle Creek Road
Leavenworth, WA 98826-9113
phone: 509-548-7668
web: www.eaglecreekwinery.com
e-mail: info@eaglecreekwinery.com
picnic area: Yes
gift shop: Yes
fee: Complimentary wine tasting
hours: 11–4 weekends and holidays from May
through October, or by appointment

BEST Destination

DIRECTIONS: **From Leavenworth center**, take US-2 (east) for .3 miles. Turn left (north) onto Chumstick Hwy and go 2.1 miles. Turn right (east) onto County Rd 112 [Eagle Creek Rd] and go 2.5 miles. Eagle Creek Winery & Cottage is on the right.

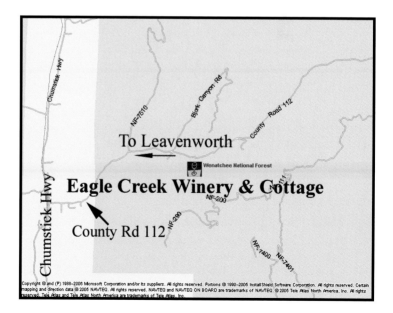

Cascadia Winery

New to the north-central Washington wine region is Peshastin's Cascadia
Winery. Although a fresh face, winemaker/owner Alan Yanagimachi is not new
to winemaking. In 2005, Alan came north from California following a stint

at Monterey
Wine Co., where
he learned the
technologies
necessary
to produce
1.5 million
gallons of wine
annually. That's
fermentation on a
grand scale. Now
he looks forward
to producing
1,500 cases per
year and relishes
the idea of creating
"artisan" wines.

Among other winemaking stops, Alan worked at Arbor Crest Wine Cellar in
Spokane (where he met his wife, Lilith). He also traveled to the former Soviet
Republic of Georgia and, for 18 months, experienced winemaking in one of the
oldest winemaking areas in the world. He also worked for a winery near Angels
Camp in California, made famous by Mark Twain's short story "The Celebrated
Jumping Frog of Calaveras County." Alan doesn't mention if the winery's sales
leapfrogged over its competitors.

Added to his working experience is a degree in fermentation science/enology
from the University of California–Davis. The degree came about after a chance
meeting with Robert Mondavi in 1985 at a dinner/jazz concert at Mondavi
Cellars. Because of his science background, Alan has found it helpful to offer
lab services to other wineries as well as wine enthusiasts while he gets Cascadia
Winery off and running.

Despite his recent migration from California, Alan hasn't wasted any time
getting started. Already, his '07 offerings include a dry "Pinnacle Rosé," a
riesling, a wine labeled "Apple Andy," made from Gala and Golden Delicious
apples, and a chardonnay with tropical flavors and full finish. His plans are to
produce a larger portfolio of wines, in particular, red wines, but those will take
time to age. Still, Alan loves the idea of staying small and producing handcrafted
wines relying on fruit from his new home, Washington.

CASCADIA WINERY
opened: 2006
winemaker(s): Alan Yanagimachi
location: 10090 Main Street
Peshastin, WA 98847
phone: 509-548-7900
web: www.cascadiawinery.com
e-mail: alany@cascadiawinery.com
picnic area: No
gift shop: Yes
fee: Complimentary wine tasting
hours: 11–5 Thursday through Saturday, 11–5
Monday, 12–5 Sunday

Alan Yanagimachi

DIRECTIONS: From US-2 heading east or west, take Main St. exit for Peshastin. Road name changes to Peshastin Rd. Turn left (northwest) onto Depot Rd. The road name changes to Main St. within .1 miles. Arrive at Cascadia Winery on your right.

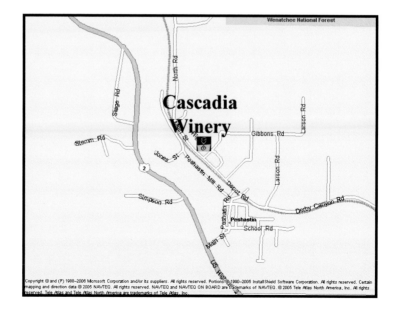

Icicle Ridge Winery

Most winery owners feel right at home in their wineries. But in the case of the Wagoners, the feeling is quite literal: Icicle Ridge Winery is their home. Not only do they live in it, but Louis Wagoner actually built the log-style home, along with much of the rustic furniture that graces the winery. Situated outside of Leavenworth, this jewel of a winery is a wonderful surprise for WineTrails

trekkers. As you arrive, you will be greeted by 40 acres of pear trees that are slowly giving way to a variety of Bordeaux varietals. No need to ring the front doorbell—visitors can come right in and enjoy wine tasting in the kitchen.

On the way in, please note the family photo featuring the Wagoners' three daughters: They are an integral part of the winery, handling marketing, event coordinating, bottling, and myriad other jobs. Much of the art you see on the walls was created by the family. You can circulate comfortably from living room to dining room to kitchen area with glass in hand while you sample premium wine. Icicle Ridge's winemaker, Don Woods, is often assisting and can explain how he went from a chemical engineering job to become the chief winemaker at Icicle Ridge Winery. By the way, Don is married to one of the three blond daughters mentioned above. As Don noted, "This has been the greatest experience of my life."

The family relies on estate-grown grapes as well as Columbia Valley grapes to produce a wide variety of white and red wines. Currently, the winery produces about 2,500 cases per year, but as the pear trees give way to grape vines, don't be surprised to see that number double in the not too distant future. However, the family's goal is to remain a small winery devoted to the production of premium wines. For whites, check out the white riesling and the "Three Blondes" gewürztraminer. Among the reds, the syrah and "Romanze" were soft and fruity.

Icicle Ridge has gained a reputation for hosting a summer event known as Jazzamatazz (see www.icicleridgewinery.com for details) as well as being a great spot for a wedding. At Icicle Ridge, Eddie Bauer meets premium wine, and you'll feel right at home.

ICICLE RIDGE WINERY
opened: 2002
winemaker(s): Dan Woods
location: 8977 North Road
Peshastin, WA 98847-9521
phone: 509-548-6156 Tasting room in Leavenworth
web: www.icicleridgewinery.com
e-mail: info@icicleridgewinery.com
picnic area: Yes
gift shop: Yes
fee: Complimentary wine tasting
hours: Daily 12–5

BEST Picnicking and weddings

DIRECTIONS: Take US-2 to Peshastin. Turn left (east) onto Main St. (road name changes to Peshastin Rd). Turn left (northwest) onto Depot Rd. Road name changes to Main St. for .5 miles. Road name changes again to North Rd. Continue .5 miles. Turn right (east) onto Anderson Canyon Rd and follow signs to Icicle Ridge Winery (.2 miles).

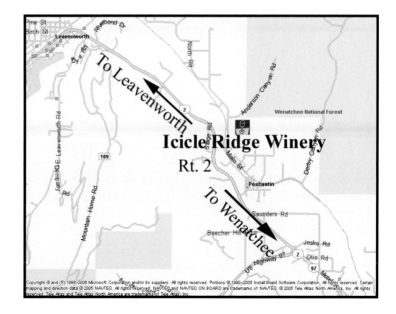

211

Wedge Mountain Winery

The plaque at Wedge Mountain Winery's entrance says it all: "A passion for the vine; a passion for the grape; a passion for the wine." This "impassioned" message from Charlie and Mary Ann McKee explains their drive to create estate wines from the Riverbend Ranch Vineyard, located about 5 miles east of Leavenworth off Highway 2.

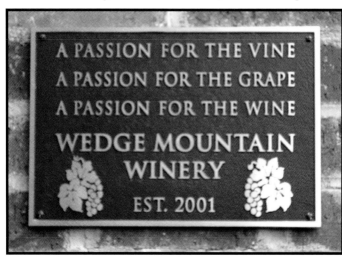

Upon arriving at the winery, and if weather permits, you should first spend some time walking around the property, through the apple and pear trees, past the horses and cows, to the vineyard next to the meandering Wenatchee River. Towering above you is beautiful Wedge Mountain, with the Enchantments to the west. Take in the smells, the sights, the sounds. You're now ready to taste some great wine.

The Wedge Mountain Winery's tasting room is located in a rather unusual wine cellar. Long after your visit, you'll still recall the tasting room built in the side of a knoll. In the fall, the top of the knoll becomes the crush pad. Mary Ann works the tasting room, while Charlie manages the winemaking duties. Mary Ann's relaxed manner encourages questions, which typically involve the origin of their grapes and Charlie's winemaking style. Complimentary samples of a wide variety of reds (cabernet sauvignon, merlot and syrah) and whites (chardonnay, white riesling, and a blend of riesling and chardonnay called "Deux Chevaux Blancs") are available, along with a selection of fruit wines, such as pear, cherry, and raspberry. (Note: The McKees were fruit growers before becoming entwined with the vine.) Although most Wedge Mountain wines are made from grapes acquired from the Columbia Valley, several of its wines rely on Riverbend Ranch Vineyard fruit. Your mission is to sniff out which are the estate wines and which are not.

Mary Ann McKee

WEDGE MOUNTAIN WINERY
opened: 2001
winemaker(s): Charlie McKee
location: 9534 Saunders Road
Peshastin, WA 98847
phone: 509-548-7068
web: www.wedgemountainwinery.com
e-mail: charliem@nwi.net
picnic area: Yes
gift shop: No
fee: Complimentary wine tasting
hours: 10–6 Thursdays through Mondays

 BEST Views

DIRECTIONS: From Leavenworth go east on US-2 5 miles and turn left onto Saunders Rd. After approximately .5 miles look for Wedge Mountain Winery sign.

From the south go north on Hwy 97A (Blewett Pass) to intersection with US-2. Cross over Hwy 2 to Jesky Rd. Proceed straight to Saunders Rd. Turn left onto Saunders Rd. Look for Wedge Mountain Winery sign, turn right onto gravel driveway.

From the east go west on Hwy 2/97 17 miles west of Wenatchee. Turn right onto Saunders Rd for approximately 1+ miles. Look for Wedge Mountain Winery sign.

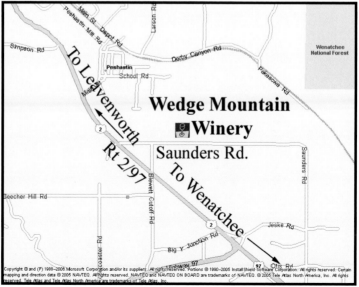

213

Wenatchee-Quincy-Wilbur
WineTrail

Chateau Faire Le Pont tasting room

Have you ever been to Wilbur? Well, here is your chance, my fellow
WineTrail enthusiast. The Wenatchee-Quincy-Wilbur WineTrail
features wineries found along the hillside of the mighty Columbia
River. In terms of views, this is the most spectacular of all tours. From
Wenatchee, you travel south along the Columbia River to Mattawa,
where premier vineyards populate the Wahluke Slope. Along this
WineTrail is Washington's leading destination winery—Cave B at
the Gorge. If you haven't been there, you are in for a just-what-the-
doctor-ordered magical getaway. In short, it's gorgeous.

Wenatchee-Quincy-Wilbur WineTrail

1 Chateau Faire Le Pont
Winery
2 Martin-Scott Winery

3 Saint Laurent Winery
4 White Heron Cellars
5 Cave B Estate Winery

6 Fox Estate Winery
7 Whitestone Winery

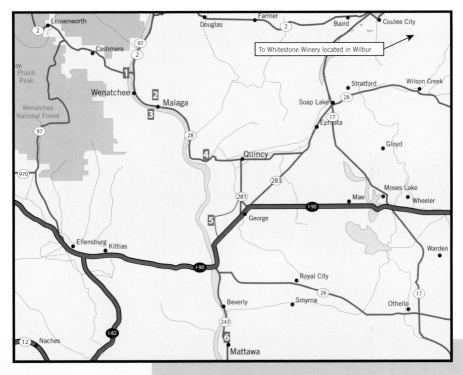

Region:	**North Central Washington Wine Country**
# of tasting rooms on tour:	**7**
Estimated # of days for tour:	**2 or 3**
Getting around:	**Car**
Key events:	❑ **Red Wine and Chocolate (mid-February) sponsored by the Columbia Cascade Winery Association. See www.columbiacascadewines.com for details.**
Tips:	❑ **Consider hiring a limousine service (e.g., Northwest Limousine 509-670-4952).**
Best:	❑ **Best Destination: Cave B Estate Winery** ❑ **Best Eats: Cave B Estate Winery** ❑ **Best View: Cave B Estate Winery, Saint Laurent Winery, and Martin-Scott Winery** ❑ **Best Picnicking: Cave B Estate Winery** ❑ **Best for Weddings: Cave B Estate Winery**

215

Chateau Faire Le Pont Winery

Wenatchee-based Chateau Faire Le Pont Winery is housed in a restored 1920s fruit packing warehouse. The restoration preserved the original hardwood-plank flooring and gently arching windows. Behind the wine bar, a mural by local artist Sarah Morgan depicts grapes growing amongst apple and cherry orchards of the Wenatchee Valley. The 6,000-square-foot winery easily holds 150 guests

for weddings, corporate events, class reunions, and wine-tasting geeks like me. A full-service kitchen supports its Vineyard Café, which serves up light and full fare. During the summer, a generous-sized patio offers a great place to relax and enjoy the view.

In short, Faire Le Pont is Wenatchee's destination winery.

The English translation of "Faire Le Pont" is "to bridge the gap." We're not sure what gap is being bridged, but it certainly makes sense that Wenatchee would sport a premium winery. After all, within a 100-mile radius you have premier vineyards in Lake Chelan, Wahluke Slope, and the Yakima Valley. Located next to the winery, an "educational vineyard" is a key component of Faire Le Pont's Adopt-a-Vine Club. Would-be vintners join the club to prune, pick, and crush an adopted vine. In this hands-on learning lab, you get to bottle your own wine.

The sources of Faire Le Pont winemaker Doug Brazil's fruit are the Alderdale and Mattawa growers of Yakima Valley. With this fruit, Doug produces a full slate of dry and sweet white wines as well as classic French-style red wines. Among other critically acclaimed wines, Doug's red blend "Confluence" has won high praise. This red gets its name from the winery's location near the meeting of the Wenatchee and Columbia rivers. When wine critics gush over their favorite wines, they often note the winemaker's attention to detail as the primary ingredient for making great wine. We're certain that Doug's 21-year background as a Navy helicopter pilot demanded attention to detail, and that ingrained attention is still paying off. Although young in wine years, Faire Le Pont will undoubtedly win many more awards, medals, and high praise well into the future.

CHATEAU FAIRE LE PONT WINERY
opened: 2004
winemaker(s): Doug Brazil
location: 389 Technology Center Way
Wenatchee, WA 98801-8117
phone: 509-667-WINE (9463)
web: www.fairelepont.net
e-mail: info@fairelepont.net
picnic area: Yes
gift shop: Yes
fee: Small tasting fee
hours: 11–6 Monday through Sunday, 11–8 Friday

DIRECTIONS: From US Hwy 2 east take the 2/97 exit toward Chelan. Turn right at the first light on Easy St. Turn left at the next light on E. Penny. Take the second right on Technology Center Way. Chateau Faire Le Pont is located at 389 Technology Center Way.

217

Martin-Scott Winery

Located above the Columbia River in east Wenatchee, Martin-Scott Winery enjoys a stunning view, one that easily qualifies as one of the top 10 in the state. Come for the wine, but stay for the view.

Mike and Judi Scott host guests in their downstairs tasting room and are often behind the bar introducing visitors to Martin-Scott wines. They make a cute

couple. While sipping their full-flavored reds and whites check out their oft-dry estate riesling, with its distinct apple taste.

Mike takes care of the agricultural side of the business by farming their 55-acre estate vineyard and fruit farm. Judi, along with her other tasks, manages the tasting room and coordinates events (of which there are many). With the chemistry and microbiology inherent in winemaking, Judy's work as a laboratory technician also comes in handy.

When visiting Martin-Scott, be sure to check out the banquet room with its oversized dining table and accompanying dining-room details. With the table's capacity to seat 20 guests, many a family and business has reserved the space for catered events.

The running of Martin-Scott Winery is a family affair. In addition to Mike and Judi, oldest son Tim Scott helps his dad manage the 55-acre farm. Youngest son Chris Scott pitches in with the marketing of their wines. Daughter-in-law Becky Scott is the artist-in-residence and is responsible for the beautiful wrought iron Martin-Scott sign at the winery's entrance. Even granddaughter Grace Scott gets in the act: "Grace's Gewürztraminer" bears her name.

MARTIN-SCOTT WINERY
opened: 2000
winemaker(s): Michael Scott
location: 3400 SE 10th Street
East Wenatchee, WA 98802
phone: 509-886-4596
web: www.martinscottwinery.com
e-mail: martinscott@martinscottwinery.com
picnic area: Yes
gift shop: No
fee: Complimentary wine tasting
hours: 12–5 Saturdays, or by appointment

BEST Views

DIRECTIONS: From SR-28 about 3 miles south of Wenatchee, turn North onto S. Nile Ave. Go .7 miles. Turn right (east) onto 8th St. SE and go 1 mile. Turn right (south) onto S. Union Ave. and continue .2 miles. Bear left (east) onto 10th St. SE and continue about 100 yards. Follow signs to Martin-Scott Winery on the right.

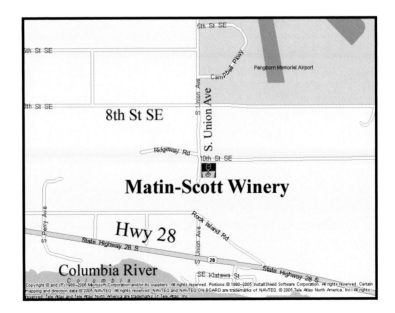

219

Saint Laurent Winery

The views from Saint Laurent Winery are truly stunning. So stunning that you'll need to remind yourself you're here for the wine. Still, if you didn't bring a picnic, make a mental note to bring food next time, so you can eat al fresco and take in the scenery.

An interesting fact about Saint Laurent Winery is that Laura Laurent-Mrachek is its horticulturist and her husband, Mike Mrachek, is the vintner. This great pairing has succeeded in growing 240 acres of amazing fruit and transforming

their wine grapes into award-winning wines 3,500 cases strong.

Visiting Saint Laurent is great anytime, but you can plan your tour to coincide with one of many events offered. For example, Saint Laurent hosts a "Dinner and a Movie Night" during the summer, which may pair barbecued chicken and cornbread with cabernet sauvignon while

watching *Walk the Line*. The winery's summer concert series showcases local bands performing with a backdrop of the Wenatchee Valley; it's nice to watch the valley fade as night sets in and the stars take over. During the summer, take time to stroll through the winery's European-style garden. When the weather gets cooler, many of the winery events shift to a rustic barn. For example, you can sip wine and enjoy the Apple Cup, toasty warm, with the Dawgs and the Cougs. But Saint Laurent's tasting room itself is one of the highlights of the visit. Housed in a Victorian-style house, the room is "cozy comfortable." Laura often takes off her horticultural hat to pour wine and entertain the winery's many visitors.

By the way, did you know that Saint Laurent is the patron saint of vintners and cooks? In the month of August, A.D. 25, Saint Laurent (aka Laurence, Laurent, Laurentius, Lawrence of Rome, Lorenzo) was roasted to death on a gridiron. Since then, cooks and vintners have claimed Saint Laurent as their patron saint. If you look closely at the Saint Laurent wine label, you will find a replica of the gridiron on which Saint Laurent was barbecued. Ouch. Yes, we know it's gruesome, but it does get you thinking about barbecued ribs to pair with Saint Laurent cabernet sauvignon.

SAINT LAURENT WINERY
winemaker(s): Craig Mitrakul
location: 4147 Hamlin Road
Malaga, WA 98828
phone: 509-888-9463
web: www.saintlaurent.net
e-mail: sarah@saintlaurent.net
picnic area: Yes
gift shop: Yes
fee: Small fee waived upon purchase
hours: Daily 12–5

Visitors at Saint Laurent tasting room

BEST Views

DIRECTIONS: From Wenatchee go south on S. Wenatchee Ave.—this will turn in to Malaga Alcoa Hwy. From the underpass go 4 miles and turn right on "West Malaga Rd—Three Lakes". Then go 1.2 miles and turn right on Hamlin Rd. After .7 miles, see address "4147 Hamlin Rd" and sign "Saint Laurent" on left. Tasting room is in the front of large brown building on left.
From east Wenatchee/Quincy, after crossing Columbia River Bridge follow signs towards Malaga (left at light, left on Marr St., right on S. Wenatchee Ave.), go 4 mi and turn right on "West Malaga Rd—Three Lakes". Then go 1.2 miles and turn right on Hamlin Rd. After .7 miles see address "4147 Hamlin Rd" and sign "Saint Laurent" on left. Tasting room is in front of large brown building on left.

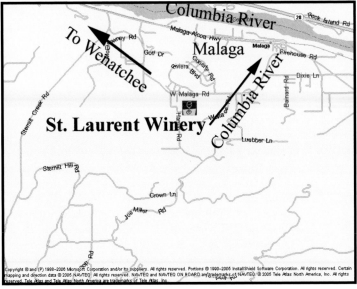

White Heron Cellars

Located in the ghost town of Trinidad, White Heron Cellars is the creation of Swiss-trained vintners Phyllis and Cameron Fries. The winery is about 1,000 feet above the Columbia River Gorge between Wenatchee and Quincy. If your wine travels include Cave B Estate Winery, then you will want to add White

Heron Cellars to your itinerary; it's a mere 30-minute drive away. Dry weather, the moderating influence of the Columbia River, the slope of the land, and the soil itself all conspire to create a unique *terroir* that's perfect for growing wine grapes.

As you enter the White Heron property, you're forgiven if you suddenly stop and fish for your camera. Perched on the hillside, the White Heron Cellars winery and the Fries' contemporary-style home pop out from the rest of the scenery. With acres of vineyard rows between your lens and the winery, you have a perfect picture moment.

Well over 6 feet tall, Cameron possesses a big, toothy smile and a deep voice to match his height. In the winemaking community, he's a bit of an iconoclast, using techniques he learned in Switzerland. For example, he doesn't believe in using fresh oak. He wants the wines to express the true taste of the grape rather than reflecting the taste of the oak. Most of White Heron's wines are estate wines and include cabernet sauvignon, cabernet franc, malbec, petit verdot, pinot noir, gamy, syrah, rousanne, and viognier. As you sample his rousanne, Cameron notes that it is more popular than viognier in the Rhone region of France, and he characterizes it as a "syrah in drag." His wines are refreshingly honest, devoid of the puckering power of tannins you find at other wineries.

Because their winery is off the beaten path, Cameron and Phyllis began hosting summer concert series, guest-chef nights, and shellfish festivals long before other wineries got in on the act. They also built a *Pétanque* court (a French game similar to bocce) and each summer they sponsor a *Pétanque* tournament at the winery. We told you White Heron Cellars is unique. Cameron is a self-described "stupid optimist," and we suspect that with the emergence of the surrounding wine industry, White Heron Cellars will become a popular stop along the North Central WineTrail.

Cameron S. Fries

WHITE HERON CELLARS
opened: 1986
winemaker(s): Phyllis and Cameron Fries
location: 10035 Stuhlmiller Road
Quincy, WA 98848
phone: 509-797-9463
web: www.whiteheronwine.com
e-mail: info@whiteheronwine.com
picnic area: Yes
gift shop: No
fee: Tasting fee may apply
hours: 11–6 Thursdays through Mondays

DIRECTIONS: Heading **south on SR-28** (from Wenatchee area) travel about 21 miles. Turn left onto Stuhlmiller Rd. NW and follow signs to White Heron Winery up the hill. From I-90, take exit 149 and go west on SR-28 about 8 miles. Turn right onto Stuhlmiller Rd NW and follow signs to White Heron Winery up the hill.

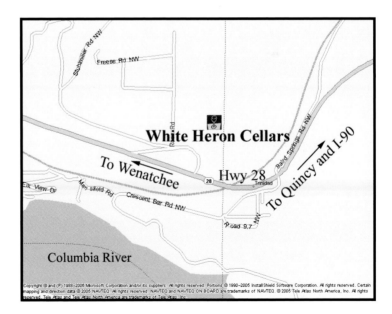

Cave B Estate Winery

Few Washington wineries can boast that they are a "destination winery." But Cave B Inn and Cave B Winery are in a position to brag. Most reviewers consider Cave B to be the no. 1 destination wine resort in the state—and for good reason.

Halfway between Spokane and Seattle, near Vantage, lies Cave B Inn and Cave B Winery. Just follow the signs to the Gorge Amphitheater off I-90. Once there, you will marvel at the stunning views of the Columbia River Gorge and the surrounding vineyard. The Inn's grand lobby, with its iron-turned chandeliers

hanging from the soaring ceiling, huge wrap-around fireplaces and eager staff at your service, will quickly squash any concerns you had about your getaway. Inside the Inn the critically acclaimed Tendrils Restaurant at SageCliffe offers elegant Northwest cuisine prepared by Fernando Divina. The menu includes suggested wine pairings for each course, always a nice touch for WineTrail travelers. Reservations are highly recommended.

If you are staying at the Inn for any length of time, you may want to turn off the flat-screen plasma TV and get off the all-too-comfortable bed, with its 300-threadcount Egyptian cotton linens, and head for the spa. Whether it's a massage, a facial or getting your nails done, you will be pampered and made to feel like a wet noodle—just in time to hit the tasting room.

The Cave B Winery tasting room features the wonderfully rich, full-bodied wines of Cave B as well as its second label, SageCliffe. Located in the RoundHouse, the Cave B tasting room houses a 17-foot-long tasting bar, handcrafted from used French oak wine barrel staves crafted by highly skilled local artists. It's a comfortable space in which to relax and sample Rusty Figgins' (of Walla Walla fame) reds and whites, both the Cave B and SageCliffe vintages. If they are still in stock, you might experience the chardonnay, semillon, semillon ice, cabernet sauvignon, merlot, and a Bordeaux-style blend called "Cuvée de Soleil."

CAVE B ESTATE WINERY
opened: 2002
winemaker(s): Berle "Rusty" Figgins
location: 348 Silica Road NW
Quincy, WA 98848-9468
phone: 509-785-3500
web: www.caveb.com
e-mail: info@caveb.com
picnic area: Yes
gift shop: Yes
fee: Complimentary wine tasting
hours: Daily 11–5:30 from January through March;
11–5:30 Sunday through Thursday, 11–6 Friday and
Saturday, from April through December

BEST Destination, eats, views, picnicking and weddings

DIRECTIONS: From I-90 take exit 143 and head west toward Columbia River on Road U SW [Silica Rd SW]. Continue for about 5.5 miles and follow signs to Cave B Estate Winery at 348 Silica Rd NW.

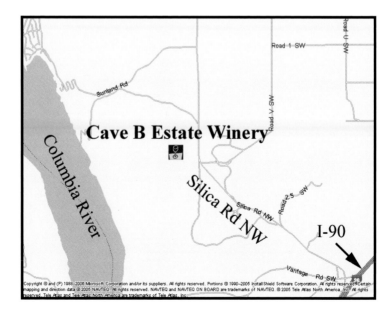

Fox Estate Winery

In the science of agriculture, diversification is a good thing, especially if you are dependent upon apples. Such was the situation in the late '70s when Jerry Fox decided to convert some of his apple acreage to vineyards, beginning

with riesling and gewürztraminer varietals. Little did Jerry know then that his Mattawa location would one day become a designated American Viticulture Area (AVA) with the enviable "Wahluke Slope" moniker. His prized grapes thrive in the sun-drenched arid slopes of Saddle Mountain. Across the highway from his winery and tasting room is Chateau Ste. Michelle's famed Indian Wells Vineyard, bordered by Milbrandt Vineyards. Talk about prized real estate!

Jerry Fox is quick to point out that without the marketing muscle and vision of Chateau Ste. Michelle, the Washington wine industry and his wine venture would be dormant, or nearly so. Nevertheless, with the emergence of Cave B not too far to the north and plenty of "206ers" moving to the eastern side of the Columbia River, Jerry can envision a day in the not-too-distant future when a dozen wineries line the highway near Fox Estate Winery. And with that comes the infrastructure to meet tourist needs: hotels, restaurants, and water slides.

With more than 250 acres of wine grapes, Fox Estate Winery manages to sell more grape juice to other wine producers, but it reserves enough to produce a reported 8,000 cases under the Fox Estate Winery label. Fortunately, with more than 600 acres of apples to process, Jerry has the labor and the production facilities to take on the challenge. In addition, Fox Estate Winery is a family affair, with son Don managing the apple/wine production facility and daughter Julie taking on marketing initiatives from her Walla Walla home. Currently, the Fox Estate Winery tasting room is housed in a doublewide situated next to the winery's huge processing facility. However, it is Jerry's intention to one day build a new tasting room at the entrance to the property. No doubt it will lure many a Western Washington visitor to stop and discover Fox Estate wine and perhaps decide to resettle in nearby Desert Aire.

FOX ESTATE WINERY
opened: 1981
winemaker(s): Jerry Fox and consultant winemaker
location: 24962 Highway 243 South
Mattawa, WA 99349-2009
phone: 509-932-5818
web: www.foxestatewinery.com
e-mail: support@foxestatewinery.com
picnic area: No
gift shop: Yes
fee: Complimentary wine tasting
hours: 10–5 Monday through Friday, 12–4 Saturday
and Sunday, summer and holidays

DIRECTIONS: From I-90, take exit 137 onto SR-26 (Wanapum Dam / Richland) and travel 1.1 miles. Continue straight on SR-243 and continue 14.7 miles and look for Fox Estate Winery at 24962 Hwy 243 on the right.
From Mattawa town center, go west on 24-SW Rd [Government Rd] for less than a mile. Turn left on SR-243 and arrive at 24962 Hwy 243 S. Fox Estate Winery's tasting room is next to the large production facility.

Whitestone Winery

Washington State is full of surprises when it comes to wine. Take exhibit A for example—Whitestone Winery. The reason? Who would have guessed that you can find a winery in Wilbur, Washington, let alone that they use their own grapes to make wine? And, if you are trying to figure out where Wilbur is, you're not alone. Wilbur is located just south of Roosevelt Lake and about halfway

Whitestone's converted gas station

between Coulee City and Davenport along US-2. It's the home of Wild Goose Bill Days held the second Saturday in June. You mean you haven't experienced Wild Goose Bill Days?

Walter and Judy Haig planted Whitestone Winery's vineyard in 1992 with the help of Washington State University. WSU researchers knew that the area was the perfect fusion of climate and soil for premium wine grapes. Historically, nearby Whitestone Rock was the site of one of the largest vineyards in Eastern Washington. Then in 1941, the newly built Grand Coulee Dam put the vineyard underwater and created Roosevelt Lake. Nearly fifty years later the Haigs turned back the clock with the planting of merlot, cabernet sauvignon, and syrah.

In 2005, Whitestone Winery opened in a renovated gas station in the heart of Wilbur. There you can experience Whitestone's big red wines and visit with one of the Haig family members pouring and providing background about their estate wines. Their son, Michael Haig, is the winemaker and vineyard manager and welcomes the opportunity to showcase the Whitestone Rock flavor profile. It's a true family affair from tending the vineyard, harvesting, crushing, bottling, and labeling. There you can "filler up" but instead of premium gas, it's premium Bordeaux-style reds.

Whitestone Winery's team

WHITESTONE WINERY
opened: 2005
winemaker(s): Walter Haig and Michael Haig
location: 115 NE Main Street
Wilbur, WA 99185
phone: 509-647-5325
web: www.whitestonewinery.com
e-mail: msh@whitestonewinery.com
picnic area: No
gift shop: No
fee: Complimentary wine tasting
hours: 10–6 Thursdays through Saturdays

DIRECTIONS: From US-2 heading east or west through Wilbur town center find Whitestone Winery on north side of E. Main St. [US-2]. Look for the converted gas station and Whitestone sign.

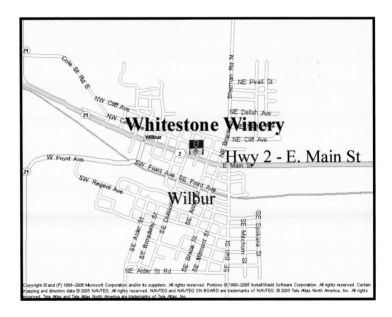

Lake Chelan South Shore
WineTrail

Summer concert at Tsillan Cellars, Lake Chelan

Most visitors come into Lake Chelan via Highway 97-Alt and are surprised to find rows of vineyards climbing up the hillside from the Lake. One such vineyard is home to Tsillan (pronounced "Chelan") Cellars, where the Italian-style architecture and distinct clock tower host a steady flow of WineTrail enthusiasts. They are there for the great wine, outdoor concerts, and marvelous restaurant. But don't leave the South Shore without visiting other nearby wineries—from delicious pinot noir to delightful chardonnay, many feature estate-grown grapes.

Lake Chelan South Shore WineTrail

1 Chelan Estate Vineyards & Winery   **2** Nefarious Cellars   **4** Tsillan Cellars

3 Tunnel Hill Winery

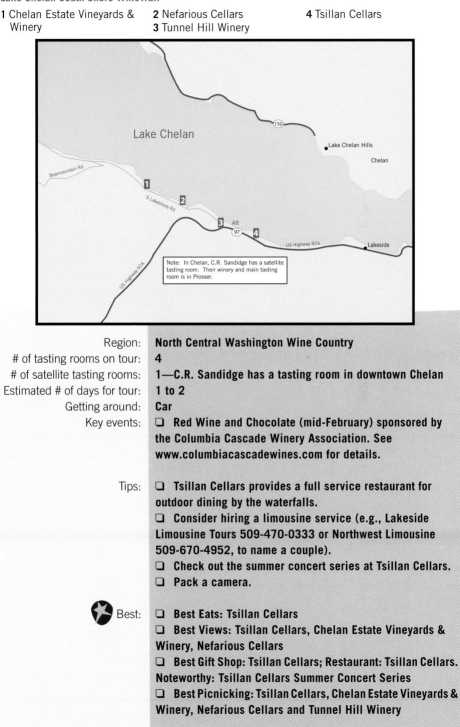

Note: In Chelan, C.R. Sandidge has a satellite tasting room. Their winery and main tasting room is in Prosser.

Region:	**North Central Washington Wine Country**
# of tasting rooms on tour:	**4**
# of satellite tasting rooms:	**1—C.R. Sandidge has a tasting room in downtown Chelan**
Estimated # of days for tour:	**1 to 2**
Getting around:	**Car**
Key events:	❑ **Red Wine and Chocolate (mid-February) sponsored by the Columbia Cascade Winery Association. See www.columbiacascadewines.com for details.**
Tips:	❑ **Tsillan Cellars provides a full service restaurant for outdoor dining by the waterfalls.** ❑ **Consider hiring a limousine service (e.g., Lakeside Limousine Tours 509-470-0333 or Northwest Limousine 509-670-4952, to name a couple).** ❑ **Check out the summer concert series at Tsillan Cellars.** ❑ **Pack a camera.**
Best:	❑ **Best Eats: Tsillan Cellars** ❑ **Best Views: Tsillan Cellars, Chelan Estate Vineyards & Winery, Nefarious Cellars** ❑ **Best Gift Shop: Tsillan Cellars; Restaurant: Tsillan Cellars. Noteworthy: Tsillan Cellars Summer Concert Series** ❑ **Best Picnicking: Tsillan Cellars, Chelan Estate Vineyards & Winery, Nefarious Cellars and Tunnel Hill Winery**

Chelan Estate Vineyards & Winery

The popular belief is that it is simply too hot to grow pinot noir in Eastern Washington, particularly in the area around Lake Chelan. However, because of an interesting meteorological phenomenon known as a microclimate, Bob Broderick and Rich Nestor of Chelan Estate Vineyards & Winery have discovered fertile ground for pinot noir on the south shore of Lake Chelan. The

lake provides cooler summers and warmer winters. Thus, of the 14 acres of grapes Broderick and Nestor cultivate, 65 percent is pinot noir and the remainder is chardonnay.

Broderick and Nestor must be doing something right. The lighter-colored pinot noir is deceptively elegant and stylish—a rich reward for these growers/winemakers, considering this grape demands more time and attention than most. Chelan Estate's 2003 pinot noir has received high praise from wine critics.

From the deck of Chelan Estate Vineyards & Winery, you enjoy a stunning view of Lake Chelan. Pack a picnic, because you'll want to make a leisurely day of it. Your most difficult decision may be whether to uncork the Columbia Valley chardonnay, the merlot, or the estate pinot noir. Chelan Estate's chardonnay proves amazing thanks to the use of super-sized oak barrels called puncheons. Aging in these puncheons translates into a very fruit-forward white wine that is the perfect accompaniment to grilled halibut. You might end up doing what I did: uncorking both a white and a red. The view from Chelan Estate's doublewide manufactured home just got even better. Cheers.

Rich Nestor

CHELAN ESTATE VINEYARDS & WINERY
opened: 2004
winemaker(s): Bob Broderick and Rich Nestor
location: 755 S. Lakeshore Road
Chelan, WA 98816-9228
phone: 509-682-5454
e-mail: chelanestatewinery@verizon.net
picnic area: Yes
gift shop: No
fee: $3 refundable with purchase
hours: 11–6 Saturday, 11–5 Sunday; call for
weekday appointment

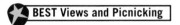 **BEST Views and Picnicking**

DIRECTIONS: From Chelan, take US-97 Alt (west) and go about 4 miles. Bear right onto SR-971 [South Lakeshore Rd]. Turn left (south) at winery sign and go up driveway.

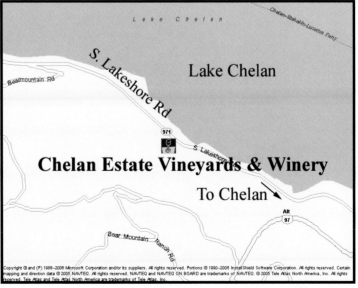

Nefarious Cellars

Hang around Lake Chelan a day or two and you might overhear someone mention "that cute couple from Oregon" in reference to Nefarious Winery. At the local information center, your question about Nefarious will be greeted with a resounding, "Oh, you must visit that winery. The owners are from Oregon and they are a lot of fun." While it is a fact that Dean and Heather Neff's last stop

was a five-year stint in Oregon, the reality is they are both originally from Lake Chelan. They may be Chelan born, but when it comes to winemaking, they're Oregon trained.

A visit to the winery reveals that Heather creates the white wines, and Dean makes the reds. In Heather's world, fruit is separated quickly from the skins

Patio view of Lake Chelan from Nefarious Winery

and bathed in stainless steel. In Dean's world of red, skins and pulp, touched by oak, commingle for long periods. A sample of "Heather's Consequence" (a blend of 90 percent sauvignon blanc and 10 percent riesling) will encourage you to take your glass outside to the patio and enjoy the magnificent view of Lake Chelan. However, as you progress to the reds, Dean's jammy and tannin-tamed "Wahluke Slope" syrah will have you wanting New York strip steak to pair with this wine. Whether you are a red fan or a white aficionado, Nefarious wines will delight.

A recently completed red-and-gray dwelling houses both the wine production facility and the living quarters for Dean, Heather, and their new addition to the family and future cellar rat, son George. The walkway leads to a generous door that opens to a spacious tasting room. The tasting room takes advantage of a spectacular view of Lake Chelan and the surrounding hills. Outside the tasting room is a large patio, complete with Adirondack-style deck furniture—a perfect setting in which to uncork a bottle of Nefarious and take in the view. The view itself is clearly among the top 10 in Washington.

Overall a swirl and taste of the Neffs' wine provides a wickedly good experience. It's simply Nefarious.

Dean and Heather Neff

NEFARIOUS CELLARS
opened: 2005
winemaker(s): Dean and Heather Neff
location: 495 South Lakeshore Road
Chelan, WA 98816
phone: 509-682-9505
web: www.nefariouscellars.com
e-mail: getsome@nefariouscellars.com
picnic area: Yes
gift shop: No
fee: $2 tasting fee
hours: Daily 11–6 from May through October;
11–6 on Saturday and Sunday from November
through April

 BEST Views and picnicking

DIRECTIONS: From Chelan, take US-97 Alt (southwest) and go about 4 miles. Bear right (northwest) onto SR-971 [S. Lakeshore Rd]. Continue about .8 mile—Nefarious Cellars is on the left up the hill. Follow signs to parking lot.
From Wenatchee, take US-97 Alt (northeast) to Lake Chelan. As you come down the hill to Lake Chelan, go left at SR-971 [S. Lakeshore Rd]. Continue about .8 mile. Winery and vineyard are on the left up the hill. Follow signs to winery.

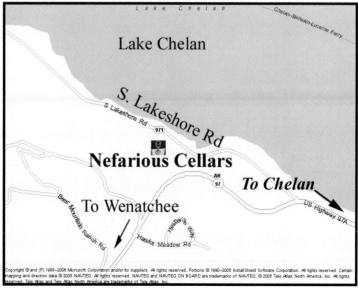

Tunnel Hill Winery

The structure that houses Tunnel Hill Winery is made of granite, harvested from the excavation of nearby Knapps Tunnel. At first glance, you could easily picture this building in the Normandy region of France. However, a quick look around at nearby Lake Chelan and the surrounding hills reminds you that you

are smack dab in the middle of Washington's vacationland. The slopes above the winery have been producing award-winning apples for generations, but now these hills are the estate vineyards for Tunnel Hill. Rows of pinot noir, riesling, and syrah grapes stripe the hillside.

Tunnel Hill's owner and winemaker, Denny Evans, is producing small lots of estate pinot noir. Making fewer than 500 cases of wine annually requires Denny to wear many hats: grape grower, winemaker, production manager, head of marketing, and chief bottle washer. However, understanding Tunnel Hill Winery is appreciating the road that brought Denny here, one man's version of the phoenix myth.

If you have been lucky enough to have seen the Emmy-nominated documentary *Broken Limbs*, you might recognize that a "star" of the show is Denny himself. Guy Evans, Denny's son, made *Broken Limbs* to explain the sudden demise of Washington's apple industry and to highlight how this downturn has affected families in the Chelan-Wenatchee area. Denny's orchard was once one of the largest apple-producing farms in the state. Seemingly overnight, it fell on hard times, the result of foreign competition.

When 6'4" Denny is pouring, you raise your glass. He locks you in with his blue eyes and patiently explains the winemaking style and vision of Tunnel Hill. Being a "dirt guy," he is most comfortable being in the fields. However, reinventing yourself comes easily when you are a quick study, and Denny has taken advantage of Washington's rich educational resources and its community of supportive winemakers and viticulturists. Now he can proudly state on his website, "On the shores of Lake Chelan, in a cool, quiet cellar under the hillside, we create handcrafted wines using age-old techniques." From the ashes of burning applewood, Tunnel Hill Winery has risen.

WineTrail Note: If your group needs lodging while visiting the Chelan area, check out Denny's FarmHouse at www.sunshineorchards.com. It's easy to imagine that this would be the ideal place to explore the pairing of Tunnel Hill pinot noir with apples and pears from nearby orchards.

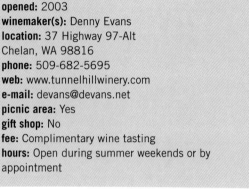

TUNNEL HILL WINERY
opened: 2003
winemaker(s): Denny Evans
location: 37 Highway 97-Alt
Chelan, WA 98816
phone: 509-682-5695
web: www.tunnelhillwinery.com
e-mail: devans@devans.net
picnic area: Yes
gift shop: No
fee: Complimentary wine tasting
hours: Open during summer weekends or by
appointment

BEST Picnicking

DIRECTIONS: From Chelan, drive west on US-97 Alt along the north shore of Lake Chelan. Go 3.9 miles and as the road turns left the Tunnel Hill Winery is located on the left side of the road next to the fruit and vegetable stand. Arrive at 37 US-97 Alt.

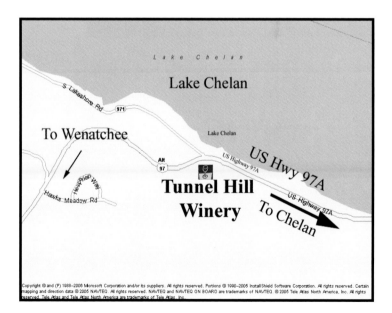

Tsillan Cellars

Tsillan Cellars is the crown jewel of a growing number of young wineries that have popped up in the Chelan-Manson area in recent years. With spectacular views of Lake Chelan as well as the scenic mountains in the distance, there is little doubt that Tsillan (pronounced "Chelan") Cellars is the destination winery on this area's WineTrail.

Dr. Robert Jankelson, a dentist and the owner of Tsillan Cellars, has a special love for Italy, having made 47 separate sojourns to that country over the years. As you turn off the highway and make your way up the gentle hill to Tsillan's

135-acre estate, you spy the Tuscan-inspired architecture of the winery and tasting room. The majestic 35-foot bell tower houses a 650-pound cast-bronze bell. The surrounding vineyard is composed of more than 40 acres of syrah, merlot, malbec, chardonnay, pinot grigio, riesling, and gewürztraminer. Not far from the tasting room is a spectacular amphitheater, where live musical performances are hosted during the summer. Three waterfalls surround the island stage, creating a sense of harmony and offering a spectacular backdrop for the performers.

This sense of elegance continues into the tasting room itself, which features a wine bar stretching 40 feet in length. No need to rub elbows with strangers here. Behind the bar is plenty of cellar space to house many of the 7,000 cases of wine produced annually. It is clear that the Tsillan goal is to sell as much of its wine as possible directly from its tasting room rather than at wine shops and grocery stores. Dr. Jankelson and his staff want you to experience the beauties of life—be it food, music, architecture, lovely grounds, or the wine itself—in a setting reminiscent of Italy's Lake Como. To this end, tasting room manager Lupe Peterson and her staff possess excellent training and patient smiles as they respond to myriad visitors wondering how to pronounce "gewürztraminer."

This is a destination winery where you can easily while away an afternoon tasting great wine, strolling through the well-manicured grounds, exploring the vineyards (and noting that a rose bush is planted at the head of each row), and most certainly uncorking a bottle of Tsillan Cellars wine to enjoy with a picnic.

TSILLAN CELLARS
opened: 2004
winemaker(s): Peter Devison
location: 3875 Highway 97 Alt, PO Box 1759
Chelan, WA 98816
phone: 509-682-9463
web: www.tsillancellars.com
e-mail: info@tsillancellars.com
picnic area: Yes
gift shop: Yes
fee: Small tasting fee
hours: Daily 11–7 summer, 11–5 winter; tours of
winery and tasting room conducted twice daily at
1 and 3

BEST Eats, views, gift shop, restaurants and Picnicking

DIRECTIONS: From Chelan, head west on US-97 Alt about 3.5 miles. The winery is on the left up
the hill.
From Wenatchee take US-97 Alt toward Entiat/Chelan, proceed 33 miles north to the shores of
Lake Chelan. The Tuscan style winery will be on the right at 3875 US-97 Alt.

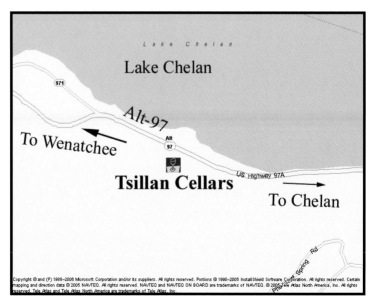

Lake Chelan North Shore
WineTrail

Benson Vineyards at Lake Chelan

Few places in Washington can boast that they offer great places to eat, stay and sample wine, but Lake Chelan easily meets these needs. The North Shore is the perfect place to recreate and check out outstanding wines from a variety of wineries. Your WineTrail excursion can start with outdoor bistro fare and a white blend at Vin du Lac, and end at Wapato Point Cellars with a hearty steak and cabernet sauvignon. In between, you will experience award-winning wines and spectacular views. Speaking of which, the view from Benson Estate Vineyards and Winery is clearly top ten in the state. See if you agree. Because this WineTrail also includes Lost River Winery, 75 miles to the north in Winthrop, budget at least two days for this tour.

Lake Chelan North Shore WineTrail

1 Vin du Lac Winery
2 Lake Chelan Winery
3 Benson Vineyards Estate
  Winery

4 Balsamroot Winery and
  Vineyard
5 Tildio Winery

6 Chelangr'La Winery
7 Wapato Point Cellars
8 Lost River Winery

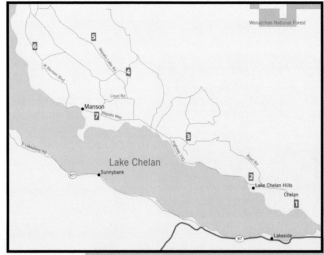

Region:	**North Central Washington Wine Country**
# of tasting rooms on tour:	**8**
Estimated # of days for tour:	**2 to 3**
Getting around:	**Car**
Key events:	❏ **Red Wine and Chocolate (mid-February) sponsored by the Columbia Cascade Winery Association. See www.columbiacascadewines.com for details.**
Tips:	❏ **Vin du Lac Winery, Lake Chelan Winery and Wapato Point Cellars offer food service.** ❏ **Consider hiring a limousine service (e.g., Lakeside Limousine Tours 509-470-0333 or Northwest Limousine 509-670-4952, to name a couple).** ❏ **Plenty of choices for eating and sleeping in Manson and nearby Chelan, however, make reservations well in advance—especially around Memorial Day, July 4th and Labor Day Weekends.** ❏ **Take Lady of the Lake to Stehekin for a great escape.**

 Best:
❏ **Best Eats: Vin du Lac, Lake Chelan Winery, and Wapato Point Cellars**
❏ **Best Views: Benson Vineyards Estate Winery and Tildio Winery**
❏ **Best Gift Shop: Lake Chelan Winery**
❏ **Best Picnicking: Benson Vineyards Estate Winery, Vin du Lac Winery and Tildio Winery**

241

Vin du Lac Winery

Vin du Lac, which is French for "wine of the lake," is the creation of Larry Lehmbecker and Michaela (Micki) Markusson. After visiting Paris and the French countryside, and venturing to Lake Chelan innumerable times, they decided to take the plunge and launch Vin du Lac Winery in 1998.

Larry and Micki figured that if you can't be in Europe, you might as well re-create it, and that's exactly what they did with the establishment of Vin du Lac. With its eye-pleasing yellows and striped awning, the Vin du Lac tasting room has the look and feel of a French countryside bistro. When the weather's warm, visitors can enjoy the outdoor patio and order from a menu with a decidedly French and Vietnamese slant. A certain joie de vivre is likely to come over you as you stroll through the surrounding orchards and vineyards—especially if you're toting a glass of one of Larry's critically acclaimed reds or whites.

We don't often go out of our way to comment on wine labels, but with Vin du Lac, we make an exception. Its whimsical labels are the creation of Lisa Pettit, a Seattle-based designer known for her carefree designs that often portray stick figures enjoying life—bicycling, kayaking, and picnicking. As WineTrail enthusiasts know, you can look at an entire wall of wines at the local grocery store, but very few wine bottles stand out. Thanks to Lisa Pettit, that is not the case with Vin du Lac. Her award-winning designs help separate Vin du Lac from the throng.

The old orchard farmhouse that now serves as the winery's tasting room offers a relaxed space in which to enjoy Vin du Lac's whites, sweet whites, and reds. The names chosen for the wines demonstrate the passion that Larry and Micki have put into each vintage. With names such as "Grisant" (French for "exhilarating") for their pinot gris, "Les Amis" for their riesling, and "Red Café" for their cabernet sauvignon, it's clear the couple wants the drinker to experience and remember their wines as a signature moment. Larry is a self-described *vigneron*, or vine grower, and he excels at blending small lots of hand-picked grapes from different vineyards to meet his tasting standards.

Serene and romantic surroundings, a shimmering lake below you, and great wines to pair with delectable bistro fare: This is Larry Lehmbecker and Michaela Markusson's vision for celebrating the joy of living.

VIN DU LAC WINERY
opened: 1998
winemaker(s): Larry Lehmbecker
location: 105 Hwy 150
Chelan, WA 98816-9505
phone: 509-682-2882
web: www.vindulac.com
e-mail: info@vindulac.com
picnic area: Yes
gift shop: Yes
fee: Complimentary wine tasting
hours: Tastings/bistro 11:30–6 Friday through
Sunday, retail shop daily 11:30–5 from October
through March; daily 11–7 April through September

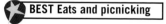

BEST Eats and picnicking

DIRECTIONS: The winery is located within the city limits of Chelan, .5 miles northwest of downtown off of Hwy 150 [Chelan-Manson Hwy]. Take a left at Spader Bay Drive, across from No-See-Um Rd, and drive up to the bright yellow buildings.

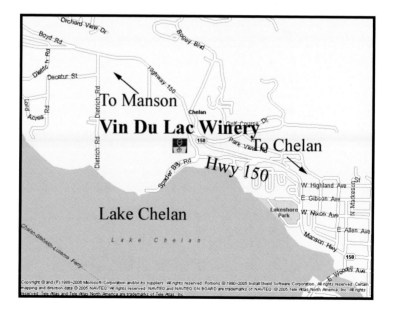

Lake Chelan Winery

Lake Chelan Winery distinguishes itself on many fronts. First, WineTrail enthusiasts might be interested to know that Lake Chelan Winery was the first of its kind in the Lake Chelan area. Since 1998, Lake Chelan Winery has been serving premium wines from its Chelan-Manson Highway location. Second, its tasting room is located in what was the last privately owned apple-packing operation in Chelan. This might surprise you when you visit the 3,000-square-foot tasting room with its generously sized gift shop. The transformation from packing shed to tasting room is nothing short of spectacular. Third, Lake Chelan Winery is in the top 10 in the gift shop category. We're not talking about the sheer number of items for sale (there are plenty), but the quality of the merchandise.

The winery also distinguishes itself with a wine garden situated next to the winery. During the summer, the winery features a nightly barbecue in the Vineyard. You can pick up a bottle of Lake Chelan wine and order up baby back pork ribs, chicken breasts, salmon, bratwurst or hot dogs (for the kids) and side of corn on the cob, coleslaw, or baked beans. Get ready to go through a pile of napkins devouring this barbecue, or simply jump in the lake afterward to wash away that barbecue sauce.

Bobbi and Steve Kludt are co-owners of Lake Chelan Winery, along with Spencer Bell and John and Dawn Abbott. To assist with winemaking, Ray Sandidge (of C.R. Sandidge Winery fame) acts as consultant winemaker. Complimentary wine tasting provides visitors with a taste-bud tour of the winery's chardonnay, muscat, pinot noir, syrah, gewürztraminer, cabernet sauvignon, and a luscious red blend called "Storm Mountain Red," composed of pinot noir, syrah, and small doses of cabernet franc and cabernet sauvignon. Note the prevalence of pinot noir. You find an increasing number of wineries in the Lake Chelan area using locally grown pinot noir grapes. It remains to be seen how the Lake Chelan pinot noirs measure up to the great pinots produced in the Willamette Valley.

By the way, if the name "Kludt" sounds familiar, it may be because Steve and Bobbi's son, Jonathon Kludt, is the winemaker for Wapato Point Cellars, located a few miles down the road in Manson.

LAKE CHELAN WINERY
opened: 1998
winemaker(s): Ray Sandidge
location: 3519 Chelan-Manson Highway (SR-150)
Chelan, WA 98816-0000
phone: 509-687-9463
web: www.lakechelanwinery.com
e-mail: lakechelanwinery@verizon.net
picnic area: Yes
gift shop: Yes
fee: Complimentary wine tasting
hours: 11–8:30 from May through October; 11–5
from November through April

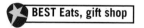
BEST Eats, gift shop

DIRECTIONS: From Chelan, head northwest toward Manson on SR-150 [Manson Hwy] for about 4.5 miles. The winery is on the right at 3519 SR-150.
From Manson head toward Chelan on SR-150 going southeast. The winery is on the left at 3519 SR-150 in the historic Harding Packing Shed.

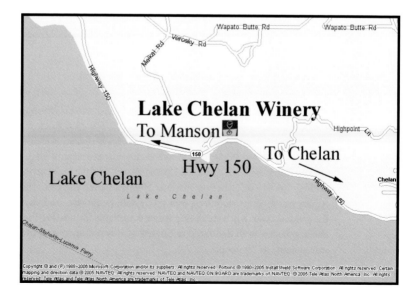

245

Benson Vineyards Estate Winery

The name is important: Benson Vineyards Estate Winery. No other winery in the Lake Chelan area can boast a production of 100 percent estate wines. Located on Lake Chelan's North Shore, the Benson 30-acre vineyard has the

look of northern Italy with its hills, tall spindly trees, terra-cotta homes and deep blues of the pristine lake below.

Although the winery is relatively new (established in 2005), the vineyards began much earlier. The Bensons knew that to be true vintners, they needed to know the land first. To this day, they require that all their staff—tasting room personnel included—work the vineyard during the year pruning, picking, and getting dirt under their fingernails.

Interestingly, the land area apportioned to growing grapes in the Lake Chelan Valley is smaller than other American Viticultural Areas in Washington. However, Lake Chelan has something other viticultural areas lack; namely, infrastructure. There are plenty of places to eat, sleep, and recreate in Lake Chelan. The Bensons obviously have a good thing going.

When the Bensons note on their website that their wine is "from our family to yours," they're not kidding. The entire family gets in on the act, with son Scott assuming the role of winemaker and the parents managing the tasting room and other day-to-day operations. The new facility for tasting and storing wine offers a stunning exterior view of Lake Chelan as well as a unique interior view of the facility's lower level, where as many as 500 oak barrels can rest. This is where the winery produces its viognier, pinot gris, syrah, sangiovese, and chardonnay. On the ground floor, a private tasting room is available for hosting functions. There's also a separate room dedicated to catered sit-down dinners that can comfortably seat as many as 25 people.

Benson's new tasting room under construction

BENSON VINEYARDS ESTATE WINERY
opened: 2005
winemaker(s): Scott Benson
location: 754 Winesap Avenue
Manson, WA 98831-9581
phone: 509-687-0313
web: www.bensonvineyards.com
e-mail: info@bensonvineyards.com
picnic area: Yes
gift shop: No
fee: Complimentary wine tasting
hours: Daily 11–5 in season

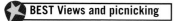

BEST Views and picnicking

DIRECTIONS: From Chelan, head northwest on SR-150 [Manson Hwy] for about 2.5 miles. Turn right (northeast) onto Winesap Ave. and go about .5 miles up the hill. Follow signs to winery. **From Manson**, head southwest on Hwy 150 and turn onto Winesap Ave. Go about .5 miles up the hill. Follow signs to winery. Arrive 754 Winesap Ave.

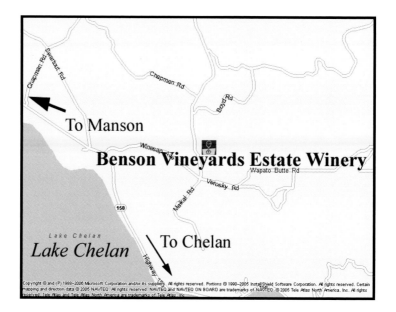

Balsamroot Winery and Vineyard

As you drive up Ivan Morse Road in Manson, you have the beauty of Lake Chelan behind you and the promise of a new winery before you. You know you've arrived at Balsamroot when you see the yellow-logo-emblazoned SUV parked at the entrance. A 2006 start-up, Balsamroot Vineyard and Winery is the creation of Don and Judy Phelps. Don's background as an engineer comes in handy nurturing their 4-acre vineyard. Judy's mathematical mind (she's a

biostatistician) is often exercised in the science of winemaking. She can readily tell you that 30 tons of grapes translate into 2,000 cases of wine.

A visit with Don and Judy quickly dispels any notion that a mathematician and an engineer are devoid of passion. As you swirl and sip their chardonnay, viognier, riesling, syrah, cabernet sauvignon, and "Ivan the Red" blend, you can't help but notice that they poured their collective hearts into the creation of these wines.

If time permits, you can relax on the outside deck (hopefully with a glass of wine in hand) and enjoy the view of the backyard hillside. During the spring, the native arrowleaf balsamroot wildflower is in its full yellow splendor. If you notice strange little animals scurrying around the dirt-encrusted hillside, please don't be concerned that you've imbibed too much wine. Those critters are a colony of marmots that entertain visitors throughout the day.

BALSAMROOT WINERY AND VINEYARD
opened: 2006
winemaker(s): Judy Phelps
location: 300 Ivan Morse Road
Manson, WA 98831
phone: 509-687-3000
web: www.balsomrootwinery.com
e-mail: info@balsomrootwinery.com
picnic area: Yes
gift shop: No
fee: $3 tasting fee for 6 tastes
hours: Daily 12–6

Don and Judy Phelps (l to r) with tasting room assistant

DIRECTIONS: From Chelan follow SR-150 towards Manson. Take a right at Mill Bay Casino onto Wapato Lake Rd. Ivan Morse Rd is the second right. Look for winery sign on right.

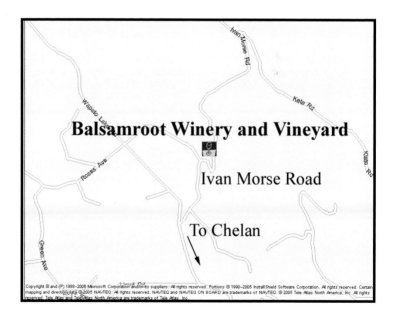

Balsamroot Winery and Vineyard

Ivan Morse Road

To Chelan

Tildio Winery

It's not unusual for friends and neighbors to stop by and spend the afternoon drinking wine, munching on cheese and assorted fruit, and yakking with Tildio Winery owners Milum and Katy Perry. The shaded patio offers an inviting place to relax and enjoy the view of nearby Roses Lake. Here, the sounds of laughter,

uncorking wine bottles, and Katy asking what wine you wish to try next is the order of the day. The fact is, Milum and Katy pay as much loving attention to their guests as they do their vintages.

Both Milum and Katy cut their winemaking teeth in California before they ventured north in 2000 to stake a claim in the burgeoning Washington wine industry. They named their winery Tildio, which is the Spanish word for killdeer, a shorebird that breeds in large numbers in the Perrys' 8-acre vineyard. Having the vineyard gives them control, from vine bud to bottling, and allows Katy to exercise her degree in enology and viticulture from the University of California at Davis. Yes, the art of winemaking is crucial, but science spells the difference between acceptable and outstanding.

Pack a picnic for your visit to Tildio and budget time to visit with the Perrys. If weather permits, enjoy Tildio's chardonnay, viognier, malbec (our favorite), cabernet sauvignon, merlot, and zinfandel out on the patio. But even with a foot of snow outside, pack a picnic anyway. You're going to enjoy your visit with Milum and Katy and get to know their red and white offerings.

TILDIO WINERY
opened: 2000
winemaker(s): Milum and Katy Perry
location: 70 East Wapato Lake Road
Manson, WA 98831
phone: 509-687-8463
web: www.tildio.com
e-mail: milum@tildio.com
picnic area: Yes
gift shop: Yes
fee: $2 tasting fee refunded with purchase
hours: Daily 12–7 in summer, 12–5 weekends in winter

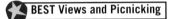 **BEST Views and Picnicking**

DIRECTIONS: Located on the scenic Manson Scenic Loop Rd. **From Chelan**, head northwest on SR-150. Go about 5 miles and turn right onto East Wapato Lake Rd. Arrive 70 E. Wapato Lake Rd in Manson across from Roses Lake.

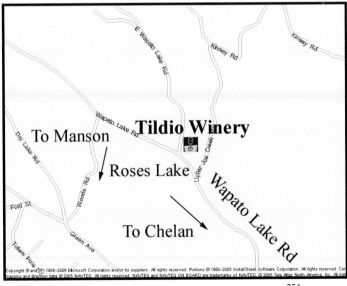

Chelangr'La Winery

Located in the town of Manson, Chelangr'La Winery is one of the smallest wineries in the Lake Chelan Valley, which makes perfect sense with this winery's emphasis on "quality above quantity." Jim Berg is Chelangr'La's owner/winemaker and is responsible for the eye-popping label and unusual name for

the winery. But if you visit the Lake Chelan Valley for any length of time, perhaps it does feel like Chelangr'La.

Jim offers a combination of berry wines and classic wines such as chardonnay, merlot, and cabernet franc, and christens them with high-falutin' names such as "Grandpa's Dirty Belly" gewürztraminer, "Very Berry Razz," and "Red Ink" merlot. For a winery started in 2005, this is an ambitious list of wines to offer, but Jim likes to make wine. It's that simple. He's not out to win awards and accolades per se; he's out to satisfy his passion—fermenting fruit.

Jim converted his home's garage into a tasting room, which offers a cool respite during hot summer days. Chelangr'La Winery is located on the Lake Chelan North Shore WineTrail and makes for a quick but enjoyable wine-tasting stop.

CHELANGR'LA WINERY
opened: 2005
winemaker(s): Jim Berg
location: 3310 Manson Boulevard
Manson, WA 98831
phone: 509-687-9746
web: www.chelangrla.com
picnic area: Yes
gift shop: No
fee: $2 tasting fee for 5 tastings
hours: Daily 12–6

DIRECTIONS: From Chelan, take SR-150 toward Manson. Go through Manson. The road name changes to W. Manson Blvd. Arrive 3310 W. Manson Blvd. Winery is on the right.

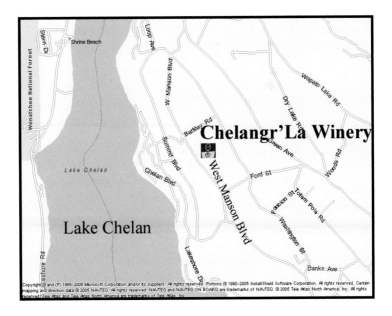

Wapato Point Cellars

Jonathon Kludt is a mature young man. At 26, his youth may explain the unbridled energy he's used to create a destination where visitors can enjoy great cuisine and great wine. Yet his résumé includes extensive experience in the wine industry. He is the son of Steve and Bobbi Kludt of Lake Chelan Winery fame. Jonathon also spent time in Santa Barbara working at Fess Parker Winery and Vineyards. Moreover, he is wise enough to realize the advantage of surrounding

himself with talented staff and family, and in particular, relying on the sage winemaking advice of Ray Sandidge.

Fundamental to Wapato Point Cellars' success is its wine, which includes a full slate of red and whites, many of which have won awards. Several vintages are created from grapes grown in the family's own Cougar Ridge Vineyard. This estate vineyard is within the soon-to-be-named Lake Chelan Valley viticulture area, and for Jonathon, it is a great source of pride.

Located in the heart of Wapato Point Resort, the winery is family friendly, with a huge yard that includes playground equipment for kids—or adults who act like kids. There's plenty of space for picnicking and tossing a Frisbee. Even the menu at the Winemaker's Grill is kid friendly, with menu items geared to appeal to young taste buds. This family-oriented approach reflects Jonathon's own beliefs about the importance of family; he is very involved in both the Kludt family and his spouse's family, the Williams.

Many WineTrail trekkers time their visit to Wapato Point Cellars for the evening, so that they can dine at the casually elegant Winemaker's Grill and enjoy live music from local talent. **WineTrail Note:** For a great evening meal, try the New York strip steak with the estate merlot. The winery hosts numerous special events and offers a spacious banquet room and patio for family and corporate events. Family owned and operated, Wapato Point Cellars is a destination winery not to be missed along the Lake Chelan North Shore WineTrail.

Jonathon Kludt

WAPATO POINT CELLARS
opened: 2003
winemaker(s): Jonathon Kludt
location: 200 Quetilquasoon Road
Manson, WA 98831
phone: 509-687-4000
web: www.wapatopointcellars.com
e-mail: jkludt@wapatopointcellars.com
picnic area: Yes
gift shop: Yes
fee: Complimentary wine tasting
hours: Daily 11–9 summer; 12–6 Thursday through
Sunday winter

 BEST Eat

DIRECTIONS: From Chelan, head toward Manson on SR-150. Go about 5 miles. Turn left (south) onto S. Quetilquasoon Rd at the 76 Station. Arrive 200 S. Quetilquasoon Rd. Wapato Point Cellars is on the right.

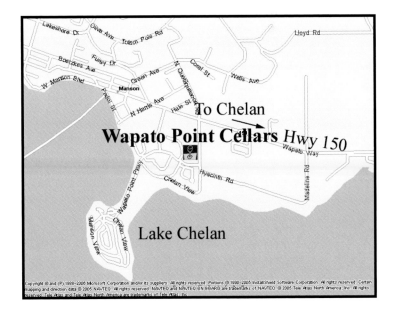

Lost River Winery

A river is "lost" when its runoff dwindles and it seemingly disappears. In fact, however, the river is still active and running strong below the pebbles and bedrock of the riverbed. The Lost River Winery is not apparent either, unless you happen to appreciate outstanding wine and find yourself in the frontier town of Winthrop. Tucked in the northern tip of the north-central wine country

region, this gem of a winery is where John Morgan and company "produce fine wine at a fair price."

A civil engineer by background, John and his spouse, Barbara House, moved to the Methow Valley in 2001 to create fine wines. With no vineyards to consume his time, John can focus on the art of winemaking. However, for an engineer, the biochemistry of winemaking is always at the forefront, presenting a "solving for x" problem. With engaging eyes and a sturdy demeanor, John patiently explains the art and science of winemaking to a steady stream of visitors to the tasting room. Don't be surprised when he waxes eloquently about the thickness of the staves, a wine's length of time in the barrel, and the frequency of racking to control such aspects as the amount of oxygen in the wine. John is passionate about winemaking. Not to worry though; the only test you will have is to swirl and taste his finished product.

Barbara and her son Liam Doyle (who is also a partner in the winery) are usually in the tasting room pouring samples and explaining how Lost River Winery produces such excellent wine. While Winthrop may not be the winemaking center of the universe, it is in fact close to the wine cornucopia of the famed Okanagan Valley in British Columbia. It is also just an hour's drive north of the Chelan Valley wine region. Being the only winery in this funky frontier town has its distinct advantages. After you park your horse and mosey around the town, with its wooden sidewalks and cowboy-friendly storefronts, you will likely develop a powerful thirst for a delicious cabernet or syrah. The relaxed atmosphere of the Lost River Winery offers the perfect place to quench your thirst, learn about winemaking, and meet some very good people. Giddy up, partner!

John Morgan, Barbara House and Liam Doyle
(l to r)

LOST RIVER WINERY
opened: 2002
winemaker(s): John Morgan
location: 26 Highway 20
Winthrop, WA 98622
phone: 509-996-2888
web: www.lostriverwinery.com
e-mail: info@lostriverwinery.com
picnic area: Yes
gift shop: No
fee: Complimentary wine tasting
hours: 11–5 Friday and Saturday, or by appointment;
open 11–5 on Mondays during summer

DIRECTIONS: Heading west on Hwy 20 (when the highway is open), the winery will be the first large building on your left before Winthrop's archway. If you've passed the baseball field, you've gone too far.
In the winter (during pass closure) from Wenatchee take Hwy 97 north to Pateros. Then travel north on Hwy 153. At Twisp, connect with Hwy 20. Go west 12 miles to the western edge of Winthrop. The winery is 100 yards past the ball field on the right.

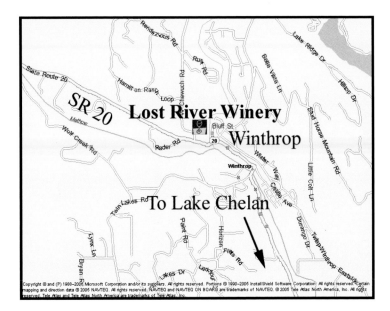

Yakima Valley
WINE COUNTRY

Yakima
WineTrail

Yakima WineTrail is a weekend getaway that is complete with quaint lodging, hidden restaurants, and wineries that display the fruit of this prosperous valley. Several tasting rooms are located in downtown Yakima within easy walking distance of each other. A short car drive takes to you other wineries in nearby Selah and Natches. Also, with great restaurants like the Barrel House Restaurant, Greystone Restaurant, and Zesta Cucina, it's hard to neglect your tummy. All these restaurants feature local wines from the Yakima Valley.

From "Catch the Crush" to "Thanksgiving in Wine Country," don't be surprised if your visit coincides with a weekend event. These people know how to celebrate life's finer things.

Yakima WineTrail

1 Kana Winery
2 Donitelia Winery

3 Yakima Cellars
4 Desert Hills

5 Selah Heights Winery
6 Running Springs Wine
Tasting Room

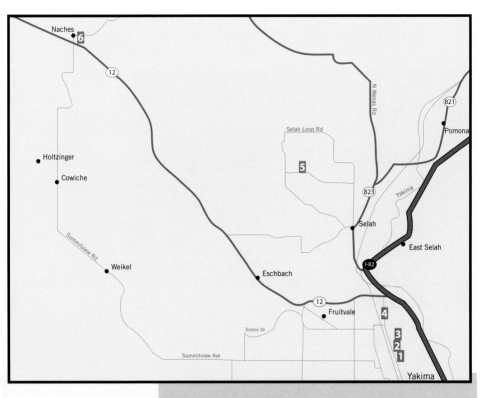

Region:	**Yakima Valley Wine Country**
# of tasting rooms on tour:	**6**
Estimated # of days for tour:	**1 to 2**
Getting around:	**Car and foot**
Key events:	❑ **Spring Barrel Tasting in the Yakima Valley (last weekend in April); Red Wine and Chocolate (mid-February); and Catch the Crush (October) sponsored by Wine Yakima Valley. See www.wineyakimavalley.org.**
Tips:	❑ **Park or stay downtown and experience three tasting rooms within easy walking distance.** ❑ **Looking for a romantic getaway weekend? Stay at the nearby Birchfield Manor Country Inn for great food and cozy rooms.**

Kana Winery

Located in the historic Larson Building on South Second Street, Kana's tasting room offers complimentary wine tasting and rotating art on the wall. As an added bonus, Kana Winery hosts "happy hour" between 5 and 6:30 p.m. Monday through Saturday. Nearby restaurants feature one of the Northwest's most extensive wine lists.

Winemaker Mark Wysling focuses on Rhone-style wines, using varietals such as roussanne, viognier, marsanne, syrah, mourvédre, grenache, and counoise. Kana Winery does manage to produce some non-Rhone varietal wines, including a Spanish-derived tempranillo, known for its brilliant red color in the glass and long finish in the mouth.

As noted on the Kana website, "Kana" is a Native American word for the spirit, or the fire, within a mountain, referring to the perceived supernatural power of volcanic activity. With the Cascade Mountains in the distance, it's not hard to imagine why the locals would have respect for Kana. Visitors are welcome at Kana Winery throughout the year; it's known to draw particularly large crowds for special events, such as Thanksgiving in the Wine Country, Red Wine and Chocolate, and Spring Barrel Tasting. No matter what their cultural backgrounds may be, visitors will likely agree that Kana Winery is good for the spirit.

KANA WINERY
opened: 2004
winemaker(s): Mark Wysling
location: 10 South 2nd Street, Larson Building
Yakima, WA 98901-2646
phone: 509-453-6611
web: www.kanawinery.com
e-mail: kanawinery@aol.com
picnic area: No
gift shop: No
fee: Complimentary wine tasting
hours: 12–6:30 Monday through Saturday,
12–5 Sunday

DIRECTIONS: From I-82 take Yakima Ave./Terrace Hts. (city center) exit 33 and head west on E. Yakima Ave. toward city center. Arrive at 10 S 2nd St. (Historic Larson Building). Kana's tasting room is located on the street level and S. 2nd St.

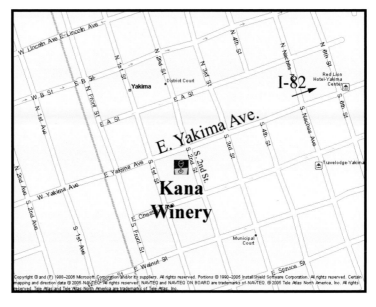

Donitelia Winery

When there is a waiting list to get into a winery's wine club, you know it must be doing something right. Such is the good fortune of Donitelia Winery, located in downtown Yakima in the heart of the theater-and-arts district, next

to the Hilton Hotel. Owner and winemaker Mark Maiocco's mission is to produce and sell the highest quality premium Italian wines in the Pacific Northwest. We're talking beautiful sangiovese, dolcetto, barbera, pinot grigio and some supremely Tuscan-style blends of cabernet and sangiovese: reserve "Megan Grace," reserve "Helen's Devotion," and reserve "Duetta." There's one Italian-sounding wine called "Pinot Nero," which is just the Italian term for the French pinot noir. As it turns out, Mark's wife loves pinot noir.

Mark is a busy guy. He is a family-practice physician by day and a vintner by night (and weekends). While wearing these different hats, Mark still manages to produce approximately 2,000 cases of wine annually for Donitelia.

Donitelia Winery is named for Mark's great-grandmother. She's pictured on the bottles and her smiling face is prevalent throughout the Donitelia tasting room. We're sure she would be very proud of Mark's continuation of family tradition: making handcrafted wines in the Italian style.

DONITELIA WINERY
opened: 2004
winemaker(s): Mark Maiocco
location: 321 E. Yakima Ave., Suite B
Yakima, WA 98901
phone: 509-452-9900
web: www.donitelia.com
e-mail: nicole@donitelia.com
picnic area: No
gift shop: No
fee: Complimentary wine tasting
hours: 4–7 Friday, 12–5 Saturday; special events or
by appointment

DIRECTIONS: From I-82 take Yakima City Center exit 33 and head west on E. Yakima Ave. Arrive at 321 E. Yakima Ave. (Great Western Building) on the right hand side next to the Hilton Hotel. Look for the black awning with Donitelia name inscribed.

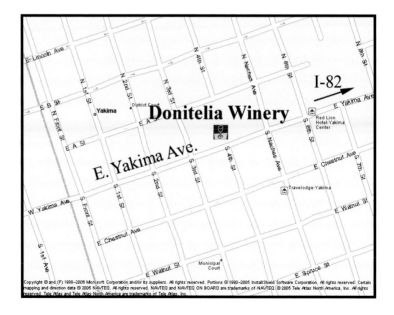

Yakima Cellars

A group of Yakima-area physicians originally started Yakima Cellars in 1999. However, with the growing demands of treating sore throats and birthing babies, the doctors chose to sell the winery in 2006 to Matt Gray and Mike

Andrews (owners of Prosser-based Coyote Canyon Winery). Although Yakima Cellars might be under new management, winemaker Mark Wysling remains at the helm making such wines as cabernet sauvignon, sangiovese, syrah, viognier, and blends with place names such as "Downtown White" and "Downtown Red."

Yakima Cellars' tasting room is located downtown in a renovated bank building on North Second Street. The former bank's safe now holds wine instead of money. The 1920s retro interior is spacious and sports hardwood floors and exposed brick walls, with selected art pieces hanging here and there. It's a place where Yakima professionals would feel right at home gathering after work for a glass of cabernet.

Yakima Cellars winery is located in the heart of Yakima's art and entertainment district and is within walking distance of fine restaurants, hotels, and the historic Capitol Theatre.

Yakima Cellar's tasting room

YAKIMA CELLARS
opened: 1999
winemaker(s): Mark Wysling
location: 32 North Second Street
Yakima, WA 98901
phone: 509-469-0621
web: www.yakimacellars.com
e-mail: TrishFYC@yahoo.com
picnic area: Yes
gift shop: No
fee: Complimentary wine tasting
hours: 11–7 Tuesday through Saturday, 1–5
Saturday and Sunday, or by appointment

DIRECTIONS: From I-82 take Yakima City Center exit 33 and head west on E. Yakima Ave. Turn right on 2nd St. and go one block. The winery is on the left side on the corner—look for the green awning.

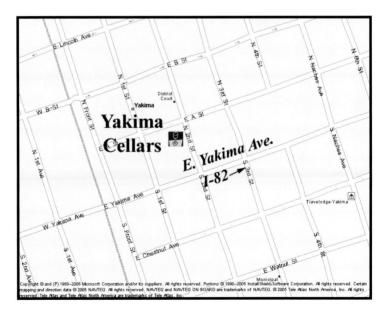

Desert Hills

For those entering Yakima wine country, a nice surprise awaits. Take exit 31 from Interstate 82 to North First St. Travel south for .5 miles and look for the Desert Hills Winery on the right. Follow the signs around back and you're

there! Congratulations, you have discovered a wine oasis one minute from the hustle and bustle of I-82. Get ready for some lovely Yakima Valley wines at Desert Hills Winery.

Bill and Lisa Burke don't need to be doing this—owning a winery, that is. A chemist by day, Bill let his passion for making wine get the better of him. In 2002, he and Lisa launched Desert Hills Winery. If you purchase quality grapes, use high-end oak, and price your wine competitively, you are bound to have a "money pit" on your hands. Such is the case for this couple. However, the "labor of love" transcends the bookkeeper's numbers, and we get to enjoy one of life's great pleasures, compliments of Bill and Lisa.

At Desert Hills, visitors can sample Bill's handcrafted sangiovese, merlot, cabernet sauvignon, and syrah. The spacious tasting room's ample light is perfect for checking out the ruby-colored sangiovese. Tables and chairs invite visitors to relax and enjoy the moment. You might be thinking that you have five other wineries in Zillah to visit. Forget about it. With cabernet sauvignon and syrah still to be tasted, your Zillah wine tour just got shorter.

DESERT HILLS
opened: 2002
winemaker(s): Bill & Lisa Burke
location: 1208 North 1st Street
Yakima, WA 98901-1906
phone: 509-453-0503
web: www.DesertHillsWinery.com
e-mail: lisa@deserthillswinery.com
picnic area: Yes
gift shop: No
fee: Complimentary wine tasting
hours: 10–4 Monday through Saturday, 12–4 Sunday,
after Spring Barrel Tasting or by appointment

DIRECTIONS: From I-82 take exit 30 and turn onto N. 1st St. toward Yakima. Proceed about .5 miles and find Desert Hills Winery at 1208 N. 1st St. Follow signs to tasting room and parking in the back of the building.

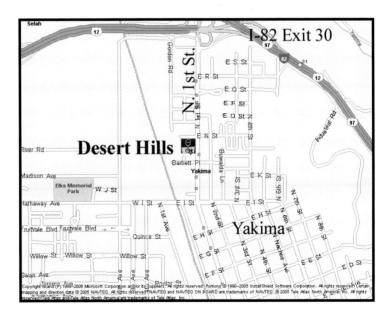

Selah Heights Winery

The story of Selah Heights Winery is one guided by beliefs: the belief that a family can relocate to a new land and find happiness, the belief that wine grapes can do just fine in the Upper Yakima Valley, and the belief that you make

wine to satisfy your own palate while disregarding the latest trends.

In the mid-'90s, Mike Clark packed up his family and moved to Selah from California. He hasn't looked back. A grade-school teacher by day, Mike works the winery at night and on weekends, assisted by his young son Jesse and his father, Royce. The winery is a side venture for the family. Mike loves being a schoolteacher and harbors no dreams of being a major wine producer. Rather, his goals are modest, focusing on handcrafted estate wines. With an annual production of approximately 1,000 cases, white wines highlight the Selah Heights portfolio, including riesling, gewürztraminer, chardonnay and a white blend Mike has named "Kaleidoscope." However, he also finds time to produce reds, including a red blend called "Tre Stelle Columbia Valley" (a blend of cabernet sauvignon, merlot and cabernet franc). Mike loves his estate pinot noir, saying that it shows early promise. By the way, a wine purchase at Selah Heights Winery won't cost you an arm and a leg. Its premier "Kaleidoscope" sells for $9 a bottle.

At 1,500 feet in elevation, Mike's vineyard enjoys cooler nights than the myriad vineyards found south of Union Gap in the lower Yakima Valley. He believes this location lends a unique flavor profile to his grapes and wonders aloud why many question the wisdom of planting grapes in the Selah area. He points out that grape growers are producing amazing fruit in British Columbia's Okanagan Valley, even though many were of the opinion that it would be too cold there, too.

The Clarks are huge fans of the rural hills of Selah and the town's friendliness, where the local hardware store employees know you by name. It's the perfect climate for a hard-working family to reach its potential—and the same could be said for the grapes.

Three generations of Clarks—Mike Clark on right

SELAH HEIGHTS WINERY
opened: 2002
winemaker(s): Mike Clark
location: 31 Katie Lane
Selah, WA 98942
phone: 509-698-6980
web: www.selahheightswinery.com
e-mail: mike@selahheightswinery.com
picnic area: No
gift shop: No
fee: Complimentary wine tasting
hours: Open weekends from Memorial Day until
Christmas, or by appointment; call for hours

DIRECTIONS: From I-82 take exit 30 toward Selah on SR-823 [S. 1st St.] and proceed about 2 miles. Continue on N. 1st St. about 1.5 miles (road name changes to Selah Loop Rd). Turn left (west) onto McGonagle Rd and go 1.5 miles. Go left on Katie Lane and find Selah Heights Winery immediately to your left.

271

Running Springs Wine Tasting Room

Running Springs is what you might call a virtual winery. The wine made from its grapes is bottled by Tefft Cellars under the private label Running Springs Vineyard wines. The wine is subsequently sold at Thompson Fruit Stand in

Naches, "the gateway to Mount Rainier." For Running Springs Vineyard, the dilemma had been what to do with all its wine grapes. Enter Tefft Cellars for production and Thompson Fruit Stand for distribution. Running Springs' goal is to produce estate wines, but in the meantime, this arrangement seems to be a good temporary solution.

In addition to sampling some fine wines, you have the pleasure of visiting Thompson Fruit Stand. John Thompson is often found at his Naches fruit stand, exuding Yakima Valley hospitality and offering much more than fresh fruit and wine. John is a bit of a farmer turned Renaissance man. At the "fruit stand," you can sit and enjoy ice cream at the traditional soda fountain, pick up a double tall mocha at the latte stand, shop for other farm produce (canned goods, honey, etc.) and merchandise, and look over John's restored "trolley tour" bus parked on the side. During October, you can visit the nearby pumpkin patch, which features two pumpkin cannons, and blast away or catch a hayride. In short, visiting Thompson Fruit Stand is down-home fun, and depending on the time of year, you are likely to cart away fresh corn, apples, peaches, cherries, as well as a bottle of Running Springs Vineyard merlot.

A word to the wise: If you are visiting Thompson Fruit Stand for the first time with the intent of sampling wine and making a quick exit, forget about it. There is a lot to explore here, and when you add in the warm hospitality, you need to budget at least a half hour, or longer if a root beer float grabs you at the soda fountain.

RUNNING SPRINGS WINE TASTING ROOM
opened: 2000
winemaker(s): Tefft Cellars
location: 9950 US-12 (Thompson Fruit Stand)
Naches, WA 98937
phone: 509-653-2848
e-mail: runningspringswine@transedge.com
picnic area: Yes
gift shop: Yes
fee: Complimentary wine tasting
hours: 10–5 weekends from April through May; daily
10–5 from June through October

DIRECTIONS: Take US-12 to Naches and look for Thompson Fruit Stand at 9950 US-12 as you get close to Naches. Running Spring Wine Tasting Room is found inside Thompson Fruit Stand.

Wapato
Wine Trail

Located at the north end of Yakima Valley, four wineries comprise the Wapato WineTrail. Although all feature fruit from the Yakima Valley, each winery is distinctly different in winemaking styles and presentation. That's what makes this venture a "can't miss" stop along I-82 from exits 40 to 44. The Wapato WineTrail will expose you to a winery owned by a world power in the spirits and wine trade, as well as to a small family-owned winery that produces less than 2,000 cases annually. You will visit a winery that relies on Frank Lloyd Wright–inspired architecture, and an old-fashioned one residing in an historic mercantile shop.

While at Windy Point Winery, be sure and soak in the panoramic view of the Yakima Valley. Framed by Rattlesnake Hills to the east and Horse Heaven Hills to the south, you can see the Yakima River at the center of the Valley snaking its way to the Columbia. With rich earth on either side of the river, you have the perfect formula for wine grapes. Just add sunlight and a winemaker's magic, and you have the ideal ingredients for premium wines.

Wapato WineTrail

1 Sagelands Vineyard   **3** Masset Winery   **4** Piety Flats Winery
2 Windy Point Vineyards

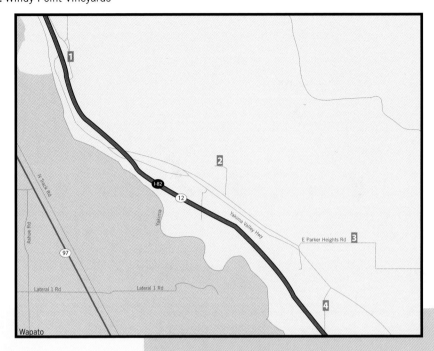

Region:	**Yakima Valley Wine Country**
# of tasting rooms on tour:	**4**
Estimated # of days for tour:	**1**
Getting around:	**Car**
Key events:	❏ **Spring Barrel Tasting in the Yakima Valley (last weekend in April); Red Wine and Chocolate (mid-February); and Catch the Crush (October) sponsored by Wine Yakima Valley. See www.wineyakimavalley.org.**
	❏ **Rattlesnake Hills Wine Trail Association sponsors events throughout the year.**
Tips:	❏ **Purchase Rattlesnake Hills Winery Association Passport and get discounts on wine purchases and more.**
	❏ **Need to do some grocery shopping? No problem, Piety Flats Winery is housed in a turn-of-the-century mercantile store.**
	❏ **Consider hiring a limousine service (e.g., S.U.V. Tours 509-783-7060, A+ Pacific Limousine 206-437-1298 or Sunset Coach Tours 800-941-2941, to name a few).**
Best:	❏ **Best Gift Shop: Sagelands Vineyard**
	❏ **Best Views: Windy Point Vineyards**

275

Sagelands Vineyard

OK, my fellow "wineaux," who's interested in visiting a first-class tasting room? Located just east of Yakima off I-82, Exit 40, the Sagelands Vineyard tasting room and winery stands as the gateway to the Yakima wine country. Of course, when the parent company of Sagelands is Diageo Chateau & Estate Wines

with multibillion-dollar holdings (perhaps you've heard of Beaulieu Vineyards, Canoe Ridge Vineyard, Smirnoff vodkas, Guinness, and Baileys Irish Cream, to name a handful of Diageo's assets), you would expect a gorgeous facility and you wouldn't be disappointed. With a view of Mount Adams to the southwest, Sagelands Vineyard provides a spacious tasting room that can readily accommodate a busload or two of tourists, which it often gets. There is plenty of space inside to converse with the pouring staff, mingle about the gift shop area, and peek inside the barrel room. Sagelands' focus is cabernet sauvignon and merlot. However, if they should be available, also check out the merlot rosé and the port-style "Ellipse." By the way, if you are a Rattlesnake Hills Passport holder, you get 10 percent off all wine purchases at the tasting room.

Sagelands' winemaker, Frederique Spencer, is a transplant from Provence, France. Frederique is refreshingly demure about her winemaking style and past accolades. She is not one to boast about her wines, preferring instead to let their fruit-forward, full-bodied tastes do the talking. Her training, however, emphasized blending grapes from different vineyards and using traditional winemaking techniques to create Bordeaux-style wines. Believing that it all starts in the vineyard, she collaborates with contracted wine growers from the area known as "The Four Corners": Wahluke Slope, Walla Walla Valley, Horse Heaven Hills, and Rattlesnake Hills.

There was a time when sage covered most of Eastern Washington. Thus, the name "Sagelands" is fitting. Nowadays, however, the sage has receded and been replaced by fields of cabernet sauvignon and merlot.

SAGELANDS VINEYARD
opened: 1999
winemaker(s): Frederique Spencer
location: 71 Gangl Road
Wapato, WA 98951
phone: 509-877-2112
web: www.sagelands.com
e-mail: Sagelands.info@sagelandsvineyard.com
picnic area: Yes
gift shop: Yes
fee: $5 waived upon purchase
hours: Daily 10–5; call ahead in winter

 BEST Gift shop

DIRECTIONS: From I-82 heading east or west take exit 40 and turn left onto Thorp Rd for .2 miles. Turn right onto Gangl Rd and go .3 miles and follow sign to Sagelands.

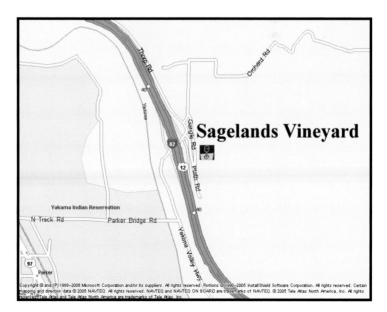

277

Windy Point Vineyards

Without doubt, Windy Point Vineyards offers one of the top 10 winery views in Washington. Situated on a hilltop in Wapato, you have a commanding view of the Yakima Valley, with mile upon mile of orchards below, and the Cascade Mountains in the distance. This is agricultural country. You can see the patchwork quilt of farms below with I-82 snaking its way southeast toward the Tri-Cities.

Featuring award-winning syrah and cabernet franc, Windy Point Vineyards is the creation of Mike and Liz Stepniewski. With three decades of farming under their belts, the Stepniewskis converted 15 acres of fruit orchards to wine grapes. Plans call for adding more grapes, with the goal to produce 100 percent estate wines. The couple is close to meeting that goal now. Regardless, they are proud that all fruit is from the Yakima Valley. Despite a huge early success with wine critics, their goal is to remain "boutique," with total annual production of 3,000 cases. While Mike tends the vineyards, Liz is the winemaker with a focus on "Pointless" wines, including "Pointless Red," "Exclamation Point," and "Pointless Cabernet." In addition to these red blends, she handcrafts other vintages, such as merlot, estate cabernet franc, syrah, estate cabernet sauvignon, gewürztraminer, and riesling.

The elegant design of the tasting room is strongly reminiscent of Frank Lloyd Wright's style, reflecting Mike's keen interest in architecture. This is especially evident in the wall facing the Yakima Valley, which incorporates plenty of glass for panoramic views. The wine tasting room features a full-service kitchen that clearly shows the Stepniewskis' devoted interest in cooking. Is there a winemaker dinner in your future? Call ahead and inquire.

Windy Point Vineyards' excellent wines, great views, and fantastic architecture add up to a highly desirable destination for a WineTrail journey.

WINDY POINT VINEYARDS
winemaker(s): Liz Stepniewski
location: 420 Windy Point Drive
Wapato, WA 98951
phone: 509-877-4446
web: www.windypointvineyards.com
e-mail: winemaker@windypointvineyards.com
picnic area: Yes
gift shop: Yes
fee: Complimentary wine tasting
hours: 10–5 Thursday through Monday; winter hours may vary

BEST Views

DIRECTIONS: From I-82 heading east or west, take exit 40 onto Yakima Valley Hwy and go 2 miles. Turn left onto W. Parker Heights Rd and go .5 miles. Turn left onto Windy Point Drive and go .3 miles to Windy Point Vineyards winery up the hill.

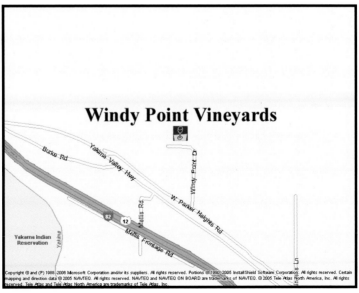

Windy Point Vineyards

Masset Winery

Dripping with French-country charm, the Masset Winery tasting room is located in a barn converted from the historic 1905 Angel Farmstead. We can only imagine what Greg and Michaela Masset felt like when they decided to transform the dilapidated barn into an inviting tasting room. However, with considerable elbow grease and buckets of paint, Michaela succeeded—if the

winery goes south, she's got a career as an interior designer. Choosing the right mix of antiques to complement the warm yellows and earthy browns, she created a perfect space to taste wine and relax in understated elegance. A hand-hewn 14-foot-long workbench separates the tasting bar area from an alluring living room. This centerpiece invites you to touch.

Michaela is also in charge of the tasting room and charmingly pours wines that have wonderful names, such as "Sandra Jean," "Love Potion #9," and "Margaret Alice." Despite being a recent startup, Masset Winery offers a full complement of reds (e.g., syrah, cabernet sauvignon, and merlot), whites (e.g., a semillon/sauvignon blanc blend, a roussane/viognier blend), and port. But the real star of the show is Masset's petit sirah, which winemaker Greg Masset is so passionate about that he is an active member of "P.S. I Love You," a petit sirah advocacy organization. Because very few of the 30,000 acres of grapes planted in Washington are petit sirah, to find a winery that specializes in this grape is indeed a treat.

Winemaker Greg Masset is an executive chef by day at the Yakima Country Club. Greg grew up in the hospitality business as a family member of the renowned Birchfield Manor Gourmet Restaurant. Armed with a degree in food science and his background in the business, Greg has the pedigree for Masset Winery to succeed.

Greg Masset is hard-working and quick to give thanks to family, friends and mentors. His quest is for elegant simplicity, creating big Yakima wines with that petit sirah difference. With all these good things going for Masset Winery, it's clear that the 1905 Angel Farmstead has been lovingly reborn.

MASSET WINERY
opened: 1999
winemaker(s): Greg Masset
location: 620 East Parker Heights Road
Wapato, WA 98951
phone: 509-877-6675
web: www.massetwinery.com/
e-mail: massetwine@nwinfo.net
picnic area: No
gift shop: No
fee: Complimentary wine tasting
hours: 11–5 Saturday and Sunday, 2–5 Thursday,
Friday, and Monday, from February through November

DIRECTIONS: From I-82 heading east or west, take exit 40 and turn right onto Yakima Valley Hwy. Go about 3.5 miles and turn left onto W. Parker Heights Rd. Continue for .75 miles to Masset Winery on the right.

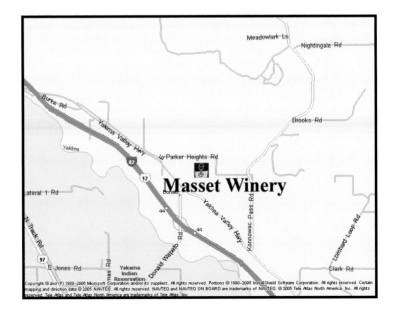

Piety Flats Winery

Get ready for some old-country-store charm. You might even decide to forgo the wine and go right to the Thomas Kemper Root Beer float served at Piety Flats! Partners Bryan Eglet and Jim Russi, along with winemaker David Minick,

produce some unique Yakima Valley wines. The tasting room is situated in the 1911 Mercantile Building, full of antiquated charm, and is famous for its peach sundaes. Conveniently located right off the I-82 freeway, this rustic store still has the appearance of the past century, "complete with creaking wooden floors, old country store fixtures and memorabilia of yesteryear." Visitors can enjoy the ambiance of bygone days while shopping from well-stocked shelves and sampling wine.

Each wine is served with pride by a very knowledgeable wine pourer. And what a line-up of wines to sample! Piety Flats produces a number of mainstay wines, including syrah, merlot, cabernet-merlot blend, and a pinot grigio–chardonnay blend. But it also features late-harvest viognier, cabernet port, black muscat, and chenin blanc. Have you ever tried black muscat? Or how about a late-harvest viognier? Or perhaps you like your cabernet port served chilled? These are some of the many distinguishing features of the Piety Flats establishment that set it apart from other wineries. By the way, as you are imbibing, check out the distinctive label and note the building across the way from the winery. Coincidence? I think not.

Many WineTrail enthusiasts like their syrah "big and intense," and the Piety Flats syrah won't disappoint. Aged 11 months in small oak barrels (30 percent new, 50 percent American, and 50 percent French), the winery has succeeded in preserving the great flavors that the Yakima Valley is known for. Think steak or even pepperoni pizza for this vintage.

Winery events are held in coordination with the Rattlesnake Hills Wine Trail Association. Visit www.rattlesnakehills.com for upcoming events, including Spring Barrel Tasting at the end of April; Going Vertical! on Labor Day Weekend; Red Wine and Chocolate in February; and the Thanksgiving Festival.

PIETY FLATS WINERY
winemaker(s): David J. Minick
location: 2560 Donald-Wapato Road
Wapato, WA 98951
phone: 509-877-3115
web: www.pietyflatswinery.com
e-mail: info@pietyflatswinery.com
picnic area: Yes
gift shop: Yes
fee: Complimentary wine tasting
hours: 10–6 Monday through Saturday, 10–5
Sunday, from March through October; daily 10–5
from November through December; 12–5 Saturday
and Sunday in January and February

DIRECTIONS: From I-82, take exit 44 and go north onto Donald-Wapato Rd .125 miles. Piety Flats
Winery is on your left.

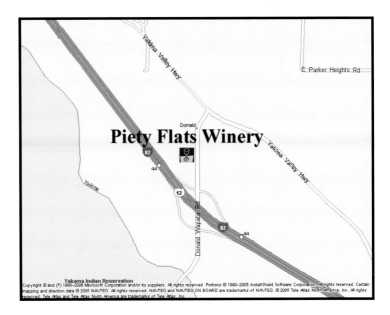

Rattlesnake Hills
WineTrail North

Viognier
Block - 2

Who would have guessed that Zillah would have stretch limousines zipping between tractors, but that's what you get when you add a couple dozen wineries to this landscape. Speaking of landscape, this is American farmland at its finest. And it reflects the transition from fruit orchards to vineyards. Many winemakers in this part of the Yakima Valley are "dirt guys," having farmed the land for many years. They know that great wine begins with great fruit.

Rattlesnake Hills WineTrail North

1 Bonair Winery
2 Wineglass Cellars
3 Two Mountain Winery
4 Hyatt Vineyards

5 Sheridan Vineyard Winery
6 Agate Field Vineyard
7 Maison de Padgett Winery
8 Paradisos del Sol

9 Silver Lake at Roza Hills
10 Portteus Vineyards & Winery

Region:	**Yakima Valley Wine Country**
# of tasting rooms on tour:	**10**
Estimated # of days for tour:	**2**
Getting around:	**Car or bike**
Key events:	❑ **Spring Barrel Tasting in the Yakima Valley (last weekend in April); Red Wine and Chocolate (mid-February); and Catch the Crush (October) sponsored by Wine Yakima Valley. See www.wineyakimavalley.org.** ❑ **Rattlesnake Hills Wine Trail Association sponsors events during the year.**
Tips:	❑ **For avid bicyclists, this WineTrail is heaven. See Wineglass Cellars website at www.wineglasscellars.com for David's 60 Miler course.** ❑ **Purchase Rattlesnake Hills Winery Association Passport and get discounts on wine purchases and more.** ❑ **Consider hiring a limousine service (e.g., S.U.V. Tours 509- 783-7060, A+ Pacific Limousine 206-437-1298 or Sunset Coach Tours 800-941-2941, to name a few).**
Best:	❑ **Best Views: Silver Lake at Roza Hills** ❑ **Best Picnic: Hyatt Vineyards and Silver Lake at Roza Hills** ❑ **Best Gift Shop: Bonair Winery** ❑ **Best for Weddings: Hyatt Vineyards**

285

Bonair Winery

Founded in 1985, the Bonair Winery and Vineyards is located in the heart of Yakima wine country: Zillah. With the Rattlesnake Hills to the east, this wine country region is a constellation of calendar-worthy images: October harvest, Fourth of July red, white and rosé tasting rooms, cases of wine under the Christmas tree, and more. Gail Puryear, owner and vintner of Bonair,

wants visitors to experience "real wineries," where you pass by vineyards on the way to the tasting room and know where the fruit comes from.

Bonair Winery and Vineyards is one of the many wineries that have banded together to create the Rattlesnake Hills Wine Trail Association. When you visit Bonair (and other participating wineries), you can purchase a $5 "passport," which gives you discounts on wine purchases, reserve-wine tasting, plus a souvenir glass at selected wineries on the Rattlesnake trail. The discount special varies from winery to winery, so you will need to ask before getting your passport stamped. The passport idea is fun. And, as it turns out, it's a great way to discover for yourself which wines you enjoy most.

With its turret and brown-trimmed white buildings, Bonair Winery may remind you of an English country estate. A koi pond positioned in front of the winery and Yakima's typical deep blue skies add to a picture-perfect composition. Soak it all in and then get ready to enjoy what Gail describes as a "hobby that got out of control." Bonair's reputation for chardonnay, elegant reds, fruity sipping wines, and mead puts it in a unique position. Yes, the chardonnay is aged in oak "the old-fashioned way." Bonair's flagship "Chateau Puryear" reserve chardonnay is big, soft, buttery. Sample the chardonnay and imagine it paired with your wine-country turkey and cranberry sauce. Wow.

BONAIR WINERY
opened: 1985
winemaker(s): Gail Puryear
location: 500 South Bonair Road
Zillah, WA 98953-9245
phone: 509-829-6027
web: www.bonairwine.com
e-mail: winemaker@bonairwine.com
picnic area: Yes
gift shop: Yes
fee: Small tasting fee
hours: Daily 10–5 from April through November;
weekends December through March, or by
appointment

BEST Gift shop

DIRECTIONS: From I-82 heading east or west, take exit 54 and turn onto Yakima Valley Hwy. Proceed about 2 miles around bend to Cheyne Rd. Turn right onto Cheyne Rd and proceed about 1 mile to Highland Drive. Turn left onto Highland Drive and proceed about 1 mile to Bonair Rd. Turn left onto Bonair Rd and proceed to the end. The winery will be straight ahead.

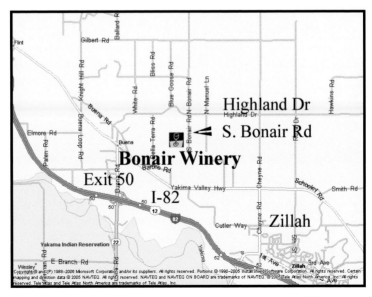

Wineglass Cellars

linger *v.*– to be slow in leaving, especially out of reluctance; tarry. See 'stay.'

Bring your picnic; you might be here awhile. Your reason for lingering will surely be David Lowe's superlative wines. (You might also want to bring your

bicycle. We'll explain why in a bit.) Many visitors to Zillah get no farther than Wineglass Cellars. Why? This description of its 2005 "In the Buff" chardonnay may provide a clue: "In the buff, as you might suppose, means no oak, no malolactic. It is nonetheless quite stacked with flavor, thick currents of pear, peach and other stone fruits, and plenty of natural acid to keep it lively in the mouth. This is the sort of honest, no-nonsense wine that chardonnay rarely can be—more like a sturdy red in the way it coats the tongue and lingers." Paul Gregutt, *Seattle Times* Wine Advisor, August 2, 2006.

The chardonnay offers a wonderful prelude to Wineglass Cellars' big, full-bodied reds. Get ready for sangiovese, merlot, "Capizimo" (a blend of cabernet sauvignon, merlot, sangiovese, and malbec), cabernet sauvignon, reserve merlot, and "Elerding Vineyard" cabernet sauvignon. We hope that owners David and Linda Lowe are there when you experience their array of reds. The Lowes are the nicest, most unassuming people you will meet in Yakima wine country. Here's your chance to discover where they acquire their grapes, why they relocated from Seattle, and what future releases are in store. Speaking of Seattle, Wineglass Cellars is a featured winery at The Tasting Room, located in Post Alley, at Pike Place Market. We know. We've made several emergency stops at The Tasting Room for a glass of Wineglass Cellars' "Capizimo." (OK, this WineTrail enthusiast admits that "Capizimo" is my personal favorite.)

Regarding that bicycle reference, David Lowe has been so kind as to post directions on the winery's website for a nice little 60-mile jaunt around Zillah wine country. That's right, a 60-miler! However, we suspect that the bicycle hanging out of your car's trunk will be ridden another day. You've lingered too long at Wineglass Cellars.

WINEGLASS CELLARS
opened: 1994
winemaker(s): David Lowe
location: 260 North Bonair Road
Zillah, WA 98953
phone: 509-829-3011
web: www.wineglasscellars.com
e-mail: sales@wineglasscellars.com
picnic area: Yes
gift shop: Yes
fee: Complimentary wines except $1 for reserve
hours: 10:30–5 Friday through Sunday (and
Monday holidays) from Presidents Day Weekend
through November

David Lowe

DIRECTIONS: Take Zillah exit 50 off of I-82 and head toward Zillah. At Cheyne Rd go north for 1.8 miles. Turn left onto Highland Drive and go .9 miles. Turn right onto N. Bonair Rd. Wineglass Cellars will be on your left.

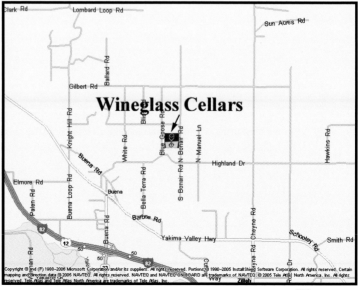

Two Mountain Winery

The closely knit Washington wine community was shaken in May 2006 when they learned that the owner and force behind Zillah's Two Mountain Winery was killed in an auto accident. Ron Schmidt was a third-generation orchardist, and it was his vision to convert a portion of the fruit in Schmidt Orchards to

vinifera wine grapes in 1999. His dream was to create a Yakima Valley winery, and that dream became a reality in 2003 with the launch of Two Mountain Winery.

Today, Matt Rawn, Ron's nephew, is Two Mountain's vineyard manager and winemaker, and the family tradition lives on with other family members involved in the business. The Schmidt Orchard contains 55 acres of grapes, and Matt is able to control the quality of wine from "the dirt to the glass." Each acre generates 3 to 4 tons of grapes, which translates to 200 tons of grapes. It takes lot of stomping feet to make 3,000 cases of chardonnay, riesling, lemberger, merlot, syrah, cabernet sauvignon, "Hidden Horse" red table wine, cabernet franc, and "Midnight Rosé." As you taste the Two Mountain riesling, imagine serving this with grilled asparagus and Black Forest ham. This is a wine to share with friends and family over a simple but elegant meal, the way Ron Schmidt would have wanted it.

As you might expect, the tasting room and winery provide a stunning view of both Mount Rainier and Mount Adams. Hanging inside the converted farm building is a local artist's painting depicting colorful vineyard rows and the two mountains in the distance. You know you are in Eastern Washington when you see Cougar paraphernalia decorating the tasting room bar. If you have a Rattlesnake Hills Passport, you get 10 percent off wine purchases.

TWO MOUNTAIN WINERY
opened: 2003
winemaker(s): Matt Rawn
location: 2151 Cheyne Road
Zillah, WA 98953
phone: 509-829-3900
web: www.twomountainwinery.com
e-mail: info@twomountainwinery.com
picnic area: Yes
gift shop: Yes
fee: Complimentary wine tasting
hours: 10–6 Friday through Monday from
Presidents Day Weekend through November, or
by appointment

Two Mountain is Coug country

DIRECTIONS: From I-82 take exit 52 toward Zillah. Go north on Cheyne Rd approximately 2 miles.
Two Mountain Winery will be on your right.

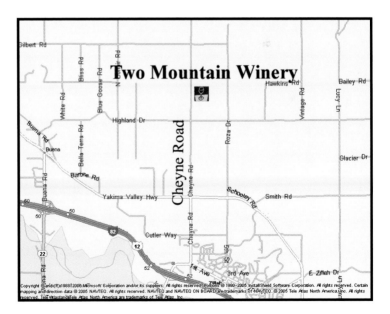

Hyatt Vineyards

Leland and Lynda Hyatt established Hyatt Vineyards in 1985 and produced their first vintage in 1987. Since that time, they have witnessed a number of changes, including the designation of their area—Rattlesnake Hills—as an American Viticultural Area (AVA). The grounds on which their winery and

Hyatt Vineyards

tasting room are situated command a large footprint of real estate, with a windmill as the centerpiece of their well-manicured lawn. Upon viewing the grounds, you might think that this would be a great place for a wedding, and you'd be right. You can book the property, arrange for chairs, caterer and a preacher, and have yourself a heck of a wedding—especially if both Mount Rainier and Mount Adams decide to make an appearance on the special day. And there's certainly plenty of wine to go around.

Hyatt's winemaker, Andy Gamache, gets most of his grapes from four estate vineyards within 2 miles of the winery. With an annual production of approximately 30,000 cases, Hyatt wines are found throughout Washington, in grocery stores and Washington State Liquor Stores. Selling at $7 to 9 a bottle for the Hyatt brand and $13 to 15 for the Roza Ridge label, the Hyatt wines are one of the best values of their kind out there. Although you can sample the "second-tier" Hyatt wines free at its tasting room, there is a small fee for sampling Hyatt Roza Ridge Wines. (This fee is waived for Rattlesnake Hills Passport holders.) It's interesting, and educational, to taste the difference between Hyatt's regular wines and its premium Roza Ridge reserves, including "Roza Ridge" syrah, cabernet sauvignon, and merlot.

If your trip takes you to Hyatt in September, you can enjoy the "Taste the Grape" event sponsored by the Rattlesnake Hills Winery Association. Here is an opportunity to taste wine grapes right before the crush. Have you ever bitten into a handful of chardonnay grapes? Well, WineTrail enthusiasts, here is your big chance.

HYATT VINEYARDS
opened: 1985
winemaker(s): Andy Gamache
location: 2020 Gilbert Road
Zillah, WA 98953-9766
phone: 509-829-6333
web: www.hyattvineyards.com
e-mail: hyattvineyards@msn.com
picnic area: Yes
gift shop: Yes
fee: No tasting fee except for Roza Ridge wines—fee waived for Rattlesnake Hills Passport ticket buyers
hours: Daily 11–5

BEST Picnicking and weddings

DIRECTIONS: Take Zillah exit 50 off I-82 and head toward Zillah. At Cheyne Rd go north for 3 miles. Turn left onto Gilbert Rd and proceed about 1 mile. The Hyatt Winery will be on your left—look for the white windmill.

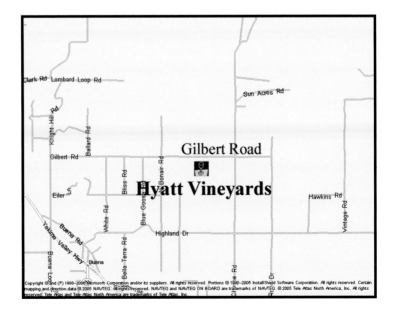

Sheridan Vineyard Winery

There are many reasons why someone would start a winery, but sometimes it just comes down to a philosophy. In the case of Sheridan Vineyard, it's a philosophy that wine should be shaped by the vineyard that surrounds the winery, and Sheridan Vineyard happens to produce excellent grapes. In 1996, owner and winemaker Scott Greer acquired 76 acres of land in the Yakima Valley known as Sheridan Vineyard. Thus began his quest to display the surprisingly intense

flavors of the grapes grown in this part of the Upper Yakima Valley by making wine under the Sheridan Vineyard label. Low yields of grapes on a per-acre basis results in fruit that is deeply red— almost black—with huge flavors.

Scott Greer is self-taught when it comes to winemaking, but after more than 10 years of making wine, his former life in finance must be a distant memory. Fortunately, Scott's winemaking skills have benefited from drawing upon the experience of a number of industry leaders. We're sure, for example, that Scott has drawn from his friendship with fellow vintner Tim Stevens of Stevens Winery fame. In fact, a look at Sheridan's wine label reveals two children stomping grapes. The two kids are a depiction of Scott's children and derived from a sculpture executed by Tim Stevens.

The distinctive über-barn in Zillah is the site of the Sheridan Winery tasting room. Often Scott is there pouring wine for eager visitors, assisting Sarah Fewel, the tasting room manager. Depending upon availability, the winery features a predominantly red portfolio, including cabernet franc, syrah, cabernet sauvignon, and red blends called "Kamiakin Red" and "L'Orage" (French for "The Storm"). A white blend called "Kamiakin White" is refreshingly crisp and a welcome relief in the summertime.

SHERIDAN VINEYARD WINERY
opened: 2005
winemaker(s): Scott Greer
location: 2980 Gilbert Road
Zillah, WA 98953
phone: 509-829-3205
web: www.sheridanvineyard.com
e-mail: info@sheridanvineyard.com
picnic area: Yes
gift shop: Yes
fee: Complimentary wine tasting
hours: 12–5 Friday, 11–5 Saturday, 12–4 Sunday

DIRECTIONS: Take exit 52 from I-82 turn north heading into Zillah. Take 2nd left on Cheyne Rd. Go 3 miles to third stop sign (corner of Cheyne and Gilbert). Turn right on Gilbert Rd for .25 miles to first building on the right and arrive at 2980 Gilbert Rd.

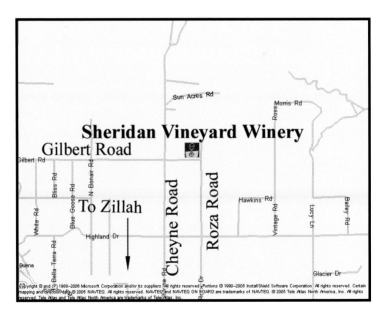

Agate Field Vineyard

This is a winery rich in tradition yet young in winemaking years. Founder Ben Rashford has been growing grapes on his 10-acre Zillah-based vineyard for more than 60 years. Yet it wasn't until his wife, Ruth, suggested that they use some

of the grapes to produce their own wine that Ben got the notion of Agate Field Vineyard wine. Fortunately, they kept it in their family by turning to their daughter, Ginger, whose husband, Bob Radke, became their winemaker. Interestingly, Bob is a law enforcement officer for the Department of Agriculture by day, so WineTrail enthusiasts are advised to keep the syrah plantings in the ground and not take them with you.

From Agate Field's second floor deck

Bob, Ginger, Ruth, and Ben often work the tasting room together serving up elegant blends of estate cabernet sauvignon, cabernet franc, and merlot as well as syrah. But with production at just 500 cases annually, don't be surprised if they are sold out of a vintage or two. The tasting room itself has a cowboy-movie rustic feel with a second-story deck overlooking the vineyards of Whiskey Canyon. Bring a picnic, uncork a bottle of Agate Fields red, and enjoy the view. Inside, the spacious tasting room provides a comfortable environment thanks in large part to the use of structurally insulated panels, which provide warmth during the winter; coolness in summer. It's a relaxing space reflecting the friendly demeanor of Agate Field Vineyard's familial staff.

AGATE FIELD VINEYARD
opened: 2004
winemaker(s): Bob Radke
location: 2911 Roza Drive
Zillah, WA 98953
phone: 509-829-6097
web: www.agatefieldvineyard.com
e-mail: Bob@agatefieldvineyard.com
picnic area: Yes
gift shop: Yes
fee: Complimentary wine tasting
hours: 11–5 Friday through Sunday, from April
through the second week in December

Bob Radke

DIRECTIONS: If traveling east on I-82 from Yakima, take exit 44 and turn left (north) onto Donald Wapato Rd. Continue for .6 miles. Turn right onto Yakima Valley Hwy and proceed 8 miles. Turn left (north) onto Roza Dr. and proceed 1.7 miles. Look for Agate Fields Winery on your right.
If traveling west on I-82 from Prosser, take exit 54 and turn right onto Yakima Valley Hwy. Proceed 2.2 miles. Turn right (north) onto Roza Dr. and continue for 1.7 miles. Look for Agate Field Winery on your right.

Maison de Padgett Winery

Are you game to explore one of Washington's most fun wineries? Then check out Maison de Padgett Winery. True, owner/winemaker David Padgett does concentrate on bringing you and other wine lovers fine wines, but what's most important to him is that you have fun. To him, wine is bottled pleasure and it needs to be approachable. To this end, he produces a full range of wines designed to meet varying palates, from those of the once-in-a-great-while wine tasters to the informed tongues of seasoned veterans. Included in his arsenal are several ports for which Maison de Padgett enjoys a large following. Check out the label on David's "Smoking Gun" coffee port; that's David pictured on the label. Regarding his labels, they are downright wacky. David comes up with the concept for the label, which a graphic artist in Portland then gets to execute. One can only imagine how David communicates his dream-like imagery, but apparently the artist gets it.

Bridal room on the grounds of Maison de Padgett

A key stop along the Rattlesnake Hills WineTrail North, the Maison de Padgett Winery is the sister winery of nearby Horizon's Edge, which David also owns. The winery is wonderfully spacious with pleasing architectural touches and includes an English-style garden large enough to host weddings and other events. In fact, the garden area includes a quaint bridal cottage for pre- and post-nuptial garment changes as well as a space for berating the caterer for confusing macaroni salad with fruit salad.

With 18 acres of grapes nearby, David handcrafts estate merlot and cabernet sauvignon. Other Maison de Padgett wines rely on nearby vineyards for grapes that are used in the production of "Singing Toad" (a late harvest white wine), "Funky Monkey" pinot noir ice wine, cabernet franc reserve port, "Sleeping Giant" port, "Lip Service" (at a whopping 8.4 percent residual sugar, it could also be called "Lip Smacking"), "Risqué" chardonnay, and "End of the Road Part III" red blend. If you delight in the names, wait till you see the labels!

As David states on his website, "Welcome to Washington's Most Unique Winery." He's not kidding. Adventurers beware: You are entering the fun zone. Get ready for some unusual ports and whimsical labels. Like other visitors, you'll leave with a smile (and, we suspect, several bottles to take home).

MAISON DE PADGETT WINERY
opened: 2002
winemaker(s): David Padgett
location: 2231 Roza Drive
Zillah, WA 98953
phone: 509-829-6412
web: www.maisondepadgettwinery.com
e-mail: yvine@aol.com
picnic area: Yes
gift shop: Yes!
fee: Small tasting fee
hours: 11–5 Thursday through Monday, Tuesday and
Wednesday by chance, from March through November;
open Presidents Day Weekend 11–5

DIRECTIONS: From I-82 take exit 52 toward Zillah. Turn left on Cheyne Rd. Turn right on Highland Drive. Head east on Highland Drive to Roza Drive. Maison de Padgett is on the corner of Highland Drive and Roza Drive.

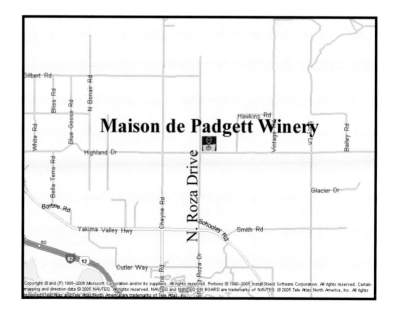

Paradisos del Sol

Paul Vandenberg, owner and winemaker for Paradisos del Sol, is mad. We're not talking "Mad Hatter" mad, but mad in the best sense of the word. He's mad about perfecting "pure and natural" wine, and views himself as a winegrower, not a winemaker.

As you approach Paradisos del Sol's tasting room outside Zillah, the colorful flags, outdoor sculpture, and chickens scampering around the backyard might have you wondering if you took a wrong turn. There may also be a strange-looking guy wearing wildly colored pants positioned by the front door greeting visitors. The greeter is Paul himself. Like one of those free-sample stands you find at Costco, Paul sets up his table and engages wine tasters to sample a couple of his wines. He does this mostly to educate the many visitors, but we suspect

that he too is learning, about the likes and dislikes of the wine-drinking public. Despite working fulltime as a winemaker since 1983, Paul still learns and evolves his practice.

Barbara Sherman, Paul's spouse, runs the tasting room as well as taking care of the myriad paperwork chores behind the scenes. To handle weekend and event crowds, the couple provides two different tasting areas featuring different wines; it's like a progressive dinner party, except that all the courses are drinkable. Depending on availability, Barbara and her team might be pouring their dry "Rosé Paradisos," their mildly sweet riesling, their ever popular "Under 10 Buck Red," a Paradisos red blend, cabernet sauvignon, or a couple of dessert wines, such as a late-harvest botrytis riesling ("The Noble Rot"), and the wonderfully named "Angelica G."

Paul and Barbara are huge believers in wine as a complement to good food and friends. To this end, we thank them for sharing the following recipe from El Ranchito Restaurant in Zillah:

Ceviche de Camaron (Shrimp Cocktail) Recipe (Serves 4)
1 lb. large shrimp (quartered)
1/2 red onion (sliced)
Fresh lime juice (8 limes)
1 or 2 jalapeño chile peppers (chopped)
1/2 cup fresh cilantro (chopped)
1/4 tsp. salt, pepper, to taste
Mix and let sit overnight.

Now, uncork a bottle of Paradisos del Sol riesling and you're good to go.

PARADISOS DEL SOL
opened: 2000
winemaker(s): Paul Vandenberg
location: 3230 Highland Drive
Zillah, WA 98953
phone: 509-829-9000
web: www.paradisosdelsol.com
e-mail: info@paradisosdelsol.com
picnic area: Yes
gift shop: Yes
fee: Complimentary wine tasting
hours: Daily 11–5; winter hours may vary—call ahead

DIRECTIONS: From I-82 take exit 52 toward Zillah. Turn left on Cheyne Rd. Turn right on Highland Drive and go .5 miles to Paradisos del Sol Winery on the right.

Silver Lake at Roza Hills

Are you interested in owning a winery but need to keep your day job? Would you like to enjoy the benefits of winery ownership (e.g., discounts on wine, dibs on new releases, and hobnobbing with other wine owners at special events)? If

so, put your money where your mouth is and buy some stock in Silver Lake Winery. It is one of the largest consumer-owned wineries in the U.S. and boasts more than 2,000 shareholders.

Silver Lake Winery is one of the top 10 producing wineries in Washington and relatively old in Washington-winery years. Starting in 1989, three University of Washington professors crushed their first vintage. As Silver Lake lore tells it, their "hobby got out of control" and today they produce more than 25,000 cases a year to diehard Silver Lake fans.

Silver Lake's tasting rooms can be found in Woodinville, Leavenworth, and Zillah. Although the three locations are quite different from one another, they all offer the same line-up of exceptional wines sold at good prices.

The Woodinville tasting room is located on the main road near the Columbia Winery. It's a rather modern, glassy-pointy structure, but don't get too comfortable with this setting. Silver Lake is in the process of building a new tasting room, which will be a part of a large complex housing its winery and retail services. Once completed, the new complex will dwarf the existing tasting room. Shareholders will be very proud to show off this new setting, and there's no doubt it will become a Woodinville destination.

On the other side of the mountains, in sparsely settled Zillah, is the Silver Lake at Roza Hills winery. Without doubt the highlight of this winery—aside from the delicious wine—is the view of the valley. One can easily imagine hosting a corporate event, a family get-together, or a wedding reception at this location. The view is overlooking the Whiskey Canyon Vineyard and the entire valley, and can be enjoyed from the "viniferanda." (What a great new word! Don't we all need a viniferanda?) Bring camera, picnic, and bottle opener to this location.

About 100 miles north of Zillah, in the Bavarian-inspired town of Leavenworth, is another Silver Lake tasting room. This quaint setting is a nice pit stop as you stroll around and visit the many shops and restaurants of Leavenworth.

If you are interested in being a co-owner of a very successful winery—and one that has a definite eye on the future—check out www.silverlakewinery.com/shareholder.htm.

SILVER LAKE AT ROZA HILLS
opened: 1988
winemaker(s): William Ammons
location: 1500 Vintage Road
Zillah, WA 98953
phone: 509-829-6235
web: www.silverlakewinery.com
e-mail: info@washingtonwine.com
picnic area: Yes
gift shop: Yes
fee: No fee except $5 charge for reserve wines
hours: Daily 11–4 from December through March;
daily 10–5 from April through November

BEST Views and picnicking

DIRECTIONS: From I-82 take exit 52 toward Zillah. Turn left on Cheyne Rd. Turn right on Highland Drive. Turn left on Vintage Rd and drive to the end of the paved road. The Silver Lake tasting room is on your left. (Note: Silver Lake also has Woodinville and Leavenworth tasting rooms.)

Copyright © and (P) 1988–2006 Microsoft Corporation and/or its suppliers. All rights reserved. Portions © 1990–2005 InstallShield Software Corporation. All rights reserved. Certain mapping and direction data © 2005 NAVTEQ. All rights reserved. NAVTEQ and NAVTEQ ON BOARD are trademarks of NAVTEQ. © 2005 Tele Atlas North America, Inc. All rights reserved. Tele Atlas and Tele Atlas North America are trademarks of Tele Atlas, Inc.

303

Portteus Vineyards & Winery

Paul Portteus is many things to many people. Depending upon to whom you are talking, Paul is a husband, father, grape grower, winemaker, and mentor. However, one thing is certain: His name is held in high regard among industry people in the Yakima Valley and wine lovers throughout the Northwest region.

As reported on Mike Lempriere's "Guide to Washington Wineries" website (www.vintners. net), "Paul Portteus first started making beer at age 19 in his home on Mercer Island, having been exposed to an uncle who was a home winemaker/brewer. While majoring in philosophy at University of Washington, he took an extended tour of Europe by motorcycle, discovering the Bordeaux region." It was from those early beginnings, and an extended visit in the Sonoma Valley, that he and his wife, Marilyn, launched Portteus Vineyards & Winery in 1981. They were the 13th bonded winery in Washington at the time.

At the Portteus tasting room, located about 7 miles from I-82, you will usually find Paul's son Seth doing the pouring honors. An artist by background (one of his paintings can be viewed at the Paradisos del Sol tasting room), Seth engages WineTrail trekkers with his relaxed demeanor. He's not out to sell you anything; he simply responds to frequent questions and makes sure your glass isn't empty. As you work your way through the lineup of estate reds, you might be surprised when you encounter the Portteus zinfandel. In true pioneer fashion, Paul became the first grower to plant zinfandel in Washington. After you swirl and enjoy the peppery notes of this wine, you will understand why zin is Portteus' number-one seller.

Paul championed the designation of the Rattlesnake Hills American Viticulture Area and obtained the official federal AVA title in early 2006. It was not easy; many argued that Rattlesnake Hills' *terroir* was no different than that of Yakima Valley. But if you have the guts to ride a motorcycle through Bordeaux in the '70s and later weather the vicissitudes of the grape industry economy, then dealing with Rattlesnake Hills AVA politics is minor. We know that Paul must have a lot of intestinal fortitude—how many winery proprietors do you know who would dress up in a wacky costume for their "Hallowine" event?

Seth Portteus

PORTTEUS VINEYARDS & WINERY
opened: 1981
winemaker(s): Paul Portteus
location: 5201 Highland Drive
Zillah, WA 98953
phone: 509-829-6970
web: www.portteus.com
e-mail: paul@portteus.com
picnic area: No
gift shop: No
fee: Complimentary wine tasting
hours: 10–5 Monday through Friday, 11–5 Saturday,
12–4:30 Sunday

DIRECTIONS: From I-82 heading east or west, take exit 52 toward Zillah. Turn left on Cheyne Rd. Turn right on Highland Drive and go about 2.5 miles—Portteus Vineyards and Winery is on your right.

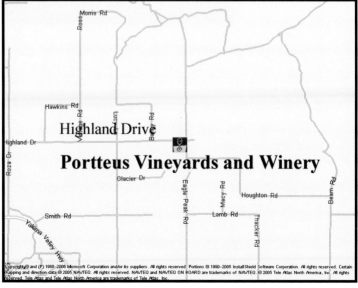

Rattlesnake Hills
WineTrail South

In 2006, the Rattlesnake Hills region of Yakima Valley obtained the American Viticultural Area (AVA) designation. Winemakers with years of experience and newcomers alike banded together to obtain this prestigious federal label. With their newly won AVA title, it wasn't long before most wineries worked together to promote their produce and sponsor a variety of events.

Beginning with Claar Cellars, situated along the I-82 exit near Zillah, to Horizon's Edge Winery, Eaton Hill Winery, Tefft Cellars, and Steppe Cellars traveling to the east, WineTrail enthusiasts will need to budget the better part of a day to experience these tasting rooms.

1 Claar Cellars

2 Horizon's Edge Winery

3 Eaton Hill Winery

4 Tefft Cellars Winery

5 Steppe Cellars

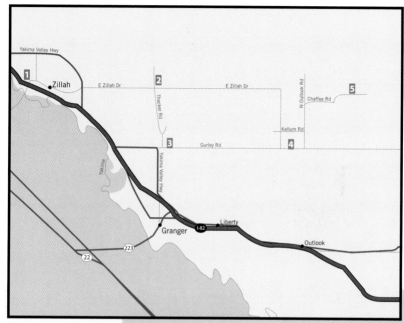

Region:	**Yakima Valley Wine Country**
# of tasting rooms on tour:	**5**
Estimated # of days for tour:	**1 or 2**
Getting around:	**Car or bike**
Key events:	❑ **Spring Barrel Tasting in the Yakima Valley (last weekend in April); Red Wine and Chocolate (mid-February); and Catch the Crush (October) sponsored by Wine Yakima Valley. See www.wineyakimavalley.org.** ❑ **Rattlesnake Hills Wine Trail Association sponsors events during the year.**
Tips:	❑ **Purchase Rattlesnake Hills Winery Association Passport and get discounts on wine purchases and more.** ❑ **Consider hiring a limousine service (e.g., S.U.V. Tours 509-783-7060, A+ Pacific Limousine 206-437-1298 or Sunset Coach Tours 800-941-2941, to name a few).** ❑ **Stay at the Outlook Inn Guest House at Tefft Cellars (two night minimum stay).** ❑ **Check out El Ranchito Restaurant in Zillah for your south-of-the-border cravings.**
Best:	❑ **Best Destination: Tefft Cellars' Outlook Inn** ❑ **Best Views: Steppe Cellars**

Claar Cellars

Few of us will be lucky enough to visit the Claar Cellars winery and vineyard, located in the White Bluffs area of the Columbia Valley Appellation. It's certainly off the beaten path. However, getting to the Claar Cellars tasting room is easy: Take Exit 52 off I-82 and you are practically there. A huge, puncheon-sized barrel, with Claar Cellars' distinctive red-lion logo embossed on its side, stands in front of the Zillah tasting room. Bob and Crista Claar Whitelatch have been farming in the White Bluffs area for more than 20 years. Early on, they found a market for their prized grapes, and in 1997, took the plunge and began crushing

their own grapes, starting out in a 10,000-square-foot facility. Over time, the couple has gradually expanded the winemaking facility, hired an experienced winemaker, and been awarded a boatload of gold, silver, and bronze hardware.

French-born Bruno Corneaux grew up in a wine-making family; it's certainly in his blood. After years of training, internships, and experience in many countries, learning various techniques and honing his abilities, Bruno took up the winemaking duties for Claar Cellars in early 2000. He's charged with converting the White Bluffs produce into excellent riesling, chardonnay, sauvignon blanc, cabernet sauvignon, merlot, sangiovese, and other wines. One particular red blend of note is called "Corneauxcopia" (of course).

John Claar Whitelatch manages the attractive tasting room and has an extensive knowledge of Claar Cellars' history and winemaking techniques. He should—he's Bob and Crista's son. With friendly aplomb and bottle in hand, John fields visitor questions and keeps the samples coming. Depending on availability, all Claar Cellars estate wines are available for tasting. If it's not sold out, check out the "Corneauxcopia" and experience why this wine has taken home the gold at prestigious wine-tasting events. Claar Cellars is an active member of the Rattlesnake Hills Winery Association and participates in its events throughout the year. If the tasting-room parking lot is nearly full when you arrive, you know that you've timed your visit with an event weekend. No worries! John and his staff efficiently handle the crowd.

CLAAR CELLARS
opened: 2000
winemaker(s): Bruno Corneaux
location: 1001 Vintage Valley Parkway
Zillah, WA 98953
phone: 509-829-6810 (Z)
web: www.claarcellars.com
e-mail: claar@claarcellars.com (P) zillah@
claarcellars.com (Z)
picnic area: Yes
gift shop: Yes
fee: Complimentary wine tasting
hours: Zillah—daily 10–6; Pasco—by
appointment only

DIRECTIONS: From I-82 heading east or west, take exit 52 onto Toppenish Zillah Rd. Head toward Zillah and take first left onto Vintage Valley Parkway. The Claar Cellar tasting room is on the right.

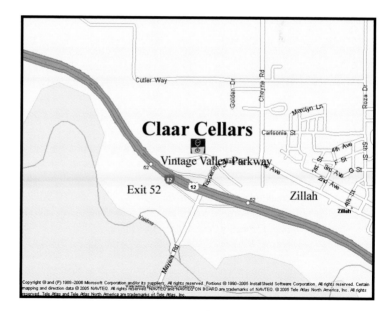

Horizon's Edge Winery

Got a sweet tooth? If so, Horizon's Edge Winery, along the Rattlesnake Hills South WineTrail, might be just what the doctor ordered. Try Horizon's Edge ice wine, Nouveaux Riche, port, or cream sherry to satisfy that sweet tooth. On the other hand, if you're not in a sweet mood, winemaker/owner David Padgett has Bordeaux-style estate wines to meet
your needs.

If you are familiar with the sister winery of Horizon's Edge—Maison de Padgett—you will recognize that the labels are unmistakably David Padgett's handiwork. Adjectives such as whacky, unorthodox, and whimsical might spring to mind as you gaze at the label of "Brittney's Butterfly" ice wine. You will also notice that this is a working winery, from vineyard to bottling. To those wine lovers who have grown used to business-park wineries, where the continuity from vineyard and winemaking is broken, Horizon's Edge will be a new experience. Adjacent to the winery are 18 acres of Yakima Valley wine grapes for Horizon's Edge use. Assuming there are 3 tons of grapes per acre, that's 108,000 pounds of grapes by our way of reckoning. Incidentally, if you hold a Rattlesnake Hills Passport, you will get 12 percent off wine purchases, increased to 15 percent for a case of wine.

While you satisfy your sweet tooth, make sure you take time to enjoy the views of Mount Rainier and Mount Adams on the horizon's edge.

HORIZON'S EDGE WINERY
opened: 2000
winemaker(s): David Padgett
location: 4530 East Zillah Drive
Zillah, WA 98953-9326
phone: 509-829-6401
e-mail: yvwine@aol.com
picnic area: Yes
gift shop: No
fee: Small tasting fee
hours: 11–5 Thursdays through Mondays, Tuesdays
and Wednesdays by chance, from March through
November; open Presidents Day Weekend 11–5

DIRECTIONS: Take I-82 to exit 54, go north on Yakima Valley Hwy .5 miles, then go east on East
Zillah Drive 3 miles. Winery is on the right.

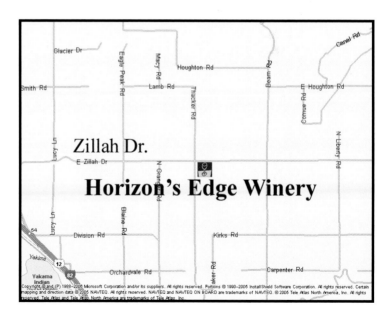

Eaton Hill Winery

Eaton Hill Winery is located in the restored Rinehold Cannery building, originally built by Floyd Rinehold for his bride, Emma Eaton, in the early 1900s. The structure itself is worth the trip, and you'll want to spend some time outside the building to study its elegant architecture. If this building looks familiar, you may have seen it on a wall calendar or a coffee-table book. Clearly,

Floyd Rinehold was a master builder of his era. The interior of this former fruit and vegetable cannery provides ample space for Eaton Hill wines and merchandise.

Ed and JoAnn Stear own both this historic Yakima Valley property and Eaton Hill Winery. Launched in 1988, Eaton Hill features a wide range of wines, including but not limited to cabernet sauvignon, chardonnay, gewürztraminer, semillon, muscat canelli, chenin blanc, and sauvignon blanc.

Eaton Hill Winery is an active member of the Rattlesnake Hills Wine Tour Passport program. Passport visitors get 10 percent off bottle purchases and 5 percent off in addition to the regular discount on case purchases. Winery events are held in coordination with the Rattlesnake Hills Winery Association and include Spring Barrel Tasting in April; Going Vertical! on Labor Day Weekend; Red Wine and Chocolate in February; and the Thanksgiving Festival in November.

EATON HILL WINERY
opened: 1988
winemaker(s): Gary Rogers
location: 530 Gurley Road
Granger, WA 98932-9432
phone: 509-854-2220
picnic area: Yes
gift shop: Yes
fee: Complimentary wine tasting
hours: Daily 10–5 from February through November;
daily 12–4 in December and January

DIRECTIONS: If heading east on I-82 take exit 54. Turn right onto Yakima Valley Hwy and go 3 miles. Keep left onto Gurley Rd, continue .5 miles and arrive at 530 Gurley Rd.
If traveling west on I-82 take exit 58 and go west on Yakima Valley Hwy and then right on Gurley Rd .5 miles. Arrive at Eaton Hill Winery at 530 Gurley Rd.

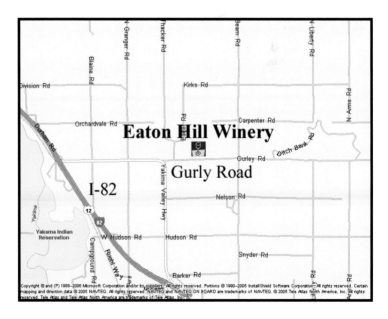

Tefft Cellars Winery

Tefft Cellars offers a treasure trove of memories. If you're like us, the number-one memory you will take from this place is a sense of ease. Tefft Cellars has a knack for making you feel special, no matter what your experience with wine

Mural outside Tefft Cellars Winery

has been. Simply stated, the owners and staff are gracious hosts. It's the type of place your wine-shy mother would enjoy.

Also memorable is Tefft's "out of the box" approach to packaging its wines. The winery offers the 4-liter cabernet sauvignon-merlot blend at $21.95 a box. That's not a typo, that's a good deal. Also, you can find "split"-size 375-milliliter bottles of wine in six packs. But, for those who still enjoy the sound of the cork pulled from a traditional 750-milliliter bottle, those are available too.

As an added bonus, the wines served in the tasting room are presented in Reidel stemware. When a winery uses Reidel in place of the small orange juice glasses, WineTrail lovers know they've come to the right place. The glasses are perfect for sampling Joel Tefft's handcrafted wines. And the names of those wines will quickly register in your Tefft Cellars memory database: "Villarocca," "Rosey Outlook," "River Mist," "Saints Wine," "Black Ice," and "Starboard."

While there, you might also want to check out the newly renovated Outlook Inn Guest House. With three full-sized bedrooms, each equipped with it's own bathroom, and a fully functional kitchen, dining area, and cozy living room, you might just want to reserve it for your next Yakima Valley wine country tour.

If you didn't notice the outside mural on your way into the tasting room, make sure you pause and experience it on your way out. The mural depicts various wine-related scenes, from crush to spring barrel tasting. Despite the bright sun, the mural's vibrant colors invite the viewer to be drawn into the scene. After a short while, one of the characters might appear to be you! However, that's a bizarre memory, and we certainly didn't mean to imply that we had that experience...certainly not.

Mural outside Tefft Cellars Winery

TEFFT CELLARS WINERY
opened: 1991
winemaker(s): Joel Tefft
location: 1320 Independence Road
Outlook, WA 98938
phone: 509-837-7651
web: www.tefftcellars.com
e-mail: tcwinery@aol.com
picnic area: Yes
gift shop: Yes
fee: Small tasting fee may apply
hours: Daily 10–5

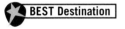

BEST Destination

DIRECTIONS: If heading east on I-82 take exit 54 and turn right (south) onto Yakima Valley Hwy. Continue about 3 miles and keep left onto Gurley Rd and proceed 3 miles. The road name changes to Independence Rd—continue another 1.3 miles and arrive at 1320 Independence Rd. Tefft Cellars is on the right.

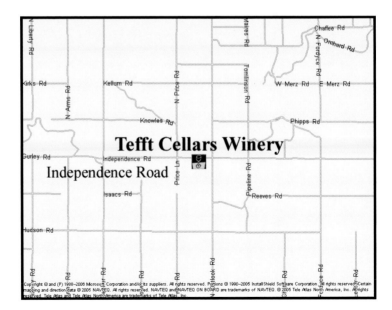

Steppe Cellars

Named after the shrub steppe environment of the surrounding ecosystem, Steppe Cellars is the creation of Tom and Susan Garrison and Terry and Anne Harrison. Although they could have easily named their winery "Harrison and Garrison," they elected to go with a name that gives credit to the land that they call home. Tom Garrison has been growing wine grapes since the early 1980s, and one of the buyers of his grapes at that time was Terry Harrison. It turns out that Terry was using Tom's grapes to fulfill his own winemaking hobby.

It was only natural that the grape-growing/winemaking relationship would cultivate discussions of launching their very own winery, and with the support

of co-conspirators Susan and Anne, Tom and Terry decided to start Steppe Cellars. However, in the beginning, they were given three pieces of advice: 1. Don't do it, 2. Don't do it, but if you do, keep your day job, and 3. Don't do it, but if you do, hire an experienced winemaker.

Well, as Terry points out, they succeeded in adhering to two out of three recommendations. In fact, they hired as their winemaker Anke Freimuth-Wildman, a native of Germany whose pedigree includes many generations of winemakers. Despite the young winery's short history, Anke has used her old-world winemaking expertise to create amazing riesling and gewürztraminer wines. Of course, it doesn't hurt to be blessed with excellent fruit from the Yakima Valley, including riesling grapes from Tom and Susan's Dalkeith Farm.

The tasting room is "Quonset hut chic"—literally—with a "swamp cooler" providing welcome relief from the summertime heat, and patio heaters strategically placed inside for wintertime comfort. It's a perfect wine tasting environment: cozy, comfortable, and inviting.

STEPPE CELLARS
opened: 2006
winemaker(s): Anke Freimuth-Wildman
location: 1991 Chaffee Road
Sunnyside, WA 98944
phone: 509-837-8281
web: www.steppecellars.com
e-mail: steppecellars@steppecellars.com
picnic area: No
gift shop: No
fee: Complimentary wine tasting
hours: 11–5 Thursday, Friday, and Sunday, 11–6
Saturday, from April through October; from November
through March, by appointment only

(l to r) Terry and Anne Harrison and Susan and Tom Garrison.

BEST Views

DIRECTIONS: From I-82 take exit 63 to Hwy 12 and turn left. Continue on Hwy 12 till you reach Outlook Rd (will turn into North Outlook Rd), then turn right. Continue on North Outlook Rd for 5 miles past Van Belle Rd and Independence Rd. Turn right onto Chaffee Rd. Go another 2 miles on Chaffee Rd. The winery is located on the left-hand side of the road at the top of the hill.

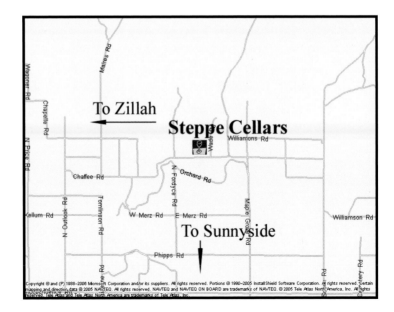

Sunnyside-Grandview
WineTrail

True WineTrail enthusiasts stop when they see a sign for a highway
with the name "Wine Country Road." Hello. We're there. With
wineries that include Apex, Bridgman (actually a second tier wine of
Apex), Tucker, and Manchego Real, your afternoon is set. Your drive
from Sunnyside to Grandview is a swivel-head experience with acre
upon acre of lush farms. Drivers need to be careful to keep their eyes
on the road with fall's bounty being especially glorious. After you
have driven a short duration, you can readily see why the Yakima
Valley became the state's first designated American Viticultural Area
in 1983.

Sunnyside-Grandview WineTrail

1A Apex Cellars
1B Bridgman Winery

2 Tucker Cellars

3 Manchego Real Winery

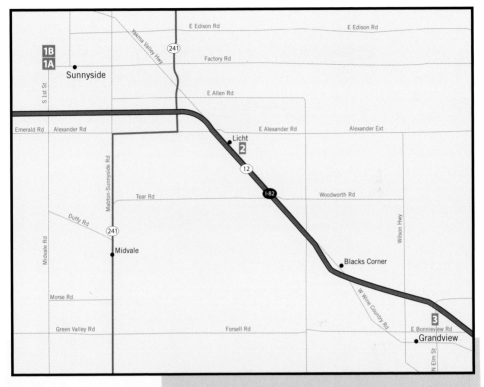

Region:	**Yakima Valley Wine Country**
# of tasting rooms on tour:	**3**
Estimated # of days for tour:	**1**
Getting around:	**Car**
Key events:	❑ **Spring Barrel Tasting in the Yakima Valley (last weekend in April); Red Wine and Chocolate (mid-February); and Catch the Crush (October) sponsored by Wine Yakima Valley. See www.wineyakimavalley.org.**
Tips:	❑ **Two for one tasting at Apex Cellars—Bridgman Cellars is the second tier wine of Apex.**
	❑ **Check out Tucker's gift shop for local fair.**

Apex Cellars and Bridgman Winery

Brian Carter, chief winemaker for Apex, Apex II, and Bridgman wines is a problem solver. He has worked with all types of fruit—from pears to cabernet sauvignon—to coax the best flavors possible from them. Given a budget and a source of grapes, he will figure out the best solution to convert the fruit to a marketable beverage. He has collected a bundle of awards along the winemaking

road and is considered one of Washington's top winemakers. Even though he recently launched Woodinville-based Brian Carter Cellars (summer 2006) he remains the winemaker for Apex, Apex II, and Bridgman wineries in Sunnyside.

A visit to the red-brick Sunnyside location is analogous to pulling into a gas station. The Bridgman label is its regular offering; the Apex II is the premium; and the Apex brand is for its very limited super premium red blends. As you would expect, the price point goes up from the regular Bridgman to the high-octane Apex. While the connoisseurs among us might agree that the Apex is the *ne plus ultra*, or highest point of excellence, most WineTrail enthusiasts would readily agree that Bridgman is the best value for the buck.

In the winery's tasting room, a large number of mouth-watering reds and whites will greet you. Bridgman and Apex II wines are complimentary, but there is a small (yet well worthwhile) tasting fee for the ultrapremium Apex. While there, take a short tour of the facility and check out the banquet room (which comfortably sits 20) for family gatherings and company events. The outside garden offers a nice spot to hold a wedding or an outdoor barbecue. Moreover, Apex is big on events and cooking classes, and the tasting room staff will be happy to share the winery's schedule of events.

Brian Carter's wines are extraordinary. Consumers trust his wines because of the high quality found in bottle after bottle. Taste this quality for yourself. Just pull up to the tasting room bar and say, "Fill 'er up." **WineTrail Note:** If you are a Seattleite and can't make the trip to beautiful downtown Sunnyside, you can experience Apex wines at The Tasting Room in Post Alley at the Pike Place Market.

APEX CELLARS AND BRIDGMAN WINERY
opened: 1988
winemaker(s): Brian Carter
location: 111 East Lincoln Avenue
Sunnyside, WA 98944-2129
phone: 509-839-9463
web: www.apexcellars.com
e-mail: tastingroom@apexcellars.com
picnic area: Yes
gift shop: Yes
fee: Complimentary for Apex II and Bridgman wines;
small fee for Apex wines
hours: Daily 10–5; winter, 11–6 Thursday through
Monday, or by appointment

DIRECTIONS: From I-82 heading east or west, take exit 67 and go north toward Sunnyside 1 miles on S. 1st St. Go right onto Lincoln Ave. and Apex Winery is located immediately on your right. (Note: This is also the location for their second tier wine—Bridgman.)

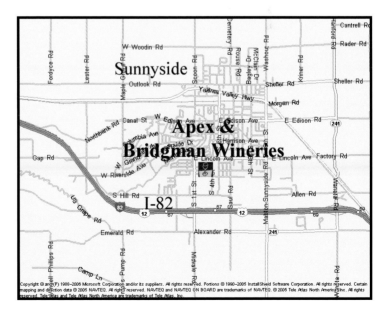

Tucker Cellars

Located on the Sunnyside-Grandview WineTrail, Tucker Cellars is just off I-82 at exit 69. This is the place to "enjoy a taste of Yakima Valley," as the Tuckers like to say. And your taste buds will likely agree: You can sample and purchase third-generation Tucker farm products, from pickled asparagus spears to White Cloud popcorn to muscat canelli.

Road sign near Tucker Cellars

Randy Tucker and his wife, Debbie, own Tucker Cellars, and rely on the fruit and vegetables of nearby Tucker Farm to produce a full array of red and white wines, as well as a variety of pickled and packaged produce. This is "one-stop shopping," Yakima Valley style. Don't pass up the opportunity to experience what Yakima Valley is famous for: great produce and down-home friendliness.

Wine snobs need to check the attitude at the door. The tasting room is a truly relaxed environment, and you are free to take a self-guided tour of the production area and barrel room, and peruse the many gift items before you sample Tucker Cellars' delicious wines. A picnic area is next to the tasting room for those so inclined.

The wines Tucker Cellars offer—and there are many—come courtesy of its 50-acre estate vineyard. Back in 1981, Randy's parents, Dean and Rose Tucker, had the foresight to plant such varietals as riesling, pinot noir, gewürztraminer, chenin blanc, chardonnay, and muscat canelli. Now, more than 25 years later, you can reap the pleasures of these mature vineyard wines, which winemaker Randy offers in the tasting room. He also produces several specialty wines that keep customers coming back, including "Indian Summer," a white pinot rosé, and a syrah port.

Tucker Cellars doesn't stand on formality. That easygoing attitude makes it a fun place to visit and experience Yakima Valley's wines and produce. And the prices will leave money in the bank for your next generation.

TUCKER CELLARS
opened: 1981
winemaker(s): Randy Tucker
location: 70 Ray Road
Sunnyside, WA 98944
phone: 509-837-8701
web: www.tuckercellars.com
e-mail: wineman@televar.com
picnic area: Yes
gift shop: Yes
fee: Complimentary wine tasting
hours: Daily 10–5 summer; daily 10–4 winter

DIRECTIONS: From I-82 heading east or west, take exit 69 and go north onto SR-241 [Waneta Rd]. Go right on Yakima Valley Hwy about 1.5 miles. Tucker Cellars is located on the left.

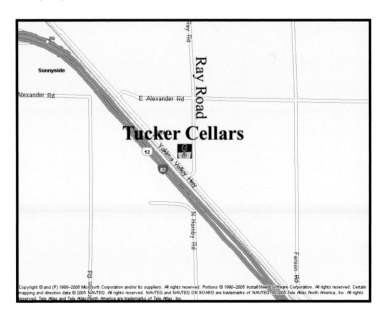

Manchego Real Winery

Formerly named Don Quixote Wines, Manchego Real is a relatively young winery located in Grandview, in the heart of Yakima Valley. The actual winery and tasting room is housed in a rather plain warehouse in an industrial park. Visitors enjoy the fact that there is no separation between barrel room and tasting area. The tasting area is surrounded by rows of barrels stacked four and five high. Consequently, you get that musty redolent smell of herbs from the oak and evaporated wine. It's a perfect setting for sampling Manchego Real wines. Surprise find: Check out the "Port de Real." At 18.2 percent alcohol, it's sweet enough to be dessert!

Jose G. Cervantes is the owner/winemaker of Manchego Real. (It's unknown if Jose is a distant relative of Miguel de Cervantes, author of *Don Quixote*.) Jose and other family members own and manage one of the state's oldest vineyards, the Roza Berge. As they proudly point out, "From its quality plantings, the finest grapes are raised." There's no one fighting windmills here. Salut!

MANCHEGO REAL WINERY
winemaker(s): Jose G. Cervantes
location: 604 North Elm Street
Grandview, WA 98930
phone: 509-882-6111
web: www.manchegoreal.com
e-mail: cervantes@futurelnk.net
picnic area: No
gift shop: No
fee: Complimentary wine tasting
hours: Daily 10–4

Tasting room at Manchego Real

DIRECTIONS: If traveling east on I-82 take exit 73 and turn left onto W. Wine Country Rd [Yakima Valley Hwy]. Go about 1.3 miles—name changes to E. Main St. [Yakima Valley Hwy]. Turn left (north) onto N. Elm St. and go .3 miles and arrive at 604 N. Elm St.
If heading west on I-82 take exit 75 and turn left onto McCreadie Rd for .2 miles. Turn right onto E. Wine Country Rd [Yakima Valley Hwy] and go .5 miles. Road name changes to E. Main St. [E. Wine Country Rd] and continue .2 miles. Turn right onto N. Elm St. and proceed .3 miles to 604 N. Elm St.

Prosser
WineTrail North

Despite having eight wineries included in Prosser WineTrail North, you just might sample all of them in one day. How is this possible? Well, when five tasting rooms are located right off I-82 exit 82 on Lee Road, you can simply park your car and go like trick-or-treaters from one winery to another—Hogue, C.R. Sandidge, Alexandria Nicole, Cowan, and Kestrel Wineries. The other three wineries included in this WineTrail, Chinook Wines, VineHeart and Pontin del Roza, are an easy drive from Lee Road. Each winery is distinctively different. Each one is memorable.

Remember, drink responsibly; drive responsibly. Those little ounces add up.

Prosser WineTrail North

1 Chinook Wines   4 Alexandria Nicole Cellars   7 Pontin del Roza Winery
2 Hogue Cellars   5 Cowan Vineyards   8 VineHeart Winery
3 C.R. Sandidge Wines   6 Kestrel Vintners

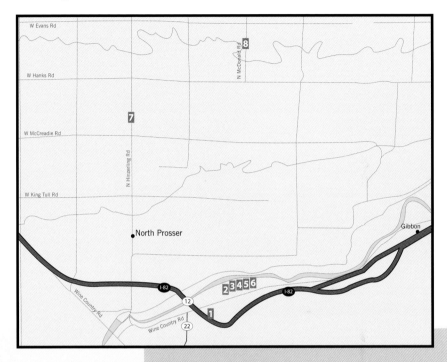

Region:	**Yakima Valley Wine Country**
# of tasting rooms on tour:	**8**
Estimated # of days for tour:	**2**
Getting around:	**Car and foot**
Key events:	❑ **Spring Barrel Tasting in the Yakima Valley (last weekend in April); Red Wine and Chocolate (mid-February); and Catch the Crush (October) sponsored by Wine Yakima Valley. See www.wineyakimavalley.org.**
Tips:	❑ **Park and walk to five winery tasting rooms at the Lee Road location.**
	❑ **Alexandria Nicole Cellars restaurant features tapas menu.**
	❑ **Consider hiring a limousine service (e.g., S.U.V. Tours 509-783-7060, A+ Pacific Limousine 206-437-1298 or Sunset Coach Tours 800-941-2941, to name a few).**

 Best:
❑ **Best Eats: Alexandria Nicole Cellars**
❑ **Best Gift Shop: Hogue Cellars**
❑ **Best Picnicking: VineHeart Winery and Chinook Wines**
❑ **Best for Weddings: VineHeart Winery**

Chinook Wines

In Prosser, at the intersection of Wittkopf Loop and Wine Country Road, the paths of winemaker and viticulturist also cross. Since 1983, Kay Simon and Clay Mackey have joined forces to create great wines under the Chinook Winery label. Their wines showcase the Yakima Valley varietals, including chardonnay,

Chinook Wines picnic area

sauvignon blanc, semillon, cabernet franc, cabernet sauvignon, and merlot. Assisted by Copper—the ever-present golden retriever— Kay and Clay warmly host winery guests in their renovated farmhouse. This is a favorite stop along the Prosser WineTrail, and it's no wonder, given the charming tasting room, a gorgeous garden for picnicking, and the surrounding vineyard, plum and cherry orchards. Pack a picnic for this WineTrail stop!

As you swirl and sip, you're struck by Kay and Clay's simple but noble vision to produce small quantities of delicious, aged wines. They have no aspirations for world domination or cranking out large quantities of wine. You might also be struck by the distinctive Chinook wine label and may recall that you have seen it before. No doubt you have. Clay routinely hops in the truck and makes deliveries to Seattle-area restaurants and wine shops.

Chinook wines are intended to complement Northwest cuisine. To encourage this pairing, Kay and Clay offer a no-fuss recipe for grilled, fennel-crusted salmon on their website. This salmon is an excellent choice for pairing with Chinook's sauvignon blanc.

Chinook Winery is a joy to visit … repeatedly.

CHINOOK WINES
opened: 1983
winemaker(s): Kay Simon
location: P.O. Box 387
Prosser, WA 99350
phone: 509-786-2725
web: www.chinookwines.com
e-mail: info@chinookwines.com
picnic area: Yes
gift shop: No
fee: Complimentary wine tasting
hours: 12–5 Saturday and Sunday from May
through October

 **BEST Picnicking**

DIRECTIONS: From I-82 traveling east or west, take exit 82 and go east onto SR-22 [Wine Country Rd] and go about .5 miles. Turn right onto Wittkopf Loop and arrive at Chinook Winery on the right.

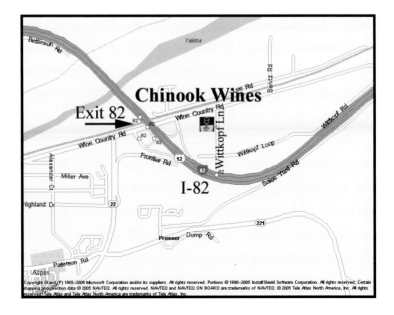

Hogue Cellars

Some tasting rooms can take an hour or more to experience. The Hogue Cellars tasting room happens to be such a place.

At the Lee Road tasting room in Prosser, visitors begin by sampling wines under three different Hogue Cellars wine labels: First is Hogue Cellars wine, which includes a full line-up of fruit-forward Yakima and Columbia Valley reds and

Original Artwork inside tasting room

whites. Next up is Hogue's pricier Genesis label, which features varietals from select vineyards. The final offerings are Hogue Reserve wines: chardonnay, merlot, and cabernet sauvignon. Among Hogue's tasting notes is the following description about its Reserve cabernet sauvignon, "Aromas of bright cherry and an undercurrent of earth are followed by flavors of intense berry and cherry, and a pleasant hint of forest floor." The "hint of forest floor" may require deep concentration to taste but the "intense berry and cherry" are unmistakable.

WineTrail Note: Hogue's limited-edition "*Terroir*" wines are sold only at the tasting room; you won't find these wines in grocery stores or wine shops. These wines also cannot be found among the standard tasting room offerings at Hogue. If you're interested in sampling the "*Terroir*" wines, ask your server.

As you work your way down the list of Hogue Cellars labels, it becomes apparent why this winery produces nearly a half-million cases of wine annually. With years of experience under the ownership of Mike and Gary Hogue, access to great fruit from the Columbia and Yakima valleys, industrial-strength winemaking equipment, and top-notch winemakers, Hogue Cellars offers consistent quality throughout its product line. Also, while you are swirling and sampling, note the original museum-quality art featured behind the wine bar, as well as Hogue's specially concocted red pepper cheese spread (which we discovered pairs wonderfully with its Reserve merlot). Assuming you don't need to dash to the next winery, check out the amply stocked gift shop. It features many unique wine-related items, including the distinctive Wine Country "Perfectly Balanced" posters.

By now, an hour has gone. My, how time flies when you're imbibing fine, fine wine!

HOGUE CELLARS
opened: 1982
winemaker(s): Co Dinn, Jordan Ferrier
location: 2800 Lee Road
Prosser, WA 99350-5520
phone: 509-786-4557
web: www.hoguecellars.com
e-mail: info@hoguecellars.com
picnic area: Yes
gift shop: Yes
fee: Complimentary wine tasting; $5 tasting fee for reserve wines waived with purchase
hours: Daily 10–5 except major holidays; call ahead for winter hours (January through Presidents Day Weekend)

BEST Gift shop

DIRECTIONS: From I-82 heading east or west, take exit 82 onto SR-22 [Wine Country Rd] and go about .75 miles. Turn left (north) onto Benitz Rd followed by a right into the Lee Rd "Wine and Food Park." Hogue Cellars tasting room is on the left.

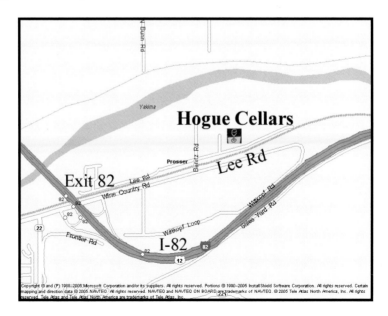

C.R. Sandidge Wines

The story behind C.R. Sandidge Wines is Ray Sandidge himself. End of story. Some wineries are more like companies and survive despite losing their winemakers. However, the heartbeat of C.R. Sandidge is Ray. We can only hope that he doesn't win the lottery, move to Australia, and start "C.R. Sandidge Down Under."

Ray's winemaking journey began at Washington State University, where he studied horticulture, using grapes as his research material. In 1985, Ray became a member of a winemaking team at Pindar Vineyards on Long Island, New York. As co-winemaker, he produced a cabernet sauvignon that was selected for George H. W. Bush's inaugural ball. In 1987, Ray traveled even farther east and

worked at Germany's 120-year-old Georg Breuer Winery. Ray honed his winemaking talents by focusing on riesling, which won him accolades from German wine critics. That's truly an amazing feat in a country with 12,000 wineries.

In 1991, Ray returned home to the Yakima Valley and worked at Apex Cellars as a co-winemaker. That was followed by a stint as Hyatt

Outside C.R. Sandidge tasting room in Prosser

Winery's chief winemaker beginning in 1995. Then, in 1998, Ray joined Prosser's Kestrel Vintners as their winemaker. It would prove to be his last job on someone else's payroll. In 2004, he launched his own winery.

At the Prosser tasting room on Lee Road, WineTrail trekkers can experience Ray's exceptional reds, including syrah, his red blend "Tri*Umph," or "Stone Tree" red. However, don't neglect Ray's viognier, with its pronounced flavors of ripe peach. If you happen to be visiting Chelan, you can also experience C.R. Sandidge wines at its new tasting room and bistro in historic downtown Chelan. Call ahead or visit its website to time your visit for when the bistro is open. During its bistro hours, you can enjoy a bottle or a glass of C.R. Sandidge and choose from a menu that features Mediterranean and European fare. Try this pairing on for size: an 8-oz. grilled lamb brochette served on sautéed apple and sweet potato slices with a glass of C.R. Sandidge "Tri*Umph." From WSU to Long Island to Germany and home again, Ray took a circuitous route to get here. You can taste those experiences in every glass of C.R. Sandidge wine you pour.

C.R. SANDIDGE WINES
opened: 2004
winemaker(s): Ray Sandidge
location: 2880 Lee Road, Suite A
Prosser, WA 99350
phone: 509-786-1100
web: www.crsandidgewines.com
e-mail: manager@crsandidgewines.com
picnic area: Yes
gift shop: No
fee: Complimentary wine tasting
hours: 10–5 from Wednesday through Sunday, or
by appointment

Proud staff at C.R. Sandidge tasting room

DIRECTIONS: From I-82 heading east or west, take exit 82 onto SR-22 [Wine Country Rd] and go about .7 miles. Turn left (north) onto Benitz Rd followed by a right into the Lee Rd "Wine and Food Park." C.R. Sandidge Wines tasting room is on the left in Suite A. (Note: Another C.R. Sandidge tasting room is found in Chelan.)

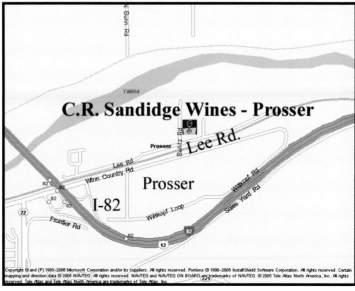

Alexandria Nicole Cellars

In terms of tasting-room experiences, the bar has now been set several notches higher in Prosser's Lee Road wine district. And Alexandria Nicole Cellars is responsible. A recent renovation of its tasting room has resulted in a warm and inviting space in which visitors can taste wine, enjoy tapas, and relax by the gas fireplace. Such details speak volumes about the quality of the winery, the staff, and how wine helps us celebrate life. In this setting, bacon-wrapped scallops with mango salsa seem to go down especially smoothly with a glass of sauvignon blanc.

The winery's mission statement is brief but meaningful: "Alexandria Nicole Cellars is dedicated to producing small lots of hand-crafted wine from our Destiny Ridge Estate Vineyard." (Yes, WineTrail enthusiasts, that's the renowned

Alexandria Nicole Cellars, Horse Heaven Hills

Destiny Ridge Vineyard: 232 acres of prime grape-growing real estate in the newly designated Horse Heaven Hills appellation overlooking the Columbia River in Patterson.) From Jarrod Boyle, Alexandria Nicole's winemaker, to its tasting-room staff, there is a collective recognition that it all begins with the fruit. This focus on the grapes of Destiny Ridge is reflected in the following quotation, posted on the cellars' web site: "There is an old expression that the best thing farmers can put on their field is their shadow. This means being out in the field and observing what is happening." In the case of Alexandria Nicole Cellars, "out in the field" means attentive viticulture management, balanced crop levels, and gentle hand-harvesting, factors that translate into quality in every bottle. It's a memorable moment when you taste the *terroir* of an estate-made wine. Alexandria Nicole Cellars offers this experience, because each sip of its wines reflects the intense flavors of Destiny Ridge.

Be prepared for simple elegance at this WineTrail location. You won't step over a golden retriever here or negotiate your way around old farm equipment to get to the wine bar. Rather, the Alexandria Nicole Cellars experience is a combination of world-class wine meets Pottery Barn, with a friendly staff at your service. (Hint: If you go on a Thursday night, you'll enjoy live music while sampling Destiny Ridge's terroir.) Cheers.

ALEXANDRIA NICOLE CELLARS
opened: 1998
winemaker(s): Jarrod Boyle
location: 2880 Lee Road, Suite C
Prosser, WA 99350
phone: 509-786-3497
web: www.alexandrianicolecellars.com
e-mail: info@alexandrianicolecellars.com
picnic area: Yes
gift shop: No
fee: $5 tasting fee refundable upon purchase
hours: Daily 11–5

 BEST Eats

DIRECTIONS: From I-82 heading east or west, take exit 82 onto SR-22 [Wine Country Rd] and go about .75 miles. Turn left (north) onto Benitz Rd followed by a right into the Lee Rd "Wine and Food Park." Alexandria Nicole Cellars tasting room is on the left in Suite C.

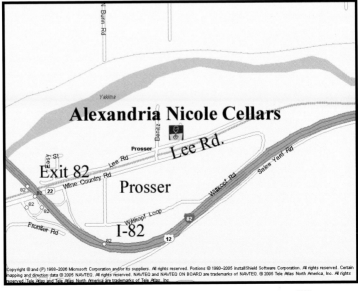

Cowan Vineyards

There's something special about a winemaker who begins his wine career as a grape grower. In Washington, to be both a viticulturist and a winemaker is unusual. On the other hand, in Italy, the concept of winemaker and grape grower as two separate vocations is downright foreign. Pose such an idea to the guys tossing bocce balls in the town square and they would look at you with raised eyebrows and think you're touched in the head. But the Cowan family began as growers first, and as David Cowan puts it, "I'm a dirt guy … I'm close to the ground." The Cowans' prized land is located near Prosser in the Yakima Valley AVA, and the grapes they grow reflect the richness and smooth softness of the area's *terroir*.

David cultivates 300 acres of fruit trees (including apple, cherry, and pear) and vineyards. Grapes alone account for 200 tons of pickings and include cabernet sauvignon, cabernet franc, merlot, gewürztraminer, and riesling. With that much fruit, David has other wineries lining up to buy his grapes. With so much demand for his grapes, it wasn't long before David realized that he had something very special, and the idea of starting his own winery using his choicest grapes took hold … or more appropriately, took root.

As David puts it, "Growing our own grapes gives us a definite advantage. We control every aspect of the grape all the way to crush. After the grapes are crushed, we decide which juice goes into what barrels and then age them at least 12 to 16 months. We decide when to bottle and have our own storage so the barrels stay at the right temperature and humidity." Sometimes it's good to be controlling.

The unique tartan label on bottles of Cowan wine reflects the family's Scottish heritage. In fact, if you happen to stop by while there is a Scottish festival in the area (as this WineTrail trekker did), there's a good chance you'll spot David wearing his kilt. David's wife, Susan, and their daughters can often be found in the tasting room serving up delicious reds (including their no. 1 seller, cabernet franc) as well as a wonderful gewürztraminer.

The Cowans' approach is summed up in their slogan: "Handcrafted from the Ground Up!"

COWAN VINEYARDS
opened: 2005
winemaker(s): David Cowan
location: 2880 Lee Road, Suite E
Prosser, WA 99350-9506
phone: 509-788-0200
web: www.cowanvineyards.com
e-mail: cowanfrt@bentonrea.com
picnic area: Yes
gift shop: Yes
fee: Complimentary wine tasting
hours: 12–5 Thursday through Monday from April
through November; winter hours, 12–5 Friday
through Sunday

David Cowan of Cowan Vineyards

DIRECTIONS: From I-82 heading east or west, take exit 82 onto SR-22 [Wine Country Rd] and go about .75 miles. Turn left (north) onto Benitz Rd followed by a right into the Lee Rd "Wine and Food Park." Cowan Vineyards tasting room is on the left in Suite E.

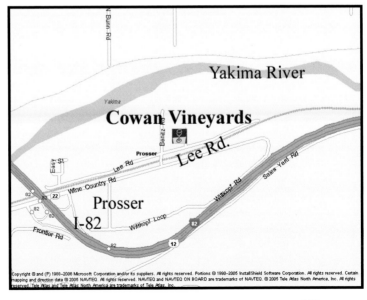

Kestrel Vintners

The common kestrel (*Falco tinnunculus*) is a bird of prey belonging to the falcon family, *Falconidae*. The bird is often found in the vineyards of Eastern Washington and is considered a great asset to the grape grower.

Located on 3 acres in the Prosser Wine and Food Park (on Lee Road), Kestrel Winery occupies 15,000 square feet comprising production space, barrel area, tasting room and gift shop. The "homey" tasting room brings us

here. Outside is a well manicured, landscaped area for picnicking, making it a definite stop along the Prosser WineTrail for unpacking something that goes well with a bottle of Yakima Valley's finest.

Of course, what's not to love about a winery whose no. 1 seller is "Lady in Red"? With its distinctive label, the "Lady in Red" series is a blend of three different grapes (merlot, syrah, and cabernet sauvignon) from three different vintages. Visitors are often seen leaving the tasting room with a case of "Lady in Red," which explains in part why, Kestrel produces 35,000 cases of wine annually. For the white-wine lovers, Kestrel offers a blend of gewürztraminer and viognier or, alternatively, chardonnay and viognier varietals, which are called "Platinum."

Ninety percent of the Kestrel wines sold are of the red persuasion, and a large percentage of the fruit comes right from the Kestrel vineyards. This 160-acre site caused Wine Enthusiast (Spring 2003) to exclaim, "A renowned vineyard, one of the ones to look out for in Washington." The remaining fruit comes from other growers in the Yakima Valley. From these intensely flavored grapes, winemaker Flint Nelson produces a variety of reds under different series labels, including Table Reds, Ultra Premium Wines, Winemaker Select, and Signature Edition.

But what makes this WineTrail stop most memorable is the tasting room itself. The owners of the winery (John and Helen Walker) believed it "should be like a living room with a relaxed and informal atmosphere, where customers could sample fine wines, learn more about the wine industry, and browse through the well-stocked gift shop." They've succeeded wonderfully in achieving this effect.

Kestrel's reserve tasting room

KESTREL VINTNERS
opened: 1999
winemaker(s): Flint Nelson
location: 2890 Lee Road
Prosser, WA 99350-5520
phone: 509-786-CORK (2675)
web: www.kestrelwines.com
e-mail: winery@kestrelwines.com
picnic area: Yes
gift shop: Yes
fee: Complimentary wine tasting
hours: Daily 10–5

DIRECTIONS: From I-82 heading east or west, take exit 82 onto SR-22 [Wine Country Rd] and go about .75 miles. Turn left (north) onto Benitz Rd followed by a right into the Lee Rd "winery row." Kestrel Vintners is in the Prosser Wine and Food Park at the east end of Lee Rd. (Note: a second Kestrel Vintners tasting room is found in Leavenworth.)

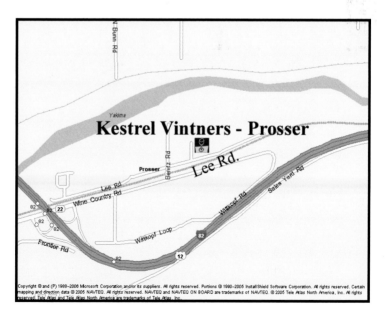

339

Pontin del Roza Winery

Scott Pontin began the Pontin Del Roza Winery as part of a Future Farmers of America project. He had yet to see his 21st birthday at the time. The Pontin (pronounced Pon-teen) family had farmed in the Yakima Valley for three generations and, with their Italian heritage, knew a thing or two about making wine. We don't know if Scott got a blue ribbon for his FFA project, but we do know that the Pontin Del Roza Winery was born in 1984.

The winery uses grapes grown only from "the Roza," an area of south-facing slopes along the north side of the Yakima Valley. Vintner Scott Pontin uses these homegrown grapes to make approximately 4,000 cases a year of white riesling, chenin blanc, cabernet, merlot, pinot gris, sangiovese, and other limited specialty wines. If you are looking for good value, make a beeline for Pontin Del Roza. Most wines sell for $15 or less.

The winery's north Prosser location on Hinzerling Road is a family affair that includes his parents and siblings. Picnic facilities are available, and the wine is complimentary. Moreover, you get a little bit of Italian/Prosser farmer wisdom when you visit the winery: Carved into a rock outside the tasting room is, "Age doesn't matter unless you are wine." That's *amore*.

PONTIN DEL ROZA WINERY
opened: 1984
winemaker(s): Scott Pontin
location: 35502 North Hinzerling Road
Prosser, WA 99350
phone: 509-786-4449
web: None
e-mail: pontindelroza@msn.com
picnic area: Yes
gift shop: Yes
fee: Complimentary wine tasting
hours: Daily 10–5

DIRECTIONS: From I-82 going east or west, take exit 80 and go north on N. Gap Rd 2.5 miles. Turn right onto W. McCreadie Rd and go 1 mile. Turn left onto N. Hinzerling Rd and go .2 miles. Pontin del Roza Winery is on the left.

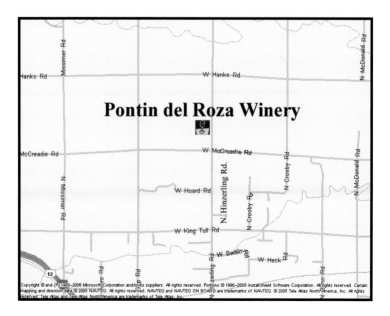

VineHeart Winery

Often, in the figurative sense of the word, there is a marriage between winemaker and grape grower. However, in the case of VineHeart Winery, the marriage between winemaker George Schneider and grape grower Patricia O'Brien is a literal one. They're hitched; and you could say it is a marriage

made in heaven, given their strong Christian beliefs. George began making wine in 1987. Patricia has been growing grapes in the Yakima Valley since 1991.

Their tasting room, located just a few miles north of Prosser, offers a spacious and inviting space to sample wine and enjoy a picnic indoors or outside, if the weather is nice. By the way, poke around outside and you'll discover a lawn vast enough to make John Deere break out in a sweat. This grassy expanse is a wonderful spot to host weddings, family reunions, and other get-togethers. If you have such an event in your future, talk to George or Patricia about your plans. There's plenty of parking space, barbecue grills, grounds, and of course, fine wine for hosting such an event.

Pat and George's goal is to create the highest-quality wines, with a hint of oak, using few additives. Add affordability to that goal; most of their wines sell for about $15 a bottle. Using estate grapes that have been handpicked and sorted, George crafts a full range of red and white wines, including a rosé named in honor of George's mother, Philomena Rose Schneider. Total annual production is approximately 2,000 cases annually. Besides the fine wine, you can also sample George's delicious smoked chicken, summer sausages, and cheeses that he sells under the Sebastian label. Try the samples of smoked cheese and sausage with the "Philomena Rose." Is this another marriage made in heaven?

George S. Schneider

VINEHEART WINERY
opened: 2000
winemaker(s): George Schneider
location: 44209 North McDonald Road
Prosser, WA 99350
phone: 509-973-2993
web: www.vineheart.com
e-mail: vinequeen@bentonrea.com
picnic area: Yes
gift shop: No
fee: Complimentary wine tasting
hours: 9–5 Thursday through Monday

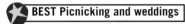

BEST Picnicking and weddings

DIRECTIONS: From I-82 going east or west, take exit 80 and go North on N. Gap Rd 3.7 miles. Turn right onto W. Hanks Rd and go 3 miles. Turn left onto N. McDonald Rd and go about .5 miles. The VineHeart Winery entrance is on the right.

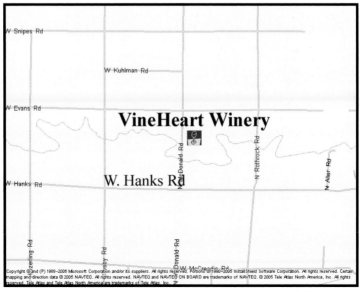

Prosser
WineTrail South

With nine wineries to choose from, your biggest challenge in touring Prosser WineTrail South will be which one to visit first.

Of course, anytime you can take Merlot Drive to Chardonnay Lane you have our attention...especially when the road takes you to Vintner's Village, where you find a varity of wineries within easy walking distance. Located near the town's center is one of the areas oldest wineries, Hinzerling. No visit here is complete without a taste or two of Hinzerling's popular ports. Snoqualmie Winery (one of the many properties of Ste. Michelle

Hangar doors to Airfield Estates Winery

Wine Estates) is strikingly beautiful in a rustic timbered way and offers wines of great value. For those who like their wines organic, check out Snoqualmie's naked brand (while wearing clothes, please). One of the newer wineries—and the grandest venue—is Desert Wind right off of exit 82 in Prosser. Finally, make sure you budget time to check out Yakima Cellars. Here you can sample premium wines and learn about the Valley's winemaking history.

Prosser WineTrail South

1 Canyon's Edge Winery   4 Willow Crest Winery   7 Hinzerling Winery
2 Airfield Estates Winery   5 Thurston Wolfe Winery   8 Snoqualmie Winery
3 Olsen Estates Winery   6 Yakima River Winery   9 Desert Wind Winery

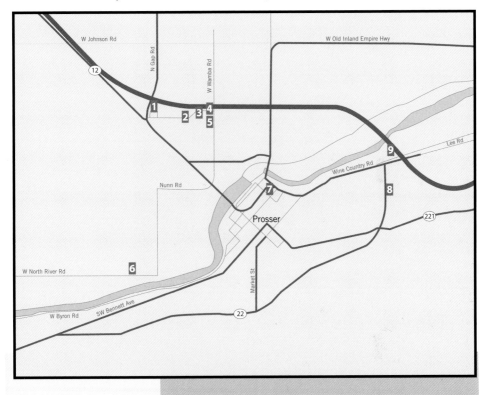

Region:	**Yakima Valley Wine Country**
# of tasting rooms on tour:	**9**
Estimated # of days for tour:	**1 to 2**
Getting around:	**Car**
Key events:	❑ **Spring Barrel Tasting in the Yakima Valley (last weekend in April); Red Wine and Chocolate (mid-February); and Catch the Crush (October) sponsored by Wine Yakima Valley. See www.wineyakimavalley.org.**
Tips:	❑ **The Vintner's Inn is Hinzerling Winery's B&B Restaurant and Wine Bar.**
	❑ **Consider hiring a limousine service (e.g., S.U.V. Tours 509- 783-7060, A+ Pacific Limousine 206-437-1298 or Sunset Coach Tours 800-941-2941, to name a few).**
	❑ **Coyote Canyon offers bistro fare.**
Best:	❑ **Best Picnicking: Snoqualmie Winery**
	❑ **Best View: Yakima River Winery**

Canyon's Edge Winery

Question: Maryhill Winery, Bookwalter, Barnard Griffin, Columbia Winery, Canoe Ridge, Gordon Brothers, and Apex Cellars are distinct wineries but they

have one big thing in common. Can you guess it?

Answer: They have all sourced their grapes from Aldercreek Vineyard in the Horse Heaven Hills and these are just a few of more than 40 wineries in total that rely on this exceptional vineyard.

At nearly 300 acres, the Aldercreek Vineyard enjoys the moderating influence of the Columbia River, arid climate, and lots of wind. The result is amazingly intense fruit sought after by many of the state's top wineries.

Now Canyon's Edge Winery has become the estate winery for Aldercreek and wine enthusiasts can experience their wines at their tasting room on Merlot Drive in Prosser opened in June of 2007. Managing owners, Dave and Brian Groth (father and son respectively) turned to experienced winemaker John P. Haw for converting their fruit into premium wine that showcases the Horse Heaven Hill's *terroir*.

Despite its winemaking youth, the portfolio of Canyon's Edge estate wines is ambitious. Featured at the tasting room are their Sage Brush Red table wine, merlot, syrah, cabernet sauvignon, cabernet franc, and Jeremiah's Chocolate Port. With the tagline, "Where Quality, the Palate and Value Meet," the tasting room is a charming stop along the Prosser WineTrail South.

CANYON'S EDGE WINERY
opened: 1998
winemaker(s): John P. Haw
location: 10 Merlot Drive; Suite D
Prosser, WA 99350
phone: 509-786-3032
web: www.canyonsedgewinery.com
e-mail: info@canyonsedgewinery.com
picnic area: No
gift shop: No
fee: Complimentary wine tasting
hours: Sunday through Wednesday 10–6;
Thursday through Saturday 10–8

DIRECTIONS: From I-82 take exit 80 and go left onto Merlot Drive. Arrive at 10 Merlot Dr., Suite D, where Canyon's Edge Winery's tasting room is located (near the drive-thru Starbucks).

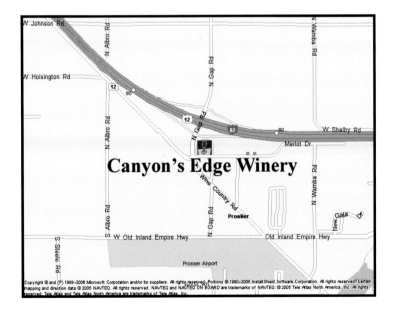

Olsen Estates Winery

(l to r) Lief Olsen, Larry and Jackie Olsen, Dick and Penny Olsen, Martin Olsen and Kyle Johnson

Winemaker Kyle Johnson must feel a little odd that his last name isn't Olsen. After all, he is surrounded by Dick and Larry Olsen who began growing grapes 30 years ago in the Yakima Valley, Martin Olsen, the winery's manager, and Leif Olsen who manages the vineyards—a remarkable 26 different farms along the Roza Canal. But Kyle Johnson's work at Chateau Ste. Michelle and a degree from Washington State University have provided the perfect ingredients to take Olsen Estates Winery to the next stage—a producer of fine wine.

Olsen Estates' sand-colored winery opened in June 2007 at the Vintner's Village in Prosser. This handsome 12,000-square-foot production facility and tasting room features a rock fireplace, a baby grand piano, and inviting thick cushioned couches. Weather permitting; visitors are encouraged to enjoy their wine on the spacious patio outside with views of nearby Airfield Estate Winery, Willow Crest, Thurston Wolfe and The Winemaker's Loft.

Although their initial vintage features a line-up of whites—chardonnay, pinot gris, and reisling—stay tuned for future releases of the red persuasion. Their reserve quality wines bear the Olsen Estates moniker and their second-tier wines have the name Olsen Hills. At a production capacity that can accommodate 14,000 cases of wine per year, Kyle Johnson and the Olsen clan will continue to be busy growing *and* making premium wine for many years to come.

OLSEN ESTATES WINERY
opened: 2007
winemaker(s): Kyle Johnson
location: 500 Merlot Drive
Prosser, WA 99350
phone: 509-786-7007
web: www.olsenestates.com
e-mail: info@olsenestates.com
picnic area: Yes
gift shop: No
fee: Complimentary wine tasting
hours: Thursday through Sunday 11–6; Tuesday and
Wednesday by appointment only

DIRECTIONS: From I-82 take exit 80 and go left onto Merlot Drive, continue past the hotels and find Olsen Estates Winery on your right at 500 Merlot Dr.

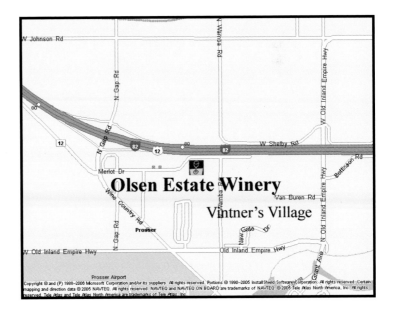

Airfield Estates Winery

Winemaker Marcus Miller's young age belies the long history he and his family have been in the wine business. Although he is only 29, you could say that winemaking is in his blood. We're not referring to his degree from Walla Walla Community College's Enology and Viticulture program or his stints at a variety

of other wineries. Rather, the Miller family has been growing premium grapes in Washington since 1960. What's more, Marcus' grandfather was friends with Walter Clore—the man generally credited as being the father of Washington's wine industry.

Mike Miller, Marcus' dad, is both grower and founder of Airfield Estates Winery. With hundreds of acres of prime vineyards, the Millers have the luxury of keeping the top 2% of the grapes for their own label.

In the spring of 2007, the Millers launched Airfield Estates Winery in Prosser's Vintage Village. Visitors to the Village will have no problems spotting Airfield Estates Winery. It's the winery with the tower that has "AIRFIELD" written on the sides. Visitors to the winery encounter several hangar doors in the front and a delightful interior featuring model airplanes, classic airfield photos and a whacky dummy's head sporting an aviator hat and goggles. It's fun and it works. But the airfield theme is no accident. It turns out that Marcus Miller's grandfather, H. Lloyd Miller, built a 1,200-acre airport ranch near Sunnyside for an air training station during World War II.

Of course, with an airfield theme under their wings, the Millers have an opportunity to come up with some great names (to go with some fabulous wines). Check out some red blends with catchy names including Mustang Red, Aviator Red, and Runway Red. It's no surprise that their wine club bears the name "Officer's Club" and offers two options—the B-17 or the B-29. You would think that an old bi-plane would drop ship your wine shipments via parachute but sadly, this is not the case. Rather, look for the more grounded UPS truck. Roger, that.

AIRFIELD ESTATES WINERY
opened: 2007
winemaker(s): Marcus Miller
location: 560 Merlot Drive
Prosser, WA 99350
phone: 509-643-1282
web: www.airfieldwines.com
e-mail: nsaomb@hotmail.com
picnic area: Yes
gift shop: No
fee: Complimentary wine tasting
hours: Friday and Saturday 11–6; Sundays 1–6

Marcus Miller

DIRECTIONS: From I-82 take exit 80 and go left onto Merlot Drive, continue past the hotels and find Airfield Estates Winery on your right at 560 Merlot Dr. just past Olsen Estates Winery.

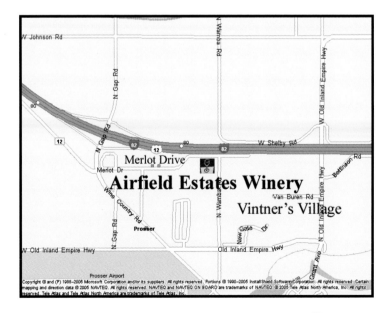

Willow Crest Winery

"It starts in the vineyard," states the Willow Crest website. It could also say it starts with the snout of a very young winemaking protégé. His name is Victor

Willow Crest tasting room

Palencia, and not long ago he was too young to drink alcohol legally. This created quite a problem at public wine tasting events where he repeatedly had to say "no thanks" to offers of wine samples. However, if you can't drink it, you can certainly smell it, and that's precisely what Victor did while learning the winemaking trade and studying at the Institute for Enology and Viticulture at Walla Walla Community College.

However, with the celebration of his 21st birthday, Victor can now taste the fruit of his labor without having to spit. Victor had the good fortune to be mentored along the way by viticulturist and winemaker David Minick, who is the owner of, and driving force behind, Willow Crest Vineyard and Winery. During most of the week, David tends the 185-acre Willow Crest Vineyard. He meticulously manages the vineyard's canopy, prunes to yield quality grapes, and harvests when the balance of fruit and sugar is just right. Early on, David spotted Victor's winemaking talent and has mentored him throughout his rookie years to the big leagues. This has freed David from his winemaking duties and allowed him to concentrate on the vineyard.

Visit Willow Crest's new tasting room in the North Prosser Business Park on Merlot Drive. You'll discover all the wines of Willow Crest; of particular note is its pinot gris (or "pinot grigio" if you're feeling Italian) as well as a number of syrahs. While there, you can find out about upcoming events, join the wine club, and sample some amazing wines. Just remember to bring your ID if you look underage.

WILLOW CREST WINERY
opened: 1995
winemaker(s): David J. Minick
location: 590 Merlot Drive
Prosser, WA 99350
phone: 509-786-7999
web: www.willowcrestwinery.com
e-mail: info@willowcrestwinery.com
picnic area: Yes
gift shop: Yes
fee: Complimentary wine tasting
hours: Daily 10–5; Leavenworth location daily 10–6

Yakima Valley vineyard

DIRECTIONS: **From I-82** take exit 80 and go left onto Merlot Drive, continue past the hotels and find Willow Crest tasting room on the right at the corner of Port Ave. (Willow Crest Winery has a second tasting room in Leavenworth on Front St.)

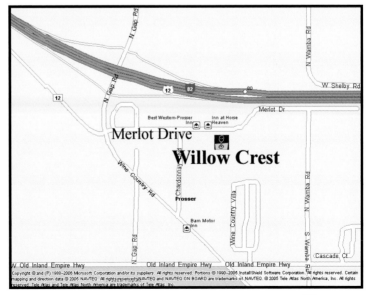

Thurston Wolfe Winery

Imagine going to a winery that has roads with names like Merlot Drive, Port Avenue, and Cabernet Court! Such is the case at the new winery/tasting room for Thurston Wolfe. Few winery owners can boast that their winery is "legendary," but with wine-industry roots that go back to the mid-'80s, Wade

Wolfe and Becky Yeaman can make that claim. Both worked closely with other pioneers in the industry, such as Dr. Walter Clore (considered to be the father of Washington's modern premium wine grape industry), to create Thurston Wolfe. With a Ph.D. from the University of California at Davis, Wade's résumé includes stints at Ste. Michelle, Hogue, and Hyatt before he launched his own winery. Now he and Becky devote all of their time to their winery.

To understand Thurston Wolfe is to appreciate its forte for making "non-mainstream" wines. Yes, you can find award-winning Bordeaux and Rhone-style wines at Thurston Wolfe, but don't pass up the opportunity to enjoy its "JTW" port (named after Wade and Becky's son), lemberger, petite sirah, sangiovese, orange muscat ("Sweet Rebecca"), rosé, and pinot gris–viognier ("PGV"). Of course, with only 3,000 cases produced annually, the winery tends to sell out quickly. Don't expect all varietals to be available when you visit the winery.

Located in the North Prosser Business Park just off I-82, the Thurston Wolfe winery features a contemporary design and a spacious tasting room. A large fireplace provides a warm and cozy environment during the winter, and the extra-long wine bar offers elbow room for weekend crowds. One of Becky's roles is that of tasting room manager, and she is there most days. With her wealth of knowledge about the wine industry in Yakima Valley, she entertains, informs, and pours, all with an engaging manner.

FYI, after you have sampled Thurston Wolfe's "PGV," don't forget to ask B.Y. about the Rattlesnake Hills AVA before you taste the "JTW."

Becky Yeamon

THURSTON WOLFE WINERY
opened: 1987
winemaker(s): Wade Wolfe
location: 588 Cabernet Court
Prosser, WA 99350
phone: 509-786-3313
web: www.thurstonwolfe.com
e-mail: whwolfe@bentonrea.com
picnic area: Yes
gift shop: No
fee: Complimentary wine tasting
hours: 11–5 Thursday through Sunday (plus Monday
holidays) from April 1 through December 8

DIRECTIONS: From I-82 take exit 80 and go left onto Merlot Drive, continue past the hotels and
find Thurston Wolfe Winery tasting room down Port Drive.

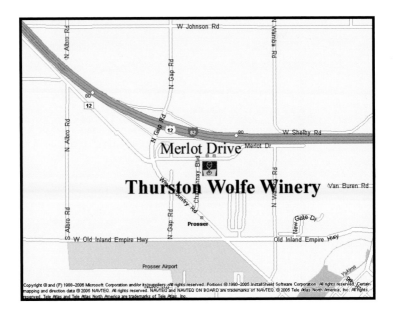

355

Yakima River Winery

John and Louise Rauner have focused on creating big, red Yakima wines for nearly 30 years. Beginning in 1977, in an unassuming winery and tasting room in Prosser, John began making wine under the Yakima River Winery label. Since those early beginnings, John has become a huge proponent of the Yakima Valley appellation; a visit with him reveals his deep love of Yakima grapes. Because of the intense concentration of flavor and deep red color of these grapes, he finds no need to go beyond his beloved Yakima Valley for fruit. Move over, Napa. Through years of perfecting his craft, John has gathered a loyal

following of Yakima River wine lovers who shun Bordeaux in favor of Yakima appellation wines.

Yakima River Winery is a white-wine-free zone. John focuses on cabernet sauvignon, merlot, syrah, petit verdot, cabernet-merlot blends, and ports. His passion for Yakima varietals overflows, and he cares for each wine as if it were his offspring. And really, they are. With nearly 30 years of wine making under his belt, John is constantly tinkering with perfecting the ultimate Yakima wines. He collaborates closely with Yakima Valley grape growers about vineyard management issues, such as canopy size, pruning, irrigation, picking, and sorting. But that's just the beginning. He also works closely with world-class coopers, paying attention to the source of the oak, toasting, the curing of the staves, and more. He's intimately involved; even the choice of yeast gets due consideration. Once the grapes have come under his control, he performs myriad time-tested tasks, from crushing to bottling. As a testament to his love of winemaking, he posted on his website an article nearly 2,000 words in length explaining his philosophy about winemaking. Now that's passion!

But to enjoy his wine, you don't need to read his treatise in advance. All you have to do is head to the winery's North River Road location, near the Yakima River, and sample his big reds. Don't forget to ask him about the source of his fruit, his choice of oak, and his philosophy about winemaking. He will turn you into a believer.

YAKIMA RIVER WINERY
opened: 1978
winemaker(s): John Rauner
location: 143302 West North River Road
Prosser, WA 99350
phone: 509-786-2805
web: www.yakimariverwinery.com
e-mail: redwine@yakimariverwinery.com
picnic area: Yes
gift shop: No
fee: Complimentary wine tasting
hours: Daily 10–5; closed Thanksgiving and
Christmas Day

Yakima River vineyard—early summer

BEST Views

DIRECTIONS: From I-82 take exit 80 and turn onto Wine Country Rd and go south about .3 miles. Turn onto N. River Rd. The road changes to W. North River Rd; follow signs to winery for about 1 mile. Yakima River Winery is on the left.

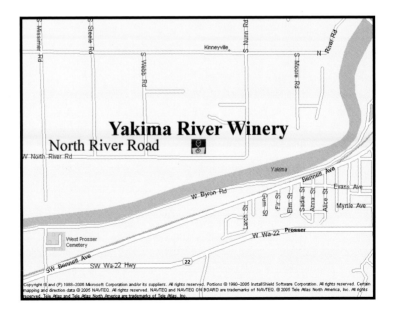

357

Hinzerling Winery

Located in the heart of Prosser, Hinzerling Winery is not your ordinary "small lot" winery. A visit to Hinzerling Winery calls for samples of Mike Wallace's port and table wines, sipped amongst winemaking implements and well-used barrels. Established in 1976 by the Wallace family, Hinzerling Winery is the Yakima Valley's oldest family-owned and -operated winery. More than a winery, Hinzerling also offers a place to eat and sleep at the Vintner's Inn Bed & Breakfast, located next door to the winery. This comfortable inn even offers two pet-friendly rooms, where well-behaved animals (weighing no more than 200 pounds) are welcome. Call 800-727-6702 for reservations to stay overnight in the heart of wine country. On Saturday nights, the Vintner's Inn Bed & Breakfast becomes a restaurant that features a six-course prix fixe menu. During the harvest season, September through October, the Vintner's Inn wine bar is open from 3:30 to 6 p.m. Tuesday through Saturday. For WineTrail enthusiasts, this is your opportunity to sample an array of some hard-to-find and interesting Yakima Valley wines. Call ahead to confirm restaurant and wine bar times and to get information about special events.

Part winery, part country inn, part restaurant and wine bar—Hinzerling Winery offers the whole Yakima Valley Wine Country package. In addition, you will also have an opportunity to sample Mike Wallace's great sense of humor and offbeat way of looking at life. Somehow, the port goes down real smooth when you're smiling.

Mike Wallace

HINZERLING WINERY
opened: 1976
winemaker(s): Mike Wallace
location: 1520 Sheridan Avenue
Prosser, WA 99350-1140
phone: 509-786-2163
web: www.hinzerling.com
e-mail: info@hinzerling.com
picnic area: Yes
gift shop: Yes
fee: $3 tasting fee
hours: 11–5 Monday through Saturday, 11–4
Sunday, from March to Christmas and most holiday
weekends; 12–4 Tuesday through Saturday in the
winter; closed New Year's Day, Easter, Christmas and
St. Swithun's Marn; open on event weekends

DIRECTIONS: From I-82 traveling east take exit 80 and go right (south) onto N. Gap Rd. Continue
on N. Gap Rd for about 1.5 miles [road name changes to Wine Country Rd]. Turn right onto 9th
St. and arrive at Hinzerling Winery on the right.
From I-82 heading west take exit 82 and take a left onto SR-22 [Wine Country Rd]. Continue on
Wine Country Rd for 1 mile and go left onto Sheridan Ave.—Hinzerling Winery is on the right.

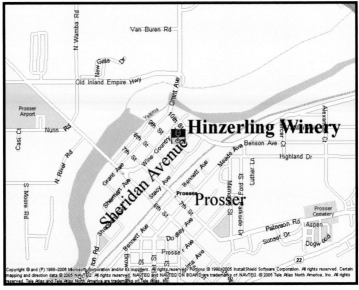

Snoqualmie Winery

Snoqualmie Winery, a subsidiary of Ste. Michelle Wine Estates, is conveniently located off I-82 in Prosser. The Snoqualmie Winery visitor center, with its rustic timbered facade and beautiful landscaping, features stylish deck chairs and tables set against a manmade waterfall. The tasting room itself reflects the "simplicity and uncomplicated goal of making approachable, food-friendly wines." You might not expect to find a Cascade-style timber lodge situated in a farming community like Prosser, where pickup trucks outnumber cars, but somehow it works. Perhaps it's because of the friendliness of the pouring staff at Snoqualmie or the simple elegance of the building itself, but in the end it is the wine that wins your heart. Snoqualmie's goal is to produce high-quality, approachable wines at an affordable price.

Be prepared to go *au naturel* at this tasting room. No, we're not talking about a nudist wine colony here (although that does conjure up an idea for a new business venture). Rather, "naked" refers to Snoqualmie's line of white wines: "Naked Riesling" and "Naked Gewürztraminer," both made with certified organically grown grapes. "Nearly Naked" wine is made from grapes grown using organic practices, but they are not certified organic. Very true to the varietals, these wines fit in perfectly with winemaker Joy Andersen's philosophy to let nature take her course and then try to capture the natural essence of the vineyard in the bottle.

Speaking of bare essentials, try the fruit-focused style of Snoqualmie's cabernet sauvignon, merlot, and syrah varietals. It's very clear that these wines are made to be paired with Northwest cuisine. We suspect that you will want to fire up the grill and try some salmon steak with Snoqualmie's "Rosebud Vineyard" cabernet sauvignon. And if you have a few extra shekels, it is well worth the price of admission ($5) to try Joy's best-of-the-best reserve reds: merlot, syrah, and cabernet sauvignon. These can stand up nicely to other Chateau Ste. Michelle labels and are sold at good prices.

WineTrail Tip: Pay your respects to Mother Nature and the staff may have some Domaine Ste. Michelle sparkling wine to pour for you. That said, clothing is not optional.

SNOQUALMIE WINERY
opened: 1983
winemaker(s): Joy Andersen
location: 660 Frontier Road
Prosser, WA 99350
phone: 509-786-5558
web: www.snoqualmie.com
e-mail: info@snoqualmie.com
picnic area: Yes
gift shop: Yes
fee: Complimentary wine tasting; $5 tasting fee for
reserve wines
hours: Daily 10–5 except Thanksgiving, Christmas,
New Year's Day, and Easter

BEST Picnicking

DIRECTIONS: From I-82 take exit 82 and go west onto SR-22 [Wine Country Rd] .1 miles. Turn left (south) onto SR-22 and go .3 miles. Turn left (east) onto Frontier Rd and find Snoqualmie Vineyards winery a short distance on the left.

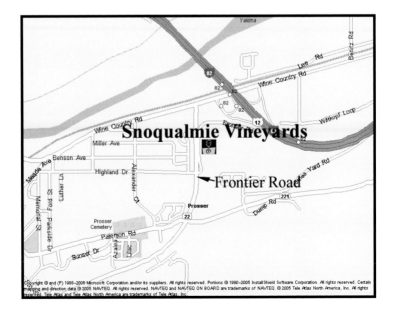

361

Desert Wind Winery

Few wineries in Washington can boast that they offer a place for wine tasting, for dining, for overnight lodging, for attending a cooking seminar, and for getting married, but the 34,000-square-foot Desert Wind Winery in Prosser offers just such amenities and more. Designed by Tate Architects of Pasco,

Washington, the Pueblo-style building opened its doors in early 2007 and readily distinguished itself from other wineries in the lower Yakima Valley in sheer size and ambiance. In a state with few destination wineries, Desert Wind sets the bar high with thoughtful touches such as flat-panel TVs in the suites, warm earth tones throughout, full-length mirrors in the bride and groom changing rooms, and a set of French doors leading to a magnificent view of the Yakima River.

Desert Wind Winery is co-owned by the Fries and Jenkins families, who started Duck Pond Cellars in Dundee, Oregon, in 1993. After considerable study, they decided to locate Desert Wind Winery conveniently off I-82 in Prosser, in the heart of wine country. Next to the winery is the yet-to-be-opened Walter Clore Wine & Culinary Center. Given the location, Desert Wind Winery can expect plenty of visitors throughout most of the year.

The spacious tasting room has a grand living room feel complete with a fireplace and a big wine bar. But perhaps the most surprising find is the wine itself: gorgeous, luscious, fruit-forward. Current offerings include barbera, merlot, cabernet sauvignon, and (my personal favorite) a Bordeaux blend called "Ruah." Full-bodied with lush fruit flavors, Ruah's price tag of $15 makes this one of the best values in the state. Total production is at 20,000 cases annually. Better hurry, wine this good will be gone with the wind.

Culinary arts and wine pairing

DESERT WIND WINERY
opened: 2001
winemaker(s): Greg Fries
location: 2256 Wine Country Road
Prosser, WA 99350-0000
phone: 800-437-3213
web: www.desertwindvineyard.com
e-mail: lisa@desertwinevineyard.com
picnic area: Yes
gift shop: Yes
fee: Complimentary wine tasting
hours: Daily 11–5 from October through; daily 10–5
May through September

DIRECTIONS: Desert Wind's southwest style winery is located just off I-82 in Prosser. **From I-82 heading east or west**, take exit 82 and head toward Prosser. Take the first right and arrive at Desert Wind Winery (just past the Walter Core Center) overlooking the Yakima River.

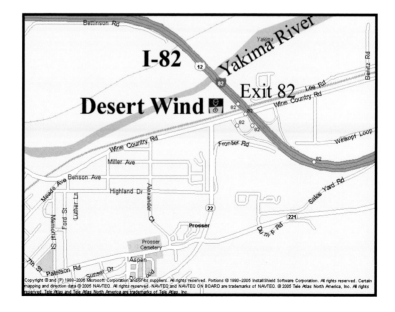

Red Mountain
WINE COUNTRY

Chocolatier at Terra Blanca Winery & Estate Vineyard

Visitors to Red Mountain aren't here for the overnight lodging or fabulous restaurants. You won't find these amenities here. Instead what you will find are fields of grapes and a number of wineries dotting the land. Red Mountain is zoned for agriculture. The Red Mountain WineTrail offers incredibly intense cabernet sauvignon grapes. With names like Hedges, Taptiel, Terra Blanca, and Kiona, you're in for a great day (or two). In between tasting rooms, you will pass some of the state's most distinctive vineyards including Ciel du Cheval, Klipsun, Hedges, Kiona, and Artz.

Red Mountain WineTrail is just a dot on the map lying between Prosser and Richland off I-82. Nevertheless, what a dot it is. In terms of places to stay and eat, nearby Prosser and the Tri-Cities offer plenty of choices.

1 Chandler Reach Vineyard
2 Oakwood Cellars Winery
3 Terra Blanca Winery &
   Estate Vineyard

4 Seth Ryan Winery
5 Kiona Vineyards Winery
6 Sandhill Winery
7 Fidelitas Wines

8 Blackwood Canyon Vintners
9 Hedges Family Estate
10 Tapteil Vineyard and Winery
11 Hightower Cellars

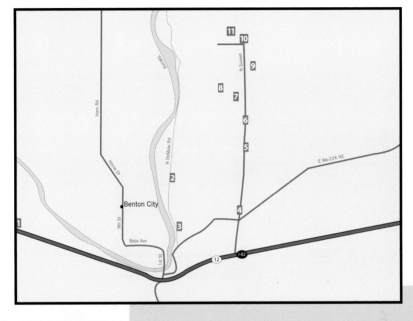

Region:	**Red Mountain Wine Country**
# of tasting rooms on tour:	**11**
Estimated # of days for tour:	**2**
Getting around:	**Car**
Key events:	❑ **Spring Barrel Tasting in the Yakima Valley (last weekend in April); Red Wine and Chocolate (mid-February); and Catch the Crush (October) sponsored by Wine Yakima Valley. See www.wineyakimavalley.org.**
Tips:	❑ **Restaurants and lodging are found in nearby Prosser or the Tri-Cities.**
	❑ **Consider hiring a limousine service (e.g., S.U.V. Tours 509-783-7060, A+ Pacific Limousine 206-437-1298 or Sunset Coach Tours 800-941-2941, to name a few).**
Best:	❑ **Best Views: Terra Blanca Winery & Estate Vineyard, Hedges Family Estate, Hightower Cellars and Tapteil Vineyards Winery**
	❑ **Best Gift Shop: Kiona Vineyards Winery**
	❑ **Best Picnicking: Terra Blanca Winery & Estate Vineyard, Oakwood Cellars Winery**

367

Chandler Reach Vineyard

If you have ever traveled on I-82 between Richland and Prosser, you may have wondered about the Tuscan-style villa near exit 93. Wonder no more. That, my wine-tasting friend, is the site of Chandler Reach Vineyard. Inspired by a trip to Tuscany in 1997, owner/winemaker Len Parris decided to create a Tuscan-style

winery/tasting room at his Benton City location. Although the winery is a work in progress, Len's ultimate vision is to provide luxury suites for overnight lodging and banquet facilities that would comfortably sit 60.

Located on a north-facing slope overlooking Red Mountain, the 42-acre Chandler Reach

Chandler Reach Vineyards' red truck

Vineyard supplies the fruit for a number of wineries. The heat index in this part of the state is high and this could be responsible for the intensity of Len's fruit. However, not all the ripe grapes leave the Chandler Reach Vineyard. Select lots become the fruit for 2,500 cases of Chandler Reach's own estate wines: cabernet sauvignon, cabernet franc, merlot, syrah, and sangiovese.

If your taste buds are seeking something other than intense, full-flavored wines, keep driving. However, if you are ready to try some serious reds, take exit 93 and head for the villa. The tasting room downstairs provides a warm environment for sampling the estate wines. After all, you are here to taste the *terroir*. Juxtaposed against Red Mountain, an area famous for its cabernet sauvignon, Chandler Reach is all about the "taste of the land." *Bellissimo!*

CHANDLER REACH VINEYARD
opened: 2002
winemaker(s): Len Parris
location: 9506 West Chandler Road
Benton City, WA 99320-7852
phone: 509-588-8800
web: www.chandlerreach.com
e-mail: chandlerreach@comcast.net
picnic area: Yes
gift shop: No
fee: Complimentary wine tasting
hours: 11–5 Friday through Sunday; call for
winter hours

DIRECTIONS: From I-82 east or west, take exit 93 and go right onto Chandler Rd. Go approximately .75 miles, and arrive at Chandler Reach Vineyard on left side of road.

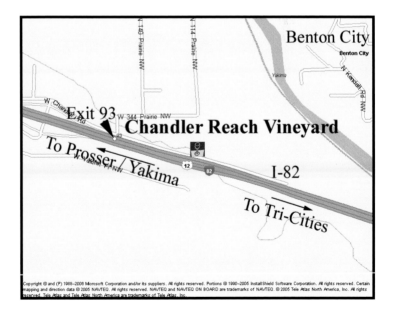

Oakwood Cellars Winery

Many a communications specialist says, "Tell it by the numbers." When it comes to Oakwood Cellars, we agree, and in order to appreciate Oakwood Cellars you need to understand five key things. Not in order of importance, we submit the following:

1. Location—Not only is Oakwood Cellars located smack dab in the middle of Red Mountain, right down the road from Terra Blanca, but it resides next to the picturesque Yakima River. In a word, it's lovely, and if you packed a picnic for your wine-tasting getaway, this is the place to enjoy it.

2. Lemberger—Not just lemberger wine as you know it (assuming you share our lemberger passion) but also an unusual lemberger white wine. A lemberger white? Yep, and to our reckoning, you won't find this anywhere else.

3. History—Proprietor and vintner Evelyn "Eppie" Skelton has been making award-winning wines since 1986. That's ancient history by Washington state standards and it's also very unusual that a woman winemaker has thrived in this male-dominated business.

4. Patience—From crush to bottle, Eppie believes that longer is better. Her cabernet sauvignon is aged in the barrel for 36 months. From a small-business perspective with inherent cash flow concerns, that's a long time.

5. Homey—The tasting room and gift shop are small in size but large on charm; you feel at home in this space.

WineTrail enthusiasts will want to budget plenty of time for Oakwood Cellars. We've given you five good reasons why you should, and we're sure you will add to the numbers.

OAKWOOD CELLARS WINERY
opened: 1986
winemaker(s): Eppie Skelton
location: 40504 North Demoss Road
Benton City, WA 99320
phone: 509-588-5332
web: www.oakwoodcellars.com
e-mail: oakwoodcellars@aol.com
picnic area: Yes
gift shop: Yes
fee: Complimentary wine tasting
hours: 12–5 Saturday and Sunday; closed from second week in December until Presidents Day weekend

BEST Picnicking

DIRECTIONS: From I-82 east or west, take exit 96 and turn onto SR-224 toward Benton City. Turn right (east) onto SR-224 [E. Kennedy Rd NE] and continue for .75 miles. Turn left (north) onto N. Demoss Rd and go 1 mile and arrive at Oakwood Cellars Winery on your left.

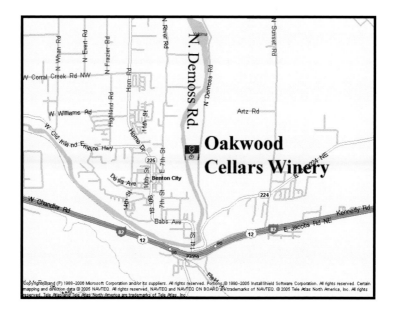

Terra Blanca Winery & Estate Vineyard

Terra Blanca has it all, with the exception, perhaps, of communal jackets and sweaters. So don't forget to bring your own when you visit, even if it's 100 degrees outside. Puzzled? The reason for the warm clothing is Terra Blanca's cave system, which retains a constant temperature of 57 degrees for housing barrel upon barrel of aging wine. However, be sure to call ahead if you decide you want to experience the caves; cave tours are by appointment only.

Terra Blanca Winery with Horse Heaven Hills in the distance

Inspired by the extensive use of natural caves in Europe, Terra Blanca's creators built two extensive cave systems to store row after row of French oak barrels. Fabricated in 1997, the first cave houses 1,000 58-gallon barrels. In 2004, the construction of a second, larger cave system, with a capacity of 3,000 barrels, was completed. If you're looking for stalagmites, head for Carlsbad Caverns National Park, but if you're curious to see cave barrels, head to Red Mountain.

We mentioned that Terra Blanca has it all and we think you will agree. Its Tuscan-inspired architecture includes a tasting room complete with a baby grand piano and large enough to accommodate busloads of weekend visitors. Remaining indoors, you will discover a wine library with shelving systems rising at least 15 feet high, a complete gourmet-style kitchen, and several banquet rooms. One banquet room seats as many as 180 guests and would make an excellent venue for a high school reunion or corporate affair. Speaking of such events, the winery points out both online and onsite: No weddings, please.

Outside, a cobblestone path leads you to a waterfall, a recently completed amphitheater for summer concerts, and, of course, Terra Blanca's famous caves. Its patio is huge and well appointed, with furniture reminiscent of the Smith & Hawken brand. From the patio, enjoy what *Wine Trails Northwest* rates as a "Top 10 View." With the vineyards of Red Mountain behind you and the beautiful Horse Heaven Hills in front, you won't want to leave.

Winemaker Keith Pilgrim is in the enviable position of having access to Red Mountain fruit, state-of-the-art equipment, and those caves to produce a full range of reds and whites. There is a $5 fee for tasting Terra Blanca's reserves. Fork it over. A mere $5 brings you samples of roussanne, reserve merlot, "Onyx" (a red blend), chenin blanc ice wine, estate chardonnay, reserve cabernet sauvignon, and reserve syrah. Now you understand why you witnessed a half-dozen visitors carting boxes of wine to their cars as you entered the parking lot.

Keith Pilgrim

TERRA BLANCA WINERY & ESTATE VINEYARD
opened: 1993
winemaker(s): Keith Pilgrim
location: 34715 North Demoss Road
Benton City, WA 99320
phone: 509-588-6082
web: www.terrablanca.com
e-mail: info@terrablanca.com
picnic area: Yes
gift shop: Yes
fee: Complimentary wine tasting, $5 fee for
reserve wines
hours: Daily 11–6

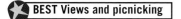

BEST Views and picnicking

DIRECTIONS: From I-82 east or west, take exit 96 and turn onto SR-224 toward Benton City. Turn right (east) onto SR-224 [E. Kennedy Rd NE] and continue for .75 miles. Turn left (north) onto N. Demoss Rd and go .3 miles and arrive at Terra Blanca Winery & Estate Vineyard entrance on your right.

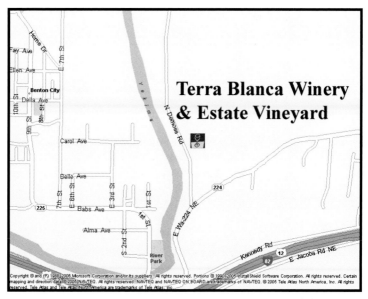

Seth Ryan Winery

Owned and operated by the Brodzinski family—Ron and Jo and their son, Kirk—Seth Ryan Winery is just 1.4 miles from I-82 and at the turnoff for Sunset Road. From the labels used on the bottles, to the gifts selected for the

well-stocked gift shop, to the pruning of the vineyards, this winery is a family affair. One of the Brodzinski family members is typically working the tasting room and can readily field questions while pouring with one eye on a wayward grandchild. The feeling a visitor gets is "from our family to your family." This is a place where it seems like you are sitting around the kitchen table engaged in a lively discussion with your siblings while mom is flipping pancakes. As the Brodzinskis say on their website, "Spirited discussions are welcome."

Seth Ryan provides complimentary tasting of most wines with a refundable fee for select reserves. Whether you are a red or a white wine enthusiast, there are plenty of varietals to taste. Of course, with Red Mountain's reputation for intense cabernet sauvignon, no visit is complete without a sampling of this varietal. Seth Ryan winery produces a full slate of wines, served "straight up" or blended with other noble varietals, including merlot, cabernet franc, pinot gris, chardonnay, gewürztraminer, petit verdot, syrah, malbec, viognier, tempranillo, and carmenère. As a nice touch, soft drinks are available at no charge for designated drivers. Annual production is limited to 3,000 cases.

Tours of the facilities are usually available, especially on event weekends such as Catch the Crush in September or Thanksgiving in Wine Country in November. During these event weekends, the Brodzinskis open the production area to better handle the large crowds. Located next to the boutique winery, Ryan Park is available for picnicking or rental for company gatherings, parties, anniversary and wedding receptions, or other special occasions or events. As writer Jane Howard stated, "Call it a clan, call it a network, call it a tribe, call it a family. Whatever you call it, whoever you are, you need one."

SETH RYAN WINERY
opened: 1985
winemaker(s): Ron and Jo Brodzinski
location: 35306 Sunset Road
Benton City, WA 99320
phone: 509-588-6780
web: www.sethryan.com
e-mail: grandmajo9@aol.com
picnic area: Yes
gift shop: Yes
fee: Complimentary wine tasting, $5 charge for reserve wine tasting, refunded with purchase of $25 or more of reserve wines
hours: Daily 10–6 from April through October

DIRECTIONS: From I-82 east or west, take exit 96 and turn onto SR-224 toward Benton City. Turn right (east) onto SR-224 [E. Kennedy Rd NE] and continue for 1.5 miles. Turn left (north) onto N. Sunset Rd and Seth Ryan Winery is immediately to your left.

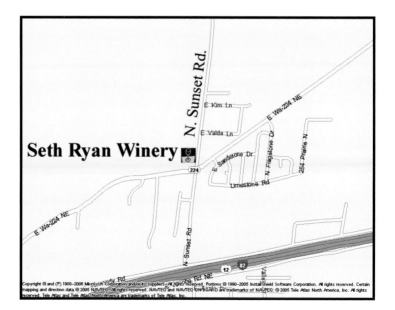

Kiona Vineyards Winery

Before Red Mountain became vineyard green, it was dusty brown. In fact, local Native Americans referred to this area as "Kiona," which means "brown hills." Hey, good name for a winery, don't you think?

It must have taken a lot of intestinal fortitude for the Williams and Holmes families to set roots down on this tract of land on Red Mountain in 1972. No roads, no electricity, and the nearest water was located more than 500 feet below solid rock. Talk about your Maalox moment; indeed, there must have been times when they questioned their sanity as they surveyed miles of sagebrush and dry, crusty-looking land. However, there was water, and the roads and electric

wires did come, and by 1975, through much hard work, the families succeeded in planting a small vineyard. They named it Kiona Vineyards.

If we fast-forward some 30 years later to the present, the Williams and their offspring continue to evolve their grape asset.

With the recent completion of a 20,000-square-foot tasting and banquet facility, equipped with a full kitchen, Kiona Vineyards and Winery is a mandatory stop along the Red Mountain WineTrail. Built underground is the new barrel room, where wine is aged in oak at a constant temperature. In the new tasting room, you can sample Kiona's full slate of red and white estate wines produced by second-generation winemaker Scott Williams. In keeping with the Williams family's belief that wine should add to life's pleasures, Scott named his second label "Vivacious Vicky," after his wife. According to Scott, his spouse has "put up with long hours, busy harvests, lost weekends, strangers for dinner, and fruit flies for 20 years and counting." As you will discover, this Vivacious Vicky has legs. Give the "Nice Legs" merlot a swirl, then a taste, and imagine what this place must have been like 30 years ago.

KIONA VINEYARDS WINERY
opened: 1972
winemaker(s): Scott Williams
location: 44612 North Sunset Road
Benton City, WA 99320-7500
phone: 509-588-6716
web: www.kionawine.com
e-mail: info@kionawine.com
picnic area: Yes
gift shop: Yes
fee: Complimentary wine tasting
hours: Daily 12–5

John Williams

 **BEST Gift shop**

DIRECTIONS: From I-82 east or west, take exit 96 and turn onto SR-224 toward Benton City. Turn right (east) onto SR-224 [E. Kennedy Rd NE] and continue for 1.5 miles. Turn left (north) onto N. Sunset Rd and go 1 mile and arrive at Kiona Vineyards Winery on your left.

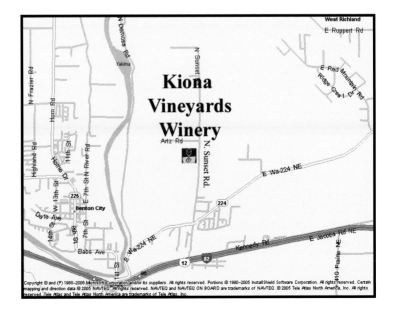

Sandhill Winery

There is one subtle but noteworthy feature about Sandhill Winery's tasting room: It has a dedicated space for kids, complete with toys, games, and pint-sized furniture. We realize that may not be a big deal to most, but after you have visited more than 200 wineries in Washington and only this one offers

View from Sandhill

a play area for children, the Sandhill space is commendable for its kid friendliness.

Actually diverting the offspring's attention to Mr. Potato Head is a wonderful strategy for allowing the adults to focus on Sandhill's renowned cabernet sauvignon, merlot, or pinot gris. However, its number-one seller is its "Cinnamon Teal" red table wine ($10 a bottle), bottled under the Ridgefield label. A portion of the proceeds from the sale of the "Cinnamon Teal" is donated to the Ridgefield National Wildlife Refuge in Ridgefield, Washington. Winemaker Pete Hedges produces more than 7,000 cases annually, using fruit exclusively from Red Mountain. And, yes, Pete Hedges is the brother of Sandhill's next-door neighbor Tom Hedges, owner of Hedges Family Estate Winery.

WineTrails Note: We love *Wine and Spirits*' description of Sandhill's 2001 merlot: "Beautiful, precise Merlot. With its evergreen and mulling spice aromas, the wine is savory in its special red berry flavors. The structure is brisk and fresh, with a clean tannic grip that lifts and lengthens the wine." We read this description and immediately thought of leg of lamb to pair with this merlot.

There are major advantages when a winemaker can focus on a few select varietals, especially when the vintner is blessed with what many consider to be the best grapes in the state. With wine this good, you will want to savor it. Enjoy the complex, full-flavored cabernet sauvignon and let the finish linger a little longer while your spouse finds the 5,000-piece jigsaw puzzle for your restless kids.

SANDHILL WINERY
opened: 2001
winemaker(s): Pete Hedges
location: 48313 North Sunset Road
Benton City, WA 99320
phone: 509-588-2699
web: www.columbiavalleywine.com/sandhill.htm
e-mail: sandhillwinery@aol.com
picnic area: No
gift shop: No
fee: Complimentary wine tasting
hours: 11–5 Saturdays and Sundays

DIRECTIONS: From I-82 east or west, take exit 96 and turn onto SR-224 toward Benton City. Turn right (east) onto SR-224 [E. Kennedy Rd NE] and continue for 1.5 miles. Turn left (north) onto N. Sunset Rd and go 1.5 miles to Sandhill Winery on the right.

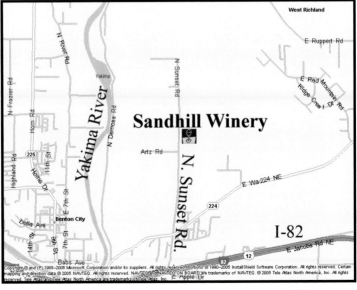

Fidelitas Wines

"I love using grapes from different regions of Washington. It's like being a chef and having access to a variety of spices that I can use to create amazing flavors," noted winemaker/owner Charlie Hoppes at his new Red Mountain tasting room. Since 2001 Hoppes has produced wines under his Fidelitas label but many know Hoppes as the consultant winemaker for Canon De Sol, Goose Ridge, Ryan Patrick Winery, Three Rivers, Alder Ridge, Gamache Vintners and others. Now with his new location, he is poised to further his identity with Fidelitas Wines.

In his early career, Hoppes (pronounced hop-pas) cut his teeth working with Mike Januik (current winemaker for Woodinville-based Novelty Hills Wines and Januik Winery) and then gained experience at Ste. Michelle Estates, first at Snoqualmie then at Chateau Ste. Michelle. But since the early 1980s, Hoppes has dreamed of establishing his winery in Red Mountain. With his acquisition of a 5-acre plot of land in 2005, Hoppes finally had his chance to create his signature Bordeaux-blends (including Optu, a red wine lover's dream), luscious red varietals and amazing whites. The eco-friendly winery and tasting room offers visitors plenty of space to sample wine and take in the views of Horse Heaven Hills in the distance. Currently, sagebrush surrounds the property but soon we suspect the desert-like vegetation will be replaced by that most wonderful of Red Mountain fruits—cabernet sauvignon.

Fidelitas wine bottles wear the distinguished circle labels – the circle is reminiscent of a wedding ring and reflects a commitment to a long-lasting marriage. Also found on the label is the tagline, "Faithful, Loyal, and True." Certainly, fans of Fidelitas Wines will be loyal and faithful for many years.

(l to r) Charlie Hoppes and Ron Pearson (Wine Consultant)

FIDELITAS WINES
opened: 2001
winemaker(s): Charlie Hoppes
location: 51810 North Sunset Road
Benton City, WA 99320
phone: 509-521-4433
web: www.fidelitaswines.com
e-mail: wine@fidelitaswines.com
picnic area: Yes
gift shop: No
fee: Complimentary wine tasting
hours: Friday through Sunday 11–5

DIRECTIONS: From I-82 east or west, take exit 96 and turn onto SR-224 toward Benton City. Turn right (east) onto SR-224 [E. Kennedy Rd NE] and continue for 1.5 miles. Turn left (north) onto N. Sunset Rd and go 1.7 miles to Fidelitas Wines on the left.

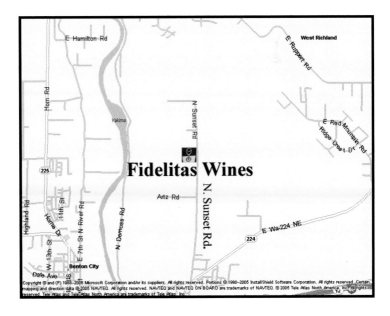

Blackwood Canyon Vintners

Paying a visit to Michael Moore, owner of Blackwood Canyon Vineyards and Winery, is a trip—in more than one sense of the word. Michael has a reputation for being a little over the top in his zeal to create wine using Old World

European techniques, techniques handed down to him during his training at the University of California–Davis and from the winemaking experience he gained in California. Call him slightly eccentric or call him certifiably nuts, Michael is truly passionate about his wine and his techniques for growing grapes.

Located on a dirt road in the prized Red Mountain viticulture area, the winery's secluded site might give you cause to think you are on the wrong trail. However, after a bumpy couple of miles, you'll know you have arrived when you pull up to Michael's somewhat disheveled tasting room/ winery. An assortment of farming implements and other equipment are strewn around the outside of the winery. As you enter the tasting room, you will likely be greeted by Michael's friendly weimaraner, with his striking blue-gray coat and inquisitive eyes, a table with literally 50 half-empty bottles of wine, and Michael himself sporting a well-worn cap and a two-day growth of beard.

For Michael, Blackwood Canyon represents a winery that "exists today as one of the last strongholds of old-school, traditional winemaking dedicated to world-class excellence." He'll immediately engage you in a discussion of his winemaking style and the number of years his wines have rested in storage. Pretty soon, he'll weave into the conversation a flattering quote from a Tom Clancy novel as well as an undated accolade from Robert Parker himself. Time passes quickly, and an hour later you find yourself thinking that maybe Michael has hit the perfect winemaking formula and that all the other wineries are producing juice for the masses—because his wine is truly different.

WineTrail Note: WineTrail adventurers are in for a memorable visit at Blackwood Canyon. This is not like any tasting room in Washington. You may like it, you may not, but you will never forget it. At the end of the day, when you are reviewing the four or five wineries that you visited, Blackwood Canyon will consume a third of the conversation. Because when it comes to Blackwood Canyon, there's much Moore to discuss.

BLACKWOOD CANYON VINTNERS
opened: 1982
winemaker(s): Michael Moore
location: 53258 North Sunset Road
Benton City, WA 99320-7598
phone: 509-588-6249
web: www.blackwoodwine.com
e-mail: info@blackwoodwine.com
picnic area: No
gift shop: No
fee: Complimentary wine tasting
hours: 10–6 Monday through Saturday;
12–6 Sunday

Michael Moore

DIRECTIONS: From I-82 east or west, take exit 96 and turn onto SR-224 toward Benton City. Turn right (east) onto SR-224 [E. Kennedy Rd NE] and continue for 1.5 miles. Turn left (north) onto N. Sunset Rd and go 1.7 miles to Blackwood Canyon Winery entrance on your left. Continue on dirt local access road about 1 mile and follow signs to winery.

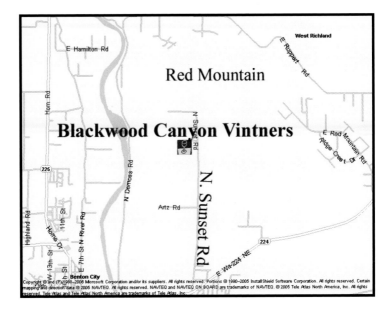

383

Hedges Family Estate

Talk about winning the vineyard lottery: In 1990, Tom Hedges and his French-born wife, Anne-Marie, purchased a parcel of land in an obscure area called Red Mountain. Now they are sitting on a viticultural "goldmine," and the price tag for land in this newly designated American Viticultural Area has gone up considerably. However, such are the spoils for those with vision, passion, and a willingness to take a big risk.

Now considered a destination winery, the Hedges Chateau presents a visual landmark on Red Mountain and offers a commanding view of miles of vineyards, with wineries dotting the land and Horse Heaven Hills in the distance. From the elegant outdoor furniture outside one of its tasting rooms, Hedges Family Estate is the perfect place to enjoy one of its award-winning blends and soak in one of the top views in Washington. That's right, we said *one* of the tasting rooms.

This is the only Washington winery where you have a choice of tasting rooms to enter. As you drive up to the winery, a sign directs you either to the free tasting room or to the upscale chateau, where you can sample the winery's top-tier wines for a small fee. The free tasting room features Hedges' popular blended whites and reds, known for their great value. The CMS white is a blend of chardonnay, marsanne, and sauvignon blanc, and is a perfect match for Northwest seafood. The CMS red blend combines cabernet, merlot, and syrah. The principal ingredient—cabernet sauvignon from Red Mountain grapes—informs your palate that you are about to experience a wonderfully intense yet balanced wine.

It's no wonder many WineTrail trekkers don't make it out of the free tasting room—the wines are that good.

However, to sample the best of the best Hedges has to offer, visit the chateau tasting room and pay the fee. This tasting room features a baby grand piano, museum-quality art, and an exquisite tasting bar. It's here that you can experience Hedges' "Three Vineyards" and "Two Vineyards" red blends, which consistently receive high praise. A few samples will reveal that many of these vintages are most fully appreciated only after being cellared for several years. Other vintages are ready to take on a peppered steak later that evening.

HEDGES FAMILY ESTATE
opened: 1987
winemaker(s): Pete Hedges
location: 53511 North Sunset Road
Benton City, WA 99320
phone: 509-588-3155
web: www.hedgescellars.com
e-mail: hedgescellarswinery@msn.com
picnic area: Yes
gift shop: No
fee: Complimentary for CMS, small tasting fee for
Hedges Estate wines refunded with purchase
hours: 11–5 Friday through Sunday or by appointment

 BEST Views

DIRECTIONS: From I-82 east or west, take exit 96 and turn onto SR-224 toward Benton City. Turn right (east) onto SR-224 [E. Kennedy Rd NE] and continue for 1.5 miles. Turn left (north) onto N. Sunset Rd and go 1.8 miles to Hedges Estate Vineyard on the right.

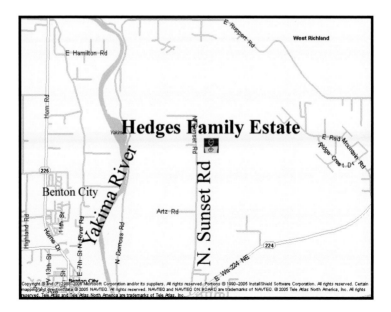

Tapteil Vineyard and Winery

It's interesting to contemplate what drives people to create businesses. Often it is the hope of making lots of money. For others, it's a mission of the heart, and the money is secondary. Take one Lawrence "Larry" Pearson.

Equipped with a solid civil engineering background, Larry dreamed of growing cabernet sauvignon. When you visit with him, you perceive a person who, despite his very analytical nature, set about satisfying a big itch without the benefit of a detailed business plan and financial projections. This itch motivated him and his spouse, Jane, to purchase a parcel of land in a relatively obscure part of Washington called Red Mountain. In 1985, Larry realized his dream of "getting his fingernails dirty" by planting his first cabernet sauvignon vines. He named his vineyard Tapteil, after the lower portion of the Yakima River where

the Tapteilmin, or "narrow river people," once lived. Today, 25 acres later and endless days managing the vineyards, Larry and his vineyard team now grow merlot, syrah, and cabernet franc amongst the rows of cabernet sauvignon on the south slope of his property.

Still learning, still reinventing, Larry continues to produce the intense, full-flavored cabernet sauvignon that has come to define Red Mountain. Larry is an active member of Vinewise, a suborganization of the Washington Association of Wine Grape Growers that focuses on sustainable, environmentally friendly, vineyard management practices.

Did we mention that Larry transforms his fruit into great wines? Located at the north end of Sunset Road, Tapteil Vineyard and Winery commands a sweeping veiw of the Red Mountain table and a panoramic view of Horse Heaven Hills in the distance. Rumor has it that if you come all this way without sampling Tapteil's cabernet sauvignon, you might be spending a night in the Benton City jail, or at least getting your head examined. While you are enjoying Larry's other Tapteil wines, please take time to introduce your palate to the wines under his second label, Spilya, a local Native American word for "coyote."

From Tapteil's hilltop terrace, complete with a basalt fountain, you can enjoy a picnic. If you do, be sure to pack some fresh artisan bread to soak up the select virgin olive oil and balsamic vinegar that Jane sells in the tasting room. Like others who have come before you to Tapteil, you might catch yourself daydreaming about quitting your day job and planting vines.

TAPTEIL VINEYARD AND WINERY
opened: 1984
winemaker(s): Larry Pearson
location: 20206 East 583 PR NE
Benton City, WA 99320
phone: 509-588-4460
web: www.tapteil.com
e-mail: winery@tapteil.com
picnic area: Yes
gift shop: Yes
fee: Complimentary wine tasting
hours: 11–5 Saturdays from April through December,
or by appointment

Larry and Jane Pearson

 BEST Views

DIRECTIONS: From I-82 east or west, take exit 96 and turn onto SR-224 toward Benton City. Turn right (east) onto SR-224 [E. Kennedy Rd NE] and continue for 1.5 miles. Turn left (north) onto N. Sunset Rd and go 2.4 miles to the end of the road. Turn left onto local access road and find Tapteil Winery on your right.

Hightower Cellars

"Service only a smaller winery can provide....A perfect example is Hightower Cellars, located in Eastern Washington's Red Mountain growing region. Tim and Kelly Hightower literally run the entire winemaking process from start to finish. They're

also wonderful hosts and you'll be hard pressed to find a nicer pair of people in the wine business." —Dan Radil, The Bellingham Herald.

I couldn't have said it better … so I didn't. Tim and Kelly Hightower and their dog, Murray, are the nicest family. Yes, Murray is a member of the family, as you will see once you drive to the end of the North Sunset Road in Red Mountain and follow the signs to Hightower Cellars.

Tim and Kelly Hightower have the rare distinction of being a husband-and-wife winemaking duo. Beginning in the mid-'90s, they honed their winemaking skills in one of Woodinville's business parks that cater to suburban "garagistes." However, the temptation to own real estate in one of the world's most acclaimed grape-growing locations proved too much, and in 2002, the Hightowers decided to move to the agricultural land of Red Mountain. What cinched the deal for them was the fact that the land they purchased includes water rights to support a 10-acre vineyard.

While their vines mature, the Hightowers are reliant on other growers for their fruit, and fortunately they don't have far to go. To date, they have acquired their grapes from nearby Artz and E & E Shaw vineyards, Alder Ridge in Horse Heaven Hills, and Pepper Bridge in Walla Walla Valley. Even when their own vines produce cabernet sauvignon, cabernet franc, merlot, malbec, and petit verdot, the Hightowers will continue to rely on other growers for their fruit. In the meantime, Murray, their yellow lab, will continue to guard the vineyard, pose for pictures from adoring fans, and allow the Hightowers to use his name on their red-blend cuvée.

HIGHTOWER CELLARS
opened: 1997
winemaker(s): Tim and Kelly Hightower
location: 19418 East 583 PR NE
Benton City, WA 99320-8598
phone: 509-588-2867
web: www.hightowercellars.com
e-mail: handsorted@hightowercellars.com
picnic area: No
gift shop: No
fee: Complimentary wine tasting
hours: 11–5 Saturday and Sunday from April through October

Tim and Kelly Hightower (and dog Murray)

 BEST Views

DIRECTIONS: From I-82 east or west, take exit 96 and turn onto SR-224 toward Benton City. Turn right (east) onto SR-224 [E. Kennedy Rd NE] and continue for 1.5 miles. Turn left (north) onto N. Sunset Rd and go 2.4 miles to the end of the road. Turn left onto local access road and follow signs to Hightower Cellars.

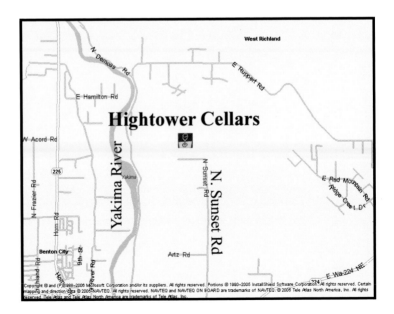

389

Horse Heaven Hills
WINE COUNTRY

Horse Heaven
WineTrail

Columbia Crest

Bordered on the north by the Yakima Valley and on the south by the majestic Columbia River, this area is home to some of the state's most celebrated vineyards, including Champoux Vineyard, Destiny Ridge, Andrew Vineyard, Alder Ridge, Canoe Ridge, and Zephyr Ridge. The soil, wind (lots of it), low moisture, gentle southern slopes and proximity to the Columbia River all conspire to create intense wine grapes.

It is a required field trip for all WineTrail enthusiasts to visit Columbia Crest at Paterson. Close by is the family-owned McKinley Springs Winery. The scenery will stun you if you are an urban dweller. Don't forget your camera. Pack a good lunch and make sure you have plenty of gas. Those kinds of necessities are rare in the Horse Heaven Hills. Besides, when you see the picnic grounds at Columbia Crest you will kick yourself if you are sans lunch. Bon voyage!

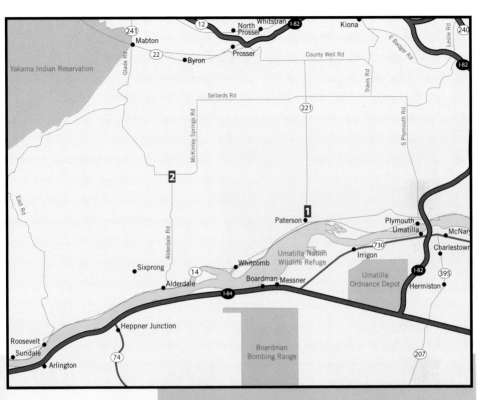

Region:	**Horse Heaven Hills Wine Country**
# of tasting rooms on tour:	**2**
Estimated # of days for tour:	**1**
Getting around:	**Car**
Key events:	❑ **Columbia Crest sponsors events throughout the year—check website for details.**
Tips:	❑ **Pack a picnic and make sure you have plenty of gas—Horse Heaven Hills is about agriculture.** ❑ **Columbia Crest offers a self-guided tour taking you from vineyard to barrel room to tasting room.** ❑ **Check out Champoux Vineyards for wine tasting and vineyard tours. By appointment only—call 509-894-5005.**
Best:	❑ **Best Views: Columbia Crest and McKinley Springs Winery** ❑ **Best Picnicking: Columbia Crest**

Columbia Crest Winery

Can you name Washington's largest producer of wine? It's Columbia Crest, and it leaves its closest competitor in the dust. Owned by Ste. Michelle Wine Estates, Columbia Crest Winery bottles 1.7 million cases per year. How does Columbia Crest produce such volume without compromising quality? To find the answer, WineTrail trekkers need to visit Columbia Crest's Horse Heaven

Hills production facility and take the self-guided tour. From surrounding vineyards, to crush pad, to the immense barrel room, the winery's Boeing-like assembly line will amaze you. It will also bring a sense of reassurance witnessing the consistent quality that goes into each bottle.

However, before you jettison the word "artisan" from your vocabulary, realize that Columbia Crest is actually three wineries in one. The vast majority of the wine it produces leaves its Paterson facility with the Two Vines label. Known for consistent quality and great value, you see the Two Vines brand in most grocery stores and chain restaurants throughout the US. If you're looking for a higher-quality wine and have a few more shekels, Columbia Crest offers its Grand Estate wines. Select vineyards in Columbia Valley supply the grapes for its Grand Estate. And, for the best of the best—in terms of both grapes and artisan winemaking practices—Columbia Crest offers its Reserve label. Chief winemaker Ray Einberger manages a team-within-a-team approach to produce limited quantities of the Reserve wines. With this kind of dedication to quality, it's no wonder Columbia Crest has achieved 90+ ratings from *Wine Spectator*, *Wine Enthusiast*, *Wine & Spirits*, *Wine News*, and others.

Don't forget to pack a picnic before heading to Columbia Crest. The surrounding grounds and spacious patio offer a spectacular setting for taking a meal al fresco. Besides, not having food on hand to pair with the Grand Estate cabernet sauvignon would be a definite *faux pas*.

For wine purchases, the spacious tasting room offers a wide variety of Columbia Crest wines—both of the red and the white persuasions. Featuring two tasting bars, the tasting room can readily accommodate the occasional onslaught of visitors disgorged from tour buses. As you would expect from any Ste. Michelle–owned asset, the staff is exceptionally well trained and affable. No wine snobbery here; Columbia Crest's staff is happy to answer even the simplest of wine-related questions.

COLUMBIA CREST WINERY
opened: 1982
winemaker(s): Ray Einberger (Juan Munoz Orca, red winemaker)
location: Highway 221, Columbia Crest Drive Paterson, WA 99345
phone: 509-875-2061
web: www.columbia-crest.com
e-mail: info@columbia-crest.com
picnic area: Yes
gift shop: Yes
fee: Complimentary wine tasting
hours: Daily 10–4:30 except for major holidays

BEST View and picnicking

DIRECTIONS: **From Prosser**, take 7th St. (southeast). The road name changes to Paterson Rd [SR-221]. Go about 24.5 miles and turn right (west) onto Columbia Crest Drive. Arrive at winery. From the Tri-Cities, take US-395 south to I-82 [US-395]. Go 19.9 miles and at exit 131, turn right onto ramp. Turn right (west) onto SR-14 for 13.4 miles. Turn right (north) onto SR-221 and go 1.4 miles. Turn left (west) onto Columbia Crest Drive.
From Vancouver/Portland area travel on I-84 about 170 miles east. At exit 179, take ramp to I-82 heading north into Washington. At exit 131, take ramp to SR-14. Turn left onto SR-14 and head west for 13.5 miles. Turn right onto SR-221 and go about 1.4 miles. Turn left onto Columbia Crest Drive.

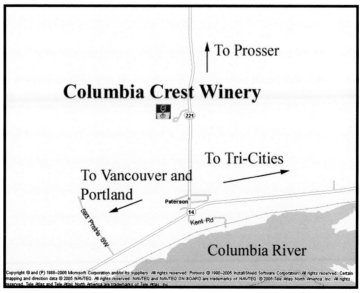

McKinley Springs Winery

Imagine being the trusty engine-maker for such auto greats as Ferrari, Mercedes, and Cadillac. Then, one day, it dawns on you that your little venture is capable of making high-end cars too. Or, from a wine perspective: Imagine selling your grapes for many years to such wineries as Bookwalters, Columbia Crest, Hogue Cellars, Northstar, Sagelands, Syncline Cellars, and Thurston Wolfe and one day realizing that you too can turn grapes into fine wine. Such is the case with

McKinley Springs Vineyards in the Horse Heaven Hills American Viticultural Area. Without McKinley Springs' wonderful fruit, 18 wineries would need to find another "engine manufacturer" for their premium wines.

After more than 25 years of growing premium grapes, the Andrews family made the decision to take the next step: to ferment their product into premium wine. However, a wise person knows their limits, and the owners of McKinley Springs called upon established winemaker James Mantone of Syncline Wine Cellars fame to do the honors.

The McKinley Springs address indicates Prosser, but the vineyard and winery are many miles to the south in the Horse Heaven Hills (named for the once-prevalent wild horses that inhabited them). It's rural here; agriculture abounds, and from the McKinley Springs tasting room you can look south to Alder Ridge and Chateaux Champoux Vineyards. Surrounding the Andrews' farm are 900 acres of carefully nurtured grapes. The plan is to double the vineyard size in the coming years. Sadie, the resident Australian sheep dog, is in keeping with the vineyard's history.

The new tasting room offers an airy space to sample its landmark offerings. Fortunately for WineTrail enthusiasts, there are plenty of large picture windows to view the windswept vineyards and hillsides. Dana Andrews is typically working the tasting room and, as a native, can readily point out distant landmarks, relate the history of the area, and, with developers moving in, offer a forecast of the future. Although changes abound, the one constant are the grapes outside—they're not going anywhere.

MCKINLEY SPRINGS WINERY
opened: 2002
winemaker(s): James Mantone
location: 1201 Alderdale Road
Prosser, WA 99350
phone: 509-894-4528
web: www.mckinleysprings.com
e-mail: rowell@mckinleysprings.com
picnic area: Yes
gift shop: Yes
fee: Complimentary wine tasting
hours: 12–6 Friday and Saturday, 1:30–5 Sunday, or
by appointment

Horse Heaven Hills

DIRECTIONS: From Prosser, take Bennett Ave. going southwest. Turn left (south) onto S. Kinney Way. Road name changes to S. Lincoln Rd. Go about 5 miles. Turn right (west) onto Sellards Rd and go about 4 miles. Road name changes to McKinley Springs Rd. Go 10.7 miles. Turn left onto Alderdale Rd and go .8 miles. Arrive at 1201 Alderdale Rd.

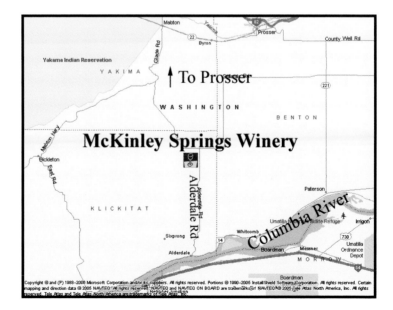

Tri-Cities
WINE COUNTRY

Tri-Cities
Wine Trail

Preston Premium Wines tasting room

The Tri-Cities WineTrail appeals to different preferences, from a focus on organic wines to tasting rooms with fine dining. Set in the heart of Columbia Valley, many of these establishments, like Preston Premium Wines, bottle estate wines. You can also sample 100% organic wine from Badger Mountain Vineyard. At Goose Ridge, the tasting room looks out on an immense 1,000-acre vineyard. Along the route, Barnard Griffin Winery is a must-see stop. Here your taste buds will experience first hand why *Wine Press Northwest* voted them "Winery of the Year for 2006." Your wallet will also appreciate the fact that you can purchase award-winning wines from the mid to high teens. During the summer, Bookwalter Winery hosts live music on Wednesday nights and the price tag won't set you back—it's free. Also offered is bistro fare for the tummy, but if hunger is the driving force, check out nearby Tagaris Winery & Taverna Tagaris for delectables paired with Tagaris Wine.

Tri-Cities WineTrail

1 Bookwalter Winery	**3** Tagaris Winery & Taverna Tagaris	**5** Badger Mountain Vineyard
2 Barnard Griffin Winery	**4** Goose Ridge Estate Vineyard and Winery	**6** Preston Premium Wines

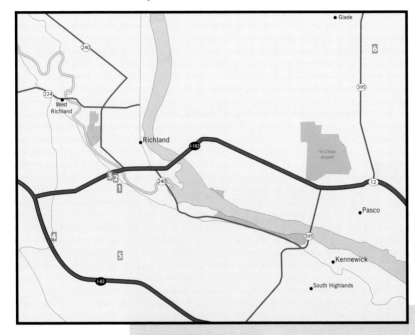

Region:	**Tri-Cities Wine Country**
# of tasting rooms on tour:	**6**
Estimated # of days for tour:	**1 or 2**
Getting around:	**Car and foot**
Key events:	❑ **Tri-Cities Wine Festival (second weekend in November). See www.tricitieswinefestival.com for details.**
Tips:	❑ **Bookwalter Winery provides bistro fare.**
	❑ **Tagaris Winery & Taverna Tagaris offers both wine tasting and restaurant price.**
	❑ **Pack a picnic for Preston Premium Wines and enjoy the outdoor deck.**
	❑ **Preston Premium Wines also has a satellite tasting room in downtown Walla Walla.**
	❑ **Consider hiring a limousine service (e.g., S.U.V. Tours 509-783-7060, A+ Pacific Limousine 206-437-1298 or Sunset Coach Tours 800-941-2941, to name a few).**
Best:	❑ **Best Eats: Bookwalter Winery and Tagaris Winery & Taverna Tagaris**
	❑ **Best Views: Preston Premium Wines**
	❑ **Best Gift Shop: Preston Premium Wines**

Bookwalter Winery

innovation *n.*– The act of introducing something new.

Despite the fact that Bookwalter Winery is approaching 25 years of age, it continues to reinvent itself and pleasantly surprise its loyal followers. Jerry Bookwalter started the winery in 1983 in the heart of Washington's Columbia Valley wine region. The winery was the first in Washington state to use a gold-embossed, full-color wine label. Early on, Jerry produced a number of "vineyard-designated vintages" before they became widely popular. Time marches on, and in 1997 Jerry and Jean Bookwalter's son, John, joined the family winery. Every bit as innovative as his father, John secured the services of consulting winemaker

Zelma Long. A number of prestigious awards and honors have followed, including the 2005 Winery of the Year award presented by Northwest Press.

In 2002, Bookwalter Winery opened a trendy "wine lounge" next door to Barnard Griffin in Richland. The hip atmosphere has succeeded in attracting a younger audience with a taste for premium wine, handcrafted cheeses, and artisan breads. The definition of a "tasting room" shifts in this contemporary ambiance. Here you can order a glass of wine to pair with regional cheeses while listening to live music, which more often than not is the sound of jazz. A full assortment of red and white wines is available to order by the glass or by the bottle. Varietals produced include cabernet sauvignon, merlot, chardonnay, riesling, gewürztraminer, chenin blanc, and muscat blanc.

Now here's something new: Bookwalter offers Wine Down Wednesdays. On Wednesday evenings, you can "relax, chill out, and unwind" at the winery until 10 p.m. It is an innovative way to bring "over the hump" day to a close with friends and loved ones.

BOOKWALTER WINERY
opened: 1983
winemaker(s): John Bookwalter and Zelma Long
location: 894 Tulip Lane
Richland, WA 99352-8588
phone: 509-627-5000
web: www.bookwalterwines.com
e-mail: info@bookwalterwines.com
picnic area: Yes
gift shop: No
fee: $5 tasting fee refundable with purchase
hours: 10–8 Sundays through Thursday, 10–11
Wednesday through Saturday

 BEST Eats

DIRECTIONS: From I-182 (heading east or west) take exit 3 onto Queensgate Drive. Take left onto Columbia Park Trail and go .2 miles. Turn left onto Windmill Rd and then bear right onto Tulip Lane. Bookwalter Winery is the first winery on the right just before Barnard Griffin Winery.

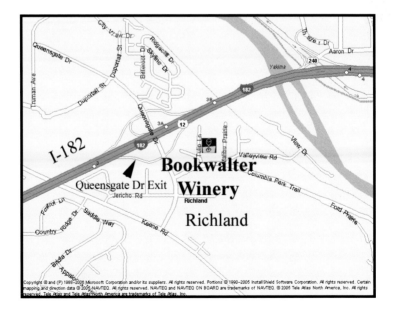

Barnard Griffin Winery

OK, OK, we're biased. We love Barnard Griffin. Why? Because it makes fabulous wine! There's a reason why it won "Winery of the Year" from Wine Press Northwest in 2006. In addition, it has accumulated enough gold and silver medals over the years to start a precious metals company. Accolades aside, Barnard Griffin continues to offer great wine at affordable prices. For example, its Tulip Label cabernet sauvignon sells for $17 a bottle.

Founded in 1983 by Rob Griffin and Deborah Barnard, the winery and tasting room are located in Richland, just off I-182, in the heart of south-central Washington wine country. More than 20 years later, and now producing

65,000 cases of wine annually, Barnard Griffin is the state's largest family-owned winery. During this time, the focus has doggedly remained on the quality in the bottle. Winemaker Rob Griffin's boyhood home is Napa Valley, where he grew up surrounded by the burgeoning wine industry. Graduating from the University of California–Davis' Department of Viticulture & Enology program, Rob understands the science of making wine. His scientific background is at the heart of Barnard Griffin's success.

Barnard Griffin's tasting room on Tulip Lane is sandwiched between the Bookwalter and Tagaris wineries. A distinctive clock tower marks the location of the tasting room/winery. During warm weather, a garden patio beckons picnickers to relax for a while and enjoy life's pleasures. There is often a small crowd to contend with in the tasting room, but the tasting room staff works the audience efficiently and with genuine friendliness. Depending upon supply, Barnard Griffin's popular "Tulip Label" wines include chardonnay, fumé blanc, riesling, semillon, merlot, syrah, and cabernet sauvignon. For port lovers, check out the syrah port (if available)—it's one of the more delectable ports in the Northwest. There is a $5 tasting fee for the winery's limited-production reserve wines (including the syrah port). We heartily recommend springing for it. Why come all this way and deny yourself such a treat?

BARNARD GRIFFIN WINERY
opened: 1983
winemaker(s): Rob Griffin
location: 878 Tulip Lane
Richland, WA 99352-8588
phone: 509-627-0266
web: www.barnardgriffin.com
e-mail: kim@barnardgriffin.com
picnic area: Yes
gift shop: Yes
fee: Complimentary wine tasting; $5 tasting fee for
reserve wines
hours: Daily 10–6

DIRECTIONS: **From I-182** (heading east or west) take exit 3 onto Queensgate Drive. Take left onto Columbia Park Trail and go .2 miles. Turn left onto Windmill Rd and then bear right onto Tulip Lane. Barnard Griffin is on the right just past Bookwalter Winery.

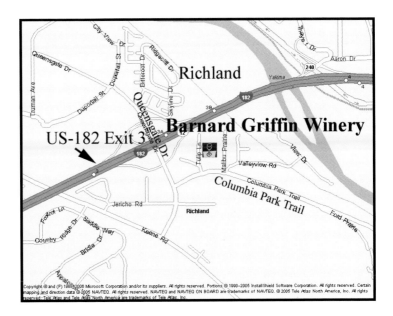

Tagaris Winery & Taverna Tagaris

Petit verdot meets heirloom-tomato-and-pancetta tart at Tagaris Winery & Taverna Tagaris.

Located on Tulip Lane in Richland, next to Barnard Griffin, both Tagaris Winery & Taverna Tagaris restaurant are the brainchild of Michael Taggares, who started the winery in 1987. The spelling of the winery and the restaurant

honors the correct spelling of the family's last name, Tagaris. The original name changed when Michael's grandfather, Pete, immigrated to America through Ellis Island. Eventually moving west and settling in Prosser, Pete Taggares became very successful in both farming and business. Today, the Taggares family is responsible for a number of successful enterprises, including Michael's 1,400-acre farm, 700 of those acres dedicated to varietal grapes. The Taggareses grow 18 different varietals, including petit verdot, counoise, malbec, mouvédre, grenache, and tempranillo, to name a few. These grapes are the primary source of fruit used by winemakers Michael Taggares and Frank Roth for Tagaris Winery.

For centuries, Greek villages have had their tavernas, popular watering holes where friends gather to enjoy wine, hearty fare, and music. To that end, Michael established Taverna Tagaris restaurant at the winery. Elegance is the word that comes to mind upon entering the restaurant. A full Mediterranean-influenced menu offers small to large plates designed to match any appetite. In warmer weather, the 9,000-square-foot Patio Kouzina provides bistro-style fare and is a perfect accompaniment to cold wine served up sangria-style. The young restaurant staff is smartly dressed and can readily suggest which wine to pair with, for example, the goat cheese tortelli.

Taverna Tagaris also features live music from Northwest bands. During most summer weekends, visitors to the winery/restaurant can enjoy contemporary-style music, jazz, and blues from a variety of popular bands. The taverna is a *ménage à trois* of wine, music, and food with a distinct Mediterranean flair.

TAGARIS WINERY & TAVERNA TAGARIS
opened: 1986
winemaker(s): Michael Taggares and Frank Roth
location: 844 Tulip Lane
Richland, WA 99352
phone: 509-628-0020
web: www.tagariswines.com
e-mail: info@tagariswines.com
picnic area: No
gift shop: No
fee: $6.50 tasting fee waived with purchase
hours: 11–4 Tuesday through Saturday; 12–6 Sundays

Tagaris Winery & Taverna Tagaris

BEST Eats

DIRECTIONS: From I-182 (heading east or west) take exit 3 onto Queensgate Drive. Take left onto Columbia Park Trail and go .2 miles. Turn left onto Windmill Rd and then bear right onto Tulip Lane. Tagaris Winery is just past Barnard Griffin on the right.

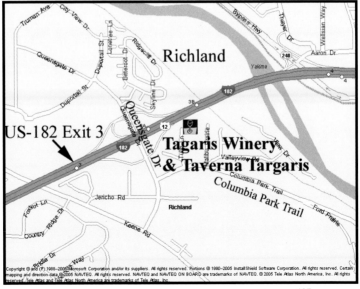

Goose Ridge Estate Vineyard and Winery

What's in a name?

If it's the name Clore, as in Dr. Walter Clore, it refers to "the father of the Washington wine industry." In the 1990s, Dr. Clore consulted with the Monson family to help plan the 1,400-acre south slope facing Goose Ridge Estate Vineyards. (Note: That's not a typo. Goose Ridge Estate Vineyards consumes

1,400 acres of prime grape-growing real estate adjacent to Red Mountain.) In addition to selecting the best blocks of grapes for Goose Ridge Estate Winery's own production, the Monsons sell some of its annual harvest to the likes of Columbia Crest and Stimpson Lane for their own wine production.

What's in a name? If it's the name Hoppes, as in Charlie Hoppes, it refers to the famed Columbia Valley winemaker. Never one to let accolades go to his head, Charlie Hoppes is usually described as "that really nice guy" and, oh yeah, an acclaimed winemaker. Charlie is the winemaker for Goose Ridge Estate Winery. The 1,400 acres are his playground, and he gets to work closely with the viticulturist to select the best-of-the-best blocks for viognier, chardonnay, pinot gris, syrah, cabernet sauvignon, and merlot.

Located just 4 miles east of Benton City on the "ridge" of Goose Hill, the winery's tasting room is situated adjacent to the expansive vineyards, and from its interior you get a bird's-eye view of the well-groomed rows of grapes. It's a tastefully decorated room with warm, neutral colors and little to distract you from enjoying Charlie's varietal and blended vintages.

What's in a name? If the name is "Sol Duc Meritage," it's a blend of 88 percent cabernet sauvignon and 12 percent merlot. Named for the sparkling waters that nourish the sun-drenched Columbia Valley, the "Sol Duc Meritage" is, according to the winemaker's notes, "a concentrated classic red wine with nice integration of rich black cherry, cassis, and notes of vanilla and spice." By any other name, this wine would taste "as sweet."

GOOSE RIDGE ESTATE VINEYARD AND WINERY
opened: 1999
winemaker(s): Charlie Hoppes
location: 16304 North Dallas Road
Richland, WA 99352-7750
phone: 509-628-3880
web: www.gooseridge.com
e-mail: info@gooseridge.com
picnic area: Yes
gift shop: No
fee: Complimentary wine tasting
hours: 11–5 Fridays through Sundays in spring, summer and fall; winter, by appointment

DIRECTIONS: **From Richland**, take I-182 west toward Yakima/Pendleton. Take I-82 south toward Umatilla/Pendleton for 3 miles. Take exit 104 onto N. Dallas Rd and go left. Continue on N. Dallas Rd for 2 miles and look for winery on the left.

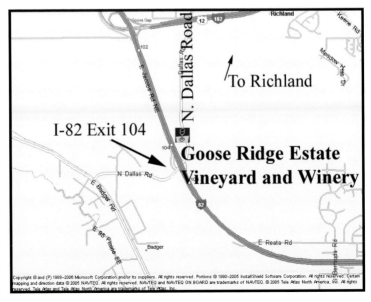

409

Badger Mountain Vineyard

When you visit Badger Mountain Vineyard, you're in for a two-for-one treat. Not only do you have the opportunity to sample certified 100 percent organic Badger Mountain wine, but you can also taste wine under the Powers label, which is made from grapes grown in select Columbia Valley vineyards.

The 82-acre Badger Mountain Vineyard serves as the backdrop to its tasting room, located a few miles off I-82 in Kennewick. The vineyard is certified 100 percent organic, which means that no chemical herbicides, insecticides, fungicides, or synthetic fertilizers touch the vineyard. Only organic and naturally occurring substances are applied. What's more, there are no added sulfites in the production of Badger Mountain wine.

Father and son Bill and Greg Powers established Badger Mountain Vineyard in 1982. In 1983, Tim DeCook, an anesthesiologist from Seattle, became their partner and together they began producing premier wines at their estate winery. From those early years, they have steadily ramped up production to nearly 50,000 cases annually. As testimony to their success, Badger Mountain wines were featured on a segment of NBC's *Today* show highlighting organic foods.

Badger Mountain's story is also one of innovation and adaptation. In 1992, the Powers/DeCook team began producing wine from local growers under the Powers Winery label. This move ultimately won them a place on *Wine Enthusiast*'s list of "50 Great U.S. Cabernet Producers." Nice job.

At Badger Mountain's tasting room, you may be faced with a dilemma: Which of the many wines offered should you sample? Here's a thought: Give those synapses a rest and enjoy them all! Ever the innovator, Badger Mountain Winery also began offering wine-in-a-box under the names Pure White and Pure Red. This method of packaging essentially negates that annoying little oxidation problem, and there's no need to worry about cork failure either. In keeping with the winery's philosophy of offering affordable wines, these attractive 3-liter boxes sell for approximately $22 a box.

WineTrail Note: Badger Mountain's cabernet sauvignon sells for a mere $15 a bottle. This is an amazingly low price, especially when compared to the reds of Walla Walla. It was no surprise when, at the inaugural 2006 Seattle Wine Awards, Badger Mountain took the silver medal in the "$10 and under" category for its cabernet-merlot blend.

BADGER MOUNTAIN VINEYARD
opened: 1982
winemaker(s): Greg Powers
location: 1106 South Jurupa Street
Kennewick, WA 99338-9392
phone: 509-627-4986
web: www.badgermtnvineyard.com
e-mail: winery@badgermtnvineyard.com
picnic area: Yes
gift shop: Yes
fee: Complimentary wine tasting
hours: Daily 10–5

Badger Mountain and Powers Wineries

DIRECTIONS: From I-82 take exit 109 (Badger Rd), turn left on Leslie. Go north on Leslie to Rachel Rd. Go west on Rachel, up the hill, 1.5 miles. Turn right on Jurupa St. The parking lot is at the end. In Kennewick go south on Leslie to Rachel Rd. Turn right (west) on Rachel. Proceed up the hill 1.5 miles. Turn right on Jurupa. Parking lot is at the end.

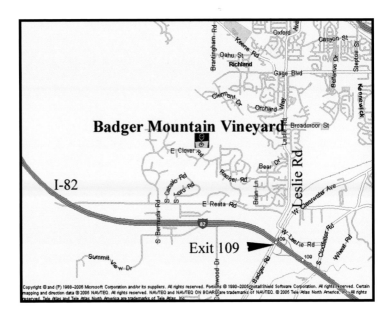

Preston Premium Wines

Preston Premium Wines was the third bonded winery in Washington state when it took root in 1976. That is ancient by Washington wine standards. However, it was the dream of Bill and Joann Preston to establish a 160-acre vineyard and put Washington on the map for premium wine production. They also saw it as their

duty to educate the public about winemaking. To this end, they created a mini-museum at their winery, where, among other items of note, visitors can get an overview of cork production in Portugal and examine Joann's extensive collection of corkscrews.

The elevated tasting room provides a commanding view of the Preston vineyard, where mature vines produce such varietals as merlot, chardonnay, sauvignon blanc, cabernet sauvignon, cabernet franc, gewürztraminer, and white riesling. Winemaker Dave Harvey can boast that most of its wines are estate wines, with the exception of the syrah, which comes from Gamache Vineyard. For port fans, Dave is also responsible for producing Preston's very successful "Tenrebac" port ("Tenrebac" is cabernet spelled backwards).

The winery's spacious tasting room also features a well-stocked gift shop and is the portal to the wine museum downstairs. Of particular note, however, is the large outdoor seating area used for picnicking and listening to live music on Friday nights during the summer. These summer concerts, known as "Vino Notte" (Italian for "wine night"), include hors d'oeuvres and desserts in addition to Preston's current vintage releases. So be sure to bring your appetite with you.

For those WineTrail trekkers seeking a winery for a corporate event, family hoedown, or wedding, take note of the winery's many amenities. From the deck outside the tasting room, you can see Preston's manicured park, which includes a gazebo, a pond, an amphitheater, and a waterfall.

View of vineyard from second story tasting room

PRESTON PREMIUM WINES
opened: 1976
winemaker(s): Dave Harvey
location: 502 East Vineyard Drive
Pasco, WA 99301
phone: 509-545-1990 ext 10
web: www.prestonwines.com
e-mail: info@prestonwines.com
picnic area: Yes
gift shop: Yes
fee: Complimentary wine tasting for up to 4 wines except $8 for reserves
hours: Daily 10–5:30 except major holidays

 **BEST Views and gift shop**

DIRECTIONS: From I-182 [US-12] take exit 14B onto US-395 toward Spokane. Go 5 miles on US-395 (north) and turn right onto E. Vineyard Drive. Go .5 miles on E. Vineyard Drive and look for Preston Premium Wines entrance on right.

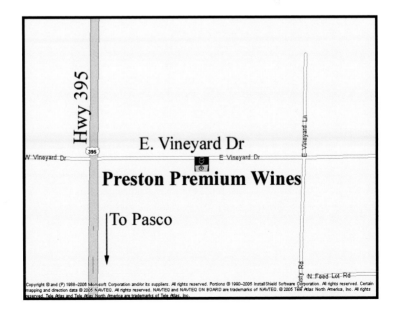

Walla Walla
WINE COUNTRY

Be sure and slow down going through Lowden on Highway 12, and not just because of the speed limit. Lowden is the home of L'Ecole N° 41 and Woodward Canyon wineries, and with their side-by-side location, they are a convenient stop traveling to or from Walla Walla for most visitors. But Walla Walla WineTrail West also features three more tasting rooms just off Highway 12, Skylite Cellars, Three Rivers Winery and Reininger Winery. Thus, you can easily enjoy a full day of tasting along the WineTrail and not even hit the Walla Walla City Center exit.

Each winery is unique in terms of winemaking styles and amenities. At the end of the day, your biggest challenge might be identifying your favorite. They're all good and offer Kodak-like moments. **WineTrail Note:** If you do plan to spend the better part of a day experiencing Walla Walla WineTrail West, pack a picnic and plan to visit the Whitman Mission National Historic Site located just off Highway 12.

1 Woodward Canyon Winery   **3** Reininger Winery   **5** Skylite Cellars
2 L'Ecole N° 41   **4** Three Rivers Winery

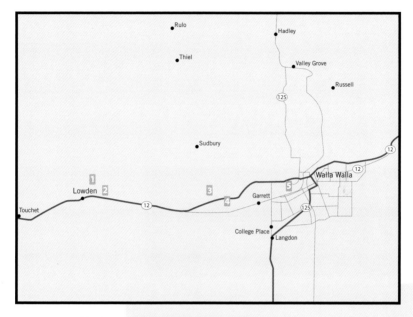

Region:	**Walla Walla Wine Country**
# of tasting rooms on tour:	**5**
Estimated # of days for tour:	**1 to 2**
Getting around:	**Car**
Key events:	❏ **Events sponsored by Walla Walla Valley Wine Alliance: Spring Release Weekend (first full weekend of May); Balloon Stampede Weekend (second full weekend of May); Vintage Walla Walla (first full weekend of June); Entwine: An Auction to Support Walla Walla Arts, Wine, and Education (mid-October); and Holiday Barrel Tasting (first full weekend of December). See www.wallawallawine.com/events for details and ticketing.**
Tips:	❏ **Three Rivers Winery offers a mini 3-hole golf course (free).** ❏ **Be sure and view the artwork at Woodward Canyon.** ❏ **Consider using a limousine service (e.g., Black Tie Limo 509-525-8585, Blue Stocking Tours 509-522-4717, Sunset Coach Tours 509-303-0355, or Four Star Limousine Service 509-521-7849 are some of the many services to contact).**
Best:	❏ **Best Gift Shop: Three Rivers Winery and L'Ecole N° 41** ❏ **Best Picnicking: Three Rivers Winery**

417

Woodward Canyon Winery

Located right off Highway 12 in Lowden is the 1870s farmhouse that serves as Woodward Canyon's tasting room. Lowden is a postage-stamp-size town, and you'll need to slow down and abide by the posted speed signs. So you might as well swing into Woodward Canyon and sample what many consider to be one of the top wines in Washington. Located right next to L'Ecole N° 41, Woodward Canyon's tasting room is hard to miss.

Started in 1981 by Rick Small and his wife, Darcey Fugman-Small, Woodward Canyon is one in the band of original wineries that served as the "starter dough" for the whole Walla Walla Valley wine experience. Rick honed his self-taught winemaking skills in the mid-'70s by collaborating with Gary Figgins, who would go on to create famed Leonetti Cellars. Believing that "intensity is key," Rick is passionate about Woodward Canyon's vineyard and spends a great deal of time there as well as working with select vineyards in Columbia Valley, Horse Heaven Hills and, of course, Walla Walla Valley. His philosophy remains quality over quantity, and the number of awards and accolades throughout the years speaks volumes about Woodward Canyon's success.

Art-adorned labels

Woodward Canyon's winemaker, Kevin Mott, produces about 15,000 cases annually. Its premium wines include cabernet sauvignon, merlot, pinot noir, cabernet franc, chardonnay, sauvignon blanc, and riesling. In addition, it makes dolcetto and barbera wines—not well known in the U.S., but very popular elsewhere. You don't need to store these wines in the cellar; enjoy them today with Italian-style food or red-meat dishes, including your everyday backyard-grilled burger. Woodward Canyon also makes a second-label wine called Nelms Road, known for its excellent value.

Each year since 1992, Woodward Canyon has selected an artist to execute a painting to adorn the bottle of its top-quality cabernet sauvignon. The painting itself hangs in the tasting room during the year. Also found in the tasting room is the full line-up of the artist series of vintage wine bottles, with their distinctive labels. As noted on the winery website, the great French painter Cezanne, in a letter written later in his life, asked, "Is art a kind of priesthood where only the most pure of heart are allowed to enter?" At Woodward Canyon, art is for everyone. For WineTrail enthusiasts visiting this winery, it can be seen on a canvas and tasted from a bottle.

WOODWARD CANYON WINERY
opened: 1981
winemaker(s): Kevin Mott
location: 11920 West Highway 12
Lowden, WA 99360
phone: 509-525-4129
web: www.woodwardcanyon.com
e-mail: info@woodwardcanyon.com
picnic area: Yes
gift shop: Yes
fee: Complimentary wine tasting
hours: Daily 10–5

One of the original bonded wineries in the Walla Walla Valley

DIRECTIONS: From Walla Walla go east on Route 12 for about 17 miles to Lowden. Woodward Canyon Winery is on the right next to L'Ecole N° 41 in a restored farmhouse.
From the west, take Route 12 from the Tri-Cities and continue on Route 12 for about 34 miles to Lowden. Woodward Canyon Winery is located on the left next to L'Ecole N° 41 in a restored farmhouse.

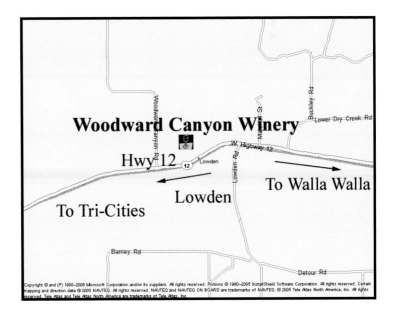

L'Ecole N⁰ 41

It is back to school whenever you pass through Lowden on Highway 12. Located about 12 miles west of Walla Walla, L'Ecole N⁰ 41 is a definitive landmark inviting those passing by to stop in and sample great wine. Established in 1983, L'Ecole N⁰ 41 is the Walla Walla Valley's third-oldest winery, with

only Woodward Canyon and Leonetti Cellar a little older. Today, L'Ecole N⁰ 41 produces about 35,000 cases annually, guided by a philosophy of traditional hands-on winemaking. The owners, Megan and Martin Clubb, are clear about their goal: "To achieve clean, ripe, stylistically expressive and aromatic wines that let the individual site characteristics of our vineyards shine through." While Martin spends most of his time these days managing the vineyards, winemaker Mike Sharon is usually at the winery overseeing the punching, bottling, labeling, tasting, racking, de-stemming, and an ever-growing mountain of other chores that go into creating wine from grapes.

Built in 1915, the former "Frenchtown" schoolhouse will take you back in time; the sounds, the smells, and even the fine craftsmanship of the building itself will have you imagining the sounds of laughing children playing at recess. On the way in, check out the cast-iron school bell outside the entrance. In the upstairs tasting room, you will notice an old chalkboard now used to list L'Ecole N⁰ 41's wines and prices. A stained-glass replica of L'Ecole N⁰ 41 gracefully sits center stage behind the wine bar. The gift shop offers a variety of wine-related items and L'Ecole N⁰ 41 logo—inspired items.

L'Ecole N⁰ 41 produces a variety of red and white wines using estate grapes and fruit acquired from Columbia Valley and local vineyards. You will want to budget a good half-hour to sample these wines and visit with the friendly and well-trained tasting room staff. Fielding questions about L'Ecole N⁰ 41 and the winemaking process with patience and an engaging smile, they appear to be very well schooled.

L'ECOLE Nº 41
opened: 1983
winemaker(s): Mike Sharon
location: 41 Lowden School Road
Lowden, WA 99360-0000
phone: 509-525-0940
web: www.lecole.com
e-mail: info@lecole.com
picnic area: Yes
gift shop: Yes
fee: Complimentary wine tasting
hours: Daily 10–5; closed New Year's Day, Easter, 4th
of July, Thanksgiving and Christmas; closed 1 pm
December 24 and 31

BEST Gift shop

DIRECTIONS: Drive west on Hwy 12 for 13 miles. The school house sits on the north side just at the entrance (40 mph sign) to Lowden where Dry Creek Rd meets the highway. A sign depicting their label is located just off the highway in front of the winery.

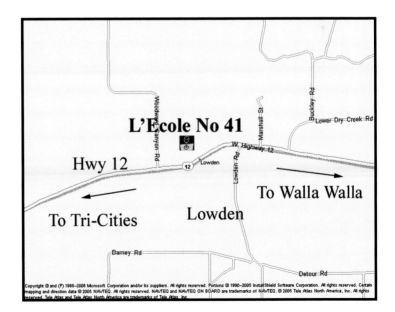

Reininger Winery

Winemaking has a way of attracting people from different fields. A half-dozen Walla Walla winemakers have backgrounds as pharmacists. Engineers also seem to gravitate toward winemaking. In addition, along Washington's WineTrails you will discover a number of winemakers who were mountaineers and climbing guides in their past life. Such is the case with Charles Reininger of Reininger Winery.

After working as a mountain guide for many years, Charles hung up his ice axe, moved to the Walla Walla Valley, and married Tracy Tucker, a Walla Walla native, in the early '90s. It was around this time that he caught the wine bug and began assisting at Waterbrook Winery and dabbling in home winemaking. As is often the case with being a mountain guide, the journey itself is the reward. In winemaking, it is the drive to create the ultimate expression of the grape … the flavor of its *terroir*. As Charles Reininger notes on the winery's website, "Wine is the adventure of the soul." We submit, however, that the destination can be great too, whether it is a mountain summit or being named one of America's top 40 wineries by Wine & Spirits in 2005. The Reiningers are surely on the right path!

WineTrail Note: Check out Reininger's red blend wine called "Cima"—assuming it's not sold out. The name "Cima" means summit or mountain peak in Italian.

Reininger produces small lots of Walla Walla Valley merlot, cabernet sauvignon and syrah, while its Helix-labeled wine focuses on fruit from the Columbia Valley. Much of the fruit for the Reininger label comes from nearby Ash Hollow Vineyard, owned, in part, by the Reiningers. Ash Hollow Vineyard focuses on cabernet sauvignon, merlot and syrah grapes.

Located right off Highway 12, a few miles west of Walla Walla, the 15,000-square-foot Reininger winery/tasting room is actually a converted potato shed. However, you won't find any potatoes here or, for that matter, Walla Walla onions. Rather, the Reininger tasting room is really all about the wine. This is intentional; the Reiningers never planned to be a "destination winery" for sponsoring the next corporate event or family shindig. Nor will you find a gift shop here. It's about experiencing the wine, and what great wine they make.

REININGER WINERY
opened: 1997
winemaker(s): Chuck Reininger
location: 5858 West Highway 12
Walla Walla, WA 99362
phone: 509-522-1994
web: www.reiningerwinery.com
e-mail: info@reiningerwinery.com
picnic area: No
gift shop: No
fee: Complimentary wine tasting
hours: Daily 10–6 from May through December; daily
10–5 from January through April

DIRECTIONS: **From Tri-Cities**, travel east on US-12 about 40 miles. Reininger Winery is on the left at 5858 W. Hwy 12. **From Walla Walla**, depart on US-12 west and go about 5 miles. Arrive at Reininger Winery on the right (look for winery sign).

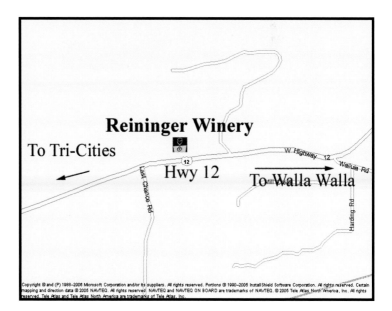

Three Rivers Winery

Midway between Lowden and Walla Walla sits the 16-acre site of Three Rivers Winery. Plenty of space to sample wine, shop for merchandise, and play golf. Golf? Yes, Three Rivers is unique among Washington wineries; it comes equipped with a short three-hole golf course. (The local community college supplied the turf.) What's more, the golfing is free.

This is a destination winery for a variety of reasons. Foremost is the sheer size of the winery/tasting room/gift shop/conference room and outdoor deck. At 18,000 square feet, there is plenty of room to host your next corporate event

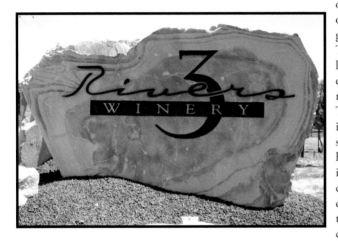

or join a swarm of other wine tasters at the generous tasting room bar. The gift shop is one of the largest in the state, with enough stock to supply next year's Christmas list. The structure itself is an inviting contemporary-style building with huge entrance doors; an interior with high-trussed ceilings; and an ample deck featuring one of the top views in Washington, courtesy of the Blue Mountains in the distance. With its features of corporate meeting space, wine tasting, shopping, picnicking, and golfing, Three Rivers is a must stop. That said, don't plan to have a wedding here. According to our tasting-room host, there's "too much bride drama."

Although many of the wines are "complimentary," there is a small fee for the select wines produced by winemaker Holly Turner. We recommend that you indulge, because these wines are special. Heck, you've taken all the time and expense to get this far, why deny yourself the winemaker's finest?

So why was the name Three Rivers Winery chosen? The name represents the three most prominent rivers in the two appellations from which the winery purchases its grapes: the Columbia, Snake, and Walla Walla rivers.

Fore!

Three Rivers Winery

THREE RIVERS WINERY
opened: 1999
winemaker(s): Holly Turner
location: 5641 West Highway 12
Walla Walla, WA 99362
phone: 509-526-9463
web: www.threeriverswinery.com
e-mail: info@threeriverswinery.com
picnic area: Yes
gift shop: Yes
fee: Complimentary wine tasting except reserves are
$5 for 3 pours
hours: Daily 10–6

BEST Gift shop and picnicking

DIRECTIONS: **From Walla Walla** travel west on US-12 for about 5 miles. Three Rivers Winery is on the left at 5641 W. Hwy 12.
From the Tri-Cities, travel east about 40 miles on US-12. Look for Three Rivers Winery sign and entrance on right.

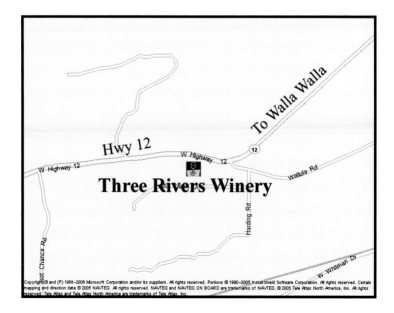

Skylite Cellars

With Skylite Cellars, you get a two-for-one taste experience. Skylite Cellars has both a downtown Walla Walla tasting room location as well as the newer location just west of town off Highway 12. It also produces under two different labels: the Skylite Cellars brand and the Hiney Wine label.

The downtown tasting room location is on Second Street, across from the JLC and Ash Hollow tasting rooms. The in-laws of proprietor Tom Hodgins own the

eclectic antiques/art shop where the downtown tasting room is located. While there, check out the distinctive wine-barrel bar and the surrounding art (particularly the painting of a tasting room scene). Upstairs, you'll discover a skylight that bathes the upstairs gallery with warm light, hence the winery's name. The skylight was discovered during the renovation of the property. It's such a wonderful architectural feature, you have to wonder why anyone would have covered it up. One of the family members is usually working the tasting room and can take you on a field trip through the gallery. Unfortunately, Washington state law won't allow you to take your wine glass with you.

Just west of town, on Campbell Road, is the newly dedicated Skylite winery/tasting room, which has ample parking, high ceilings, and a terrific mural on an interior wall of the tasting room. Tom can usually be found at his FM radio station next door. The winery is a hop, skip, and a jump from Three Rivers and Reininger wineries. When you walk into this tasting room, your first reaction will likely be "wow." It is readily apparent that a lot of creative energy went into this space.

Winemaker Robert Smasne produces small quantities "of distinctive tasting wines for the discerning wine lover." Much of Skylite's fruit is derived from Yakima Valley and local growers and made into an array of white and red wines. Even though it is relatively new, a Skylite Cellars syrah took top honors in a Marcus Whitman blind tasting contest. But Hiney Wine, Skylite's second label, is the real showstopper. With its "world-famous" Hiney red wine and slogans such as "You only go around once in life so grab all the Hiney Wine you can get!" "Feel my Hiney," and "Uncork the Hiney," it's obvious that Tom and his cohorts don't take themselves too seriously. They are about having fun. Consequently they make the wine-tasting experience accessible to most folks who just want to get out and enjoy wine.

Bottoms up!

Original painting in downtown tasting room

SKYLITE CELLARS
opened: 2005
winemaker(s): Robert Smasne
location: Highway 12 & Campbell Road
Walla Walla, WA 99362
phone: 509-529-8000
web: www.skylitecellars.com
e-mail: info@skylitecellars.com
picnic area: No
gift shop: No
fee: Complimentary wine tasting
hours: Daily 10–6

DIRECTIONS: **From US-12 traveling east** continue past Lowden about 8 miles. Go past Three Rivers and Reininger Wineries about 1 mile and turn onto Campbell Rd. The Skylite Winery and tasting room is immediately on your left. (Note: Skylite Cellars also has a tasting room in downtown Walla Walla on North 2nd Ave.)

From Walla Walla head west on US-12 about 3 miles and turn left onto Campbell Rd. The Skylite tasting room is immediately on your left.

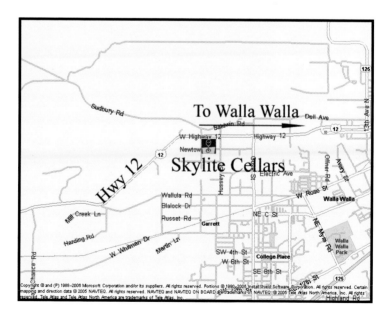

Walla Walla Downtown
WineTrail

Inside Seven Hills tasting room

Walla Walla is *the* place to go. Many people are surprised to learn that *Sunset Magazine* voted Walla Walla the 2005 Wine Destination of the Year.

The downtown has over a dozen wineries—many you can experience on foot. The remaining tasting rooms are a short drive west. Along the route, you will discover wonderful restaurants, delis to purchase picnic supplies, wine bar bistros (as if you need that), historic sites, and interesting architecture.

1 Waters Winery
2 Seven Hills Winery
3 Ash Hollow Winery
4 Waterbrook Winery
5 Fort Walla Walla Cellars
6 Morrison Lane Winery
7 Spring Valley Vineyard
8 Walla Walla Village Winery
9 Mannina Cellars
10 Forgeron Cellars
11 Whitman Cellars
12 Canoe Ridge Vineyard
13 Amavi Cellars
14 Foundry Vineyards
15 Bergevin Lane Vineyards
16 Lowden Hills Winery

Region:	**Walla Walla Wine Country**
# of tasting rooms on tour:	**16**
# of satellite tasting rooms:	**3—satellite tasting rooms for Skylite Cellars, Preston Premium Wines and Patit Creek Winery.**
Estimated # of days for tour:	**3 or 4**
Getting around:	**Car and foot**
Key events:	❏ **Events sponsored by Walla Walla Valley Wine Alliance: Spring Release Weekend (first full weekend of May); Balloon Stampede Weekend (second full weekend of May); Vintage Walla Walla (first full weekend of June); Entwine: An Auction to Support Walla Walla Arts, Wine, and Education (mid-October); and Holiday Barrel Tasting (first full weekend of December). See www.wallawallawine.com/events for details and ticketing.**
Tips:	❏ **Saturdays are the best times to experience tasting rooms—most are open.** ❏ **Great restaurants to choose from—including 26brix, The Marc Restaurant, Backstage Bistro, CreekTown Café, Grapefields Wine Bar and Café, Vineyard Wine Bar, T. Maccarone's, and Whtehouse-Crawford, to name a few.** ❏ **Consider using a limousine service (e.g., Black Tie Limo 509- 525-8585, Blue Stocking Tours 509-522-4717, Sunset Coach Tours 509-303-0355, or Four Star Limousine Service 509-521-7849 are some of the many services to contact).**

Waters Winery

WineTrail enthusiasts know it's always good to phone ahead. Especially if the winery in question makes small quantities of premium wine and has a history of selling out quickly. Waters Winery is one such winery—we suggest you call before you hit the WineTrail.

Waters Winery is conveniently located in the Depot Building near the Second Avenue exit of Route 12 in downtown Walla Walla. Chances are, if you're in the area, you will be going by there. We'll cross our fingers that Waters is open when you stop by, because with its focus on syrah, cabernet sauvignon, and a Bordeaux-style blend called "Interlude," it's a great start (or finish) for a WineTrail adventure.

Founder Jason Huntley and winemaker Jamie Brown use grapes from their own vineyard as well as other local fruit to produce small lots of wine that meet their high standards. If the wine doesn't measure up, they won't sell it. Thus, you can feel confident in leaving these bottles down in the cellar for years. Though with the distinctive calligraphy on the Waters label, you may be tempted to keep the bottle upstairs and in plain view, where it can be appreciated.

WATERS WINERY
winemaker(s): Jamie Brown
location: 416 North Second Avenue, Suite A
Walla Walla, WA 99362
phone: 509-525-1590
web: www.waterswinery.com
e-mail: jbrown@waterswinery.com
picnic area: No
gift shop: No
fee: Small tasting fee may apply
hours: 10–5 Friday and Saturday

DIRECTIONS: **From US-12** take N. 2nd Ave. (City Center) exit. Go about .2 miles and the Waters Winery tasting room is on the left in the restored train depot building.

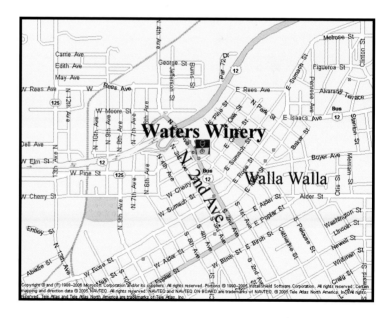

431

Seven Hills Winery

Perhaps you thought only Rome is known for its "Seven Hills." Not so fast, Rome. Walla Walla also has its Seven Hills, in the form of a winery.

The Seven Hills Winery is located in the recently renovated and restored Whitehouse-Crawford building in downtown Walla Walla. The award-winning restoration of this former lumber mill preserved the 100-year-old brick building, including its posts, its beams, and most important, its charm. You can find

it listed in the National Historic Register. It turns out that this historic building is an excellent venue for making fine wine and tasting the finished product. You can view the sky-lit temperature- and humidity-controlled barrel room from the tasting room itself, thanks to a strategically placed picture window. The barrels themselves are the traditional Bordeaux-style 225-liter oak barrels that are prevalent throughout the industry. The barrels are also the source of the Seven Hills wine club's name, the Barrique Society. Nice touch.

Seven Hills Winery focuses on reds and enjoys a reputation for great balance, which it states is a "trinity of fruit, acidity, and tannin." This trinity of ingredients inspired the use of seven Irish trinity cross-knot symbols as part of the winery's logo—at least we at WineTrails Northwest choose to think so. Enjoy the wine right out of the bottle now or order it with your meal at the gourmet Whitehouse-Crawford Restaurant, also housed in the building. Alternatively, you can cellar this wine for years. Working closely with the grape growers of Red Mountain, Columbia Valley, and Walla Walla (especially the distinguished Seven Hills Vineyard), winemaker Casey McClellan makes single vineyard wines and blends selectively to achieve, you guessed it, "harmony among fruit, acidity and tannin." He also uses fruit from Oregon to make charmingly crisp rieslings and pinot gris.

It's a good thing the winery doesn't use the 300-liter barrels prevalently used in Australia to age its wines. Otherwise, the name of the wine club would have to be the "Hogshead Society."

Seven Hills tasting room in the restored
Whitehouse-Crawford building

SEVEN HILLS WINERY
opened: 2000
winemaker(s): Casey McClellan
location: 212 North 3rd Avenue
Walla Walla, WA 99362
phone: 877-777-7870
web: www.sevenhillswinery.com
e-mail: info@sevenhillswinery.com
picnic area: No
gift shop: No
fee: Complimentary wine tasting
hours: 11–4 Thursday through Saturday from May 1
through September 1, or by appointment

DIRECTIONS: Seven Hills Winery is located in downtown Walla Walla in the historic Whitehouse-Crawford Building. **From US-12**, take the 2nd Ave./City Center exit and continue southeast on 2nd Ave. toward City Center for .3 miles. Turn right (west) onto W. Sumach St. and arrive at 212 N. 3rd Ave.

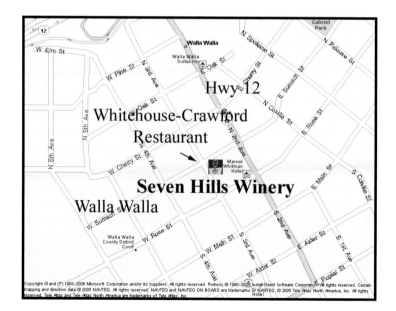

Ash Hollow Winery

If you ever find yourself driving east on Highway 12 towards Walla Walla, keep an eye out for a sign reading "Ash Hollow Vineyard," just a few miles outside of town. It will lead you to a wine experience you'll savor for a long time to come.

Great wines start with great grapes, and the fact that a number of top-notch wineries purchase their grapes from Ash Hollow is testimony to this winery's premium bounty.

Ash Hollow's mantra is "Family, Friends, Food, Fun, and Great Wine," and its quaint downtown tasting room reflects that sentiment. Situated between Main and Rose streets, a half-block from the Marcus Whitman Hotel, this storefront tasting room is a wonderful place to sample wine, with its warm atmosphere and sense of place. Co-owners John Turner (managing partner) and Steve Clifton (winemaker) grew up in Southern California and attended college together. Their goal in launching Ash Hollow has always been to create an experience that celebrates family, friends, food, and fun.

Art and fine wine converge at Ash Hallow

But John and Steve have other goals as well: Of particular interest to WineTrail enthusiasts would be their mission to create ultrapremium wines. And they accomplish this by using Ash Hollow Vineyard grapes along with fruit from other Washington state vineyards. Keep in mind that Ash Hollow wines are not destined for the cellar. Rather, enjoy them with friends and family right away.

Ash Hollow's charming tasting room displays the paintings of Walla Walla native Jeffrey Hill. If you have visited other wineries, Hill's distinctive style may look familiar to you; at least a dozen other wineries exhibit his paintings, sculptures, and murals. One of Hill's most recognized pieces is the 10-foot-high sculpture of a wine-grape harvester that graces the entrance to the Center for Enology and Viticulture at Walla Walla Community College.

Speaking of art, note that the glass object on the tasting bar is not a work of art. Please don't make the same mistake that others have made by picking it up and turning it over in search of the price tag. Do so, and wine will flow—all over the bar and probably all over you. The glass object is actually the tasting room's spittoon!

ASH HOLLOW WINERY
opened: 2002
winemaker(s): Steve Clifton
location: 14 North 2nd Avenue
Walla Walla, WA 99362
phone: 509-529-7565
web: www.ashhollow.com
e-mail: info@ashhollow.com
picnic area: No
gift shop: Yes
fee: Complimentary wine tasting
hours: 11–7 Wednesday through Saturday, 11–4
Sunday through Tuesday, from May through
September; 11–4 Wednesday through Sunday from
October through April

DIRECTIONS: Ash Hollow's tasting room is located in downtown Walla Walla on 2nd Ave.
From US-12, take the 2nd Ave./City Center exit and continue southeast on 2nd Avenue toward City
Center for .3 miles. Arrive at 14 North 2nd Ave.—the Ash Hollow tasting room is on the left. The
tasting room is located between E. Rose and E. Main Sts. across from the Marcus Whitman Hotel.

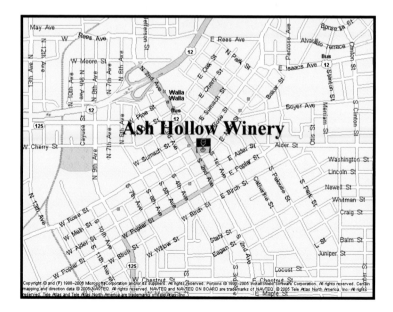

Waterbrook Winery

Waterbrook Winery was named such to complement "Walla Walla," a word in the Nez Perce Indian dialect meaning "running water." Founded in 1984, Waterbrook is one of the original four wineries in Walla Walla. This is old by current Walla Walla standards, but fortunately for us, Waterbrook's founder and original winemaker, Eric Rindal, was pretty young when he caught the wine bug and began Waterbrook Winery.

The Waterbrook Winery tasting room is housed in a brick building located in downtown Walla Walla, across from Starbucks. There are several great reasons for stopping at Waterbrook. First, of course, is the great wine it offers year after year, now made under the guidance of winemaker John Freeman. While production has steadily grown to 50,000 cases annually, the wines, produced from both Waterbrook's own vineyards and Columbia Valley vineyards, continue to win high praise.

Today, the winery offers a number of reds and whites to choose from: sauvignon blanc, chardonnay, viognier, merlot, cabernet sauvignon, syrah and a "Mélange" red wine are some of its typical stars. By the way, Waterbrook's goal for its red wines has been "softer, fleshier wines for early enjoyment while still maintaining the wines' depth and structure." It must be doing something right, because demand continues to outstrip supply. Waterbrook chardonnay (which relies on traditional oak barrel fermentation) is especially popular, with current production set at 14,000 cases per year. That's not too shabby in a field crowded with competing chardonnays.

But the tasting room experience itself is a rich reward. Waterbrook celebrates fine art, not just in the bottle but also on its walls. Every six weeks the staff rotates the artwork to feature a particular artist. For this reason, the facility is referred to as the "Tasting Room & Gallery." In addition, from May through September, WineTrail visitors are welcome to sit in the patio area with a bottle of Waterbrook wine and enjoy live music on Thursday evenings. Essentially, Waterbrook pairs fine wine with fine art and music. All you need to bring are the bread and cheese to pair with the Waterbrook chardonnay.

WATERBROOK WINERY
opened: 1984
winemaker(s): John Freeman
location: 31 East Main
Walla Walla, WA 99362
phone: 509-522-1262
web: www.waterbrook.com
e-mail: info@waterbrook.com
picnic area: Yes
gift shop: Yes
fee: Complimentary wine tasting
hours: Daily 10:30–4:30 excluding major holidays

DIRECTIONS: Waterbrook Winery is located in downtown Walla Walla. **From US-12** take 2nd Ave. toward city center and go about .5 miles. Turn left onto E. Main St. and go 1 block—the tasting room is located in a red brick building on the left-hand side across from Starbucks.

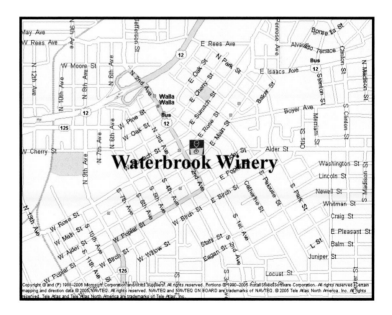

Fort Walla Walla Cellars

Sometimes misfortune results in unexpected benefits. Such was the case in 2004 when owners and winemakers Jim Moyer and Cliff Kontos experienced the big freeze that essentially killed the Walla Walla grape harvest. Like all the winemakers in the valley, they had to seek fruit elsewhere. Jim and Cliff turned

to Crawford Vineyard in the Columbia Valley Appellation, and with Crawford's fruit, their first red table wine was born: "Trapper Red." At about $18 a bottle, "Trapper Red" is one of the best values around.

The name Fort Walla Walla pays homage to the area's heritage. According to the Fort Walla Walla Cellars website, a man by the name of Frank Orselli, who was stationed at the original Fort Walla Walla, opened what many historians agree was the area's first commercial winery. It produced approximately 1,000 cases of wine annually. Study Fort Walla Walla Cellars' wine labels and you'll see an illustration of Fort Walla Walla itself. The labels even have that "aged look," as if the bottles they adorn had been kept all this time in Orselli's own wine cellar. With Jim and Cliff's penchant for history, it comes as no surprise that they stick to a traditional winemaking style, using tried and true techniques passed down from generations of winemakers. Using these methods, they produce approximately 2,000 cases per year.

Located in the heart of downtown Walla Walla, the winery's fort-like red brick tasting room enjoys a steady stream of visitors. WineTrail enthusiasts will have an opportunity to swirl and taste premium cabernet sauvignon, merlot, syrah, and, of course, "Trapper Red." Even with a dozen visitors, the tasting room manager finds time to pour, chat, and work the cash register with ease. Rarely do we see tasting room staff serving up second helpings. But at Fort Walla Walla Cellars, a second taste is often offered to guests. Yes, there is a spittoon on the wine bar, but we suspect it's an historical artifact put there to lend ambiance. Fort Walla Walla wines are too luscious to waste in a spittoon.

WineTrail Note: History comes alive at the Fort Walla Walla Museum on Myra Road through historical portrayals. For example, local Walla Wallan Rusty Figgins portrays his grandfather Francesco Leonetti, who immigrated to Walla Walla in 1901 and planted an acre of Black Prince grapes. A visit to the museum is a great way to discover Walla Walla's roots (pun intended).

Cliff Kontos

FORT WALLA WALLA CELLARS
opened: 2001
winemaker(s): Jim Moyer and Cliff Kontos
location: 127 East Main Street
Walla Walla, WA 99362
phone: 509-520-1095
web: www.fortwallawallacellars.com
e-mail: info@fortwallawallacellars.com
picnic area: Yes
gift shop: Yes
fee: Complimentary wine tasting
hours: 11–4:30 Thursday through Monday, or by
appointment

DIRECTIONS: From US-12 take N. 2nd Ave. exit (city center). Turn left onto E. Main St. and go 2 blocks. Arrive at 127 E. Main St.—Fort Walla Walla's tasting room is on the left on the corner of Main and N. Colville St.

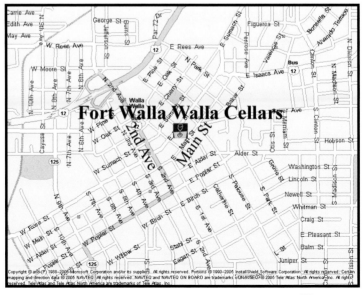

Morrison Lane Winery

Often wineries are successful because the owner and winemaker march to the beat of a different drummer. So when your lineup of wines includes cinsault, carmenère, barbera, and counoise, you distinguish yourself immediately. Such is the case with Morrison Lane.

Since 1997, Dean and Verdie Morrison have supplied a number of wineries with excellent grapes of Rhone and Italian origin from their 23-acre vineyard, located just west of Walla Walla. In 2002, the couple took the plunge themselves and

Music and wine blend at Morrison Lane

went vertical, not only growing the fruit but also turning it into fine wine. Native to the Walla Walla Valley, Dean was able to hone his winemaking skills under the tutelage of John Abbot, who, at the time, was the chief winemaker at Canoe Ridge before he launched Abeja. The Morrisons still use the winemaking facilities of Canoe Ridge and therefore technically can't refer to their wines as "estate" on the Morrison Lane labels. The Federal Bureau of Alcohol, Tobacco and Firearms would slap their wrists. Nevertheless, by any other name, the Rhone varietal counoise (pronounced koon-WAHZ) would taste just as good. It actually tastes like syrup from canned Bing cherries—very fruit-forward but not sweet.

Situated downtown in the historic Dacres Building, Morrison Lane tasting room is on the corner of Main and Fourth streets next to the trendy 26brix restaurant. Wine pairs wonderfully with music, and it's no accident that a baby grand piano graces the tasting room. The Morrisons often host musical evenings with the sounds of jazz and the blues spilling outside. Because Morrison Lane is a small, family-owned and -operated winery (youngest son Dan is its winemaker), you can often find Verdie working the tasting room. In addition to some unusual Italian and French varietals, Morrison Lane also produces wonderfully balanced yet intensely flavored syrahs, sangiovese and, in keeping with the musical theme, a red blend called "33 1/3." Verdie has a charming disposition, bright eyes, and a good sense of humor. She notes "We don't have a wine club per se, but we do have a baseball bat under the bar." She's kidding, of course … we think.

Verdie Morrison

MORRISON LANE WINERY
opened: 2002
winemaker(s): Dan Morrison
location: 201 West Main Street
Walla Walla, WA 99362
phone: 509-526-0229
web: www.morrisonlane.com
e-mail: morrisonlane@charter.net
picnic area: No
gift shop: No
fee: Complimentary wine tasting
hours: 12–6 Friday through Monday, or by appointment;
January and February by appointment only

DIRECTIONS: The Morrison Lane tasting room is located in the historic Dacres Building next to 26brix Restaurant. **From N. 2nd Ave. (US-12 Business)** turn right onto W. Main St. and go .1 miles. Arrive at Morrison Lane tasting room on the corner.

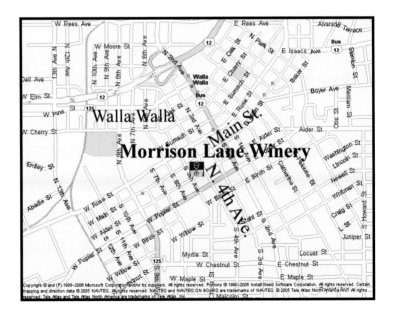

Spring Valley Vineyard

The tasting room of Spring Valley Vineyard is immersed in history. It is the story of a homesteading farm family, the Corkrums, who settled in Walla Walla Valley in 1865. Their offspring were later to marry and introduce the family names of Derby and Elvin into the mix. On the tasting room walls, you see enlarged photos of the Spring Valley Vineyard, neatly kept rows of vineyards surrounded by golden wheatfields. Pictures of key family figures adorn the wine labels as

do their names, such as Uriah, Frederick, and Derby. Don't be surprised if one of the relatives is working the tasting room. Recently, a Derby granddaughter, Katherine Derby Elvin, relocated from Minnesota to learn the trade and manage the tasting room. **WineTrail Note:** Be sure and pick up an historical fact sheet that presents a chronology of the Spring Valley Vineyard story. It's chockfull of interesting factoids, including the wonderful tidbit that Dean Derby still holds the University of Washington record for the longest touchdown run from scrimmage (92 yards) set in 1956.

After the tragic death of winemaker/manager Devin Corkrum Derby in 2004, the Derbys turned to Ste. Michelle Wine Estates for assistance. In 2005, Ste. Michelle Wine Estates agreed to lease the vineyard and winery, and purchase the Spring Valley Vineyard wine brand. Hats off to Ste. Michelle Wine Estates for stepping up to the plate. In the end, we the consumers are the benefactors of this new relationship.

But let's get real. Ste. Michelle's decision to purchase the brand was a smart business decision. Over the past few years, Spring Valley Vineyard wines have placed no. 13 and no. 17 on the prestigious *Wine Spectator* Top 100 list. In addition, its wines have received an outstanding rating by virtually all of the major wine publications in the world. Be sure to sample the "Uriah," a blend of merlot, cabernet franc, cabernet sauvignon, and petit verdot that *Wine Advocate* described as "A complex fruitful mouth of blackberry, currant, and cherry with a hint of licorice and leather." Yummy. And, if you have the opportunity to sample them, the "Frederick," "Derby," and "Muleskinner" vintages demonstrate the powerful and firm finish intensity of these 100 percent estate wines.

If time permits, take the short 20-minute drive out of town and check out the 1,100-acre Spring Valley Vineyard and wheat farm. And take your camera. You may very well want to enlarge these pictures for one of your walls at home. Cheers to five generations!

Katherine Derby Elvin

SPRING VALLEY VINEYARD
opened: 1999
winemaker(s): Serge LaVille
location: 7 South 4th Avenue
Walla Walla, WA 99362
phone: 509-525-1506
web: www.springvalleyvineyard.com
e-mail: info@springvalleyvineyard.com
picnic area: No
gift shop: No
fee: $5 tasting fee
hours: Tasting room 11–4 Friday and Saturday, 12–4
Sundays; winery open by appointment only

DIRECTIONS: **From downtown Walla Walla** head south on W. Main St. Turn left onto S. 4th Ave.— Spring Valley Vineyard's tasting room is on the left across from Patit Creek's downtown tasting room.

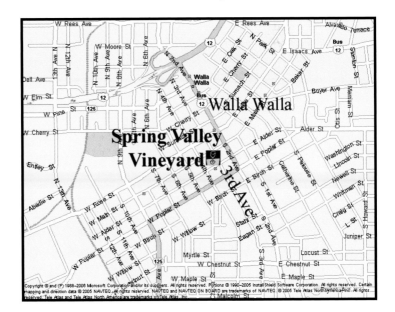

Walla Walla Village Winery

I was 15 when my dad and mom threw two of my three sisters and me in the two-tone blue Ford Fairlane 500 to drive from Spokane to the Bay Area. We were visiting my older brother stationed at Fort Ord. The nightly news reported body counts from Vietnam. Eric Burdon and The Animals' "San Francisco Nights" was a huge hit on the radio, and my dad begrudgingly turned up the volume when the song played. We were heading to music mecca, where the Fillmore was the venue for Jefferson Airplane, The Doors, Janis Joplin, The

Grateful Dead, and others. Our city tour included Haight-Ashbury and I saw plenty of hippies and psychedelic posters announcing upcoming concerts. I was to learn later that Stanley Mouse was the artistic creator behind many of the posters. Today, serious collectors wage bidding battles on eBay for his work. It was the summer of 1967.

So imagine my delight nearly 40 years later when I walked into the Walla Walla Village Winery tasting room and saw its labels designed by none other than Stanley Mouse. The same guy whose art embodied quintessential '60s rock had lent his talents to the creation of Walla Walla Village's wine labels. Just as his music posters can evoke memories of events, feelings, and ideas, a wine label can define a moment in time—be it with friends, loved ones, food, or the taste sensations of a first sip.

Barb and Lynn Irish Clark, owners of Walla Walla Village Winery, had Mouse create the label for their first 2003 release of gewürztraminer. His designs are also captured on other wines they offer. I later discovered that the eye-popping sunburst label paired perfectly with the spiciness of the gewürztraminer as well as the luscious rich flavor of their "Equinox II" cabernet sauvignon. Their son, Joel Clark, is the winemaker who creates, in addition to the cabernet sauvignon, merlot, syrah, and chardonnay varieties.

Located in a renovated 1900 building, the Walla Walla Village Winery tasting room is a beautiful complement to Walla Walla's downtown architecture. Inside, the high ceilings feature copper tiles, and the refurbished tasting bar dates back to an era that honored artisanship. As you sample the delectable offerings, you may look through the arched windows and imagine a horse-drawn carriage passing by. Incongruous as it may seem, it would be the perfect moment to hear "On a warm San Francisco night…"

WALLA WALLA VILLAGE WINERY
opened: 2003
winemaker(s): Joel Clark
location: 107 South 3rd Avenue
Walla Walla, WA 99362
phone: 509-525-WINE (9463)
web: www.wallawallavillagewinery.com
e-mail: irish@wallawallavillagewinery.com
picnic area: No
gift shop: No
fee: Complimentary wine tasting
hours: 11–5 Monday through Saturday, 1–5
Sunday, from May through November; 1–5 Sunday
through Thursday from December through April;
closed Wednesday

DIRECTIONS: From US-12 take 2nd Ave. toward city center and go about .5 miles. Turn right onto W. Alder St. and continue to 3rd Ave.—the tasting room is just around the corner on the right-hand side.

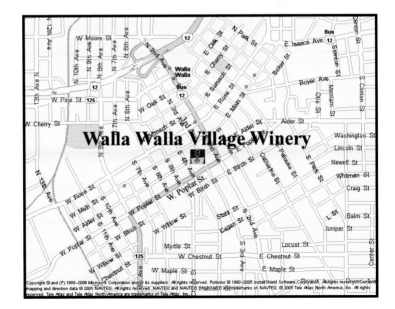

445

Mannina Cellars

Palouse hills in early spring

Truth be told, I didn't actually make it to Mannina Cellars. Not that I didn't try. I made my attempt just before press time for this book, and Mannina Cellars had just opened to the public. But when I showed up on a Sunday, I found it had been open on Saturday only. So, I leave it up to you, dear WineTrail trekker, to venture forth and discover for yourself what Mannina Cellars is all about: What is its winemaker's vision? To what style of winemaking does the winemaker adhere? And in what direction does Mannina Cellars' owner want to take the winery? Hey, you can pretend to be me!

Please let me know what to look for, sample, and experience. I would be most appreciative. I promise, in the second edition of the book, to incorporate your feedback into a description of the winery and share with other WineTrail enthusiasts the nuances and unique character that define Mannina Cellars.

MANNINA CELLARS
opened: 2006
winemaker(s): Don Redman
location: 7 West Poplar Street
Walla Walla, WA 99362
phone: 509-529-5760
web: www.manninacellars.com
e-mail: info@manninacellars.com
picnic area: No
gift shop: No
fee: Tasting fee may apply
hours: 11–4 Saturday, or by appointment

Mannina's downtown tasting room

DIRECTIONS: **From US-12**, take 2nd Ave. exit toward city center. Continue about 1 mile and turn right on Poplar St. Winery is at 7 W. Poplar St.

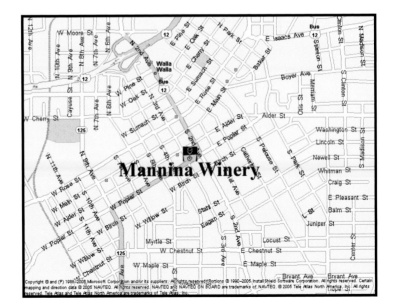

Forgeron Cellars

If you are a fan of chardonnay, you've arrived at the right place. Early on, winemaker and co-owner Marie-Eve Gilla insisted that Forgeron Cellars make chardonnay. At the time, this decision was somewhat controversial; after all, Walla Walla is home to big, intense reds. Fortunately for the other 50-plus investors, she got her way. Today, if you ask the locals where to find

great chardonnay, they would steer you to Forgeron. With chardonnay production at 5,000 cases a year, those same owners are celebrating Marie-Eve's success.

Forgeron's chardonnay uses grapes from the Columbia Valley. These grapes are 100 percent chardonnay and aged in Burgundian oak. Forgeron chardonnay sells for a little more than $20 a bottle, and is great by itself or paired with (our favorite) seared ahi and jasmine rice. By the way, you won't lose out if you enjoy the reds. Forgeron Cellars also creates luscious, full-bodied Bordeaux wines.

Forgeron's winery/tasting room was once the site of a blacksmith's workshop, hence its name, which is French for "blacksmith." The word "forgeron" also has a slightly different meaning in French, referring to artisans who build with their hands, combining experience with an extensive knowledge of their trade. This is the vision that Marie-Eve brings to the winery and participating vineyards each day. **WineTrail Note:** Marie-Eve is married to one of the distinguished vintners of Long Shadows Vintners, Gilles Nicault.

Red and black flags adorn the winery entrance and serve as a landmark for WineTrail seekers. As you step into Forgeron's tasting room, you will most likely find yourself in the presence of a dog; the lab's name is Salsa. A Mexican crew working in one of the vineyards discovered the lost dog and fed her tortilla chips. When Marie-Eve came to the dog's rescue and offered her a home, she named her Salsa.

Rumor has it that horseshoes were discovered during the renovation of the former blacksmith site. As you are swirling, sipping, and kibitzing with the friendly staff, you might just ask to see one of the horseshoes. Some of the good luck it's brought Forgeron is bound to rub off.

Marie-Eve Gilla

FORGERON CELLARS
opened: 2001
winemaker(s): Marie-Eve Gilla
location: 33 West Birch Street
Walla Walla, WA 99362-3004
phone: 509-522-9463
web: www.forgeroncellars.com
e-mail: info@forgeroncellars.com
picnic area: No
gift shop: Yes
fee: Complimentary wine tasting
hours: Daily 11–4 excluding major holidays

DIRECTIONS: **From US-12** take S. 2nd Ave. exit and go about .5 miles. Turn right onto W. Birch St. and arrive at 33 W. Birch St. on the corner—look for Forgeron's red and black flags marking the entrance.

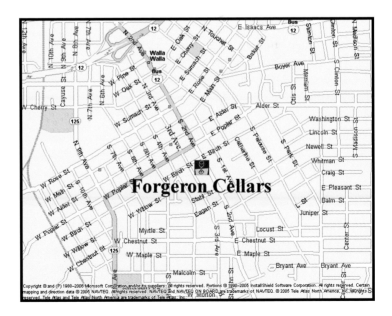

Whitman Cellars

In 1990, Sally and John Thomason delivered two trucks to Gary Figgins at Leonetti Cellars. That experience introduced them to the winemaking world and ignited their love affair with wine. The eventual result was the creation

of Whitman Cellars with business partner John Edwards.

Located on the outskirts of town very close to Amavi Cellars and Canoe Ridge Winery, Whitman Cellars is a boutique winery (about 7,500 cases annually) that has gained a loyal following and a long list of awards. As Sally Thomason explains it, "We're the Olympics of wineries—we medal well." The long list of golds, silvers, and bronzes is the signature of winemaker and partner Steve Lessard, who brings to the mix a rich background in food science and a résumé that includes a period at California's Stag's Leap Wine Cellar as an enologist (wine chemist).

A few minutes with Steve informs you how serious he is about winemaking and the real secret to making great wine is paying attention to the details. As he states on the Whitman Cellars website, "The most important word used in describing my wines is balance. A wine reflects balance in a similar way to a vineyard or I should say—its fruit reflects its *terroir*. It's an all encompassing word in which the character of the varietal, the vineyard terroir, the structure of the wine, the chemistry of the wine and the oak integration all harmonize together to produce a wine of seamless depth and interest."

In the tasting room, you will experience traditional Bordeaux and Rhone-style wines. Be prepared to taste the "balance" of Whitman Cellars' viognier, syrah, cabernet sauvignon, merlot, a proprietary blend called "Narcissa," and a port-style wine. And you will likely discover that there is a balance struck in the tasting room itself. Yes, the Thomasons are serious about their wines, but they are equally concerned that your experience at Whitman Cellars is joyful. The tasting room finds that balance with a relaxed, friendly atmosphere suitable for even the neophyte wine drinker.

Sally Thomason

WHITMAN CELLARS
opened: 1998
winemaker(s): Steve Lessard
location: 1015 West Pine Street
Walla Walla, WA 99362
phone: 509-529-1142
web: www.whitmancellars.com
e-mail: info@whitmancellars.com
picnic area: No
gift shop: Yes
fee: $5 applied to purchase of wine
hours: Daily 11–5

DIRECTIONS: **Heading east on State Hwy 12**, take the W. Pine St. exit. Follow to 13th Ave., and you will find us on the right hand side. Coming in to Walla Walla from State Hwy 125, follow to 9th Ave., turn left on Rose St. Take a right on 13th Ave. and you will find Whitman Cellars about .25 miles down on the right-hand side at the stop sign.

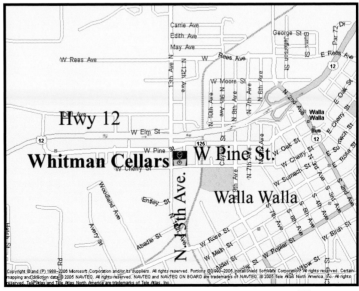

451

Canoe Ridge Vineyard

Merlot is such an elegant wine, great by itself or paired with food. Rich and velvety, with flavors of chocolate, cherry, and raspberry—what's not to like? Merlot loves to grow in Eastern Washington, particularly in the Horse Heaven Hills American Viticultural Area, which also happens to be the home of Canoe Ridge Vineyard. **WineTrail Note:** Canoe Ridge was named by explorers Lewis and Clark on their historic journey, which brought them through Eastern Washington. From the Columbia River, the massive ridge looks like an upside-down canoe. Here the proximity to the weather-moderating Columbia River,

hot summers, cool nights, and dry conditions all conspire to create the perfect growing conditions for merlot and cabernet sauvignon.

A visit to the Canoe Ridge winery near downtown Walla Walla (close to Amavi and Whitman Cellars—hey, three for one!) is a study in merlot. Yes, you can find Canoe Ridge Vineyard wines in grocery stores and wine shops, but at the winery you can sample merlot from different years and different qualities as deemed by their winemaker, Christophe Paubert. Although owned by the giant Diageo Corporation (perhaps you've heard of Tanqueray, Smirnoff, J&B, Guinness, and Sagelands, to name a few Diageo properties), Christophe has the independence he needs to craft premium wines. To this end we understand the common refrain from all winemakers: It all starts in the vineyard. What better source than the Canoe Ridge Vineyard itself for top-notch merlot?

Canoe Ridge Vineyard is also perfect for the heat-loving varietal cabernet sauvignon. While the winery focuses on red wines, it does make a limited quantity of white wines. Chardonnay was the winery's first white varietal, and it is produced in a style that allows the varietal to show through. The influence of oak barrels and malolactic fermentation is applied very judiciously. Canoe Ridge's gewürztraminer was produced in 1996.

Canoe Ridge's winemaking philosophy begins in the vineyard, where the level and quality of ripeness become the foundation of every new vintage. Each winemaking effort aims at honoring the uniqueness of the Canoe Ridge vineyard site, reflecting its individuality through the depth, nuance, concentration, and balance of Canoe Ridge wines.

Canoe Ridge—Good Friends, Good Wine, Good Times

CANOE RIDGE VINEYARD
opened: 1989
winemaker(s): Christophe Paubert
location: 1102 West Cherry Street
Walla Walla, WA 99362
phone: 509-527-0885
web: www.canoeridgevineyard.com
e-mail: CRVinfo@canoeridgevineyard.com
picnic area: No
gift shop: Yes
fee: Small tasting fee
hours: Daily 11–5 from May through September; daily 11–4 from October through April; closed major holidays and December 24 through January 1

DIRECTIONS: **Heading east US-12**, take the W. Pine St. exit. Follow to 13th Ave., take a right and you will find Canoe Ridge Winery 1 block down on the right-hand side.
From downtown Walla Walla, go west on W. Pine St. for about .5 miles. Turn left (south) onto SR-125 [N. 9th Ave.] followed by a quick right (west) onto W. Cherry St. and continue .3 miles to 1102 W. Cherry St. and arrive at winery.

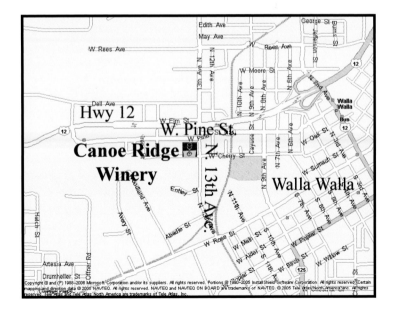

453

Amavi Cellars

At Amavi Cellars, Latin meets log cabin. A sister winery to the prestigious Pepper Bridge Winery, Amavi Cellars has adopted as its slogan "*Amor, vita, vinum,*" which in English means "Love, life, and wine." And that is the winery's goal: to capture the best of love and life in every bottle of wine. Though its slogan is Latin, the winery's architecture is decidedly American rustic. A log cabin, originally built in the 1890s in Montana, has been reconstructed and

now houses the tasting room for Amavi. Take a moment to scrutinize the old newspapers left on the cabin wall. Originally used to insulate the building, they now lend a sense of history to the place. One paper is a Chicago publication dating back to 1890.

Amavi (rhymes with "momma me") shares a winemaker with Pepper Bridge Winery: Jean-François Pellet. Amavi also relies on grapes from the 600 Pepper Bridge Vineyard as well as Seven Hills and Les Collines. However, Amavi's grapes are grown in different blocks of the vineyard, and Jean-François uses a different winemaking style to produce Amavi Cellars wines. As you might expect, Amavi Cellars specializes in red wines, including syrah and cabernet sauvignon. It also produces a rosé that this WineTrail enthusiast purchased to accompany roasted lamb and rosemary potatoes. The winery also features an award-winning semillon, which, when sampled, dances lively on the taste buds.

Located just south of downtown Walla Walla, within a stone's throw of Canoe Ridge Cellars and Whitman Cellars, Amavi Cellars is a fun stop along the Walla Walla WineTrail. Go for the *amor*, the *vita*, and the *vinum*, but don't be surprised if your spouse elbows you and says, "*Re vera, potas bene!*" ("Say, you sure are drinking a lot!")

"*In vino veritas*": In wine, there is truth.

Inside the tasting room

AMAVI CELLARS
opened: 2001
winemaker(s): Jean-François Pellet
location: 635 North 13th Avenue
Walla Walla, WA 99362-1769
phone: 509-525-3541
web: www.amavicellars.com
e-mail: info@amavicellars.com
picnic area: No
gift shop: No
fee: Complimentary wine tasting
hours: 11–5 Tuesday through Sunday from March through December; 11–4:30 from December through March, or by appointment

DIRECTIONS: **From downtown Walla Walla** go west on W. Pine St. about .5 miles. Turn left (south) onto N. 13th Ave. Arrive at 635 N. 13th Ave.—Amavi Cellars tasting room is on the right. **Coming in to Walla Walla from State Hwy 125,** follow to 9th Ave., turn left on Rose St. Take a right on 13th Ave. and find Amavi Cellars about .25 miles down on the left hand side.

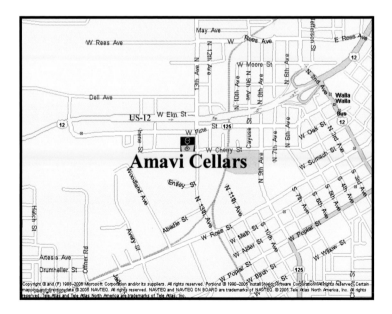

Foundry Vineyards

"Wine to me is passion. It's family and friends. It's warmth of heart and generosity of spirit. Wine is art. It's culture. It's the essence of civilization and the art of living." Robert Mondavi, *Harvests of Joy* autobiography.

Foundry Vineyards' motto is "Art takes many forms," and in the case of Foundry Vineyards, its art takes liquid form. However, Foundry Vineyards promotes

Foundry grounds

other art forms as well, in particular, über sculpture and Guggenheim-worthy paintings. It's not often that you can pick up a case of cabernet sauvignon and a Deborah Butterfield cast bronze horse or a Jim Dine painting. Just remember to bring your Visa, the one that accrues frequent-flyer miles with your purchase.

As far as Foundry Vineyards' own artistic techniques, winemaker Mark Anderson uses grapes from the Walla Walla Valley to produce just one cabernet sauvignon–merlot blend per year. Limiting annual production to 500 cases, Mark has gained a reputation for creating tannin-tamed, well-balanced wines that are great with food or without.

In keeping with its artistic focus, Foundry Vineyards selects paintings to adorn its wine labels. Essentially, it's a two-for-one purchase: a museum-quality label and great wine.

The new Foundry tasting room is located about 2 miles west of downtown Walla Walla. You'll need a car, but for those who like to mix their wine tasting with fine art, the venture is very rewarding. After all, how many times do you visit a winery where the person pouring the wine is both the tasting room manager and the curator of the museum?

WineTrail Note: the Foundry art complex is relatively close to the tasting room off Woodland Avenue. Here you can walk the grounds, visit with resident artists, and discover amazing sculpture.

Tasting room staff at Foundry Vineyards

FOUNDRY VINEYARDS
opened: 2006
winemaker(s): Mark Anderson
location: 13th & Abadie Street
Walla Walla, WA 99362
phone: 509-529-0736
web: www.foundryvineyards.com
e-mail: info@foundryvineyards.com
picnic area: Yes
gift shop: No
fee: Complimentary wine tasting
hours: 11–5 from Tuesday through Saturday

DIRECTIONS: **From downtown Walla Walla** go west on W. Rose Avenue to 13th Avenue. At 13th Avenue go right approximately 4 blocks to 13th and Abadie. Foundry Vineyard's tasting room is at the corner of 13th and Abadie.

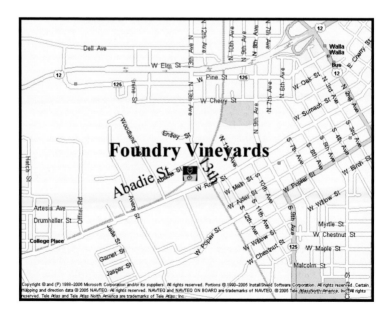

Bergevin Lane Vineyards

If you spend any time in Walla Walla and dine at some of the city's finer restaurants, you may notice that one establishment serves a Bergevin Lane viognier. Another offers a Bergevin "Calico Red". A trip to a nice bottle shop in town reveals a row of Bergevin wines, which includes the winery's top-selling cabernet franc and its reserve-blend "Intuition." You might find yourself in the

downtown Starbucks and overhear someone mention that they had Bergevin Lane's semillon last night with their fresh halibut. By day three, you begin to detect a pattern and you ask, "'Where the hell is this Bergevin Lane Vineyards?"

Bergevin Lane is a key stop on the downtown Walla Walla WineTrail, but you won't arrive by foot. To get to 1215 West Poplar, you will need to get into

the car and drive. As you pull up, you'll see that, unlike the many other tasting rooms found in downtown Walla Walla, Bergevin Lane's tasting room shares a space with the winery's production facility. The facility comes fully equipped with a spacious winemaking/testing area and barrel storage area. Co-owner Gary Bergevin has learned from his experience with other wineries, including Canoe Ridge Vineyards, that size *does* matter. So there's no need to play real-world Tetris with the barrels here.

Bergevin Lane's story is one of a collaborative effort between two women to produce world-class wines. Gary's daughter, Annette Bergevin, and her partner, Amber Lane, have formed a hugely successful team to manage the sales and marketing, as well as the day-to-day operations, of Bergevin Lane. Their passion for sharing great wine with others comes through in Bergevin's inviting tasting room, the packaging of its wines, its wine club (which clearly wins in the best name category: Club Swirl), and the partners' vision for the future. They must be doing something right. The Emperor of Wine himself, Robert M. Parker, Jr., had this to say about Bergevin Lane's cabernet sauvignon, "Edge-free, fruit-driven decadence." Five simple words, but certainly just the right verbiage to convince WineTrail enthusiasts to stop in and swirl.

BERGEVIN LANE VINEYARDS
opened: 2001
winemaker(s): Gordy Hill (winemaker consultant)
location: 1215 West Poplar Street
Walla Walla, WA 99362-2780
phone: 509-526-4300
web: www.bergevinlane.com
e-mail: info@bergevinlane.com
picnic area: No
gift shop: Yes
fee: $5 tasting fee refundable with purchase
hours: 11–4 Monday through Saturday, or
by appointment

Amber Lane

DIRECTIONS: **From downtown Walla Walla** head west on W. Poplar St. and continue about 1 mile. Arrive at 1215 W. Poplar St.—the winery and tasting room is on the left.

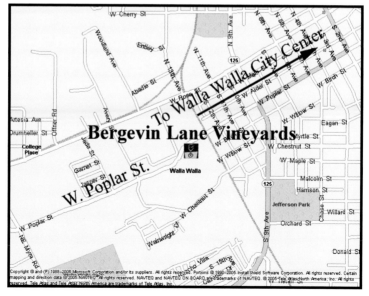

Lowden Hills Winery

Lowden Hills Winery is a labor of love from the husband-and-wife team of Jim and Sonja Henderson. A visit to the winery/tasting room finds soft-spoken Jim managing the tasting room in between the many chores associated with making wine. Jim's well-developed upper body is testimony to the physical labor associated with moving barrels and tending an 18-acre vineyard. He's a very patient man as well. If a visitor states up front that they don't like red wines, for example, Jim won't try to talk them into sampling his reds. Rather, it's typically

the visitor's spouse or friend who convinces the obstinate visitor to try the wine. It's usually then that the visitor becomes a convert to the red.

The winery and tasting room is located three blocks west of the Blue Mountain Mall on Spitzenburg Road. The site is actually a renovated red barn and stands out amongst the surrounding 1950s-style houses. The original barn, built in 1938 by Emilio Gugliemelli, Sr., stored vegetables and other crops. As Jim notes, "What once housed workhorses and livestock is now the main-floor barrel room." The foundation footprint is rather small but a cellar door leads down a steep set of stairs to the barrel room below. It's in these tight quarters that Jim plays Tetris with the barrels, racking and topping off the barrels as needed.

To understand Lowden Hills Winery is to appreciate family history. The Hendersons' vineyard, Win Chester Vineyard, is just outside the small town of Lowden on Woodward Canyon Road. On these 18 acres, they grow merlot, cabernet sauvignon, syrah, and viognier. The vineyard's name honors Sonja's mother, Susanne Estes, and her mother's late husband, Win Chester Estes. Win was a well-respected wheat farmer with a true pioneering spirit, whose family homesteaded in the Clyde area of Walla Walla County in the 1860s. A picture of Win Chester Estes is on the wall at the winery.

Honoring the past with great wines of today is the driving force behind Jim and Sonja's labor of love.

LOWDEN HILLS WINERY
opened: 2002
winemaker(s): Jim Henderson
location: 535 NE Spitzenburg Road
College Place, WA 99324-0000
phone: 509-527-1040
web: www.lowdenhillswinery.com
e-mail: info@lowdenhillswinery.com
picnic area: Yes
gift shop: No
fee: Complimentary wine tasting
hours: 11–4:30 Saturdays from mid-February to mid-December; Friday and Sunday from March through October by appointment only; closed mid-December through mid-February

Jim Henderson

DIRECTIONS: From downtown Walla Walla take W. Rose St. (west) and travel about 2 miles. Turn left onto Damson St. Go 1 block and turn left onto Spitzenburg. Lowden Hills Winery is located on the left side in the red barn.

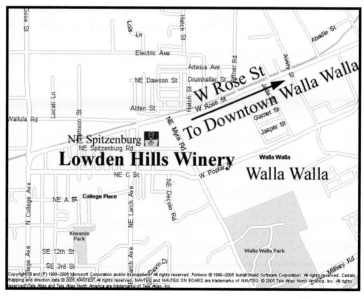

461

Walla Walla Airport
WineTrail

During World War II, the regional airport location near Walla Walla housed over 10,000 military personnel. After the war, most of these properties sat idle, and the Port of Walla Walla had a major problem deciding what to do with all the properties left behind, including barracks, mess halls and fire stations. Answer: provide a low cost solution for start-up businesses to rent space. Today over a dozen wineries are located at the Walla Walla regional airport complex, and more are on the way. You can easily spend a weekend trekking Walla Walla Airport WineTrail, and unless you bring a bike or a good pair of hiking boots, plan to use your car to get from one tasting room to another.

Walla Walla Airport WineTrail

1 Cougar Crest	6 Stephenson Cellars	11 Tamarack Cellars
2 Patrick M. Paul Vineyards	7 Trio Vintners	12 Bradenview Cellars
3 JLC Winery	8 Adamant Cellars	13 Buty Winery
4 Dunham Cellars	9 Five Star Cellars	14 SYZYGY
5 El Mirador Winery	10 Colvin Vineyards	15 Russell Creek Winery

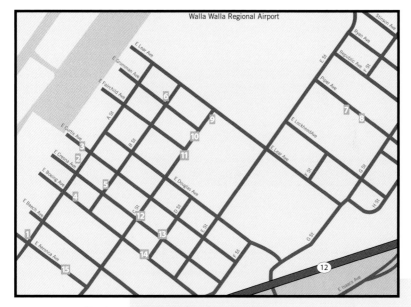

Region:	**Walla Walla Wine Country**
# of tasting rooms on tour:	**15**
Estimated # of days for tour:	**2 or 3**
Getting around:	**Car and foot**
Key events:	❑ **Events sponsored by Walla Walla Valley Wine Alliance: Spring Release Weekend (first full weekend of May); Balloon Stampede Weekend (second full weekend of May); Vintage Walla Walla (first full weekend of June); Entwine: An Auction to Support Walla Walla Arts, Wine, and Education (mid-October); and Holiday Barrel Tasting (first full weekend of December). See www.wallawallawine.com/events for details and ticketing.**
Tips:	❑ **Purchase one or two inexpensive Styrofoam chests to store your wine purchases. In the summer, interior car temperatures easily get over 100°F.** ❑ **Consider using a limousine service (e.g., Black Tie Limo 509-525-8585, Blue Stocking Tours 509-522-4717, Sunset Coach Tours 509-303-0355, or Four Star Limousine Service 509-521-7849 are some of the many services to contact).** ❑ **Looking for a gift? Check out Dunham Cellars gift shop.**

Cougar Crest

Walla Walla has many wineries, but very few of them can claim their wine production is 100 percent estate wine. Cougar Crest Winery, however, is "vertically integrated" from vineyard to bottle. In the mid-'90s, winemaker/owner Deborah Hansen, together with her husband, viticulturist David Hansen, uprooted some of their apple orchard in the Walla Walla Valley and planted

Cougar Crest tasting room

viniferous grapes. In 2001, with 50 acres of grapes and many wineries lining up to purchase their fruit, the Hansens decided to launch their own winery. This was a natural extension of their hard-science backgrounds from Washington State University: Deborah studied pharmaceutical science, and David focused on veterinary medicine. During an 18-year stint in the Bay Area, the Hansens developed a love of wine, and what grew from that love was Cougar Crest Winery. Of course, both being graduates of WSU, it was only natural that the winery be called Cougar Crest.

You'll find the Cougar Crest winery/tasting room next to the Walla Walla Regional Airport on A Street. The tasting room is small but quaint and a pleasure to visit, thanks to gregarious tasting room manager Boone Allan. Be prepared to experience intensely flavored and well-balanced red wines: merlot, cabernet sauvignon, syrah, a Bordeaux-blend cuvée, and cabernet franc (assuming these wines aren't sold out). However, don't ignore Deborah's viognier. Packed with citrus and floral flavors and possessing a long finish, this viognier will have you dreaming how perfectly it would complement Northwest seafood.

Cougar Crest wines are 100 percent estate—and 100 percent delicious. Even diehard Huskies will need to brake for this Cougar.

COUGAR CREST
opened: 2001
winemaker(s): Deborah Hansen
location: 202 A Street
Walla Walla, WA 99362-8497
phone: 509-529-5980
web: www.cougarcrestwinery.com
e-mail: info@cougarcrestwinery.com
picnic area: Yes
gift shop: No
fee: $5 refundable upon purchase
hours: 11–4 Thursday through Saturday

DIRECTIONS: Cougar Crest Winery is located at the Walla Walla Regional Airport Complex. **From Walla Walla,** take US-12 east about 3 miles. Take exit to Walla Walla Airport and go left (north) onto Airport Rd. Airport Rd becomes A St. Arrive at 202 A St.— Cougar Crest Winery is on the right.

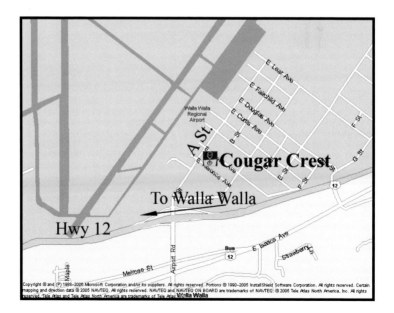

465

Patrick M. Paul Vineyards

WineTrail fans know that when they find a good cabernet franc to pounce on it. Although many wineries often use cabernet franc for blending, few wineries have risen to the top for stand-alone cabernet franc. Patrick M. Paul Vineyards, however, is Exhibit A.

In the early 1980s, Mike Paul planted 3 acres of cabernet franc, intended for Leonetti Cellar. However, four years and considerable experimentation later,

Mike decided to launch his own winery, and in 1988 Patrick M. Paul Vineyards was born. Although he produces small lots of cabernet sauvignon and merlot, Mike has gained a reputation for his cabernet franc, and a visit to the winery's attractive tasting room reveals why. Here's what *Wine Press Northwest* magazine had to say, "A pioneer in cabernet franc is Mike Paul, owner and winemaker of Patrick M. Paul Vineyards. He planted his first vines in the early 1980s and has produced stellar versions for nearly two decades."

Chances are that Mike will be pouring when you visit, and it won't take long for you to realize that Mike has a wealth of knowledge about the wine industry in general and Walla Walla Valley in particular. Mike still has a fire in his belly about wine, and he brings it with him every day as winemaker and owner of Patrick M. Paul Vineyards. Mike talks about the experience of drinking wine, with friends, with food, and at events. He would never trade the experience of uncorking a bottle of wine, hearing the pop of the cork, and delighting in the swirling and smelling. You won't see any "bag in the box" wines coming out of Patrick M. Paul.

PATRICK M. PAUL VINEYARDS
opened: 1988
winemaker(s): Mike Paul
location: 124 W. Boeing Ave. #3
Walla Walla, WA 99362
phone: 509-526-0676
web: www.wallawallawine.com/wineries/winerydtl1.
cfm?ID=30
e-mail: paulte@wwics.com
picnic area: No
gift shop: No
fee: Complimentary wine tasting
hours: 11–4 Friday through Monday

Mike Paul

DIRECTIONS: Patrick M. Paul Vineyards is located at the Walla Walla Regional Airport Complex. **From Walla Walla**, take US-12 east about 3 miles. Take exit to Walla Walla Airport and go left (north) onto Airport Rd. Airport Rd becomes A St. Proceed about .2 miles and arrive at 124 W. Boeing Ave. The tasting room is on your left.

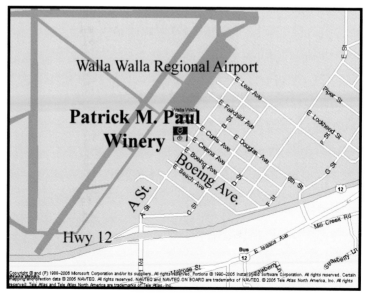

467

JLC Winery

Formerly James Leigh Cellars, the resurrected JLC Winery stands for Just Lynne Chamberlain. Lynne, who returned home after a prolonged sojourn in Washington, D.C., is first and foremost a person who understands farming. Her

500-acre farm, located on the Oregon side of the Walla Walla American Viticultural Area, is home to the celebrated 40-acre Spofford Station Vineyard. The farm also produces other crops, such as mint and wheat. It's also the place where she grew up.

WineTrail Note: The word "station" refers to where trains would stop and load grain and other farm produce for transport.

There are a number of stations around the Walla Walla area, including Rulo Station, which explains the grain elevator label on the Rulo wine label.

The JLC tasting room, elegantly decorated with vintage armoire pieces, is located near the entrance to the Walla Walla Regional Airport. Here at the tasting room, you can sample JLC's premium red wines, including "Palette," Lynne's Walla Walla red table wine. The label on the "Palette" wine is an angel enjoying her "Angels' Share," and the original painting, created by a local artist, sold for $3,500 in a Portland benefit auction. As noted in the Angels Share Club member pamphlet, "In the days of old, before science grabbed attention, the winemaker left the cellar at evensong. His cellar rats continued to care for the precious elixirs as he rested. On returning, he noted that the juice in the barrel had been lowered. 'You have stolen my precious nectar!' The reply, 'No, master, a mere sip is promised the Angels.' What is now called evaporation was known as "Angels' Share."

JLC WINERY
opened: 2002
winemaker(s): Lynne Chamberlain
location: 124 W. Boeing Ave. #4
Walla Walla, WA 99362
phone: 509-529-1398
web: www.jlcwinery.com
e-mail: info@jlcwinery.com
picnic area: No
gift shop: Yes
fee: $5 tasting fee applied to purchase
hours: 12–4 Saturdays, or by appointment

Lynne Chamberlain

DIRECTIONS: JLC's tasting room is located at the Walla Walla Regional Airport Complex. **From Walla Walla,** take US-12 east about 3 miles. Take exit to Walla Walla Airport and go left (north) onto Airport Rd. Airport Rd becomes A St. Proceed about .2 miles and arrive at 124 W. Boeing Ave. The tasting room is on your left.

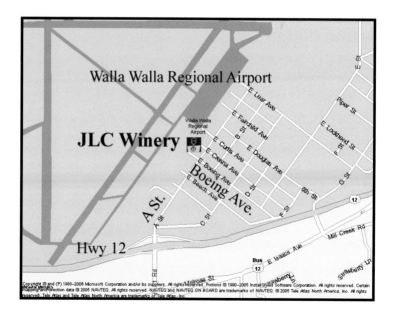

Dunham Cellars

The dog's name is Port. Found by winemaker Eric Dunham, the canine is usually lying on the tasting room floor greeting visitors with his inquisitive eyes. The tasting room itself is located at the Walla Walla Airport Complex and, with its warm Tuscan colors and engaging staff, is one of the favorite wine stops along the Walla Walla Airport WineTrail. Be sure to note the picture on the label of

the "Three Legged Red Table Wine" bottle—it's Port himself. You'll do a double take from bottle label to Port, who, in all likelihood, hasn't taken his eyes off you, as if willing you to come rub his belly.

Eric is often at the winery tending to the never-ending duties of winemaking, but he still manages to find time to visit with guests, whether they are novice wine drinkers or experienced connoisseurs. Eric is one of the friendliest winemakers in the valley. His roots are in Walla Walla, and in 1999, together with his parents, Mike and Joanne Dunham, he began the winery in the former World War II airplane hangar. Fortunately, they don't need to go far and wide in search of the best fruit; they own several vineyards that produce renowned grapes. Indeed, theirs must be excellent grapes, because they possess a laundry list of prestigious awards too numerous to list here. In addition to the "Three Legged Red," you have an opportunity to sample their renowned syrah, cabernet sauvignon, semillon, "Shirley Mays" chardonnay, a rosé wine as well as a Bordeaux-blend called "Trutina" (the Latin word for "balance"). By the way, the vivid artwork that graces the Lewis Vineyard syrah wine label is the artwork of Eric himself—the guy is multitalented. We don't doubt that he is a terrific cook, too.

As the saying goes, "The passion is in the bottle," and from harvest and bottling, Eric practices a minimalist approach. Through gentle crushing and pressing, and bottling without the use of filtration or fining, Dunham Cellars succeeds in coaxing the best flavors out of the juice. The Dunhams state on their website that "you are on your way to a wonderful wine experience." That's no exaggeration, but we encourage you to find out for yourself.

Eric Dunham

DUNHAM CELLARS
opened: 1999
winemaker(s): Eric Dunham
location: 150 East Boeing Avenue
Walla Walla, WA 99362-7400
phone: 509-529-4685
web: www.dunhamcellars.com
e-mail: wine@dunhamcellars.com
picnic area: Yes
gift shop: Yes
fee: $5 refundable upon purchase
hours: Daily 11–4

DIRECTIONS: Dunham Cellars is located at the Walla Walla Regional Airport Complex. **From Walla Walla**, take US-12 east about 3 miles. Take exit to Walla Walla Airport and go left (north) onto Airport Rd. Airport Rd becomes A St. Turn right onto E. Boeing Ave. and arrive at 150 E. Boeing Ave.—Dunham Cellars is on the right.

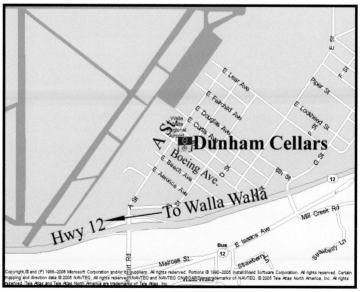

El Mirador Winery

A surprising little jewel of a winery is found at the Walla Walla Airport Complex. It's called El Mirador, and its focus is on handcrafted wines.

In the fall of 2003, El Mirador Winery owners Joe and Amy Donnow released their "Roja" red table wine and merlot. They've since added syrah and chardonnay to their line-up. Their focus is on quality, not quantity, and they rely on traditional methods that never cut corners. For example, their grapes are crushed in small lots and basket-pressed by hand to make certain the highest quality is achieved. The term "El Mirador" refers to "the lookout," but the name came from the house in which co-owner Amy Donnow's grandfather grew up in the Ojai Valley of California. Tradition is alive and well at the boutique winery El Mirador.

EL MIRADOR WINERY
opened: 2003
winemaker(s): Joseph Donnow
location: 425 B Street
Walla Walla, WA 99362-0000
phone: 509-526-0233
web: www.elmiradorwinery.com
e-mail: jdonnow@elmiradorwinery.com
picnic area: Yes
gift shop: No
fee: Complimentary wine tasting
hours: 11–4 Tuesday through Sunday from March
through December, or by appointment

DIRECTIONS: El Mirador is located at the Walla Walla Regional Airport Complex. **From Walla Walla**, take US-12 east about 3 miles. Take exit to Walla Walla Airport and go left (north) onto Airport Rd. Airport Rd becomes A St. Turn right onto E. Cessna Ave., then immediately turn left onto B St. Arrive 425 B St.—El Mirador is on the left.

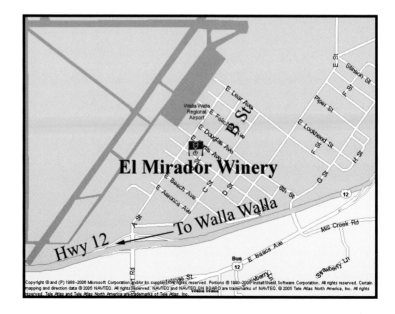

473

Stephenson Cellars

Stephenson Cellars is a relatively new winery located in the Walla Walla Airport Complex. It is a little off the beaten path and, with its diminutive size, easy to overlook. Moreover, with a production of 1,000 cases per year, it's a blip on the radar screen. Still, after Dave Stephenson achieved a double gold award at the 2005 Tri-Cities Wine Festival, WineTrail enthusiasts took note. Dan Radil, wine critic for *The Bellingham Herald*, nicknamed David Stephenson "Mr. Syrah" and referred to his 2003 syrah as "mind-boggling, with an incredible nose of violets and smoky undertones and lush flavors of blackberry."

A few years ago, while still in his early forties, Dave quit his lucrative stock market job, rolled the dice, and launched Stephenson Cellars on a shoestring. Passion overcame whatever trepidation he felt and with a goal to create "graceful wines" from Washington state fruit, Dave focuses on syrah, cabernet sauvignon, and merlot. Keep it simple, win an occasional double gold, and grow slowly… such was his formula for success.

Open only on Saturdays and Walla Walla Valley Wine Alliance event weekends, Stephenson Cellars is a quick but memorable stop along the Walla Walla Airport WineTrail. After a day of touring wineries, you might remember the architecture of the tasting room, the friendliness of the Labrador retriever, or the view from the outside deck. However, in the case of Stephenson Cellars, we suspect that you will remember the taste of Dave's wines. We believe that is exactly what he intended.

STEPHENSON CELLARS
opened: 2004
winemaker(s): Dave Stephenson
location: 755 B Street
Walla Walla, WA 99362
phone: 509-301-9004
web: www.stephensoncellars.com
e-mail: stephenson@bmi.net
picnic area: No
gift shop: No
fee: Complimentary wine tasting
hours: 11–4 Saturday, or by appointment

DIRECTIONS: Stephenson Cellars is located at the Walla Walla Regional Airport Complex. **From Walla Walla**, take US-12 east about 3 miles. Take exit to Walla Walla Airport and go left (north) onto Airport Rd. Airport Rd becomes A St. Turn right onto E. Grumman Ave. Arrive 755 B St.—Stephenson Cellars is on the left.

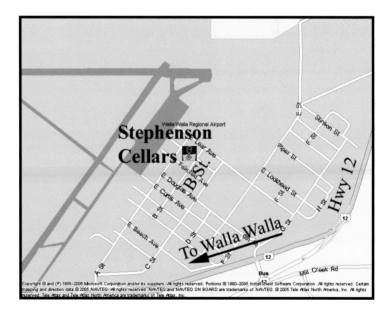

Trio Vintners

incubator *n.* — A company or facility designed to foster entrepreneurship and help startup companies, usually technology-related, to grow using shared resources and intellectual capital.

Rather than relating to technology, it seems only fitting that this definition of incubator be applied to winemaking in Walla Walla. Such is the case at the Walla Walla Regional Airport, where three incubator buildings emerged on Piper Road fostered by state grant money. Each 1,600-square-foot building provides adequate space specifically designed for producing 1,000 cases of wine annually.

Although the space is provided, the winemakers bring the equipment, the winemaking know-how, and a fair dose of entrepreneurial guts.

Enter Trio Vintners, a new winery owned by Denise Slattery, her husband, Steve Michener, and partner Tim Boushey, to take up residence at one end of a brick-colored building. In late 2006, the partners inked a six-year nonrenewable lease to fulfill their dream of creating great wine. All three are graduates of Walla Walla Community College's Institute for Enology & Viticulture.

Despite their short tenure (which included the myriad paperwork required by the federal government's Alcohol, Tax & Trade Bureau), they have released a riesling, a syrah, a sangiovese and a rosé made from mourvedre and sangiovese varieties. While each wine is remarkably pleasing, you can't help but notice the distinctive label showcasing the nearby Wallula Gap. As graduates of the Enology & Viticulture program, the winemaking trio knows that the narrow Wallula Gap between present day Oregon and Washington was the culprit of a massive flood that occurred thousands of years ago. Without that flood, the soil that wine grapes so love would not be there. No flood, no soil and hence no Trio Vintners. Little wonder that their use of the Wallula Gap image is not by accident. Given their knowledge and focused energy, we suspect that the incubation period will be less than 6 years.

TRIO VINTNERS
opened: 2007
winemaker(s): Tim Boushey, Denise Slattery, and
Steve Michener
location: 596 Piper Avenue
Walla Walla, WA 99362
phone: 509-529-8746
web: www.triovintners.com
e-mail: wine@triovintners.com
picnic area: Yes
gift shop: No
fee: Complimentary wine tasting
hours: 11–4:30 Saturday and Sunday, or
by appointment

DIRECTIONS: Trio Vintners is located at the Walla Walla Regional Airport Complex. **From Walla Walla**, take US-12 east about 3.5 miles. Take G St./Interchange Rd exit to Walla Walla Airport and go left (north) on G St. Proceed about .5 miles and turn left onto Piper Ave. Trio Vintners is found in the red brick colored "incubator" building on the left.

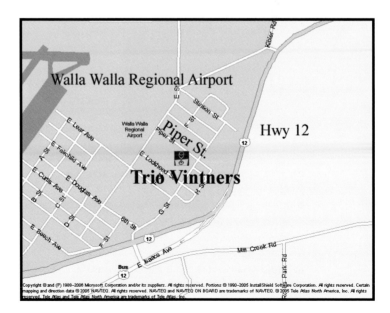

Adamant Cellars

You've spent more than a half-dozen years preparing, planning, investing, and dreaming. With a rush of adrenaline, you open your doors to the public and hope for the best. Like a young actor in your first major performance, you wait for the reviews to come. Such is the "scary-excited" feeling that Devin and Debra Stinger, owners of Adamant Cellars, must have had in early 2007 when they released their first wines, semillon and rosé. Maturing in French oak are reds that rely exclusively on Walla Walla Valley AVA fruit. Look for cabernet sauvignon, merlot, syrah, and Bordeaux blends in the future.

The couple began their winemaking adventure in 2000 in the basement of their Portland house, where they made their first wine. Adamant Cellars is the fulfillment of their dream to join the ranks of other well-known artisan wineries in Walla Walla. However, they do so in a crowded field of other start-ups, such as Trio Vintners, àMaurice Cellars, Skylite Cellars, Balboa Winery, Ensemble Cellars, Terulia Cellars, and Gifford Hirlinger. All of them are eager to establish their mark in the Walla Walla wine scene.

The Stingers embarked on their winemaking business venture in late 2006 when they began leasing space in a bright red, state-of-the-art "incubator" building at the Walla Walla Regional Airport and Industrial Park. They join another incubator winery, Trio Vintners, which set up shop at the other end of the brick-colored building. In this case, they provide the winemaking equipment (e.g., tanks, pumps, and barrels) and long hours to create wine in a 1,600-foot space specifically created for making wine. The six-year lease is not renewable. Translation: Sink or swim.

For wine-tasting trekkers, it's fun to revisit new wineries such as Adamant Cellars and discover how their wines have matured and, if luck has been with them, how a consistent track record has brought them those good reviews.

ADAMANT CELLARS
opened: 2006
winemaker(s): Devin Stinger
location: 600 Piper Avenue
Walla Walla, WA 99362
phone: 509-529-4161
web: www.adamantcellars.com
e-mail: devin@adamantcellars.com
picnic area: No
gift shop: No
fee: Complimentary wine tasting
hours: Open most days 11–5; call ahead to confirm

DIRECTIONS: Adamant Cellars is located at the Walla Walla Regional Airport Complex. **From Walla Walla**, take US-12 east about 3.5 miles. Take G St./Interchange Rd exit to Walla Walla Airport and go left (north) on G St. Proceed about .5 miles and turn left onto Piper Ave. Adamant Cellars is found in the red colored "incubator" building on the left.

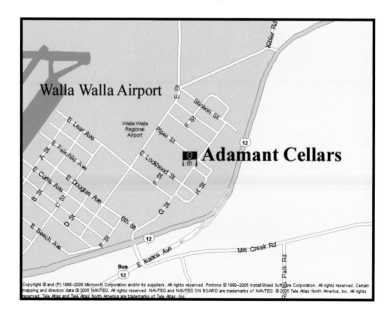

479

Five Star Cellars

"It is a wise father that knows his own child."—William Shakespeare, The Merchant of Venice

Along the WineTrails of Washington, you come across a number of retirees who traded in the tedium of retirement to create fine wines. Such is the story of David Huse. He didn't need to launch Five Star Cellars, but his passion won out. In 2000, following his career as a farm equipment provider and a few stints assisting at other wineries, David started Five Star Cellars. He hasn't looked back.

Of course, when you name a winery "Five Star," you'd better deliver wines worthy of that premier rating. To achieve this level of quality, David needed a helping hand. He didn't have far to look. In 2002, his son Matt signed on to assist with winemaking, and Matt's timing couldn't have been better: Production had doubled to more than 1,000 cases per year. He enrolled in the Enology and Viticulture Program at Walla Walla Community College and was a member of the first graduating class. Today, Matt is Five Star's chief winemaker. This has freed David to assume the duties of operations manager, marketing director, and chief bottle-washer.

Located at the Walla Walla Airport Complex near the Colvin and Tamarack wineries, Five Star Cellars offers an inviting space to sample its ultra premium wines: merlot, syrah, and cabernet sauvignon. Matt and David have made significant improvements on the leased space. It's "their nickel" so to speak—they didn't have to do it—but they chose to make the changes to improve the tasting experience. These improvements reflect their commitment to excellence. As part of this renovation, they've added a wood stove. Imagine visiting on a cold winter day with the stove blazing, keeping you toasty warm. By christening their winery "Five Star" the Huses have set the bar high, but it's proven worthy of the name.

David Huse and Matt Huse (l to r)

FIVE STAR CELLARS
opened: 2000
winemaker(s): Matt Huse
location: 840 C Street
Walla Walla, WA 99362-7423
phone: 509-527-8400
web: www.fivestarcellars.com
e-mail: info@fivestarcellars.com
picnic area: No
gift shop: Yes
fee: Complimentary wine tasting; tasting fee may apply during event weekends
hours: 10–4 Saturdays, or by appointment

DIRECTIONS: Five Star Cellars is located at the Walla Walla Regional Airport Complex. **From Walla Walla**, take US-12 east about 3 miles. Take exit to Walla Walla Airport and go left (north) onto Airport Way and go about 1 mile. Turn right onto Douglas Ave. and continue to C St. Turn right onto C St. and continue about .25 miles. Five Star Cellars is on the right at 840 C St.

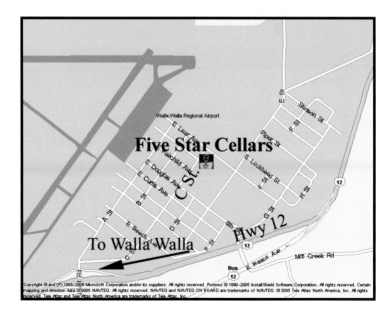

481

Colvin Vineyards

It's not often that we make a recommendation to visit a winery with the goal of seeing a rock. However, such is the case with Colvin Vineyards winery. If you have ever had the great fortune of uncorking a bottle of Colvin Vineyards wine, you might have wondered about the unusual picture on its wine label. Wonder no longer. The image is actually that of a rock that owners Mark and JoAnne Colvin's then-7-year-old daughter Katherine discovered in the vineyard in August 1998. The rock, which is the size of a softball, had a golf-ball-size section gouged out, revealing a "delicate yet powerful image." Mark immediately recognized the image as a perfect logo for the winery. Later, Katherine found the missing piece of rock, which bears the reverse image found on the original rock. Both pieces are at the Walla Walla Airport winery/tasting room location

and shown for the asking. However, be advised that if you do ask to see it, it will cost Mark Colvin a dollar. Mark promised Katherine that he would add $1 to her college fund each time he showed the rock to a tasting room visitor. He's going broke ... but it's for a good cause.

Mark and JoAnne are transplants from Steamboat, Colorado, where the lack of any wine industry spurred Mark to start scouting out a new locale. A visit to Walla Walla in the early '90s was all it took for Mark to convince JoAnne to make the move. A pharmacist by trade, Mark combines his scientific background with the art of creating ultrapremium wines. We don't toss around the term "ultrapremium" lightly; as you enter the tasting room, check out the prize ribbons that festoon an entire table of Colvin Vineyards wines.

Colvin was the first winery in Washington state to use a Bordeaux varietal called carmenère. The joy of being a WineTrail enthusiast is discovering an unusual varietal, a different taste, a new sensation. Mark succeeds in delighting many a wine lover with his carmenère, with production now at 2,000 cases per year.

If you have an itch to get away one Saturday afternoon, Colvin Vineyards Winery offers the perfect prescription.

COLVIN VINEYARDS
opened: 1999
winemaker(s): Mark Colvin
location: 720 C Street, Building 805
Walla Walla, WA 99362-0000
phone: 509-527-9463
web: www.ColvinVineyards.com
e-mail: mark@colvinvineyards.com or
colvinmj@bmi.net
picnic area: No
gift shop: Yes
fee: Small tasting fee
hours: 11–4 Fridays; 10–4 Saturdays; private
tastings may also be scheduled

Mark Colvin

DIRECTIONS: Colvin Vineyards Winery is located at the Walla Walla Regional Airport Complex. **From Walla Walla,** take US-12 east about 3 miles. Take exit to Walla Walla Airport and go left (north) onto Airport Rd. Turn right (east) onto C St. and go about .5 miles and arrive at 720 C St. Colvin Vineyards Winery is on the right.

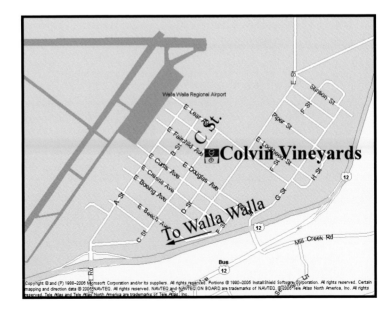

483

Tamarack Cellars

Ron Coleman has the nicest smile, and he's not fazed by visitors to this winery who turn up their noses at the thought of trying his chardonnay or wince when they sample his "Firehouse Red." He just smiles and conveys a "to each his or her own" attitude. Ironically, his *c'est la vie* approach wins over a lot of converts.

It's fairly obvious that Ron's career background includes other wine industry experience. He has worked as a wine sales representative and served as a sommelier. Tamarack Cellars is a convergence of his past experiences and his creative juices.

Established in 1998 by Ron and his wife, Jamie, the winery is located in a restored World War II fire station and barracks at the Walla Walla Airport Complex. Ron is dedicated to making handcrafted wines using varietals from select vineyards in the Walla Walla Valley, the Yakima Valley and Red Mountain. Current production is approximately 11,000 cases a year, give or take a few pallets. One of his most popular wines is the "Firehouse Red," with the number of varietals used corresponding to each vintage. For example, his 2006 "Firehouse Red" features a blend of six varietals; his 2007 will be a combination of seven varietals, and so on. Ron notes with a grin that he cannot wait for the 2009 release. In fact, Robert Parker's *Wine Advocate* praises the 2004 "Firehouse Red," calling it "highly expressive" and "bursting with flavor." If available for tasting, other got-to-try wines are sangiovese, merlot, syrah, cabernet franc, cabernet sauvignon, chardonnay, DuBrul Vineyard Reserve, and Seven Hills Vineyard Reserve. Ron's winemaking style is big and bold, yet very smooth and approachable—in a word, balanced.

A tamarack is a deciduous North American larch tree (*Larix laricina*) having short needles borne on spur shoots. Admittedly, this WineTrail enthusiast forgot to ask Ron why he named his winery Tamarack Cellars, but keeping a little mystery in life is not such a bad thing. Besides, this gives other WineTrail explorers something to discover.

TAMARACK CELLARS
opened: 1998
winemaker(s): Ron Coleman
location: 700 C Street
Walla Walla, WA 99362
phone: 509-526-3533
web: www.tamarackcellars.com
e-mail: ron@tamarackcellars.com
picnic area: No
gift shop: No
fee: Complimentary wine tasting
hours: 10–4 Saturdays from March through
December, weekend events, or by appointment;
closed January and February

Ron Coleman

DIRECTIONS: Tamarack Cellars is located at the Walla Walla Regional Airport Complex. **From Walla Walla**, take US-12 east about 3 miles. Take exit to Walla Walla Airport and go left (north) onto Airport Rd and go about .1 miles. Turn right onto C St. and continue for .7 miles. Tamarack Cellars is on the right at 700 C St.

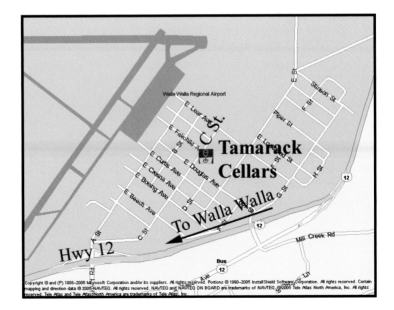

485

Bradenview Cellars

Let's face it, when it comes to Walla Walla, other areas of Washington harbor a certain amount of "vino envy." When you are the no. 1 destination for WineTrail enthusiasts, you are bound to catch a little flack from non-Walla

Wallans. You might hear, "Wineries in Walla Walla don't use their own fruit; they get most of it from us." In this case, the "us" is Yakima Valley. But in reality, there are many vineyards in Walla Walla that produce intense, outstanding varietals, especially merlot and cabernet sauvignon.

One such vineyard is BradenView Vineyards, owned by Ron and Lyla Reibel. The Reibels' 20-acre vineyard is located south of Walla Walla, where the soil, heat, and underground water all conspire to create a distinctive *terroir*. Of course, with an increasing demand for their grapes, it wasn't long before the Reibels went vertical—from bud to bottle—and Bradenview Cellars was born.

Located on Boeing Avenue in the Walla Walla Airport Complex (just down the street from SYZYGY), the winery/tasting room is housed in former military quarters. It's small but quaint, and in the summer time, it offers welcome respite from the hot sun. At Bradenview Cellars, you have an opportunity to sample some truly wonderful wine—assuming it hasn't sold out.

As the Reibels state on their website, "*Terroir*: Keystone to Quality." They could just as well have written, "Thank you very much, Yakima, we'll use our own grapes."

BRADENVIEW CELLARS
opened: 2002
winemaker(s): Ron Reibel
location: 305 East Boeing Avenue
Walla Walla, WA 99362
phone: 509-529-7264
web: www.bradenview.com
e-mail: grapes@bradenview.com
picnic area: No
gift shop: No
fee: Small tasting fee may apply
hours: 11–4 Saturdays, or by appointment

DIRECTIONS: Bradenview's tasting room is located at the Walla Walla Regional Airport Complex. **From Walla Walla**, take US-12 east about 3 miles. Take exit to Walla Walla Airport and go left (north) onto Airport Rd. Turn right (east) onto C St. and go about .5 miles and arrive at 305 E. Boeing Ave. BradenView's tasting room is on the left.

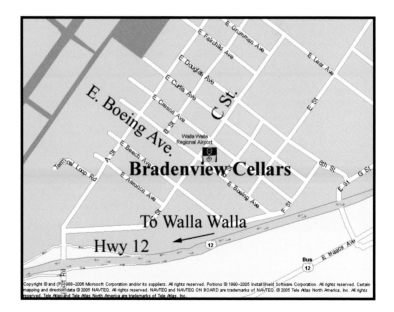

Buty Winery

Occasionally, WineTrails Northwest advises our fellow trekkers to call the winery before getting into the car. Take this advice before going to the Buty Winery, because its shelves may be empty. This boutique winery, located at the Walla Walla Airport Complex, has gained a loyal following, and the 3,000 cases it produces annually go quickly. In 2000, owners Caleb Foster and Nina Buty Foster opened the winery on a shoestring budget and, using borrowed equipment, managed to release their initial vintages. Despite a relatively high price tag ($40 for a bottle of their blended red wine), Buty's growing reputation has translated into quick sales. As my father would say, "There are good problems and bad problems ... that's a good problem."

Surrounding hills of Walla Walla

Buty (pronounced "beauty") Winery focuses on red blends, or cuvées, as well as a low-oaked chardonnay and a Bordeaux white blend of semillon/sauvignon blanc. For eight years, winemaker/owner Caleb Foster cut his teeth as an apprentice at Woodward Canyon Winery working for Rick Small, did a stint at Mount Baker Winery, and spent time overseas in New Zealand and South Africa, where he cultivated his predilection for blends. During this period, Caleb and Nina fine-tuned their own style of making wine. However, Caleb, aware that great wine all starts in the vineyard, now collaborates with well-known Washington grape growers who supply his fruit. When it comes to the grapes themselves, balanced yields and high ripeness are Caleb's goals.

Most of the buzz about Buty wines surrounds Caleb's cuvées, particularly his "Rediviva of the Stones" and his "Columbia Rediviva". Both are blends of cabernet sauvignon and syrah with the alcohol level checking in at less than 14 percent. Buty also makes a cabernet franc/merlot blend. As the Fosters state on their website, "Buty is all about family, creativity, being tied to the land, intriguing wines, and having a lot of fun." If you go to the winery, we suggest that you get your name on the Buty mailing list. You can be the first on your block to order next year's release of "Rediviva of the Stones"!

BUTY WINERY
opened: 2000
winemaker(s): Caleb Foster
location: 535 East Cessna Avenue
Walla Walla, WA 99362-7412
phone: 509-527-0901
web: www.butywinery.com
e-mail: info@butywinery.com
picnic area: No
gift shop: No
fee: Complimentary wine tasting
hours: Daily 11–4, but call ahead to confirm

DIRECTIONS: Buty is located at the Walla Walla Regional Airport. Eastbound on US-12, take the airport exit. Turn left from the off-ramp onto Airport Way, which turns into A St. Turn right onto Cessna Ave., and follow it nearly to its end. After crossing E St., Buty is on your left.

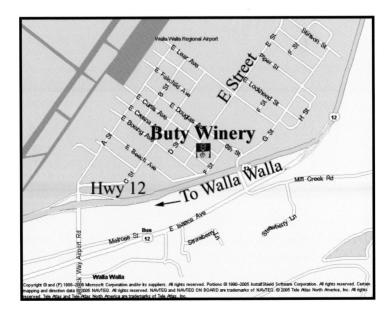

SYZYGY

OK, you're having a dream and you've been called upon to spell "syzygy" in a national spelling bee. Phew, you breathe a sigh of relief, because you are a big fan of SYZYGY! Moreover, as you spell out S-Y-Z-Y-G-Y, you recall that the word means the alignment of earth, moon and sun. Such was the inspiration of Zach Brettler and Kelsey Harmon when they launched SYZYGY in 2002—the

convergence of different Walla Walla and Columbia Valley vineyards and varietals to create the perfect blend of red wine.

With its distinctive orange-and-blue color scheme, the labeling of its wines clearly distinguishes SYZYGY from the pack. Even the orange T-shirts it sells along with the logo-adorned underwear will have you standing out from the pack (well, maybe not if you put your pants on). But more than the great packaging, it's the liquid art in the bottle that will leave the lasting impression. You can store this wine in the cellar for many years or pop the cork and enjoy it now. By itself or as a complement to that just-purchased Oregon natural beef, SYZYGY wine celebrates the moment.

Winemaker Zach Brettler gets his grapes from a list of who's who of Washington grape growers: Conner Lee, Minnick Hills, Sagemoor and Charbonneau, Six Prong, Sagemoor/Bacchus, Milbrandt, Wooded Isle, Morrison Lane, Les Collines, and Seven Hills. The label on the bottle could indicate that the wine is 100 percent syrah or 100 percent cabernet sauvignon, but the wine is actually a blend of the same grape varietal from different sources. The goal is syzygy—an optimal blend of vineyards to achieve just the right balance, taste, and finish. Zach brings this artistic aspect to his craft, and we get to enjoy.

The tasting room/winery is located toward the end of Boeing Avenue in a former military barracks. The original golden-colored hardwood floors are a distinctive complement to the orange walls. It gives the room an airy feel. It's a pleasurable space meant to be shared with friends, family, and lovers—that's SYZYGY.

Kelsey and Zach Brettler

SYZYGY
opened: 2002
winemaker(s): Zach Brettler
location: 405 East Boeing Avenue
Walla Walla, WA 99362
phone: 509-522-0484
web: www.syzygywines.com
e-mail: info@syzygywines.com
picnic area: Yes
gift shop: No
fee: Complimentary wine tasting
hours: 11–4 Saturdays from March through December,
or by appointment

DIRECTIONS: SYZYGY is located at the Walla Walla Regional Airport Complex. **From Walla Walla**, take US-12 east about 3 miles. Take exit to Walla Walla Airport and go left (north) onto Airport Rd. Airport Rd becomes A St. Turn right onto E. Boeing Ave. and arrive at 405 E. Boeing Ave.—SYZYGY is on the left.

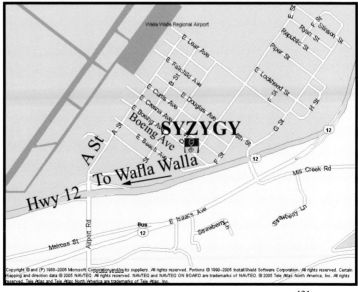

491

Russell Creek Winery

The story behind Russell Creek Winery is that of the winemaker and owner himself, Larry Krivoshein. His friends affectionately call him "Digger," a nod to his former career as a funeral director. In fact, when Larry first went public with his wines in 1998, his "Diggers" wine labels showed a map of the state of Washington with a shovel stuck in the ground near Walla Walla. In addition, the flags of the Soviet Union, Canada, and the United States adorned the label, reflecting Larry's kaleidoscopic background. In a nutshell, the man behind Russell Creek Winery is a retired funeral director originally from Saskatoon

who's blessed with a quirky sense of humor and a passion for making wine. For WineTrail lovers, what's not to love!

Fortunately, Larry put the Diggers name six feet under and adopted "Russell Creek Winery," named for the creek near his farm. Using old-world techniques (e.g., he still likes to hand-punch the grape cap at fermentation) and a healthy dose of new French oak, Larry focuses on making classic wine with a lasting finish. Russell Creek makes red wines using Columbia Valley and Walla Walla grapes: merlot, cabernet sauvignon, and sangiovese (his number-one seller).

Now in his seventies and going strong, Larry is often at his tasting room and winery, located at the Walla Walla Regional Airport and Industrial Complex. It's a labor of love for Larry; he doesn't need to be doing this. As he pours, Larry talks about his winemaking background and wonders aloud how the market can accommodate more than 100 wineries in the Walla Walla Valley. For visitors, however, it's a lot of fun to hang out amongst the wine barrels and sample his creations while studying the old "Diggers" wine bottles and other memorabilia.

A visit to Russell Creek Winery is an opportunity to taste great sangiovese, soak in Walla Walla winemaking history, and meet a living legend—Larry Krivoshein.

RUSSELL CREEK WINERY
opened: 1998
winemaker(s): Larry Krivoshein
location: 301 Aeronca Avenue
Walla Walla, WA 99362
phone: 509-386-4401
web: www.russellcreek-winery.com
e-mail: krivoslg@wwics.com
picnic area: No
gift shop: No
fee: $5 tasting fee refundable upon purchase
hours: Daily 11–4; special events 10–5

Larry Krivoshein

DIRECTIONS: Russell Creek Winery is located at the Walla Walla Regional Airport Complex. **From Walla Walla**, take US-12 east about 3 miles. Take exit to Walla Walla Airport and go left (north) onto Airport Rd. Airport Rd becomes A St. Turn right onto Aeronca Ave. and find Russell Creek on the left.

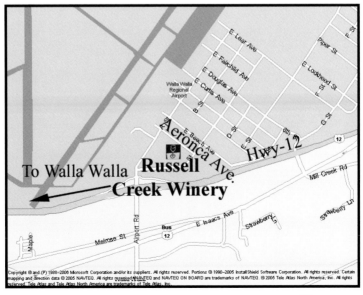

Walla Walla
WineTrail East

Abeja Winery and Inn outside Walla Walla

Although Walla Walla WineTrail East includes only five wineries—
College Cellars of Walla Walla, K Vintners, Walla Walla Vintners,
àMaurice, and Patit Creek Cellars—be sure you have enough room
in the car for a couple cases of wine. We suspect that you will need
it. Also, because Patit Creek Cellars' Dayton location is a half-hour
drive, call ahead to verify tasting room hours. If you don't have time
for a trip to Dayton, Patit Creek also has a downtown Walla Walla
tasting room.

Any time of the year is special in this city. However, in the summer,
the area east of Walla Walla with rolling hills of golden wheat and
lush green vineyards is picture perfect. **WineTrail Note:** It's a splurge, but
for a truly memorable experience, stay at The Inn at Abeja—easily a
top wine stay destination in Washington.

1 College Cellars of Walla
  Walla

2 K Vintners
3 Walla Walla Vintners

4 àMaurice Cellars
5 Patit Creek Cellars

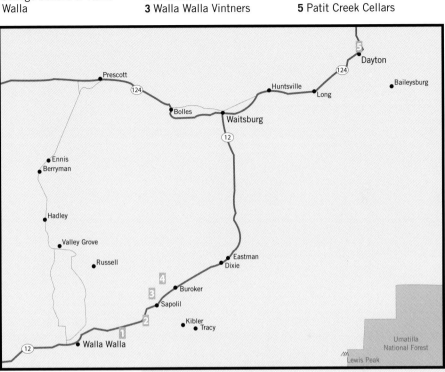

Region:	**Walla Walla Wine Country**
# of tasting rooms on tour:	**5**
Estimated # of days for tour:	**1**
Getting around:	**Car**
Key events:	❑ **Events sponsored by Walla Walla Valley Wine Alliance: Spring Release Weekend (first full weekend of May); Balloon Stampede Weekend (second full weekend of May); Vintage Walla Walla (first full weekend of June); Entwine: An Auction to Support Walla Walla Arts, Wine, and Education (mid-October); and Holiday Barrel Tasting (first full weekend of December). See www.wallawallawine.com/events for details and ticketing.**
Tips:	❑ **Restaurant suggestions: In Waitsburg—the Whoopemup Hollow Café; In Dayton—Weinhard Café or the Patit Creek Restaurant.** ❑ **Consider using a limousine service (e.g., Black Tie Limo 509-525-8585, Blue Stocking Tours 509-522-4717, Sunset Coach Tours 509-303-0355, or Four Star Limousine Service 509-521-7849 are some of the many services to contact).**

College Cellars of Walla Walla

"What do you hope to do with your degree?" I asked as my pourer offered me a sample of the cabernet sauvignon. She was a second-year student at the Institute for Enology and Viticulture in Walla Walla and with graduation on the horizon, she had some choices to make. With eyes on my glass, she smiled and said, "I

actually don't know. The great thing is I can go in a variety of directions. But I might want to try marketing wine first." She's right, I thought, she does have options. Suddenly, the lines from Dr. Seuss' *Oh, The Places You'll Go* popped into my head:

You have brains in your head
You have feet in your shoes
You can steer yourself in any direction
you choose

As you visit Walla Walla's wineries, make it a point to visit with the tasting room staff and discover their backgrounds. Chances are that many pourers you encounter are students at the Institute for Enology and Viticulture. In addition, many of the winemaking staff graduated from the program, including Matt Huse of Five Star Cellars and Tim Boushey, Denise Slattery, and Steve Michener of Trio Vintners. Farther east from the college is Walla Walla Vintners, created by Dr. Myles J. Anderson, current director of the Institute for Enology and Viticulture.

Open to the public only on Friday afternoons , College Cellars of Walla Walla is a teaching winery located at the Institute for Enology and Viticulture on the campus of Walla Walla Community College. There, you can experience the product of Walla Walla's budding winemakers and perhaps take home a few bottles (or cases) of their medium-priced wines. Proceeds from the sale of wine support the wine education program through the Walla Walla Community College Foundation.

Under the winemaking direction of the highly respected Stanley Clarke, College Cellars of Walla Walla offers students hands-on experience handcrafting wines, with most of the first year devoted to fieldwork in the vineyards. During the second year, students round out their education with additional exposure to the science associated with winemaking. And just as important is all the hands-on training students get from crushing, punching, racking, filtering, bottling, corking, labeling, and pouring for the many visitors on Fridays as well as event weekends.

Stanley Clarke

COLLEGE CELLARS OF WALLA WALLA
opened: 2003
winemaker(s): Stanley Clarke
location: 500 Tausick Way
Walla Walla, WA 99362-9270
phone: 509-524-5170
web: www.collegecellarsofwallawalla.com
e-mail: info@collegecellars.com
picnic area: No
gift shop: No
fee: Complimentary wine tasting
hours: Fridays 1–5

DIRECTIONS: **From downtown Walla Walla,** head east on E. Poplar St. Go about .3 miles. Bear right (east) onto Alder St. and proceed 1.8 miles. Road changes to Tausick Way. Arrive at College Cellars on your right at the corner of Tausick Way and Isaacs Ave.

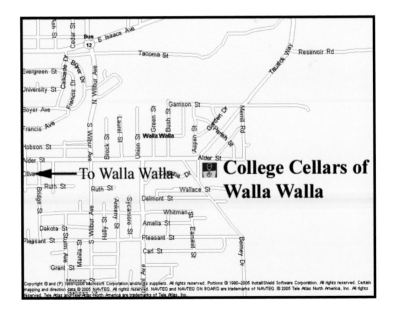

K Vintners

K Vintners' Charles Smith appreciates the philosophy that wine is a means to an end: The "end," in this case, is to enjoy life and have a glass of wine while you're at it. Life is short—too short to drink bad wine. Being a lover of good wine, wild man Charles Smith is on a quest to create exceptional syrah. Fortunately, the syrah grape finds Washington very hospitable. It thrives in places like Walla Walla and Wahluke Slope, where Charles acquires his fruit.

He has evidently succeeded in his quest. Check out some of these accolades:

"Top ten syrah in America."
– *Wine and Spirits*

"These wines offer fascinating layers of richness."
– *The San Francisco Chronicle*

"His syrahs are focused, pure and abounding with character."
– *WineStreet.com*

Enough said.

Originally from northern California, proprietor and winemaker Charles Smith managed rock 'n' roll bands in Scandinavia for 11 years before moving back to the US and launching K Vintners. He also is the creator and winemaker for a second label: The Magnificent Wine Company, whose bottle sports his boldly lettered label "House Wine." This bottle grabs your attention with its label and then keeps it with its great price.

The tasting room and winery are located a few miles east of Walla Walla on Mill Creek Road (close to Abeja). Unless your eyes are glued to the Blue Mountains ahead of you, you can't miss the giant K standing in front of the small vineyard and big old farmhouse with its massive tree next to it. Once there, be prepared to party. This isn't one of those genteel, library-quiet establishments; rather, you're here for some kick-ass wines (assuming Charles isn't sold out). Party on, dudes!

K VINTNERS
opened: 2001
winemaker(s): Charles Smith
location: 820 Mill Creek Road
Walla Walla, WA 99362-8415
phone: 509-526-5230
web: www.kvintners.com
e-mail: charles@kvintners.com
picnic area: Yes
gift shop: No
fee: Complimentary wine tasting
hours: 10–5 Saturdays from April through October,
or by appointment

Charles Smith

DIRECTIONS: **From downtown Walla Walla**, take US-12 east 4.3 miles and turn right onto Interchange Rd which becomes Mill Creek Rd. About .5 miles on the right is K Vintners—look for the large block white K sculpture. Alternatively, take E. Rose Ave. east about .5 miles. Bear to the right onto E. Isaacs Ave. and continue for about 4 miles. Bear right onto Mill Creek Rd and find K Vintners on the right at 820 Mill Creek Rd.

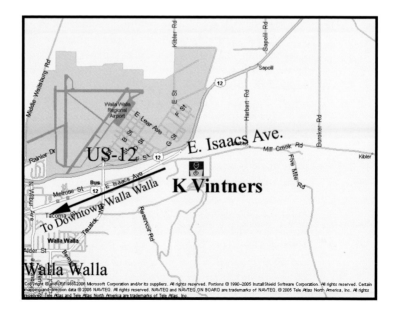

Walla Walla Vintners

Started by Myles Anderson and Gordon Venneri, Walla Walla Vintners was a "hobby business" that morphed into a very successful venture. Both men come from highly structured backgrounds. Myles helped found Walla Walla Community College's Enology and Viticulture program and serves as its director. Gordon is a retired accountant and a retired agent for Knights of Columbus Insurance. You would expect, with these backgrounds, that they

would operate from a detailed business plan, complete with financial projections that would delight a banker. Nope. Nada. Zilch.

Before launching Walla Walla Vintners in 1999 (and becoming the eighth bonded winery in Walla Walla Valley), Myles and Gordon experimented. The winery grew out of a labor of love to handcraft premium wine. It also grew out of much failure. Here's what they said on an earlier version of their website: "As winemakers we made home-crafted wines for over ten years before we considered making commercial wine. This was all done in our backyard using borrowed, makeshift equipment and for a while a small apple press. …We experimented with oak chips, used oak barrels, beer kegs, food-grade plastic buckets, plastic apple juice containers, Coca-Cola syrup stainless steel containers, and glass carboys. The yeast and chemicals came from a local drug store that specialized in stocking such items for beer and winemakers." That's passion.

Myles and Gordon have also gained a reputation for being exceptionally generous with their time, expertise, and winemaking equipment. They provide the training ground for the Enology and Viticulture program's interns, educate other would-be winemakers, and lend their production facility and equipment to start-ups such as nearby àMaurice Winery.

Located a few miles east of Walla Walla on Vineyard Lane, Walla Walla Vintners sits at the foothills of the Blue Mountains. Next door is àMaurice Cellars. Housed in a red barn (the same structure that graces the winery's wine labels), the tasting room offers an inviting space in which to sample wine and browse the interesting articles and memorabilia scattered about. Check out the clock on the wall made from a converted wine barrel—who thinks of these things?

Gordon Venneri

WALLA WALLA VINTNERS
opened: 1999
winemaker(s): Myles Anderson and Gordon Venneri
location: 225 Vineyard Lane
Walla Walla, WA 99362
phone: 509-525-4724
web: www.wallawallavintners.com
e-mail: gordy@wallawallavintners.com
or mjanders@bmi.net
picnic area: Yes
gift shop: No
fee: Complimentary wine tasting
hours: 10:30–4:30 Saturdays from March through
December; 1–4:30 in January and February, or
by appointment

DIRECTIONS: From downtown Walla Walla take US-12 about 3 miles to the Rooks Park exit. Cross Isaacs onto Mill Creek Rd. From Isaacs Ave. to the winery is 3.2 miles. Walla Walla Vintners is on the left in the distinctive red barn.

àMaurice Cellars

"Go Beavs!" àMaurice winemaker Ned Morris exclaims as we leave the winery. Ned had just discovered that a member of our party attended Oregon State University and his Beaver pride was quick to surface. Turns out a number of winemakers in the Walla Walla Valley got their winemaking education at Oregon State University, including John Abbott of Abeja Winery, where Ned Morris served as the assistant winemaker before accepting his new position at àMaurice Cellars.

Tom and Kathy Schafer may not be wearing OSU's orange and black, but they are the proprietors of àMaurice Cellars. With 13 acres of premium grapes planted next to their winery, their long-term goal is to produce their own fruit for àMaurice wines. At

the time of our visit in early spring, you could see row upon row of vines with plastic sleeves encircling each vine to keep the deer from feasting on the plants. Of note is the Schafers' strong belief in sustainable grape growing. They are charter members of Vinea, an alliance of Walla Walla wineries and vineyards that adhere to the strict guidelines of sustainable viticulture. Until their own vineyard matures, Ned and co-winemaker Anna Schafer rely on grapes from other Washington vineyards to create a rich and smooth Premier Red Blend as well as a crisp chardonnay and floral-accented viognier.

The notion of sustainable crops is nothing new to the Schafers, given their family's heritage. Tom's father, Maurice Schafer, developed a self-sustaining 20,000-acre evergreen tree farm. Because of his vision and kindness toward others, the Schafers paid homage to him with the naming of their winery—in French, àMaurice means "to Maurice."

Ned Morris

ÀMAURICE CELLARS
opened: 2006
winemaker(s): Ned Morris and Anna Schafer
location: 178 Vineyard Lane
Walla Walla, WA 99362
phone: 206-226-2624
web: www.amaurice.com
e-mail: anna@amaurice.com
picnic area: No
gift shop: No
fee: Complimentary wine tasting
hours: 10:30–4:30 Saturdays

DIRECTIONS: From downtown Walla Walla take US-12 about 3 miles to the Rooks Park exit. Cross Isaacs onto Mill Creek Rd. From Isaacs Ave. to the winery is 3.2 miles. Take a left onto Vineyard Lane and arrive at àMaurice on the right.

503

Patit Creek Cellars

The numbers can tell Patit Creek Cellars' story. Six partners (actually three couples) own Patit Creek Cellars: Larry and Marilou Cassidy, Connie and Lee Kearney, and Paul and Marcene Hendrickson. The partners launched Patit Creek Cellars in 1999, and the winery is located just 3 miles from where the famous explorers Meriwether Lewis and William Clark camped on May 2, 1805, on the journey of the Corps of Discovery. You can experience Patit Creek wine at two locations: the winery itself, located in charming Dayton, about 30 miles north of Walla Walla, and Patit Creek's spacious wine tasting room in downtown Walla Walla. The partners focus on just two wines, merlot and cabernet sauvignon.

They acquire their grapes from two Walla Walla Valley vineyards, Pepper Bridge and Seven Hills. Phew.

Wine drinkers definitely benefit from the fact that Patit Creek concentrates its winemaking talents on those quintessential wines of Washington, merlot and cabernet sauvignon. Winemaker Paul Hendrickson (another Walla Walla–area pharmacist by day, winemaker by night) and Swiss winemaking consultant Jean-François Pellet (of Pepper Bridge Vineyard fame) continue to receive high marks for their reds. Perhaps this is because of the labor-intensive practices they use, hand-sorting the already handpicked grapes and aging the wine in bottles for a full year before release. Or perhaps it is the top-notch grapes that they press. Whatever the reason, the result is sensational.

A distinctive wine also deserves an equally distinctive wrap. To that end, the partners have chosen Leslie Williams Cain's chalk-pastel drawing of Patit Creek to decorate the label. Two wines, six partners, two locations, and one great label. It all adds up to one memorable experience.

PATIT CREEK CELLARS
opened: 1999
winemaker(s): Paul Hendrickson
location: 507 East Main Street
Dayton, WA 99328
phone: 509-382-1357
web: www.patitcreekcellars.com
e-mail: info@patitcreekcellars.com
picnic area: No
gift shop: No
fee: Complimentary wine tasting
hours: 11–5 Saturdays, or by appointment

DIRECTIONS: **From Walla Walla** take US-12 east about 30 miles to Dayton. Arrive at 507 E. Main St.—Patit Creek Winery is on the left.

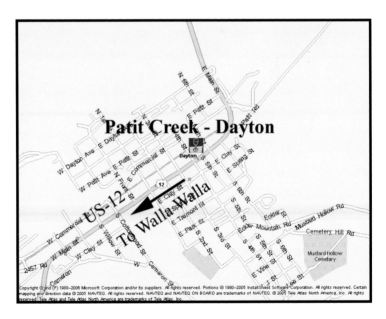

505

Walla Walla
WineTrail South

View to the south from Pepper Bridge Winery

Many would-be WineTrail enthusiasts bypass Walla Walla City Center and head south where excellent wineries abound. The Walla Walla WineTrail South can easily consume a weekend. Although, to maximize your visit, definitely check out the tasting room hours in advance.

For WineTrail trekkers who enjoy bicycling, the gentle hills of Walla Walla WineTrail South will get the heart pumping and work up an appetite. Whether you are in a car or on a bike, the views of the Blue Mountains in the distance and rows of cabernet sauvignon provide a terrific backdrop to sampling premier wines. Along the way, you will experience one of Washington's top wine country resorts, picturesque vineyards, fun people, and some intense reds.

1 Basel Cellars Estate Winery
2 Zerba Cellars
3 Saviah Cellars
4 Beresan Winery

5 Balboa Winery
6 Va Piano Vineyards
7 Pepper Bridge Winery
8 Northstar Winery

9 Gifford Hirlinger Winery
10 Glen Fiona Winery
11 Isenhower Cellars
12 Dusted Valley Vintners

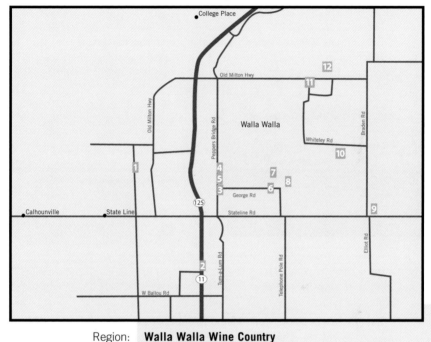

Region:	**Walla Walla Wine Country**
# of tasting rooms on tour:	**12**
Estimated # of days for tour:	**2**
Getting around:	**Car or bike**
Key events:	❏ **Events sponsored by Walla Walla Valley Wine Alliance: Spring Release Weekend (first full weekend of May); Balloon Stampede Weekend (second full weekend of May); Vintage Walla Walla (first full weekend of June); Entwine: An Auction to Support Walla Walla Arts, Wine, and Education (mid-October); and Holiday Barrel Tasting (first full weekend of December). See www.wallawallawine.com/events for details and ticketing.**
Tips:	❏ **Consider using a limousine service (e.g., Black Tie Limo 509 525-8585, Blue Stocking Tours 509-522-4717, Sunset Coach Tours 509-303-0355, or Four Star Limousine Service 509-521-7849 are some of the many services to contact.**

 Best: ❏ **Best Destination: Basel Cellars Estate Winery**
❏ **Best View: Basel Cellars Estate Winery**

507

Basel Cellars Estate Winery

One word: "Wow."

For both 2005 and 2006 "Best of Seattle" issues, *Seattle Magazine* voted Basel Cellars Estate Winery the Best Destination award. And for good reason. The winery, in its 87-acre setting on a bluff just south of town, offers more than

Pool at Basel Cellars

wine. It provides luxury accommodations, including spacious meeting rooms, a gourmet kitchen for private dinners, hot tubs, sauna, outdoor pool with poolside cabana, and much more. This is where well-heeled companies would hold corporate retreats or loving partners would take their wedding vows. The spacious 13,800-square-foot facility is a fusion of elegant artisanship and rustic timbers, and if the hand-carved entrance doors don't grab you, the views of the valley and the surrounding Blue Mountains surely will. Guests are welcome to walk through the nearby vineyards and experience the source of Basel Cellars premium wines.

Opened in 2002, Basel Cellars Estate Winery is the brainchild of Greg Basel and his business partner, Steve Hanson. At the heart of their vision is the wine itself, which features grapes harvested from Greg's local vineyard, Pheasant Run Vineyard, as well as other local and Columbia Valley vineyards. Basel's winemaking facility is housed in a 9,600-square-foot subterranean structure. Yes, Basel Cellars has a great winemaking facility and uses the finest fruit, but the added ingredient of passionate winemaking contributes substantially. To this end, Greg's son Justin is now the resident winemaker and supported in his efforts by winemaker consultants.

A visit to Basel Cellars will first take you through a secured, gated entrance at the top of the bluff where the deluxe complex is located. You'll want to budget plenty of time to enjoy Basel Cellars' stellar line-up of wines: reserve cabernet sauvignon, syrah, merlot, claret, and another red blend with a great moniker, "Merriment." You will also want to poke around and explore the grounds, at least as far as the public is allowed. You may even have an opportunity to visit with the gregarious Greg Basel and gain a little insight into his vision for the winery. Greg's résumé reflects an extensive background in the building trade and construction industry. Consequently, he takes a hands-on approach to every aspect of the winery. Combine great vision and close personal involvement and you get Washington's top destination—and a winery experience that shouldn't be missed.

BASEL CELLARS ESTATE WINERY
opened: 2002
winemaker(s): Justin Basel and consultant winemakers
location: 2901 Old Milton Highway
Walla Walla, WA 99362-7156
phone: 509-522-0200
web: www.baselcellars.com
e-mail: info@baselcellars.com
picnic area: Yes
gift shop: No
fee: $5 tasting fee refundable upon purchase
hours: 10–4 Monday through Sunday, or by appointment

Basel Cellars Estate Winery

 **BEST Destination and views**

DIRECTIONS: **From downtown Walla Walla** take Hwy 125 south toward Milton-Freewater, right onto Old Milton Hwy. Basel Cellars Estate Winery is located .8 miles on your left.

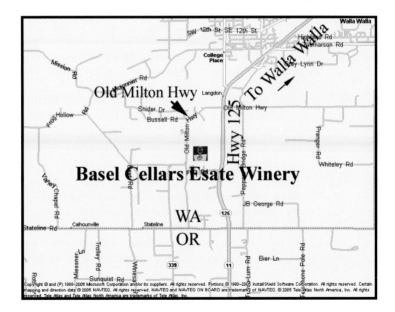

509

Zerba Cellars

OK, I realize that the book is titled *Wine Trails of Washington* and you might wonder how an Oregon winery snuck in here. The reality is that the Walla Walla Valley AVA extends into Oregon and is the home of such noted vineyards as Cayuse, Pepper Bridge, and Seven Hills. It's little wonder that one of the wineries chose to stay in Oregon and produce their own estate-made wines.

Zerba Cellars tasting room

That winery is Zerba Cellars and is within a stone's throw of the state line. More surprising is the fact that there aren't other Oregon-based wineries in the Walla Walla Valley, but that situation will likely change in the near future.

Cecil and Marilyn Zerba opened Zerba Cellars in 2004 with their estate-bottled 2002 wines. Prior to launching the wine business, they had a successful nursery business that served the Walla Walla Valley. However, love of wine and the economics of growing premium cabernet sauvignon and other varieties convinced Cecil and Marilyn to plant grapes on three different vineyards: Dad's Place, Cockburn Hills and Winesap Road. Although their 2004 release checked in at a paltry 200 cases, their 2006 production grew to a robust 6,000 cases in 2006. *Northwest Palate Magazine* in March 2006 noted that Zerba Cellars is an "Oregon Wineries to watch!" But despite this and other recent accolades, Cecil's mantra remains, "It's about the vines in the wines."

When I first met Marilyn at the tasting room, I made the same mistake that 9 out of 10 visitors make. Dyslexia must have hit me and I referred to her winery as "Zebra Cellars." The confusion is due, in part, to a drawing of a zebra prominently displayed on their "Wild Thing Red Wine" label. Marilyn explained that the zebra adorned label was "tongue in cheek" because so many people make the mistake of referring to their winery as Zebra Cellars. I wasn't the first, nor will I be the last.

The log house inspired tasting room relies on western juniper from Central Oregon. This knotty tree consumes 40 to 50 gallons of water per day and consequently vegetation is scarce surrounding a western juniper. The trees used to build the tasting room lay on the forest floor for years, allowing worms to attack and eat their way between bark and wood. The results are amazing patterns of etched wood—look closely at the wood as you sample Zerba's finest to see nature's art. No two patterns are the same; just like the reds and whites of Zerba Cellars, the wines are all distinct.

Marilyn Zerba of Zerba Cellars

ZERBA CELLARS
opened: 2004
winemaker(s): Cecil Zerba
location: 85530 Highway 11
Milton Freewater, OR 97862
phone: 541-938-9463
web: www.zerbacellars.com
e-mail: info@zerbacellars.com
picnic area: Yes
gift shop: No
fee: Complimentary wine tasting
hours: 12–5 Monday through Saturday, 12–4 Sundays

DIRECTIONS: From Walla Walla take Hwy 125 south. After you cross the State Line Rd, Hwy 125 becomes Hwy 11 in Oregon. When you cross State Line Rd, stay right, and Zerba Cellars is one block south on the right-hand side.

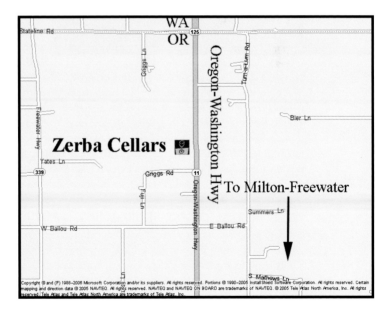

Saviah Cellars

Saviah Cellars celebrates tradition. Perhaps that is why an old wine press rests in its tasting room/winery just south of Walla Walla. Reflecting winery owners Richard and Anita Funk's roots in Montana, the wines have names that pay tribute to their heritage: a white wine called "Star Meadows" is the location of the original family homestead; its "Une Vallée" red wine derives its name from their current family homestead; and its "Big Sky" cuvée gets its name from…well, you guessed it, Montana's official nickname. They also produce

a delicious blend of Columbia Valley merlot and cabernet sauvignon that they dubbed "The Jack Lot 25." We have no idea where the name came from, but we suspect that it too has a connection with the past.

Richard and Anita moved from Montana in 1991 and, armed with a background in environmental science, Richard focused on water-quality programs. His work with the Walla Walla Health Department brought him in close contact with many of the local winemakers. He also found time to get his fingernails dirty by analyzing the soil around the valley. It wasn't long before the artistic side of winemaking captured his scientific mind. In 2000, his father and mother, Mike and Kay Funk, joined forces with Richard and Anita and launched Saviah Cellars. It's no coincidence that the name Saviah is shared by a Montana relative on Anita's side of the family.

With all winemaking, you have the rhythm of cycles from harvest through crush, fermenting, and bottling. It's all about appreciating these cycles and understanding your role, whether it be making premium wine or keeping the family legacy going. Saviah Cellars excels at both, and when you sample its "Une Vallée" red, you will come to understand that a lot more than chemistry and microbiology goes into creating this wine. It's a fusion of traditional values and good science.

SAVIAH CELLARS
opened: 2000
winemaker(s): Richard Funk
location: 1979 JB George Road
Walla Walla, WA 99362
phone: 509-520-5166
web: www.saviahcellars.com
e-mail: info@saviahcellars.com
picnic area: No
gift shop: No
fee: Complimentary wine tasting
hours: 11–5 Saturdays from May through October, or by appointment

DIRECTIONS: **From Walla Walla**, travel south for approximately 3 miles on Hwy 125. Turn left at the intersection of Hwy 125 and Old Milton Hwy. Turn right onto Peppers Bridge Rd. Saviah Cellars is located at the corner of JB George Rd and Peppers Bridge Rd. If coming from the west on US-12 go past Whitman Mission and turn right onto Last Chance Rd. Turn left onto Whitman Rd, and right on S. College Ave. Continue to SR-125 (south) and turn right. Turn left at the first light you come to, Old Milton Hwy. Go right onto Peppers Bridge Rd. Saviah Cellars is at the corner of Peppers Bridge Rd and JB George Rd.

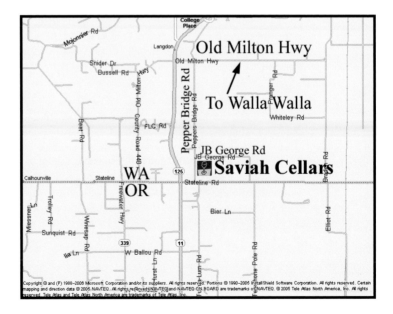

513

Beresan Winery

Located about 4 miles south of Walla Walla, Beresan Winery occupies a lovingly restored 1926 red barn. The barn is a distinctive landmark and one of our favorite stops along Walla Walla WineTrail South. Tom and Debbie Waliser, owners of Beresan Winery, meticulously renovated the old barn to serve the dual purpose of making and tasting wine. When you walk into the barn's south-end

tasting room, you are struck by the attention to detail. The barn's high ceilings, rustic colors, quality woodwork, and turn-of-the-century furnishings create an ambiance that speaks volumes about the Walisers' passion for making great wine.

Tom Waliser is first and foremost a "wine grower." He is the vineyard owner/manager for three different vineyards—Yellow Jacket Vineyard, Beresan Estate Vineyard, and Waliser Vineyard—whose combined 18 acres are the source of fruit for Beresan Winery. All the vineyards are located in the Walla Walla Valley, with the 2-acre Beresan Estate Vineyard bordering the winery itself. The Waliser family history includes many generations of farmers whose origins go back to the Beresan area of the Ukraine. Eventually, these farmers made their way to Walla Walla, where the family's farming expertise continues.

However, growing premium wine grapes is one thing. Converting the fruit to fine wine is another. For this, Tom turned to another Tom—Tom Glase, who also makes wine under his own wine label, Balboa. Together, the two Toms collaborate from vineyard to bottle to produce a portfolio of predominantly red estate wines, including syrah, merlot, cabernet sauvignon, and a red blend with the captivating name "Stone River." To date, we know of no plans to create a wine with the name "Tom Squared," but it would be fitting. Regardless of the name, all Beresan wines reflect the intense flavors and character of the estate vineyards.

BERESAN WINERY
opened: 2003
winemaker(s): Tom Glase
location: 4169 Pepper Bridge Road
Walla Walla, WA 99362-7135
phone: 509-522-9912
web: www.beresanwines.com
e-mail: info@beresanwines.com
picnic area: Yes
gift shop: No
fee: Complimentary wine tasting
hours: 11–4 Saturdays, or by appointment

Debbie Waliser in the tasting room

DIRECTIONS: **From Walla Walla**, travel south for approximately 3 miles on Hwy 125. Turn left at the intersection of Hwy 125 and Old Milton Hwy. Turn right onto Peppers Bridge Rd. Beresan Wines is located at the corner of JB George Rd and Peppers Bridge Rd.

Balboa Winery

Some people roll the dice and leave the comforts of home to resettle in a new place. These are adventurous souls, willing to take a risk and try something new. Such is the case of Tom Glase and his spouse, who gave up a comfortable existence on Bainbridge Island and moved to Walla Walla in 1997. Tom was volunteering at Walla Walla's L'Ecole N° 41 when owner/winemaker Martin Clubb asked him if he knew of anyone available to work at the winery. In fact, Tom did know of someone—himself. There was one slight problem for Tom, however. He had just accepted a loan officer position with a local bank and was expected to report to work that Monday morning. But two minutes of soul

searching convinced Tom what his course of action should be. That Monday, he called the bank and informed management that he wouldn't be taking the position.

There followed a three-year stint at L'Ecole N° 41, where Tom learned to make wine—very good wine. He then left L'Ecole N° 41 to become winemaker for Tom Waliser at Beresan Winery. With winemaking facilities and premium grapes at his disposal, it wasn't long before Tom, together with Mike Sharon of L'Ecole N° 41, created their own wine under the Balboa label. Their goal for Balboa is "to create an affordable bottle of wine without compromising quality." Employing fun label designs and screw-cap bottles, Tom has set his own course with distinctive syrahs, cabernet sauvignons, and merlots, as well as viogniers and sauvignon blancs. However, with production around 500 cases, don't be too surprised to learn that some of the wines have sold out. Bottom line: Time your visit to coincide with release dates.

At the time of this writing, Balboa's tasting room is located at Beresan Winery. But soon Tom may move his wine-tasting operations to his wife's apparel and jewelry shop in downtown Walla Walla. Thus, a word to the wise: Call ahead before venturing forth.

Tom Glase and Tom Waliser (l to r)

BALBOA WINERY
opened: 2006
winemaker(s): Tom Glase
location: 4169 Peppers Bridge Road
Walla Walla, WA 99362-7135
phone: 509-529-0461
web: www.balboawinery.com
e-mail: info@balboawinery.com
picnic area: No
gift shop: No
fee: Complimentary wine tasting
hours: Call for hours

DIRECTIONS: **From Walla Walla**, travel south for approximately 3 miles on Hwy 125. Turn left at the intersection of Hwy 125 and Old Milton Hwy. Turn right onto Peppers Bridge Rd. Balboa Winery is located at the Beresan Winery at the corner of JB George Rd and Peppers Bridge Rd.

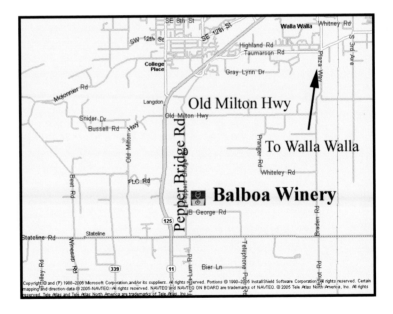

Va Piano Vineyards

Imagine drinking superb wine and contributing to a good cause while under the roof of a Tuscan-inspired estate. You can, simply by experiencing Va Piano Vineyards. Upon purchasing a bottle of Va Piano's "Bruno's Blend" at the vineyards, $2 of your purchase goes to an African-based charity that supports

children orphaned by AIDS. But how does a medium-priced wine get the name "Bruno" and why an African-based charity?

The answers have their roots in the mid-'90s when Va Piano's proprietor and winemaker, Justin Wylie, attended Gonzaga University's Florence campus during his senior year. There, Justin met and befriended Father Bruno Segatta, assistant dean of the Florence program. Bruno, as students and friends alike know him, is also an avid painter and ardent contributor to a variety of developing-country charities. Routinely, he contributes half the proceeds of his art sales to such causes. Thus, when Justin and his wife, Liz, sought to name their wine, it seemed natural to name it "Bruno's Blend" and feature Bruno's artwork on the label. What's more, the idea of contributing $2 toward one of Bruno's charities seemed only fitting.

Bruno's artwork also graces Va Piano's tasting room, where the warm earth tones and Liz's relaxed style make you feel right at home. It is the perfect setting in which to experience "Bruno's Blend" as well as Va Piano's other wines: a full-bodied, intensely flavored syrah and a cabernet sauvignon. However, to savor the moment (and wine) you need to keep Va Piano Vineyards' motto in mind, *Chi va piano, va sano e va lantano*, which translates to "He who goes slowly, goes safely and goes far." Thus the name "Va Piano," or "go slowly," reminds us to swirl, observe the deep red color, take in the aroma, and concentrate on some amazing tastes.

Liz Wylie of Va Piano

VA PIANO VINEYARDS
opened: 2003
winemaker(s): Justin Wylie
location: 1793 JB George Road
Walla Walla, WA 99362
phone: 509-529-0900
web: www.vapianovineyards.com
e-mail: info@vapianovineyards.com
picnic area: Yes
gift shop: Yes
fee: Complimentary wine tasting
hours: 11–4 Saturday and Sunday in March
and April; summer tasting room hours 10–5
Friday through Sunday beginning May 1; or
by appointment

DIRECTIONS: **From Walla Walla,** travel south for approximately 3 miles on Hwy 125. Turn left at the intersection of Hwy 125 and Old Milton Hwy. Turn right onto Peppers Bridge Rd. Turn left onto JB George Rd and go about .5 miles. Va Piano Vineyards is on the left.

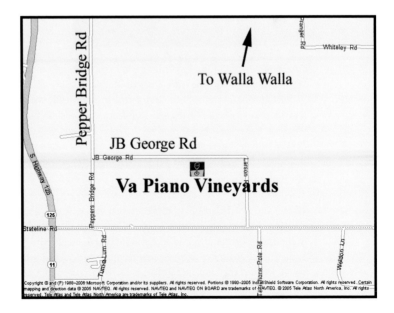

519

Pepper Bridge Winery

As you approach Pepper Bridge Winery, you are likely to see a Swiss flag flying above the handsome tri-level estate and winery. No, you haven't left the U.S.; the flag honors the home country of Pepper Bridge winemaker Jean-Francois Pellet. It was in Switzerland that Jean-Francois honed his winemaking skills, beginning at his family's winery/vineyard and later working in Spain.

However, the wonderful thing about Pepper Bridge is the team of people who have come together to create a great winery that is integrated, from "grape buds to bottle." This team is composed of managing partners, viticulturists, winemakers, marketing and sales staff, and tasting room hosts. Whomever you

visit with, you are struck by the professionalism and dedication to Pepper Bridge Winery. You come to understand that the winery is more than the personality of one individual—it is about an organization.

The winery/tasting room sits on a hill on the southern edge of Walla Walla, with Northstar Winery in view in the distance. The hill provides a panoramic vista of the Blue Mountains, but the location was chosen to take advantage of gravity. The three-story production facility allows grapes to gently flow from top to bottom, from destemming to fermentation. It is this design and attention to detail that is responsible for Pepper Bridge's 100 percent award-winning Walla Walla estate merlots and cabernet sauvignons. As testimony to Pepper Bridge's excellent grapes, more than 60 wineries purchase its grapes, including Col Solare, L'Ecole N° 41, Reininger, Woodward Canyon, Hogue, and Seven Hills, just to name a few.

WineTrails Northwest rarely advocates that you join a particular winery's wine club. But with the Pepper Bridge Vine Club, we make an exception. Using an innovative approach, Pepper Bridge Winery sells vines to its Vine Club members at the cost of $150 per year. For that fee, members receive a bottle of wine, a certificate of ownership, and a "hands-on" day in the Pepper Bridge vineyard, where they learn pruning, thinning, and harvesting techniques. What's more, your name is prominently displayed on your vine. Now that's a different kind of wine club ... *Vive la différence!*

Pepper Bridge wine club member's
dedicated vine

PEPPER BRIDGE WINERY
opened: 2000
winemaker(s): Jean-Francois Pellet
location: 1704 JB George Road
Walla Walla, WA 99362
phone: 509-525-6502
web: www.pepperbridge.com
e-mail: info@pepperbridge.com
picnic area: Yes
gift shop: No
fee: $8 tasting fee refundable upon purchase
hours: Daily 10–4

DIRECTIONS: **From downtown Walla Walla**, take SR-125 (south) [S. 9th Ave.] for about 4 miles.
Turn left onto Old Milton Hwy and continue for about .5 miles. Turn right onto Peppers Bridge Rd
and drive 1 mile. Turn left at JB George Rd and drive about .5 miles. At the end of the road, turn
left onto limited access road. Drive through grapevine-lined lane and continue straight to Pepper
Bridge Winery.

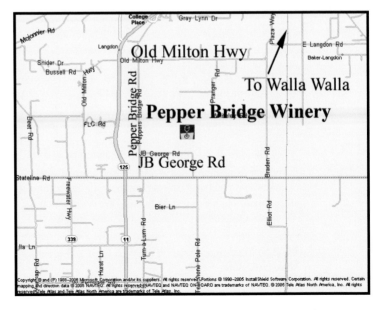

Northstar Winery

Merlot, a French black grape dating back to the 1700s, is often called Bordeaux's other red grape, cabernet sauvignon being the signature grape of the region. Merlot, however, is lighter in color, acid, and tannins than cabernet sauvignon and because of its complex flavors and smooth taste, is hugely popular on its own merits.

Northstar is all about ultrapremium merlot. It makes no whites, nor are there any other red varietals at Northstar. Even its web address is www.

northstarmerlot.com. Don't go "sideways" on us, Miles, but pinot noir is not welcomed here.

Washington is world renowned for its merlot vineyards, and Northstar derives and blends its grapes from 15 different vineyards in the Walla Walla and Columbia valleys. Most notable are the merlot grapes from the Indian Wells and Cold Creek vineyards in the Wahluke Slope subappellation. Consulting winemaker Jed Steele (of California fame) works with Northstar's resident winemaker to create "Columbia Valley" merlot, blended from a limited amount of Walla Walla merlot and a "not quite up to snuff" merlot called Stella Maris, affectionately known to locals as Stella.

The parent company of Northstar, Ste. Michelle Wine Estates Ltd., is all about elegance. This elegance is reflected in Northstar's stylish tasting room and state-of-the-art production facility. Located just south of Walla Walla within a stone's throw of Pepper Bridge Winery, Northstar offers a commanding view of the distant Blue Mountains. Fourteen acres of grapes grow next to the winery (can you guess the varietal?). The spacious tasting room offers plenty of room to mingle and enjoy the views as the well-informed tasting room staff answers your questions and attends to your sampling needs. Be sure to ask a staff person if you can view their production area. From a side door, you look down into the winemaking area. By most standards, the production area is huge, with mammoth stainless steel tanks lining the walls like sentinel soldiers. It's also kept exceptionally clean and well organized. You could eat off the floor. But don't. They'd have to "cut you off" back in the tasting room.

Make Northstar one of your destination stops as you trek along the Walla Walla WineTrail South.

NORTHSTAR WINERY
opened: 1992
winemaker(s): Jed Steele acts as a consultant to winemaking staff.
location: 1736 JB George Road
Walla Walla, WA 99362
phone: 509-525-6100
web: www.northstarmerlot.com
e-mail: info@northstarmerlot.com
picnic area: Yes
gift shop: Yes
fee: $5 tasting fee; 10% discount on purchase
hours: 10–4 Thursday through Saturday, 11–3 Sunday, or by appointment

DIRECTIONS: **From downtown Walla Walla**, take SR-125 (south) [S. 9th Ave.] for about 4 miles. Turn left onto Old Milton Hwy and continue for about .5 miles. Turn right onto Peppers Bridge Road and drive 1 mile. Turn left at JB George Rd and drive about .5 miles. At the end of the road, turn left onto limited access road. Drive through grapevine-lined lane and turn right at first driveway to Northstar Winery.

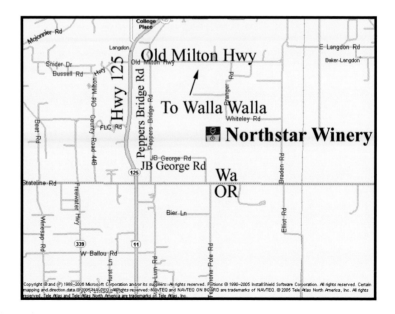

Gifford Hirlinger Winery

Located on Stateline Road on the south side of Walla Walla, Gifford Hirlinger Winery is literally a stone's throw from Oregon. Actually, it is more of a stone's lob. Housed in an ultramodern building, the winery/tasting room is home to

30-year-old Mike Berghan. The architecture is stunning and offers ample patio space to enjoy a bottle of wine with a front row seat for viewing Mike's developing vineyard.

Mike has blossomed on the scene with a red blend he appropriately named "Stateline Red," a marriage of 58 percent cabernet and 42 percent merlot. More wines are scheduled for the future. This promising beginning will evolve and include a number of estate wines featuring fruit from his vineyard. Whatever he makes, Mike is guided by a winemaking philosophy that he learned while studying in Florence, Italy: Wine is meant to complement food, not overpower it. Some call this a "wine as a condiment" approach to its extreme. Mike strives to make tannin-tamed wines that are not too big.

Originally from Sandpoint, Idaho, Mike became incredibly bored while chasing the American dream at Smith Barney in San Francisco. He did what many of us only imagine: He quit his high-paying job to get his hands dirty (literally) working for a vineyard management company in California. Eventually, he landed in Walla Walla, but not by dumb luck. His ancestors homesteaded in the Walla Walla Valley. In fact, the name Gifford Hirlinger (GH for short) derives from his not-too-distant relatives. For WineTrail enthusiasts, it will be fun to watch GH evolve and add to the tapestry of Walla Walla that his ancestors started.

GIFFORD HIRLINGER WINERY
opened: 2001
winemaker(s): Mike Berghan
location: 1450 Stateline Road
Walla Walla, WA 99362
phone: 509-301-9229
web: www.giffordhirlinger.com
e-mail: wine@GiffordHirlinger.com
picnic area: Yes
gift shop: No
fee: Tasting fee may apply
hours: 11–5 Friday through Sunday, or by appointment

Mike Berghan

DIRECTIONS: **From downtown Walla Walla,** take SR-125 (south) [S. 9th Ave.] for about 4 miles. Turn left onto Old Milton Hwy and continue for about 1 mile. Turn right onto Braden Rd and travel about 1.5 miles to Stateline Rd. Turn left and Gifford Hirlinger is found immediately on your left.

Glen Fiona Winery

syrah *n.*– A noble black grape variety thought to be indigenous to the Rhône region of France since Roman times.

Have you ever noticed how syrah tastes different from one Washington winery to another? Moreover, even in the same winery, the syrah can differ remarkably from one year to another. However, despite this difference, there is one thing WineTrail seekers can count on: The syrah at Glen Fiona is consistently good year after year.

Since 1995, Glen Fiona has staked its reputation on making top-notch syrah, first under the guidance of Caleb Foster (now Buty Winery's owner and winemaker) and Michael Carpenter, and later with winemaker Rusty Figgins (now at Cave B Winery). The ownership has changed as well. In 2004, Washington Wine & Beverage Co., owners of Silver Lake Winery, acquired Glen Fiona. Despite changing winemakers and owners, the vision of Glen Fiona has remained constant—to create premium syrah using "natural" techniques to maintain the expression of the fruit. We're talking "low intervention methodology."

Glen Fiona Winery and its tasting room are located in south Walla Walla, near the Rulo and Isenhower wineries. The Celtic-themed wine estate (Glen Fiona means "valley of the vine" in Gaelic) enjoys a stunning panoramic view of the Blue Mountains. Yes, soak in the view, but get ready to enjoy syrah with names such as "Basket Press Reserve," "Puncheon-Aged," and "Cuvee Parallel 46." Now you've found your pot of gold.

GLEN FIONA WINERY
opened: 1994
winemaker(s): Justin Neufeld (Cheryl Jones is consulting winemaker)
location: 1249 Lyday Lane
Walla Walla, WA 99362-7308
phone: 509-522-2566
web: www.glenfiona.com
e-mail: syrah@glenfiona.com
picnic area: No
gift shop: No
fee: Complimentary wine tasting
hours: 11–4 Saturday and Sunday;
first weekend in May is Spring Release; Holiday Barrel Tasting in December; or by appointment

DIRECTIONS: **From US-12** to Walla Walla exit 2nd Ave. to Rose St. Left onto 9th Ave. to SR-125. Left onto Old Milton Hwy. Right onto Braden Rd. Right onto Lyday Lane. Winery at end of Lyday Lane.

Isenhower Cellars

Occasionally wine is more than the sum of its parts. More than the grapes, more than the winemaking style, it is the passion and sense of caring the winemaker brings to the craft. These qualities are rooted in the heart, and if you care deeply for your family and friends, you have an opportunity to express it in the wine you make. Such is the case with Isenhower Cellars.

Eisenhower barrels featuring local artist Jeffrey Hill

In early 1998, Brett and Denise Isenhower left Colorado and relocated to Washington to pursue their dream of making wine. Both pharmacists by profession, their scientific backgrounds bring an understanding of the chemistry involved in turning grapes into wine. They also appreciate the importance of the fruit and work closely with their grape-growing partners at Red Mountain, Horse Heaven Hills, and Yakima Valley on a host of issues, from pruning to harvesting.

Denise takes the lead on the Bordeaux-style wines, and Brett pursues his passion for Rhône-style wines. Many of their wines have been christened after flowers, e.g., "Wild Alfalfa" (syrah), "Batchelor's Button" (cabernet sauvignon), and "Red Paintbrush" (merlot). But these wines are not named after mere garden-variety flowers. They get their names from wildflowers. The Isenhowers also create an exotic wine using a blend of roussanne and viognier, dispelling the notion that Walla Walla is all about "reds."

The winery is located just south of Walla Walla and can be seen from Old Milton Highway. Once inside the winery, you might have to step over the family's big dog, Lucy, who doesn't get too excited about the steady stream of visitors. Assisted by an able crew of volunteers, the Isenhowers have enjoyed steady growth and a loyal fan base. Stylistically, all the Isenhower wines are rich, intense, and balanced. Their hope is that you pair them with a meal in the company of friends and loved ones.

ISENHOWER CELLARS
opened: 1998
winemaker(s): Denise and Brett Isenhower
location: 3471 Pranger Road
Walla Walla, WA 99362-7307
phone: 509-526-7896
web: www.isenhowercellars.com
e-mail: winemakers@isenhowercellars.com
picnic area: No
gift shop: No
fee: Complimentary wine tasting
hours: 10:30–5 Saturdays and Sundays, or
by appointment

DIRECTIONS: From downtown Walla Walla, take SR-125 (south) [S. 9th Ave.] for about 4 miles. Turn left onto Old Milton Hwy and continue for about .75 miles. Turn right onto Pranger Rd. Eisenhower Winery is immediately to your left. If coming from the west on US-12 take go past Whitman Mission and turn right onto Last Chance Rd. Turn left onto Whitman Rd, and right on S. College Ave. Continue to SR-125 (south) and turn right. Turn left at the first light you come to, Old Milton Hwy. Isenhower Cellars will be on your right, on the corner of Old Milton Hwy and Pranger Rd.

Dusted Valley Vintners

Dateline Walla Walla: Transplanted Cheeseheads find vino a perfect complement to cheddar.

Dusted Valley Vintners is the story of two families from Wisconsin—the Johnsons and the Braunels—who relocated to Walla Walla and discovered a passion for making exquisite wines. Along with this passion came a strong desire to demystify the wine experience and turn it into a Bacchus-filled joyride. Even their wine club bears the name "Stained Tooth Society." They know, after all, that wine is just fermented grape juice. OK, we understand there's a little more to it than that, but we're up for some fun, too.

Located in a converted garage on the southern outskirts of Walla Walla, the Dusted Valley tasting room space is small, but the ambiance is warm and inviting. Even the wine neophyte will feel at ease in this setting. Outside, there's a king-size turnaround for comfortably maneuvering your stretch limo and ample deck furniture upon which to sit and enjoy a Dusted Valley Vintner white with Wisconsin cheese. As the Johnsons and Braunels state on their website, "Dusted Valley Vintners vinifies vivacious vino that will vanquish your versed palate." Alliteration aside, check out their Columbia Valley syrah. It is serious wine.

DUSTED VALLEY VINTNERS
opened: 2003
winemaker(s): Chad Johnson
location: 1248 Old Milton Highway
Walla Walla, WA 99362-8174
phone: 509-525-1337
web: www.dustedvalley.com
e-mail: info@dustedvalley.com
picnic area: Yes
gift shop: No
fee: Complimentary wine tasting
hours: 10–6 Saturday and Sunday, or by appointment

DIRECTIONS: **From downtown Walla Walla**, take SR-125 (south) [S. 9th Ave.] for about 4 miles. Turn left onto Old Milton Hwy and arrive at 1248 Old Milton Hwy—Dusted Valley Vintners is on the left.

Spokane
WINE COUNTRY

Merry Cellars 2005 Crimson

The Spokane-Pullman WineTrail offers the opportunity to put on a pair of sneakers and see many of the wineries on foot. While in downtown Spokane, you will experience rich architectural history, a rushing river and wonderful eateries. For sure, walk through the restored Davenport Hotel and linger over the photographs of turn-of-the-century Spokane. Downtown, you have the opportunity to savor the wines of Barrister, Robert Karl, Grande Ronde, and Caterina. If you throw in a meal at one of Spokane's many fine restaurants, your day is full. However, as part of this WineTrail we include a foray into the scenic Palouse to sample three distinctive wineries: Merry Cellars, Wawawai Canyon and Basalt Cellars.

Award-winning wines, terrific hosts, and wonderful amenities—the Spokane-Pullman WineTrail has it all. If you venture south to sample the fine wines of the Palouse, WineTrail enthusiasts will need to budget two full days to experience this area's delights.

1 Barrister Winery
2 Grande Ronde Cellars
3 Robert Karl Cellars
4 Caterina Winery
5 Merry Cellars
6 Wawawai Canyon
7 Basalt Cellars

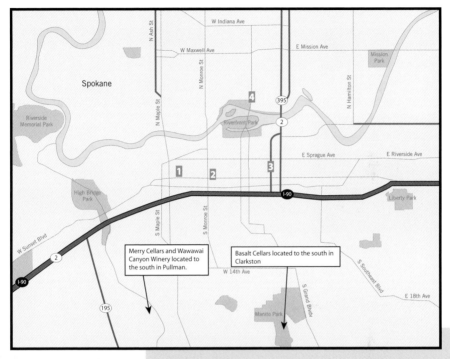

Region:	**Spokane Wine Country**
# of tasting rooms on tour:	**7**
# of satellite tasting rooms:	**1—Arbor Crest Wine Cellars downtown tasting room, 808 W. Main, 509-747-3903.**
Estimated # of days for tour:	**2**
Getting around:	**Car and foot**
Key events:	❑ **Consisting of 10 local wineries, the Spokane Winery Association features two key events: Spring Barrel Tasting (Mother's Day weekend) and Holiday Wine Festival (weekend before Thanksgiving).** ❑ **See www.spokanewineries.net/calendar.htm for more information.**
Tips:	❑ **Downtown Spokane wineries can be visited on foot.** ❑ **Caterina Winery features a restaurant with light fare.** ❑ **Grande Ronde Cellars also features wines of Vin du Lac and Masset Winery.** ❑ **Many area restaurants feature local wines.**
Best:	❑ **Best Eats: Caterina Winery**

Barrister Winery

Who doesn't love a success story about two guys toiling in their garage to make wine only to discover that their passion has taken them beyond "garagiste"? Such is the story of Barrister Winery. Founded in a garage by attorneys Greg Lipsker and Michael White, the winery produces wonderfully FULL-BODIED and supple reds. As Greg and Michael note on the winery website, "In the fall of 1997, we bought our first 5-gallon home winemaking kit. Since then, winemaking has become the 'little hobby' that got out of control. In 2001, we

Michael White (center) educating visitors

took the quantum leap from home winemaking to becoming a bonded winery. Producing only red wine, our grapes come from some of Washington's most prestigious vineyards (and a couple of sleepers)."

Barrister Winery is situated in a 100-year-old brick building in the historic Davenport Arts District of downtown Spokane. The entrance to the winery is found off an alley, and the surroundings may cause you to wonder what you have gotten yourself into. But all worries fade once you go inside and are greeted by a spacious environment featuring exposed brick, wine barrels resting bung up, and friendly pourers. In fact, don't be surprised if Greg or Michael happen to be doing the honors. Periodically, one of them will lead tours of the barrel room, which is located in the basement of the building. As you descend the stairs, your nose tells you that you are entering the barrel room; the distinct musty, damp smell hints of cabernet. Here in the low light of the room, you can see row upon row of French and American oak barrels, which nurture the wine for 16 to 24 months. In the dimness and dampness of the barrel room, the audience peppers their guide with questions about the winemaking process. Every question is handled with care, much like that taken by Greg and Michael to make hand-crafted premium wines. Although the winery has become a full-blown business now, it is still a labor of love. Their primary goals are to remain small and to focus on producing topnotch reds.

WineTrail Note: If you ever require a Spokane-area winery to host a wedding reception, a family reunion, or a corporate shindig, Barrister Winery is available for such events. I'm sure that the winery staff would sell you some wine for your affair as well.

Barrister Winery is an active member of the Spokane Winery Association and participates in both a fall tasting event (the weekend before Thanksgiving) and a spring tasting event (Mother's Day weekend). See www.spokanewineries.net for details.

Fellow WineTrail partner, I rest my case.

Greg Lipsker

BARRISTER WINERY
opened: 2001
winemaker(s): Greg Lipsker and Michael White
location: 1213 West Railroad Avenue
Spokane, WA 99201
phone: 509-465-3591
web: www.barristerwinery.com
e-mail: info@barristerwinery.com
picnic area: No
gift shop: No
fee: Complimentary wine tasting
hours: 10–4 Saturdays

DIRECTIONS: From downtown Spokane: drive west on Second Ave. to Jefferson (about 12 blocks west of Division St.). Turn right onto Jefferson and left onto Railroad Ave. immediately before going under the railroad viaduct. Note that Railroad Ave. is on the south side of the railroad overpass. Don't be confused by Railroad Alley which is on the north side of the railroad overpass. Arrive at 1213 West Railroad Ave.

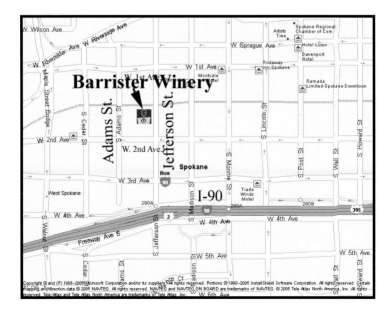

537

Grande Ronde Cellars

Started in 1997, Grande Ronde Cellars was the inspiration of four partners: Dave Westfall, Michael Manz, John Mueller, and J. David Page. It was Michael Manz, however, who became the heart and soul (and winemaker) for Grande Ronde Cellars and moonlighted as the vintner for Mountain Dome. Unfortunately, Michael's untimely death in 2007 resulted in a huge loss for Grande Ronde Cellars. Nevertheless, the remaining team is committed to producing premium wines and permitting Michael's legacy to live on.

The winery is named for eastern Oregon's Grande Ronde River. Its tasting room is located in downtown Spokane and has the distinguished feature of offering a portfolio of wines from Grande Ronde Cellars, Mountain Dome, Vin du Lac, and Masset wineries. If you don't have time to visit the Yakima Valley or Lake Chelan, Grande Ronde Cellars can bring them to you…in a bottle. That being the case, many intrepid WineTrail enthusiasts visit the tasting room to sample Grande Ronde's own cabernet sauvignon, merlot, chardonnay, and Bordeaux blends. Walla Walla Valley is the source of most of the grapes used by Grande Ronde Cellars.

The downstairs tasting room also features a banquet area that can comfortably sit 20 guests. If you have a desire to host a sit-down dinner paired with premium wines, talk to Dave Westfall at Grande Ronde Cellars.

GRANDE RONDE CELLARS
opened: 1999
winemaker(s): TBD
location: 906 West Second Avenue
Spokane, WA 99201
phone: 509-928-2788
web: www.granderondecellars.com
e-mail: dlwestfall@msn.com
picnic area: No
gift shop: Yes
fee: Small tasting fee waived upon purchase
hours: 12–6 Thursday through Saturday, or
by appointment

DIRECTIONS: Take Lincoln Street exit off I-90. Proceed 2 blocks north on Lincoln. Winery is located at 2nd and Lincoln (two blocks off freeway) in the Freeman Center.

Robert Karl Cellars

In the mid-'90s, Joseph and Rebecca Gunselman decided to cure their recently acquired wine bug and head west from Virginia. That's quite a prescription, considering that many physicians are terrible at diagnosing and treating their own ailments. Joseph Gunselman is a practicing anesthesiologist and continues his day job at Sacred Heart Hospital in Spokane. However, truth be told, his real passion is making wine.

Armed with a scientific background, Joe understood that the secret to making great wine begins with the grapes themselves. To this end, he hit a home run with his decision to acquire his grapes from the Horse Heaven Hills AVA, home to vineyards such as McKinley Springs, Alder Ridge, and Phinny Hill. Joe collaborates closely with the growers and tracks vineyard data pertaining to temperature, precipitation, sugar content, and more.

Joe's wife, Rebecca, assists with winemaking and manages the tasting room and marketing. They also enlist the cooperation of their three cellar-rat sons to help during crush, racking and bottling. Together this family produces about 2,500 cases annually of cabernet sauvignon, claret, merlot, sauvignon blanc, syrah, and a dry cabernet franc rosé. As a consequence of remaining "boutique," Robert Karl Cellars often has to inform its visitors that a particular label is sold out. We had the good fortune of tasting a recent vintage of its claret before loyal fans snapped it up. As we learned, the word "claret" originates from the French *clairet*, meaning light red wine that uses varietals from Bordeaux. We promise to get no more cork dorky than that.

The Gunselmans are bullish about the wine industry in their adopted state, because "Washington grapes continue to get better."

Rebecca Gunselman

ROBERT KARL CELLARS
opened: 1999
winemaker(s): Joe Gunselman
location: 115 West Pacific Avenue
Spokane, WA 99201
phone: 888-4-CLARET
web: www.robertkarl.com
e-mail: info@robertkarl.com
picnic area: No
gift shop: No
fee: Complimentary wine tasting
hours: Saturdays 12–4

DIRECTIONS: Exit I-90 at Division (exit 281), travel north 3 blocks, turn left on Pacific. The winery will be on your left.

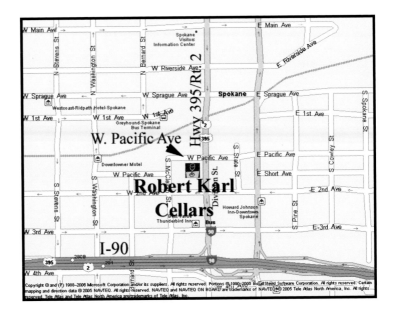

Caterina Winery

Take one charming old dairy building, add live music on weekends, throw in some great wine, and what do you get? You get Caterina Winery, a boutique winery located in the Spokane's historic Broadview Dairy Building, just off

Washington Street and across from Red Lion Inn. *WineTrail warning: Be careful not to trip over the big black Labrador as you enter. His name is Blue and he's fond of sleeping—anywhere he likes.*

Named after a founder's beloved Italian grandmother, Caterina Winery has been producing a wide range of affordable varietals since 1993. Its ambitious list of wines includes pinot grigio, riesling, viognier, chardonnay, sauvignon blanc, cabernet sauvignon, merlot, cabernet franc, sangiovese, and syrah. While the chardonnay is its best seller, Caterina Winery has developed a reputation for its delicious "break out the fish tacos" sauvignon blanc, which is characterized by its lush tropical flavors. The fruit comes from the primo Washington grape sources of Walla Walla, Columbia Valley, and Yakima Valley. Although Caterina's winemakers have come and gone over the years, its current one, Monica Meglasson,

Caterina Winery's downtown Spokane location

has continued the tradition of producing a variety of wines, from the Bohemian series of "Artistic Affordable Blends" to the "Vineyard" series of exclusive single-vineyard old-vine wines. Caterina wines range from $7 to $35 a bottle, with most wines costing around $18 a bottle. **WineTrail Note:** For those who love that "sweater on the tongue" feeling that tannins give, try the single-vineyard merlot (Willard Vineyard).

What's not to love about a winery whose motto is the Italian proverb "One barrel of wine can work more miracles than a church full of saints?" Salute!

CATERINA WINERY
opened: 1993
winemaker(s): Monica Meglasson
location: 905 N. Washington Street
Spokane, WA 99201-3210
phone: 509-328-5069
web: www.caterinawinery.com
e-mail: monica@caterina.com
picnic area: Summer
gift shop: Yes, small select items.
fee: Complimentary wine tasting
hours: Daily 12–5; wine bar open 5–midnight Friday
and Saturday for appetizers and live music

Caterina pouring staff and dog Blue

 BEST Eats

DIRECTIONS: Take exit 281 off I-90, go north on Division St. and then left on N. River Dr. and continue to N. Washington St. Caterina Winery is located across the street in the red brick building. Alternatively, from downtown Spokane, take N. Washington St. north crossing over the Spokane River. The winery is located on the left at 905 N. Washington St. A parking lot is located next to their front entrance.

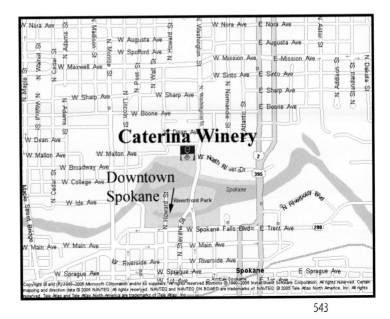

Merry Cellars

"Wine is sunlight, held together by water!"—Galileo Galilei

I believe if Galileo were a Coug he would have reworked his poetic line to read, "Wheat is sunlight, held together by undulating hills." When I think of the Palouse, I see fields of gold and green, I feel dry heat, and I hear the grasshoppers at night. However, until the emergence of Merry Cellars, wine imagery wasn't used in the same sentence with the Palouse. Then, one taste of

Merry Cellar's "Twilight Hills Red" shook my world, and I learned that the taste of the Palouse comes in a bottle. It's true. As its tasting notes make clear, Merry Cellar creates wines "comfortable and approachable, and maybe just a little rugged around the edges." That, to me, reminds me of my Eastern Washington roots.

Merry Cellars tasting room in Pullman's historic old post office

Winemaker and owner Patrick Merry is a transplanted Montanan who grew up in a family that appreciated wine. I am envious of that. My own family's experience with wine was a bottle of Cold Duck, which would be left in the refrigerator for eons after some family event. Patrick's goal is to create wines for different occasions, from backyard barbecues to elegant weddings. He respects the fruit's origin and applies a minimalist approach to his hand-picked and hand-sorted grapes in order to bring out the *terroir* of each vintage.

Located just 90 minutes south of Spokane in Pullman, Merry Cellars is a joy to visit any time of the year. Be sure to check out the WineTrails Northwest website (www.winetrailsnw.com) for event information. When Merry Cellars hosts wine-tasting and food-pairing events, there is no need for you to stop by the Coug to pick up Cougar Gold. Merry Cellars will supply the perfect wine to accompany delectable cheeses.

Kaylani Merrill and Patrick Merry

MERRY CELLARS
opened: 2004
winemaker(s): Patrick Merry
location: 245 SE Paradise Street
Pullman, WA 99163
phone: 509-338-4699
web: www.merrycellars.com
e-mail: patrick@merrycellars.com
picnic area: No
gift shop: No
fee: $5 tasting refundable with purchase
hours: 3–8 Thursday through Saturday

DIRECTIONS: **From Spokane** head south on US-195 toward Pullman and travel about 70 miles. Keep left onto SR-270 [Davis Way] and go 2.4 miles. Bear right (south) onto SR-27 [SR-270] and go only .1 miles. Turn left (east) onto SR-270 [SE Paradise St.] and arrive at 245 SE Paradise St.

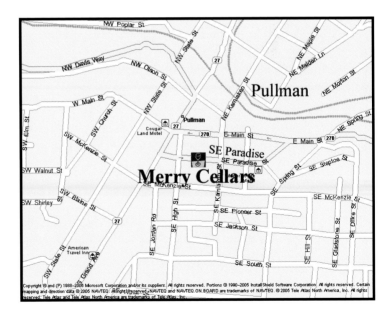

Wawawai Canyon

When it comes to winemaking, "my husband, Ben [Moffett], is the pilot and I'm the copilot," noted Christine Havens as she poured me a healthy dose of their cabernet sauvignon. No doubt Christine was being modest in terms of her winemaking involvement. After all, she met Ben while both were attending

Walla Walla Community College's Enology and Viticulture program. This was before they came home to Ben's native Pullman and established Wawawai (pronounced wah-WOW-ee) Canyon Winery.

The couple brought with them the technical expertise to make fine wine and an inherent desire to add their own unique touch. As testimony to their creative license, they released an unfiltered pinot noir using an old-world sur lies technique for aging the wine. The result is a wine that has a very different flavor profile compared to a traditional "light" pinot noir. The word "amazing" came to mind as I sipped this pinot noir. Equally impressive was a gewürztraminer that could easily pass as a dessert wine in drag.

Ben's parents, David and Stacia Moffett, both teach at nearby Washington State University and own a vineyard that borders the Snake River, about 20 miles south. The arid location provides a perfect setting to grow premium grapes. "What's the biggest challenge with growing grapes?" I asked. "Grasshoppers," Christine replied. Once every 10 years or so, a swarm of grasshoppers descend on the vineyard and devour the grapes. Nothing seems to deter them; they even eat through plastic nets. Nevertheless, despite this B-flick sci-fi scenario, the joy of producing premium grapes year after year makes up for the occasional attack of the grasshoppers.

Check out the winery's gorgeous logo created by Christine, which also serves as the image on Wawawai Canyon wine labels. Christine is also responsible for much of the artwork that hangs in the tasting room, including paintings and bronze pieces. Except for the glass of wine in hand, you might just think you were visiting an art gallery. Clearly the entire family (and this is a family affair from the vineyard to the tasting room) has many other endeavors that intrigue them. Along with teaching, painting, consulting, and cooking, producing signature wines is one of many passions they pursue.

Christine Havens and Stacia Moffett (l to r)

WAWAWAI CANYON
opened: 2004
winemaker(s): Ben Moffett
location: 5602 State Route 270
Pullman, WA 99163
phone: 509-336-9316
web: www.wawawaicanyon.com
e-mail: info@wawawaicanyon.com
picnic area: No
gift shop: No
fee: Complimentary wine tasting
hours: 1–6 Thursday through Saturday from March
through July and mid-September through December;
closed holidays; due to limited production, call ahead

DIRECTIONS: From Pullman, take SR-27 [SR-270] and head toward Moscow, ID. Go 3.2 miles and look for Wawawai Canyon's tasting room sign on your left.

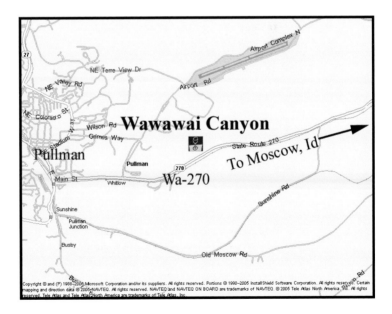

Basalt Cellars

If you live in the Pacific Northwest and haven't had the pleasure of visiting the twin cities of Lewiston-Clarkston, you need to put them on your "top 10 local places I need to visit" list. Why? How about history? This is where Lewis and Clark camped in 1805 as the guests of the Nez Perce. How about beauty? The Lewis-Clark Valley will make you pull the car over and get out to soak in the view. How about wine? At one time in the late 1800s, there was a bounty of vineyards producing premium wine grapes throughout the area. But with Prohibition, the fledging wine industry was dealt a deathblow. Now, however,

a re-emergence of the vineyards and wineries is in the offing, beginning with Clarkston's Basalt Cellars.

Owners Rick Wasem, Don McQuary, and Lynn DeVleming took enology classes at the Clarkston campus of Walla Walla Community College and discovered in one another a kindred passion for

Signage for Basalt Cellars' Port Drive location

crafting wine. It wasn't long before they bonded the winery, and Basalt Cellars was born in 2004. From just 200 cases produced in their first year, they have enjoyed phenomenal growth. In 2006, they crushed 26 tons of grapes from such vineyards as Willard, Seven Hills, Millbrandt Brothers, Sagemoor, and Pepper Bridge. That's a lot of grape stomping. By the way, if you are wondering how they came up with the name Basalt Cellars, you simply need to take your nose out of the glass and look around. The surrounding hills are composed of basalt rock, the result of past volcanic activity.

Rick Wasem is Basalt Cellars' chief winemaker and is one of a half-dozen other Washington winemakers who have backgrounds as pharmacists. (More than a pharmacy, Rick's drugstore, Wasem's Drugs, is a key retail and home medical supplier for the Lewiston-Clarkston area and employs a small army of locals.) Rick has garnered medals at San Francisco and Tri-Cities wine tasting competitions for his impressive array of white and red wines. In addition to Bordeaux and Rhone-style wines, Basalt Cellars has produced an unusual lemberger port (which quickly sold out) and is close to bottling a red blend with the cryptic name of "PVCF" (an acronym for petit verdot and cabernet franc). To sum it up, Clarkston might be the Gateway to Hells Canyon for many, but for WineTrail enthusiasts, it serves as the entrance to a heavenly selection of Basalt Cellars wines.

BASALT CELLARS
opened: 2004
winemaker(s): Rick Wasem
location: 906 Port Drive
Clarkston, WA 99403-1805
phone: 509-758-6442
web: www.basaltcellars.com
e-mail: dmcquary@smagins.com
picnic area: No
gift shop: No
fee: Complimentary wine tasting
hours: 12–4 Thursday through Saturday

DIRECTIONS: From US-195 heading south of Pullman cross into Idaho (the road name changes to US-95). Proceed on US-95 about 9 miles toward Lewiston-Clarkston. Go right onto US-12 and proceed 3.2 miles. Turn left (south) onto US-12 [1st St.] and continue into Washington .7 miles. Turn right (north) onto 5th St. and proceed .2 miles. Bear left onto Port Dr. and continue .3 miles. Arrive at Basalt Cellars on your right.

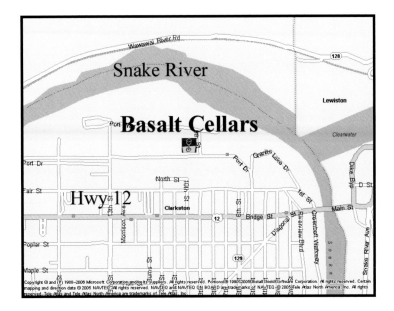

Spokane Valley–Kettle Falls
WineTrail

China Bend Winery's tasting room

The residents of the Inland Empire have become adept at hosting big events, such as the annual Bloomsday Race that brings in more than fifty thousand participants. For sure, Spokanites know how to party, and they have the accommodations to meet your needs. To WineTrail enthusiasts, this translates into great restaurants and a wide variety of hotels and motels to suit your budget and travel needs.

The Spokane Valley–Kettle Falls WineTrail highlights the diversity of wine tasting rooms—each with its own character and beauty. From a historic home "compound" overlooking the Spokane Valley to a lakeshore retreat, you will be surprised to learn that the tasting rooms of Spokane are as varied as the wines themselves. Budget at least two days to tackle this WineTrail. The journey north to China Bend easily consumes a day or more if you are one of the lucky ones to spend a night or two in this marvelous setting.

1 Lone Canary Winery   **3** Latah Creek Wine Cellars   **5** Townshend Cellar
2 Knipprath Cellars   **4** Arbor Crest Wine Cellars   **6** China Bend Winery

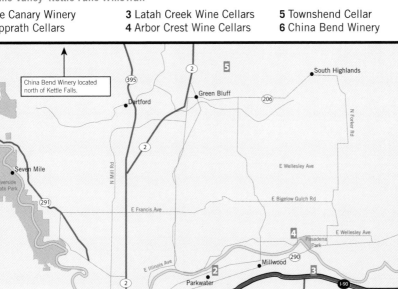

China Bend Winery located north of Kettle Falls.

Region:	**Spokane Wine Country**
# of tasting rooms on tour:	**6**
Estimated # of days for tour:	**2 to 3**
Getting around:	**Car**
Key events:	❑ **Consisting of 10 local wineries, the Spokane Winery Association features two key events: Spring Barrel Tasting (Mother's Day weekend); and Holiday Wine Festival (weekend before Thanksgiving).**
	❑ **See www.spokanewineries.net/calendar.htm for more information.**
Tips:	❑ **China Bend Winery offers a B&B complete with four-course meal.**
Best:	❑ **Best Destination: China Bend Winery**
	❑ **Best Views: China Bend Winery and Arbor Crest Wine Cellars**
	❑ **Best Gift Shop: Latah Creek Winery**
	❑ **Best Picnicking: China Bend Winery and Arbor Crest Wine Cellars**
	❑ **Best for Weddings: Arbor Crest Winery**

551

Lone Canary Winery

Visitors at Lone Canary

A visit to Lone Canary Winery is an exercise in learning to say "red" in three different languages: red, *rosso*, and *rouge*. But by any other name, a big red would taste just as good. WineTrail trekkers can find Lone Canary in the unassuming Scott-Pacific Business Park just east of downtown Spokane. The winery is a fairly bare-bones operation, but it features great signage and wine labels adorned with its distinguished Lone Canary logo: an artistic rendering of Washington's state bird, the American goldfinch, or wild canary. Forging a lone and exciting path using Washington's exemplary fruit, Lone Canary Winery has chosen to stand apart from the flock through "unique artistic expression" in its wines.

Mike Scott, winemaker and co-owner, cut his teeth at Caterina Winery, where he excelled at creating sauvignon blanc. Of course no visit to Lone Canary Winery is complete without a sample of its sauvignon blanc, with its tropical fruit flavors, sweetness, and notes of clove. It makes a perfect pairing with pecan-encrusted halibut and grilled asparagus. As the winery's website points out, Mike Scott has a long-running love affair with sauvignon blanc. But with Lone Canary, Mike Scott has been unleashed to develop some big reds and has done so with the signature blends of "Red," "Rosso," and "Rouge." "Red," an American-style red blend, is a perfect complement to barbecued burgers or London broil over a bed of greens. Whereas "Rouge" highlights a Bordeaux-style blend, and the Tuscan-style "Rosso" features sangiovese in combination with merlot and cabernet sauvignon. Also noteworthy is the DuBrul Vineyard Reserve, which comes with a $5 tasting fee that is applied to the purchase price. I walked out with a bottle.

LONE CANARY WINERY
opened: 2003
winemaker(s): Mike Scott
location: 109 S. Scott St., B2
Spokane, WA 99202-2177
phone: 509-534-9062
web: www.lonecanary.com
e-mail: info@lonecanary.com
picnic area: No
gift shop: Yes
fee: Small tasting fee for reserves refunded
with purchase
hours: 12–5 Thursday through Sunday, or
by appointment

Lone Canary

DIRECTIONS: From downtown Spokane, travel east on Sprague. About .5 miles east of Division turn right on Scott. Take first left into the Scott-Pacific Business Park. Lone Canary is located in the back—Suite B2.

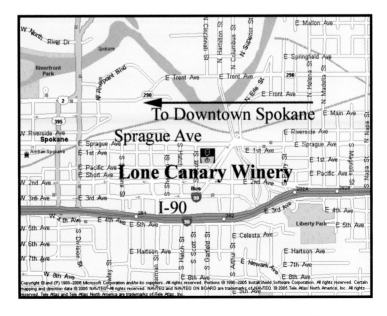

553

Knipprath Cellars

Knipprath Cellars, housed in a 1913 schoolhouse in Spokane Valley, is the offspring of a family's love affair with wine.

You might find yourself humming the Sly and the Family Stone song "Family Affair" as you take in Knipprath Cellars. While Henning Knipprath is making the wine using traditional methods from Germany, his mother, Christa, is

Knipprath's winery/tasting room

serving it in the tasting room. Knipprath Cellars is a port lover's oasis and it enjoys a solid reputation around the Northwest for its port-style wines. You can find Knipprath ports, along with many of its other wines, in select restaurants around the Northwest.

Knipprath Cellars serves as many as five different port-style wines inoculated with a extra dose of alcohol, which makes them 20 proof. So a sip here and a sip there can add up, and the tasting room can become a pretty lively place, especially when Christa shares stories about her family's winemaking adventures. Offering vanilla- and chocolate-flavored port, Knipprath can satisfy a sweet tooth. Its ports include "Northwest Positron," "Au Chocolat!," "Lagrima" white port, LaV! dessert wine (V is for vanilla), and "Matrix" port. Christa likes to pour the white port on ice with a slice of lemon, Portuguese style.

Knipprath produces a number of wines in addition to its port wine series. WineTrail enthusiasts can find its other wines under the labels Knipprath, Mica Peak, and Werner-Ernst-Friederich. The Mica Peak label offers a good value for your wine dollar. A personal favorite is the Alpine wine, which is served warm (but not too hot—you don't want to boil off the alcohol). It's great to drink as you sit by the fire après ski or with a nice holiday turkey dinner. Knipprath's Alpine wine is made from a family recipe for Glühwein, which calls for steeping the wine with assorted holiday spices. You can definitely taste the notes of clove and other spices in this full-bodied red wine.

KNIPPRATH CELLARS
opened: 1991
winemaker(s): Henning Knipprath
location: 5634 E. Commerce Avenue
Spokane, WA 99212-1307
phone: 509-534-5121
web: www.knipprath-cellars.com
e-mail: grapesoknipprath@aol.com
picnic area: Yes
gift shop: Yes
fee: Complimentary wine tasting
hours: 12–5 Wednesday through Sunday, or
by appointment

DIRECTIONS: From I-90 take exit 285 [Sprague Ave.] and travel west to Fancher (just west of freeway overpass). Turn north onto Fancher and drive to Commerce (the second left past Trent). Winery is brick building on left.

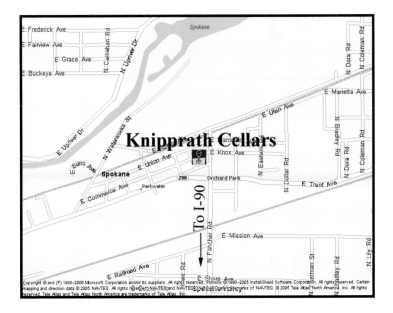

Latah Creek Wine Cellars

Latah Creek Wine Cellars has everything going for it: history, excellent white wines, great location, and a gift shop to die for. Since 1982, when Mike and Ellena Conway started Latah Creek, they have been part of a rather exclusive list of Washington wine industry founders.

To appreciate Latah Creek is to understand the philosophy that guides Mike Conway. Essentially, he believes in giving his customers the best value for their

wine dollar. Consequently, the Conways sell many of their wines at a low price point (around $10 a bottle) and rely on grapes from the same region of the state that so-called higher-end wineries use. Don't be surprised if you see loyal customers carting away cases from their tasting room visit.

WineTrail Note: Unusual for Spokane area wineries, Latah Creek features a muscat canelli wine using grapes from Wahluke Slope. For an interesting taste bud experience, sample the muscat canelli juxtaposed with the winery's reserve chardonnay. The flavors pop! Also fun is Latah Creek's huckleberry riesling, a sure-bet back-porch wine.

You won't need a GPS device to find Latah Creek. Located just off the I-90 freeway a few miles east of downtown Spokane, the winery boasts ample parking and a generously sized tasting room. A gift shop within the tasting room spills into the wine production area. Ellena Conway has an eye for wine merchandise, and there is a good chance that all your holiday gift buying for the wine lovers on your list can be achieved with a visit to Latah Creek.

LATAH CREEK WINE CELLARS
opened: 1982
winemaker(s): Mike Conway
location: 13030 East Indiana Avenue
Spokane, WA 99216-1118
phone: 509-926-0164
web: www.latahcreek.com
e-mail: mconway@latahcreek.com
picnic area: Yes
gift shop: Yes
fee: Complimentary wine tasting
hours: Daily 9–5

BEST Gift shop

DIRECTIONS: **From Spokane**, take I-90 east to exit 289 (Pines Rd) and go north to Indiana (the first street marked by a traffic light.) Turn right on Indiana and proceed east about 2 blocks to the winery on the right.

Arbor Crest Wine Cellars

Arbor Crest Wine Cellars is a labor of love from a family with a shared vision of producing high-quality wines at affordable prices. With a spectacular view overlooking the Spokane Valley, Arbor Crest Wine Cellars is a must-see. But equally gratifying at this stop are some serious wines certain to brighten anyone's day. It's no wonder *Wine Spectator* named Arbor Crest one of the "50 Great Producers Every Wine Lover Should Know" for quality and price. For example, Arbor Crest's high-end syrah sells for $20 a bottle.

Arbor Crest tasting room

Keeping things in the family, Kristina Mielke van Loben Sels is the daughter of one of the winery's founders as well as its winemaker, and her husband, Jim von Loben Sels, is the viticulturist and chief operations manager. Nice marriage. Together they produce about 20,000 cases of wine annually.

Back in 1985, the Mielke brothers purchased the Cliff House, a designated national historic landmark that sits 450 feet above the Spokane River. The mansion, which was built in 1924 by inventor Royal Riblet (honest, that was his name), houses Arbor Crest's tasting room. (The actual wine-production facility is located about a mile down the road.) The tasting room staff is well-versed in the nuances of the wines and equally adept at making WineTrails adventurers feel at ease. There is a small 5-acre vineyard at the site, and its fruit is used to produce an estate-bottled sparkling wine. All other Arbor Crest wines are made from grapes grown in the Columbia Valley AVA .

The grounds feature gardens, picnic areas, scenic views, and a man-made waterfall. But one of the unique little pleasures of this winery is the presence of a Manx cat, who can often be found lounging around the tasting room and gardens. As you may have guessed, this is a dog-free zone.

WineTrail Note: Check out Arbor Crest's website for details on its summer concert series and other events, such as the Art & Glass Fest in August.

Part of the Arbor Crest historic complex

ARBOR CREST WINE CELLARS
opened: 1982
winemaker(s): Kristina Mielke van Loben Sels
location: 4705 North Fruithill Road
Spokane, WA 99217
phone: 509-927-9463
web: www.arborcrest.com
e-mail: info@arborcrest.com
picnic area: Yes
gift shop: Yes
fee: Complimentary wine tasting
hours: Daily 12–5

★ BEST Views, picnicking and weddings

DIRECTIONS: Take I-90 (east from Spokane, west from Coeur d'Alene) to the Argonne exit 287. Travel north on Argonne and cross the Spokane River. Turn right on Upriver Drive; proceed 1 mile and as the road forks bear left onto Fruithill Rd. Make a sharp right turn at the top of the hill. You are now on Arbor Crest's private drive.

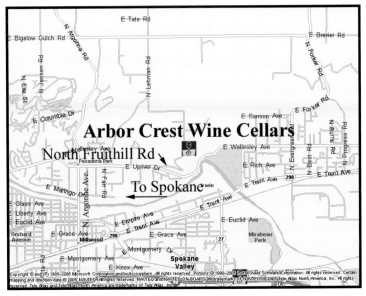

559

Townshend Cellar

Don Townshend is the mad scientist of winemaking. He's constantly tinkering to find the right blend, best grapes, and optimum oak for aging. His portfolio of table wines, dessert wines, and port-style wines is extensive, offering about 20 different reds, whites, and specialty beverages. When he's not mixing and matching in the winery, he sheds the lab coat and is often seen at events wearing

Townshend Cellars loyal guard dog

a tux as he introduces his wine to guests, pouring and getting feedback from soon-to-be-loyal fans.

Townshend Cellar winery and tasting room is located north of Spokane in the tiny hamlet of Colbert. The area's panoramic views reveal that this is rolling hills and ponderosa pine territory. Inside Townshend's comfortable tasting room, you're struck by the number of wines to sample, and it occurs to you that you're going to be here for a while. Let your taste buds work their way through the Townshend Cellar whites, which feature chardonnay and dry riesling, and then on to the reds, which are highlighted by syrah, cabernet franc, and merlot. While in the red zone, be sure you sample Don's special red blends, such as "T3" and "Vortex." The "T3" may strike a familiar note; there's a chance you imbibed this wine at one of the select Northwest restaurants that has exclusive purchasing rights to it. Also, be sure to save room for Don's very popular huckleberry port wine, made from wild huckleberries picked in northern Idaho.

With such a high ceiling, the spacious barrel room should appear airy, but with oak barrels towering five and six deep, it feels rather confined. You realize that Don must be quite expert with the forklift in this environment. From the barrel room, a flight of stairs leads to the upper-floor quarters, where you discover a fully equipped gourmet kitchen and a private dining room, which can easily handle a group of 12 guests. Indeed, the room is often reserved for corporate and other special events throughout the year.

By the end of your visit, you realize that Don Townshend lives and breathes wine, 24/7, from purchasing grapes to putting the labels on the bottle. You imagine him racing from one event to another and meeting with his distributors. Then you realize that Don has a day job as an engineer. Does this guy ever sleep?

TOWNSHEND CELLAR
opened: 1998
winemaker(s): Don Townshend
location: 16112 North Greenbluff Road
Colbert, WA 99005
phone: 509-238-1400
web: www.townshendcellar.com
e-mail: don@townshendcellar.com
picnic area: Yes
gift shop: Yes
fee: Complimentary wine tasting
hours: 12–6 Friday through Sunday

DIRECTIONS: From North Division "Y," go 5.4 miles on Hwy 2. Turn right on Day-Mt. Spokane Rd. Go 1.6 miles to Greenbluff Rd and turn left. Winery entrance is .2 miles on right side. From Spokane Valley, take Argonne Rd north to end of road and intersection with Day-Mt. Spokane Rd. Take a left and go .4 miles. Then turn right onto Greenbluff Rd. Winery entrance is .2 miles on right side.

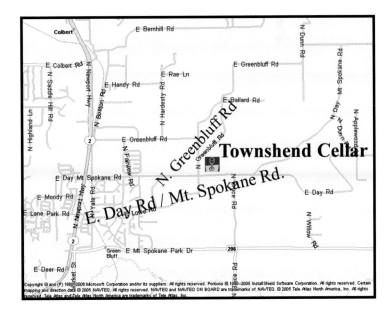

China Bend Winery

Situated on the banks of the beautiful Columbia River, China Bend offers a host of delightful surprises, not to mention stunning views of the surrounding hills and Lake Roosevelt. The Winery is the dream of owners/winemakers Bart and Victory Alexander. They had the foresight to realize that grapes would grow surprisingly well in this area's harsh winter environment. In their case, they have French oenophiles to thank for a hardy Alsatian grape varietal with the unlikely name of Marechal Foch. (Foch was a famous French general who ran the Germans out of France in World War I.) If you are from upstate New York or Québec, you might already be familiar with this varietal, but in Washington's Bordeaux-dominated landscape, Marechal Foch is a rare find. The grape produces a soft, full-bodied wine and, not surprisingly, is China Bend's no. 1 seller.

Tournament quality croquet grounds

The vineyard is certified organic, and no sulfites are used in the production of China Bend wines. According to Bart, you won't get a headache from drinking these wines.

Don't be surprised if you encounter a serious croquet match taking place at China Bend. The dedicated lawn is manicured to perfection and is the site of serious croquet play. Players from throughout the Northwest descend on China Bend to participate in major tournaments.

On your way to the tasting room, you will also go by the China Bend Bed and Breakfast. Guests wake up each morning to a full breakfast made from the bounty of Victory's organic garden. (We told you that this was a destination winery.) The attractive red-roofed tasting room is your WineTrail destination, where you can choose from Bart's portfolio of red and white wines. Increasingly, their wines rely on locally grown grapes, but some of the grapes come from Bart's native Yakima Valley. In addition to the Marechal Foch, visitors can swirl and sip China Bend lemberger, chardonnay, cabernet sauvignon, syrah, meritage, and blends with names such as "Roosevelt Red." Another highlight of the tasting room is the assortment of organic products Victory makes and sells. Check out these attractively packaged jams, pickled garlic, dill pickles, and salsas. Then grab some chips and salsa to go with the Marechal Foch you just purchased and challenge your partner to a game of croquet.

CHINA BEND WINERY
opened: 1995
winemaker(s): Bart Alexander
location: 3751 Vineyard Way
Kettle Falls, WA 99141-8852
phone: 800-700-6123
web: www.chinabend.com
e-mail: winery@chinabend.com
picnic area: Yes
gift shop: Yes
fee: Complimentary wine tasting
hours: Daily 12–5 April through October, or
by appointment

China Bend Winery

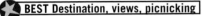

BEST Destination, views, picnicking

DIRECTIONS: **From Kettle Falls**, continue on US-395 [SR-20] (west) for 6.5 miles. Cross Columbia River/Franklin D. Roosevelt Lake and keep right onto Northport –Flat Creek Rd [River Bridge Rd]. Keep straight onto Northport–Flat Creek Rd for 20.5 miles. Bear right (east) onto Vineyard Way. Follow signs to China Bend Winery.

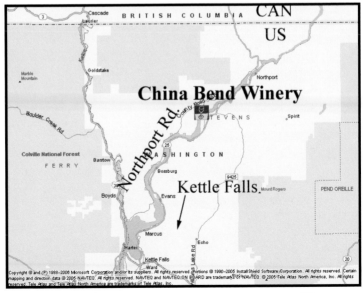

Appendix A - Wineries to Visit By Appointment Only

Wine Trails of Washington features wineries that are open to the public and have regular tasting room hours. However, there are a number of wineries that are open to the public yet do not have regular tasting room hours. These wineries welcome visitors "by appointment only." Listed by wine country region are wineries that you can visit by calling ahead and scheduling a visit. Enjoy!

Northwest Washington Wine Country

Dakota Creek Winery
3575 Haynie Road
Blaine, WA 98230-9741
www.dakotacreekwinery.com
ken@dakotacreekwinery.com
360-820-4752

Westcott Bay Orchards
43 Anderson Lane
Friday Harbor, WA 98250
www.rockisland.com/
~baylonanderson/
baylonanderson@rockisland.com
360-378-3880

Olympic Peninsula Wine Country

Blooms
5302 SE Harbor Road
Freeland, WA 98249-9534
blooms@whidbey.com
360-331-4084

Christina James Winery
205 St. James Place
Port Townsend, WA 99368
www.cjwinery.com
info@cjwinery.com
360-531-0127

Eleven Winery
12976 Roe Road NE
Bainbridge Island, WA 98110-1204
www.ElevenWinery.com
matt@elevenwinery.com
206-780-0905

Perennial Vintners
8840 Lovgreen Road
Bainbridge Island, WA 98110
www.PerennialVintners.com
info@PerenialVintners.com
206-780-2146

Puget Sound Wine Country

Andrake Cellars Winery
6315 Boston Harbor Road NE
Olympia, WA 98506
www.andrakecellars.com
bobandrake@msn.com
360-943-3746

ANIMALE
P.O. Box 70491
Seattle, WA 98127-0491
www.animalewine.com
animale@animalewine.com
206-782-8047

Camano Cellars
7420 300th Street NW
Stanwood, WA 98292
www.camanocellars.com
info@camanocellars.com
360-333-4899

Cavatappi Winery
9702 NE 120th Place
Kirkland, WA 98034-4206
www.cavatappi.com
peter@cavatappi.com
206-282-5226

Cougar Creek Wine
34307-A SE 39th Street
Fall City, WA 98024-8401
www.cougarcreekwine.com
info@cougarcreekwine.com
425-222-6546

Crutcher Family Cellars
24707 SE 45th Place
Issaquah, WA 98029-6566
www.crutchercellars.com
info@crutchercellars.com
425-417-0115

Griffins Crossing Winery
1802 131st Drive NE
Lake Stevens, WA 98258
www.griffinscrossing.com
max@griffinscrossing.com
425-334-0839

Hurricane Ridge Winery
6315 Boston Harbor Road NE
Olympia, WA 98506
www.andrakecellars.com
bobandrake@msn.com
360-459-1638

Kalamar Winery
5906 218th Avenue East
Sumner, WA 98390-8711
www.kalamarwinery.com
la-mark@msn.com
253-862-9844

Medicine Creek Winery
947 Old Pacific Highway SE
Olympia, WA 98513
www.medicinecreekwines.com
lizonthefarm@aol.com
360-701-6284

Palouse Winery
12431 Vashon Highway SW
Vashon, WA 98070
www.palousewinery.com
gkirkish@palousewinery.com
206-567-4994

Pleasant Hill Winery
32305 8th St NE
Carnation, WA 98014
www.pleasanthillestate.com
birgitr@seanet.com
425-333-6770

Quilceda Creek Vintners
11306 52nd Street SE
Snohomish, WA 98290
www.quilcedacreek.com
info@quilcedacreek.com
360-568-2389

Scatter Creek Winery
3442 180th SE Avenue
Tenino , WA 98589
www.scattercreekwinery.com/
terril@scattercreekwinery.com
360-870-4092

Soos Creek Wine Cellars
20404 140th Avenue SE
Kent, WA 98042
www.sooscreekwine.com
sooscreek@mindspring.com
253-631-8775

Sweetbread Cellars
10730 SW 116th Street
Vashon, WA 98070
www.sweetbreadcellars.com
george@seabreezefarm.com
206-567-5769

Vinland Farms
11207 206th NE Avenue
Redmond, WA 98053
goodman.s@ghc.org
425-882-0714

Ward Johnson Winery
1405 Elliott West Avenue, Suite F2
Seattle , WA 98119
www.wardjohnsonwinery.com
info@wardjohnsonwinery.com
206-229-3421

Washington Wine Company
15210 275th Avenue SE
Monroe, WA 98272
www.woodslakewinery.com
info@woodslakewinery.com
425-605-2649

Willis Hall Winery
4715 126th Street NE
Marysville, WA 98271
www.willishall.com
wine@WillisHall.com
360-653-1247
Woodinville Wine Country

Austin Robaire Vintners
19501 144th Avenue NE,
Suite D-800
Woodinville, WA 98072-4415
www.austinrobaire.com
wines@austinrobaire.com
206-406-0360

Baer Winery
9118 222nd Street SE
Woodinville, WA 98072
www.baerwinery.com
info@baerwinery.com
425-483-7060

DeLille Cellars (includes Doyenne)
PO Box 2233
Woodinville, WA 98072-8783
www.delillecellars.com
contact@delillecellars.com
425-489-0544

Domaine Ste. Michelle at Chateau Ste. Michelle
14111 NE 145th Street
Woodinville, WA 98072
www.domainestemichelle.com
info@domainestemichelle.com
866-701-3187

Gorman Winery
19501 144th Ave. NE, Suite C-500
Woodinville, WA 98072
www.gormanwinery.com
Chris@gormanwinery.com
206-351-0719

Ross Andrew Winery
18512 142nd Avenue NE
Woodinville, WA 98072
www.rossandrewwinery.com
rossandrewwinery.com
206-369-3615

William Church Winery
19495 144th NE Avenue,
Suite #A100
Woodinville, WA 98072
www.williamchurchwinery.com
info@williamchurchwinery.com
425-427-0764

Southwest Washington Wine Country

Birchfield Winery
921-B Middle Fork Road
Onalaska, WA 98570-9710
virgfox@tds.net
360-978-5224

Gibbons Lane Winery
12035 Gibbons Lane SE
Tenino, WA 98589
www.gibbonslane.com
donedei@aol.com
360-264-8466

Klickitat Canyon Winery DBA Columbia Gorge Winery
6 Lyle-Snowden Road
Lyle, WA 98635
www.klickitatcanyonwinery.com
509-365-2543

Madsen Family Cellars
1916 Allegro Drive SE
Olympia, WA 98501
dansanz@gmail.com
360-357-3015

Major Creek Cellars
White Salmon, WA 98672
www.majorcreekcellars.com
info@majorcreekcellars.com

McCrea Cellars
11515 Eagle View Lane
Rainier, WA 98576
www.mccreacellars.com
mccreawine@aol.com
800-378-6212

Scatter Creek Winery
3442 180th SE Avenue
Tenino, WA 98589
www.scattercreekwinery.com/
terril@scattercreekwinery.com
360-870-4092

Shady Grove Winery
2297 Dallesport Road
Dallesport, WA 98617
www.shadygrovewinery.com
shadygrovewinery@skyride.net
509-767-1400

White Salmon Vineyards
391 Newell Road
Underwood, WA 98651
www.WhiteSalmonVineyard.com
peter@brehmvineyards.com
509-493-4640

North Central Washington Wine Country

Fielding Hills Winery
East Wenatchee, WA 98802
www.fieldinghills.com
karen@fieldinghills.com
509-884-2221

Ginkgo Forest Winery
22561 Road T 7 SW
Mattawa, WA 99349
www.ginkgowinery.com
mthiede@smwireless.net
509-932-0082

Horan Estates Winery
470 Cross Road
Wenatchee, WA 98801
www.horanestateswinery.com
HoranEstates@direcway.com
509-662-7573

La Toscana Winery
9020 Foster Road
Cashmere, WA 98815-9417
www.latoscanawinery.com
wmoyles@nwi.net
509-548-5448

Sunset Vineyards
9224 Road South
Quincy, WA 98848
www.columbiacascadewines.com/
sunset_vineyards.html
rudy@crcwnet.com
509-787-3671
Yakima Valley Wine Country

Bunnell Family Cellars
87203 W 134 PR NW
Prosser, WA 99350
www.riveraerie.com
wineandherbs@earthlink.net
509-973-4187

Canyon's Edge Winery
255 Six Prong Ext / 1130 Hale Road
Mabton, WA 98935-9469
www.canyonsedgewinery.com
fran@canyonsedgewinery.com
509-894-2919

Cote Bonneville Winery
2841 Fordyce Road
Sunnyside, WA 98944-9771
www.cotebonneville.com
winery@cotebonneville
509-840-4596

Coventry Vale Winery
160602 Evans Road,
P. O. Box 249,
(Wilgus & Evans Roads)
Grandview, WA 98930
509-882-4100

Natches Heights Vineyard (NHV)
1857 Weikel Rd.
Yakima, WA 98908
www.NHVines.com
phil@NHVines.com
509-945-4062

St. Hilaire Cellars Winery
1340 Saint Hilaire Road
Yakima, WA 98901
garyjackson98901@yahoo.com
509-453-5987

Tanjuli Winery
East 4530 Zillah Drive
Zillah, WA 98953
tanjuli@gmail.com
509-829-6401
Red Mountain Wine Country

Beaucoup Gravier Winery
W 57705 Old Inland Empire Highway
Richland, WA 99320-7666
509-588-4977

Buckmaster Cellars
1600 Brantingham Road
Benton City, WA 99352-7626
www.buckmastercellars.com
509-628-8474

Canon De Sol Winery and Vineyard
46415 East Badger Road
Benton City, WA 99320-9589
www.canondesol.com
wine@canondesol.com
509-588-6311

Fidelitas Wines
46415 East Badger Road
Benton City, WA 99320-9589
www.fidelitaswines.com
wine@fidelitaswines.com
509-521-4433

Gamache Vintners
23509 North Dallas Road / 46415 E.
Badger Road
Richland / Benton City, WA 99352 /
99320
www.gamachevintners.com
bob@gamachevintners.com
509-546-8990

Sleeping Dog Wines
45804 North Whitmore PR NW
Benton City, WA 98320
www.sleepingdogwines.com
info@sleepingdogwines.com
509-460-2886

Horse Heaven Hills Wine Country

Chateau Champoux Vineyard Tours and Tasting
524 Alderdale Road
Prosser, WA 99350
www.chateauchampoux.com
chateaucr@bentonrea.com
509-894-5005
Tri-Cities Wine Country

Balcom & Moe Winery
2520 Commercial Avenue
Pasco, WA 99301
www.owt.com/nwwines/balcom/
balcom@owt.com
509- 547-7307

Gordon Brothers Cellars
671 Levey Road
Pasco, WA 99301-9711
www.gordonwines.com
info@gordonwines.com
509-547-6331

Moonlight Sparkling Wine Cellar
4704 West 12th Avenue
Kennewick, WA 99338
www.moonlightcellar.com
info@moonlightcellar.com
509-735-7237

Wooded Island Vineyards
91 North Columbia River Road
Pasco, WA 99301
www.woodedislandvineyards.com
terry@woodedislandvineyards.com
509-542-0201

Walla Walla Valley Wine Country

Abeja
2014 Mill Creek Road
Walla Walla, WA 99362-8424
www.abeja.net
info@abeja.net
509-526-7400

Bodega Turner
205 West Main Street
Walla Walla, WA 99362
www.bodegaturner.com
info@bodegaturner.com
509-525-5552

Bunchgrass Winery
151 Bunchgrass Lane
Walla Walla, WA 99362
www.bunchgrasswinery.com
info@BunchgrassWinery.com
509-525-1492

Cayuse Vineyards
17 East Main Street / PO Box 1602
Walla Walla, WA 99362
www.cayusevineyards.com
info@cayusevineyards.com
509-526-0686

Couvillion Winery
86 Corkrum Road
Walla Walla, WA 99362
www.couvillionwinery.com
jill@couvillionwinery.com
509-337-6133

Ensemble Cellars
145 East Curtis Avenue
Walla Walla, WA 99362
www.ensemblecellars.com
info@ensemblecellars.com
509-525-0231

Flying Trout Wines
37 South Palouse Street
Walla Walla, WA 99362
www.flyingtroutwines.com
talk@flyingtroutwines.com
509-520-7701

Harlequin Wine Cellars
1211 Sandpit Road
Touchet, WA 99360
www.harlequinwine.com
winemaker@harlequinwine.com
425-413-4633

Lahar
123 East Alder Street
Walla Walla, WA 99362
www.laharwines.com
bronk@whidbey.net
509-240-4854

Latitude 46 North
1211 Sandpit Road
Touchet, WA 99360
www.latitude46.com
info@latitude46.com
509-394-0460

Nicholas Cole Cellars
705 Berney Drive
Walla Walla, WA 99362
www.nicholascolecellars.com
info@nicholascolecellars.com
509-525-0608

Otis Kenyon Wines
1793 JB George Road; Room D,
Suite G
Walla Walla, WA 99362
www.otiskenyonwines.com
info@otiskenyonwines.com
206-463-3125

Rulo Winery
3525 Pranger Road
Walla Walla, WA 99362
www.rulowinery.com
schlick@pocketinet.com
509-525-RULO

Sapolil Cellars
1106 Sapolil Road
Walla Walla, WA 99362
www.sapolilcellars.com
sharon@sapolilcellars.com
509-520-5258

Trust Cellars
1050 Merlot Drive
Walla Walla, WA 99362
www.trustcellars.com
steve@trustcellars.com
509-529-4511

Yellow Hawk Cellar
395 Yellowhawk Street
Walla Walla, WA 99362
www.yellowhawkcellar.com
info@yellowhawkcellars.com
509-529-1714

Spokane and the Palouse Wine Country

Mountain Dome Winery
16315 East Temple Road
Spokane, WA 99217
www.mountaindome.com
manz@mountaindome.com
509-928-2788

Outdoor summer concert at Tsillan Cellars.

Appendix B - Additional Touring Resources

Tours and Limousine Service

A+ Pacific Limousine Tours–serving Yakima, Walla Walla & Columbia valleys; Red Mountain and Horse Heaven Hills
509-585-7717, www.limo01.com/winetours.html

Black Tie Limousines–serving Walla Walla Valley
509-585-8585, www.blacktielimos.net

Bon Vivant Wine Tours–serving Seattle, Woodinville, Yakima Valley, Walla Walla Valley, Red Mountain, Columbia Valley/Tri-Cities, Leavenworth/Wenatchee, Chelan, & Columbia Gorge
206-437-1298, www.bonvivanttours.com

Sacco's Ultimate Vintage Wine Tours–serving Yakima Valley, Tri Cities Area, & Walla Walla Valley
509-783-7060, www.saccotours.com

Sunset Coach Tours–serving Yakima, Walla Walla & Columbia valleys, Red Mountain and Horse Heaven Hills
800-941-2941, www.sunsetcoachtours.com

Travel Resources

AAA
800-829-5448, www.aaa.com

Alaska Airlines-City Guides
800-ALASKAAIR, www.alaskaair.com

Amtrak
800-USA-RAIL, www.amtrak.com

Prosser Chamber of Commerce
800-408-1517, www.prosserchamber.org

The Washington State Hotel & Lodging Association (WSH&LA)
877-906-1001, www.stayinwashington.com/attractions.php?region=7

Toppenish Chamber of Commerce
800-863-6375, www.toppenish.net

Tourism Walla-Walla
877-WW-VISIT, www.wallawalla.org

Tri-Cities Visitor & Convention Bureau
800-254-5824, www.visittri-cities.com

Washington State Tourism
800-544-1800, www.experiencewashington.com

Washington State Travel Counselor
800-544-1800, www.tourism@cted.wa.gov

Washington Wine Highway
425-481-8300, www.washingtonwinehighway.com

Yakima Valley Visitors & Convention Bureau.
800-221-0751, www.visityakima.com

Wine Country Regions

Columbia River Gorge wineries and events Washington and Oregon
866-413-WINE 9463, www.columbiagorgewine.com

Leavenworth, Wenatchee and Lake Chelan wineries and events
509-782-0708, www.columbiacascadewines.com

Northwest wineries and event information
509-582-1564, www.winepressnw.com

Olympic Peninsula, Whidbey Island and Kitsap Peninsula
800-785-5495, www.northsoundwineries.org

Spokane wineries and events
www.spokanewineries.net

Tri-Cities wineries and events
866-360-6611, www.columbiavalleywine.com

Walla Walla Valley wineries and events
509-526-3117, www.wallawallawine.com

Washington Wine Commission
206-667-9463, www.washingtonwine.org

WineTrails Northwest—Statewide winery database and events
206-660-5200, www.winetrailsnw.com

Woodinville wineries and events
425-482-1801, www.woodinvillewinecountry.com

Yakima Valley wineries and events
800-258-7270, www.wineyakimavalley.org

Index

This index covers cities, wineries and WineTrails. Cities are listed in bold. Wineries can be found individually in alphabetical order or under the city in which they belong.

V

W

Z

Tasting Notes

....

....

....

....

....

....

....

....

....

....

....

....

....

....

....

....

....

....

....

....

....

....

....

....

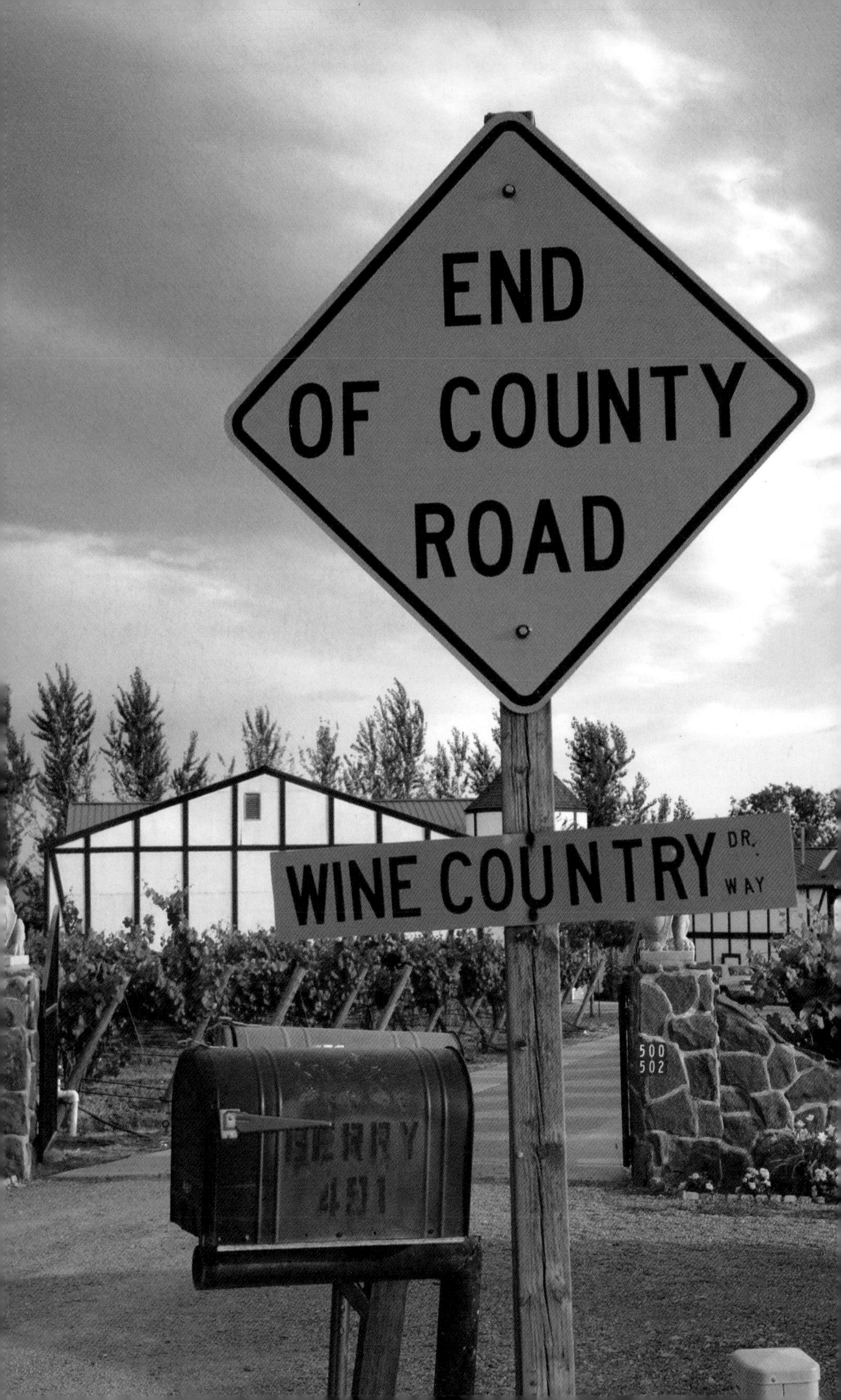
END
OF COUNTY
ROAD
WINE COUNTRY
DR.
WAY
500
502